Social Knowledge Management for Rural Empowerment

This book develops and examines the concepts and strategies for rural empowerment through the formation of a community-driven social knowledge management (SKM) framework aided by social technology. The framework is aimed at mobilizing knowledge resources to bridge the rural–urban knowledge divide while securing rural empowerment using digital connections and social collaborations built on strategies of self-sustenance and self-development. With key empirical findings supplemented by relevant theoretical structures, case studies, illustrative figures and a lucid style, the book combines social technologies and social development to derive a social knowledge management platform. It shows how the proposed SKM framework can enhance knowledge capabilities of rural actors by facilitating connection among rural–urban entities through formation of purposive virtual communities, which allow social agents to create, modify and share content collaboratively.

The volume brings forward diverse issues – such as conceptual foundations, bridging the rural–urban knowledge and information divide, issues of information and knowledge asymmetry, a knowledge-theoretic perspective of rural empowerment, knowledge capability and freedom of choice and wellbeing – to provide a comprehensive outlook on building a knowledge society through digital empowerment.

This book will be useful to scholars and researchers of development studies, rural sociology, management studies, IT/IS, knowledge management and ICT for development, public policy, sociology, political economy and development economics. It will benefit professionals and policy-makers, government and non-government bodies and international agencies involved with policy decisions related to application of technologies for rural development, social workers and those in the development sector.

Somprakash Bandyopadhyay is Professor, Management Information Systems Group, Indian Institute of Management Calcutta, Kolkata, India. With a PhD in Computer Science, he has nearly 40 years' experience in teaching, research and technology development in several organizations of international repute. He was a fellow of the Alexander von Humboldt Foundation, Germany, and fellow of the Japan Trust International Foundation. He is the Founder-Director of Social Informatics Research Group at Indian Institute of Management Calcutta.

Sneha Bhattacharyya is Research Associate, Social Informatics Research Group, Indian Institute of Management Calcutta, Kolkata, India. With an M.Phil. in Social Sciences, her interests are in applying social techniques to optimally disseminate internet-enabled technology for upliftment of marginalized communities.

Jayanta Basak is Senior Research Associate, Social Informatics Research Group, Indian Institute of Management Calcutta, Kolkata, India. He has an M.Tech. in Computer Science and works in the areas of design and development of social information systems for social development. He is also the Co-Founder-Director of NexConnect, a social business venture based in Kolkata for social inclusion through digital inclusion.

Social Knowledge Management for Rural Empowerment

Bridging the Knowledge Divide Using Social Technologies

Somprakash Bandyopadhyay,
Sneha Bhattacharyya and Jayanta Basak

LONDON AND NEW YORK

First published 2021
by Routledge
2 Park Square, Milton Park, Abingdon, Oxon OX14 4RN

and by Routledge
52 Vanderbilt Avenue, New York, NY 10017

Routledge is an imprint of the Taylor & Francis Group, an informa business

© 2021 Somprakash Bandyopadhyay, Sneha Bhattacharyya and Jayanta Basak

The right of Somprakash Bandyopadhyay, Sneha Bhattacharyya and Jayanta Basak to be identified as authors of this work has been asserted by them in accordance with sections 77 and 78 of the Copyright, Designs and Patents Act 1988.

All rights reserved. No part of this book may be reprinted or reproduced or utilised in any form or by any electronic, mechanical, or other means, now known or hereafter invented, including photocopying and recording, or in any information storage or retrieval system, without permission in writing from the publishers.

Trademark notice: Product or corporate names may be trademarks or registered trademarks, and are used only for identification and explanation without intent to infringe.

British Library Cataloguing in Publication Data
A catalogue record for this book is available from the British Library

Library of Congress Cataloging-in-Publication Data
A catalog record has been requested for this book

ISBN: 978-0-367-33493-2 (hbk)
ISBN: 978-0-367-33494-9 (pbk)
ISBN: 978-0-429-32017-0 (ebk)

Typeset in Sabon
by Taylor & Francis Books

Contents

List of illustrations   xii
Preface   xiv

1 Introduction   1

   1 Preamble 1
   2 Organization of the book 4

PART I
Rural empowerment: Bridging rural–urban knowledge and information divide   13

2 Knowledge, knowledge divide and knowledge capability: A conceptual framework   15

   1 Introduction 15
   2 Defining knowledge 16
   3 Knowledge: A social product 17
   4 Knowledge divide 20
   5 Knowledge capability 23
      5.1 The importance of knowledge in capability theory 24
      5.2 Dimensions of knowledge capability 25
   6 Managing knowledge resource to enhance knowledge capability 28

3 Rural empowerment: A knowledge–theoretic approach   33

   1 Introduction 33
   2 Empowerment and its manifestation in rural context 35
   3 Agency, opportunity structure and social capital: Facilitating empowerment 37

3.1 Empowerment and agency 37
3.2 Empowerment and opportunity structure 38
3.3 Empowerment and social capital 40
4 *Empowerment as a knowledge–theoretic concept* 42
   4.1 Conceptualizing rural empowerment through management of knowledge 42
   4.2 Facilitating rural empowerment through management of knowledge 44
5 *Conclusion* 48

4 Contemporary initiatives undertaken for rural empowerment 51

1 *Introduction* 51
2 *'Rurbanization': Promise and practice* 52
3 *United Nations' initiatives towards rural empowerment* 54
4 *Rural empowerment: Some measures taken in developing nations* 56
   4.1 Indonesia 59
   4.2 Iran 61
   4.3 India 63
   4.4 Pakistan 65
5 *Limitations of current institution-based rural empowerment paradigms* 66
6 *Conclusion* 67

5 Information asymmetry and rural producers 71

1 *Introduction* 71
2 *The need for information and the effect of information asymmetry* 72
3 *Information asymmetry of rural producers in developing nations* 73
   3.1 Information asymmetry between producers themselves 73
   3.2 Information asymmetry between producers and their prospective buyers 74
   3.3 The information asymmetry between rural producers and middlemen 75
   3.4 The information asymmetry between rural producers and government agencies 76
4 *Impact of information asymmetry on market efficiency: An Indian case study* 76
   4.1 Methodology 77

    4.2 Observation 77
    4.3 The impact of information asymmetry on Indian rural producers: Findings 82
  5 *Contemporary measures undertaken to reduce information asymmetry* 85
  6 *Conclusion* 90

6 Knowledge asymmetry and its mitigation through enhancement of knowledge capability   93

  1 *Introduction* 93
  2 *From information asymmetry to knowledge asymmetry* 96
    2.1 Information and knowledge: A comparative analysis 96
    2.2 From information asymmetry to knowledge asymmetry 97
  3 *Knowledge capability: From knowledge possession to knowledge operation* 100
  4 *Knowledge capability of rural members in mitigating knowledge asymmetry* 102
    4.1 The capability approach: Building capability set of target group 103
    4.2 A knowledge-centric capability approach for mitigating knowledge asymmetry 106
  5 *Conclusion* 108

PART II
Social knowledge management and social technologies: Conceptual foundations   113

7 Knowledge management and its evolution in organizational context   115

  1 *Introduction* 115
  2 *How society used to manage knowledge: A historical perspective* 116
  3 *Information systems and globalization: Impetus to knowledge management* 119
  4 *Knowledge management: Definitions* 121
  5 *Knowledge management: Processes and strategies* 124
    5.1 Processes of knowledge management 124
    5.2 Strategies of knowledge management in organizational context 126
  6 *Three generations of knowledge management in organizational context* 133

   6.1 First-generation knowledge management 134
   6.2 Second-generation knowledge management 135
   6.3 Third-generation knowledge management 136
  7 Conclusion 139

8 Social technology and knowledge management practices   145

  1 Introduction 145
  2 Social technology: A conceptual perspective 146
   2.1 Defining social technology 148
   2.2 Components of social technologies 149
  3 Social technology and knowledge management 154
   3.1 Networking and collaboration 154
   3.2 The social technology and SECI model-based knowledge processes 155
   3.3 Social media analytics and customer knowledge management 157
   3.4 Management of crowd knowledge for organizational benefits 158
   3.5 Enterprise social software: *Social* tools for knowledge management 159
  4 Conclusion 161

9 Efforts undertaken to manage social knowledge and information for social benefit   167

  1 Introduction 167
  2 Managing social knowledge: A historical perspective 170
  3 The first generation: Facilitating information dissemination through community information systems 172
  4 The second generation: Facilitating bi-directional information sharing 178
  5 The third generation: Facilitating multi-directional knowledge collaboration 183
  6 Conclusion 188

10 Social knowledge management: A social technology-enabled framework to bridge knowledge asymmetry of rural producers through virtual community formation   193

  1 Introduction 193
  2 Social knowledge vs. organizational knowledge 195

3 Organizational knowledge management vs. managing social
    knowledge 196
  4 Social knowledge management: A functional perspective 199
  5 A social knowledge management framework to mitigate
    rural–urban knowledge asymmetry 203
      5.1 The conceptual framework 204
      5.2 The model of intervention 206
  6 Conclusion 208

PART III
Social knowledge management in action: Some empirical studies in rural India   211

11 Cultivating online communities of practice to facilitate
   practice-oriented rural–urban knowledge exchange through
   collaborative learning spaces   213

  1 Introduction 213
  2 Conceptualizing community of practice 214
      2.1 Factors leading to the cultivation of community of
          practice 216
      2.2 Components of community of practice 216
      2.3 Structure of community of practice 217
      2.4 Factors determining sustainability of community of
          practice 217
  3 Collaborative learning spaces of early society 219
  4 Community of practice in action 220
  5 Building community of practice in organizational context 222
  6 Cultivating online communities of practice in rural context 224
      6.1 Examples from some field studies with self-help group
          women in rural India 225
      6.2 A field study with rural youth in India 236
  7 Cultivating online communities of practice using a social
    knowledge management platform 238
  8 Conclusion 240

12 Cultivating communities of purpose to enhance market
   opportunities of rural producers through collaborative
   knowledge transaction   244

  1 Introduction 244
  2 Community of purpose: A conceptual framework 246

    3 *The role of communities of purpose in bridging market separation of rural producers* 247
    4 *A digital framework towards building online community of purpose for rural producers* 252
        4.1 Conceptual foundations 252
        4.2 Operationalizing the framework: Mobilizing rural–urban community towards purposive collaboration 254
    5 *Architecting a social knowledge management platform to cultivate online communities of purpose for rural producers* 258
        5.1 NCoRe: System design 258
        5.2 Validation of the NCoRe system 263
        5.3 Discussion 263
    6 *Some field observations on cultivating communities of purpose* 264
        6.1 Objective of the study 264
        6.2 Background of the study 264
        6.3 Insights from field work 265
        6.4 Findings from field work 268
        6.5 Discussions 268
    7 *Conclusion* 270

13 **Cultivating communities of circumstance to enhance community resilience through knowledge sharing using collaboration and connections**   274

    1 *Introduction* 274
    2 *Understanding community resilience* 276
    3 *Components of community resilience* 278
    4 *A framework towards building online communities of circumstance: Mobilizing community towards resilience* 280
        4.1 Communities of circumstance 280
        4.2 An operational framework for cultivating online communities of circumstance 281
    5 *Developing resilient community through collaborative knowledge transaction: Some examples from disaster management* 282
        5.1 The role of knowledge management in disaster situations: An introduction 283
        5.2 Use of social media to engage community members during disaster for situational information and knowledge transaction 284
        5.3 Interactive community-sourcing: A participatory knowledge management practice during disaster 286

    5.4 Cultivating online communities of circumstance using a collaborative knowledge management platform: Towards a disaster-resilient community 288

  6 Conclusion 293

PART IV
What tomorrow may bring   301

14 Summary and discussions   303

    1 Introduction 303
    2 Summary of work 303
    3 Hindrances faced during the research journey and prospective solutions 304
    4 Ethical concerns addressed in the research 307
    5 Conclusion 308

15 Building a developmental ecosystem for rural empowerment   310

    1 Developmental ecosystem: Theory and practice 310
    2 The need for a developmental ecosystem for holistic rural empowerment 312
    3 Building a developmental ecosystem for rural empowerment 314

Index   318

Illustrations

Figures

7.1	SECI model of Nonaka and Takeuchi	125
10.1	Social knowledge management framework facilitating virtual community formation	205
10.2	SKM framework to mitigate rural–urban knowledge asymmetry	207
11.1	Community of practice: A conceptual framework	218
11.2	Training SHG women to use smartphones	229
11.3	Sample WhatsApp communications: Sharing information	229
11.4	Video-based asynchronous training, followed by online interactions	230
11.5	Online feedback sessions provided by urban experts to women of Kandi	230
11.6	Daily usage of WhatsApp by SHG members	231
11.7	Contribution of individual members in terms of total number of messages	232
11.8	Total response of all queries from community members	234
11.9	Screenshots of communications taking place over messaging tools	237
11.10	A social knowledge management platform to cultivate community of practice	239
12.1	Community of purpose	251
12.2	From pipeline to platform economy	253
12.3	A digital framework to cultivate online community of purpose	255
12.4	NCoRe: System design	259
12.5	Asynchronous discussions over WhatsApp during production process	266
13.1	Creating community of circumstance in emergency management	281
13.2	System architecture for CORDS: Knowledge sharing using collaboration and connection	290
13.3	Software framework of CORDS	291

Tables

5.1	Impact of information asymmetry on Indian rural producers: Findings	83
11.1	Analysis of gaps from an information-sharing perspective	226
11.2	Sample questions (translated into the native language) used to assess the impact of CoP on individual members "After becoming members of the WhatsApp community"	234
11.3	Effect of community of practice on rural SHG women (translated from Bengali)	235
11.4	Effect of community of practice on rural youth (translated from Bengali)	238
12.1	Comparative analysis of pre- and post-study conducted with rural producers in Kandi	269

Preface

This book is primarily derived from our research at the Social Informatics Research Group, Indian Institute of Management Calcutta. For the last five years we have been working on different projects with the aim to utilize the potential of social technologies and socially enabled applications in addressing problems related to marginalization and social exclusion of rural communities. We have conceptualized a *social knowledge management framework* and developed a *platform* that empowers rural communities by connecting them with urban markets, government agents, trainers, investors, etc. The suggested framework aims to digitally bridge rural–urban knowledge, information and market divide by connecting rural community members with relevant agents and opportunities online.

In this book we illustrate the motivation behind this social knowledge management framework and conceptualization of this framework and demonstrate how this conceptualization helps create a social knowledge management platform, which realizes an ICT-enabled "capability framework". We have shown how it can exploit the potential of community knowledge, making it available to the community and empowering the communities at large to interact, collaborate and participate in the development of society and transforming the way they live, learn and work.

Today, increasing proliferation of mobile devices, broadband connectivity, web technologies, social networks and cloud services enable us to share the resources, information and infrastructure available in any corner of the world. People are now living in a "digitally connected global society" where each individual in a crowd of people is a potential contributor to building a better community – they can collaborate for a social mission, participate in local governance and share their knowledge and expertise to help other underprivileged communities. We propose to study the connection and collaboration among various entities that enable formation of virtual communities to bridge knowledge, information and market divide of rural community. These virtual communities have the most positive effect on social capital when they can increase network density and facilitate the spread of knowledge and information.

Although there is a significant amount of research dealing with different models of knowledge management in the context of business organization to enhance organizational performance, there is no explicit proposal for knowledge management in the context of society at large where the objective is to manage knowledge for social development. Our innovation rests in bringing the concept of knowledge management outside formal organizational boundaries. Our book combines aspects of social technology and social development to derive a *social knowledge management framework*, addressing the challenges faced by contemporary societies to bridge the rural–urban knowledge and information divide and to ensure holistic development of society. Social knowledge management in our context is a framework for rural empowerment using knowledge creation, assimilation and dissemination through digital connections and social collaboration, enhanced by social technologies. Our aim is to craft as well as empirically validate a social knowledge management platform that would mobilize knowledge resources, bridging the gap between the urban–rural communities and creating and building social capital, leading to rural empowerment and, as a consequence, holistic development of the society.

Although this book justifies its theoretical propositions by providing case studies of rural India, its innovativeness in deploying social knowledge management to social development paradigm marks its significance beyond an Indian context. Social technology, empowerment and knowledge management are not new concepts. However, this book tries to bring about sustainable development in rural setting by premising on the cumulative potential of all the above three concepts. Knowledge management using social technology to achieve empowerment not only brings the concepts out of their traditional means of implementation, but their amalgamation offers a compelling alternative development paradigm, which can be applied to the global context following some location-specific modifications. While knowledge management using social technology offers an unstructured and democratic management of valuable information, targeting empowerment from this perspective enables the global rural mass to achieve workable levels of self-sufficiency by overcoming their civic, social and economic isolation. It is by premising on the cumulative potential of the three that the book comes up with strategies to equip the rural mass with knowledge, essential to transforming their lives and livelihood chances.

The book is organized into four parts, highlighting *the problems* (Part I), *proposed solution* (Part II), *implementation and validation* (Part III) and *future prospects* (Part IV). A detailed introduction of the book is offered in Chapter 1 to provide readers with a preliminary sense of what the book entails, what to expect from it and the broad questions guiding it. Subsequently, it enables the readers to embark on a brief, chapter-wise journey, which will help them navigate the book.

*

We would like to express our deepest appreciation to all those who are part of our research endeavour at our Social Informatics Research Group, especially the co-researchers in our group – Ms Arina Bardhan, Ms Priyadarshini Dey and Mr Rishikesan Parthiban – for their support and cooperation in writing this book. We would like to acknowledge with much appreciation the contribution of our research partner, Dr Siuli Roy, Professor, Heritage Institute of Technology, Kolkata, for her contributions in writing this book. Special thanks go to Dr Souvik Basu, Assistant Professor, Heritage Institute of Technology, Kolkata, for his contribution as a member of our research team. Finally, Mr Santosh Pal deserves special mention as a field support to our research team, who has given immense assistance in conducting extensive field studies in rural Bengal, India.

This work would not have been possible without the financial support from our institute, Indian Institute of Management Calcutta, and the Information Technology Research Academy (ITRA), Digital India Corporation, Ministry of Electronics and Information Technology, Government of India. Panasonic India also helped us by providing 50 smartphones, which were distributed among rural self-help group women at Village Kandi, West Bengal. This study was done in close collaboration with Kandi Federation (Kandi Block Mahila Cooperative Credit Society), and a Kolkata-based NGO, Calcutta Society for Professional Action in Development (SPADE). We are grateful to all of them for helping us enormously in conducting our field studies. Special thanks go to two other NGOs, namely Bagaria Relief Welfare Ambulance Society (BRWAS) at Diamond Harbour and Chandanpiri Sri Ramkrishna Ashram of Namkhana, South 24 Parganas, West Bengal, for their support in conducting our field studies.

Student interns from different academic institutes, who helped us in our primary data collection, deserve a special mention. Last, but not least, the unconditional support of our families in the journey of writing this book has served to be a true inspiration in making our journey successful.

1 Introduction

1 Preamble

This book furthers a prospective means to achieve holistic rural empowerment in developing nations by facilitating community formation among rural–urban entities by using the connecting spirit of contemporary digital technology. We would like to begin the book by explicitly making clear the need for empowerment in the context of addressing rural marginalization. With the advent and proliferation of industrialization and concentration of employment opportunities in urban areas, the rural areas in developing nations have started suffering from territorial disadvantages with respect to their urban counterparts. From a social point of view, the isolation of rural areas contributes in keeping rural communities ignorant of urban lifestyles and patterns of social exchange, while economic isolation negatively impacts their market performance. This results in a rural–urban divide where urban areas are better equipped in terms of access to both physical and non-physical resources and the capability to utilize the same in generating opportunity prospects. The rural disadvantages are not just in terms of lack of access, but characterized by the inability of the rural communities to utilize extant resources in pursuit of nurturing individual capability. In the absence of the above-mentioned credentials, the rural communities in developing countries often fall short in capitalizing on their individual capability to pronounce their opportunity scopes.

Extant rural disadvantages amount to much more than mere economic deprivation of rural communities. Lack of access to resources and exposure to unfavourable environments make rural communities victims of social discrimination and exclusion, which subsequently contribute to making the communities powerless along a socio-economic axis. Amidst this backdrop, centralized developmental policies often fall short in addressing the issue at stake. By externally thrusting forward developmental aid, without analysing whether the target group is equipped to utilize the given aid for benefit, the conventional developmental paradigms seldom take into concern empowerment of the intended beneficiaries. John Friedmann's alternative developmental model focusing on restoration of developmental aid to those in need offers a compelling way out from conventional developmental measures (Friedmann, 1992). He rightly identified empowering the marginalized as an alternative and effective developmental strategy. Empowering the marginalized refers to enhancing individual capacities of marginalized members in acquiring the means to meet their own needs. This includes possession of adequate agency among the target group, which will develop their problem-solving skills by overcoming extant hindrances and through possession of necessary social capital, skills, resources and opportunities to accomplish desired goals.

Since the majority of the rural population in developing nations can be categorized as marginalized, due to the dearth of knowledge and lucrative opportunities, empowering them in a holistic sense is the only way out in the process of addressing rural marginalization. In this context, the book tries to address the issue of rural empowerment using a *knowledge–theoretic approach*. Rural empowerment, the way we conceptualize it, can only be achieved by equipping rural communities with necessary knowledge and its operating capabilities through which the target group will derive the capacity to take informed decisions. Possession of knowledge and its operating capacities will enable the rural communities to collaborate across territories and communities: an indispensable factor in cultivating and sustaining social capital (UNESCO, 2005). The resultant collaboration and the capacity to operate knowledge in generating benefits have the potential to enhance opportunity scopes for members of rural communities. With enhanced social capital and opportunity prospects, the rural communities will be better equipped to take informed actions and decisions.

While knowledge-driven rural empowerment happens to be the focus of our book, an inter-connected spirit of contemporary digital technology has served as an implementing tool, which has made it possible for us to craft a holistic scheme for rural empowerment. Contemporary digital technologies have made today's world an integrated space. With the provision to connect easily and smoothly, the digital medium enables people to collaborate across territories and communities. With the advent of digital technology and the proliferation of the information age, attempts to include marginalized sectors within the mainstream became a major driving force. Consequently, several efforts emerged which attempted to mitigate rural–urban divide virtually by extending digital services to rural communities and thereby addressing their socio-economic marginalization (Lekoko & Semali, 2011). However, the sporadic nature of the schemes, coupled with rural communities' inability to utilize digital technologies in pursuit of generating personal benefits, contributed to making most of the initiatives ineffective. As an alternative, we have attempted to deploy the inclusive spirit of digital technologies in cultivating rural empowerment on a holistic scale. Instead of simply providing digital access to the rural marginalized, we have attempted to empower the target group to use the medium in generating opportunities. Our research endeavour uses contemporary digital technologies to usher in rural empowerment, where the medium has been used to inculcate necessary knowledge and its processing abilities among the rural target group.

The book places knowledge possession and operating abilities as the crucial prerequisites in the process of achieving holistic rural empowerment, but only after terminologically demystifying the potential of knowledge and how it happens to be a more holistic concept, distinct from data and information. Premising the research on the effectivity of knowledge as an asset, the book dedicates a significant space to discuss knowledge management as an effective strategy in enhancing organizational efficiency and innovativeness. Knowledge management is defined as the creation, assimilation and dissemination of knowledge to achieve organizational benefit (Nonaka & Takeuchi, 1995). The book attempts to expand the notion of knowledge management to *social knowledge management*, referring to the aspect and effectivity of managing *social knowledge* for rural empowerment. Social knowledge management in our context is a framework for rural empowerment using knowledge creation, assimilation and dissemination through digital connections and social collaboration, enhanced by social technologies (Bandyopadhyay et al., 2017). In our context, *social technology* is an umbrella term used to capture a wide variety of terminologies depicting internet-enabled communications, platforms and tools (for example, web 2.0, mobile 2.0, social media, social software, etc.) which have the potential to establish *collaborative connectivity* among billions of individuals across the globe. Our aim is to craft as well as empirically validate a social knowledge management platform that would mobilize knowledge resources, bridging the gap between urban–rural communities and creating and building social capital, leading to rural empowerment and, as a consequence, holistic development of the society.

The book advocates for a collaborative approach, to be realized by virtue of a social technology-driven social knowledge management platform, which will usher in rural empowerment by facilitating effective rural–urban information and knowledge exchange. The effectivity of the proposed platform rests in cultivating virtual communities, where empowerment will usher through easy and smooth knowledge exchange across rural–urban communities. This community formation is not simply derived from giving rural non-users access to digital services. It is only when rural members develop the ability to nurture individual capability through digital usage that incentives to self-prosper will evoke the need to collaborate; the prerequisite for voluntary community formation. This implies that possession of knowledge and knowledge-operating capacities in amalgamation gives rural members the ability to collaborate and subsequently form virtual communities. Knowledge exchange and effective collaboration, derivative of virtual community formation, not only offer the prospect of nurturing individual capability but also enable rural members to capitalize on the same and generate prospective opportunity outcomes. While community formation has explicit socio-economic promises, it is only effective collaboration derived from community formation that offers the prospect of mitigating rural–urban information, knowledge and opportunity divide.

While so far we have discussed why the book is important, what to expect and the broad questions guiding the book, we now embark on a brief chapter-wise journey that will help the reader navigate it.

2 Organization of the book

The book is organized into four parts: highlighting the problems (Part I), the proposed solution (Part II), implementation and validation (Part III) and future prospects (Part IV).

Following this introductory chapter, **Part I** (*Rural empowerment: Bridging the rural–urban knowledge and information divide*) takes up the issue of rural empowerment from a knowledge–theoretic angle and attempts to achieve the same through mitigation of extant rural–urban knowledge and information divide.

Part I is divided into five chapters. Chapter 2 (*Knowledge, knowledge divide and knowledge capability: A conceptual framework*) lays the groundwork for the effectivity of knowledge as an asset indispensable for human growth (Dave et al., 2012). It starts with building up a sociological conceptualization of knowledge, which sees knowledge as a social resource unevenly distributed across society. Discriminatory social rules and regulations guiding the distribution logic of knowledge as a resource inevitably pave the path for the unequal prevalence of the resource across society, thereby creating a knowledge divide. This divide leads to a hierarchical grouping – one group comprising the privileged, who possess and operate knowledge freely, and the other group devoid of similar privileges. In this context, the chapter makes an important contribution in highlighting that access by a marginalized group to a knowledge resource will not simply move them to the advantageous side of the knowledge divide. It is only when the marginalized group develops knowledge-operating capacities, or *knowledge capability* (Ning et al., 2006), along with knowledge possession, that there is a chance of mitigating knowledge divide.

Chapter 3 (*Rural empowerment: A knowledge theoretic approach*) provides a framework of rural empowerment as a knowledge theoretic concept. In this chapter we advocate for a definition of rural empowerment that is characterized by the possession of desirable levels of agency, social capital and opportunity structure by the rural members (Samman & Santos, 2009; Alsop & Heinsohn, 2005; World Bank, 2001). The endorsed definition of rural empowerment is such that equipping the marginalized population with knowledge and its operating capabilities becomes crucial in the process of empowering them. The chapter not only draws co-relations between empowerment and agency, empowerment and social capital, and empowerment and opportunity structure, but also conducts a relational study between knowledge and the three concepts: agency, social capital and opportunity structure. Such a relational study is conducted to theoretically do justice to our definition of empowerment from a knowledge–theoretic angle. The relational study theoretically justifies how possession of knowledge and knowledge capability serves to be mandatory in enhancing agency, social capital and the opportunity structure of a target group, the latter three being facilitators of empowerment. It is by making the rural population *knowledge capable* that we attempt to address rural empowerment from within, which will not only make the rural target group knowledge literate but also inculcate in them evaluative capacities to process acquired knowledge for practical benefits.

In Chapter 4 (*Contemporary initiatives undertaken for rural empowerment*) the book discusses contemporary efforts undertaken to empower marginalized rural populations. In tandem with the definition of rural empowerment postulated in Chapter 3, this chapter critically evaluates the extant measures undertaken to achieve rural empowerment. A critical evaluation reveals that a knowledge–theoretic approach is seldom incorporated within the purview of extant empowering measures. Most of the schemes have attempted to address the issue of rural marginalization by exogenously feeding crucial information and other resources considered necessary for development to the rural target group. However, amidst the backdrop of constricted agency, weak social capital and the limited opportunity structure of rural members, external feeding of information fails to secure benefits for the rural target group. The extant schemes, while making available valuable information to rural communities, do not give them the ability to process the acquired information. As a result, the acquired information remains at the level of factual data to a rural community, where lack of processing abilities and opportunities prevent the community benefiting from purposive sharing of information.

While Chapter 4 concludes by implicitly hinting at the difference between information and knowledge, and how the latter is a more holistic concept, Chapter 5 (*Information asymmetry and rural producers*) tackles the difference explicitly and analytically. The chapter begins by spelling out marginalized rural communities' need for information and justifies its propositions by providing case studies of rural Indian producers and the hindrances they face due to lack of information. Practical insights show how a dearth of information regarding markets, including tastes and preferences of contemporary customers and other market dynamics, significantly hinders rural producers' market performance. The chapter then proceeds to discuss how several schemes have been undertaken to mitigate the existing information asymmetry of rural producers because of their informationally impoverished status. However, the chapter concludes by highlighting the difference between information and knowledge and how an in-depth examination of the existing schemes undertaken to mitigate information asymmetry of rural producers has remained inadequate in delivering significant results on a holistic scale. The reason lies in their focus. The feeding of information to rural producers remains an external imposition in the presence of the target group's inability to utilize disseminated information for practical benefits. This proves that we cannot address rural communities' marginalization solely along information lines; there is a need for a more holistic concept, knowledge, which can do justice to the mission of mitigating the extant rural–urban divide.

Chapter 6 (*Knowledge asymmetry and its mitigation through enhancement of knowledge capability*) highlights that the road to holistic rural empowerment lies in mitigating knowledge asymmetry of rural participants. By providing a relational analysis between information and knowledge asymmetry (Dellemijn,

2012), the chapter spells out how the latter is a characteristic problem of marginalized rural members and how addressing knowledge asymmetry offers the prospect of mitigating rural–urban divide. It is by accrediting rural population with access to knowledge, along with developing in them knowledge capability, that knowledge asymmetry of rural participants can be both alleviated and their socio–economic prospects enhanced on a sustainable basis.

Knowledge asymmetry cannot be mitigated by ensuring access to adequate knowledge resources only. Endowing the target group with knowledge-operating capabilities is equally important in the process of empowering rural target group with knowledge resources. In this context, the following questions arise:

a   How to develop a systematic approach to capture, structure, manage and disseminate knowledge to empower the rural target group with knowledge resources and knowledge-operating capabilities?
b   How can we create a framework for managing knowledge that allows rural participants to create and modify content collaboratively to bridge the rural–urban information and knowledge divide?
c   How can the inclusive potential of contemporary digital technology, comprising internet-enabled communications, platforms and tools (for example, web 2.0, mobile 2.0, social media, social software, etc.) be exploited to establish *collaborative connectivity* among billions of individuals around the globe, to help cultivate knowledge and knowledge capabilities of rural populations?
d   How can a digital space for engagement and development of the rural population be created to manage social knowledge so that the rural users are provided with a multi-community connectivity, making it quicker and easier for members to connect, communicate, collaborate and learn by getting connected to relevant people and information in one integrated workspace?

Part II of the book (*Social knowledge management and social technologies: Conceptual foundations*) attempts to answer all these questions by proposing *social knowledge management* as an effective framework in enhancing knowledge capabilities of social actors. This part is divided into four chapters. Chapter 7 (*Knowledge management and its evolution in organizational context*) narrates what knowledge management is and how it evolved gradually over time in an organizational context to incorporate the exchange of both tacit and explicit knowledge resources within its purview (Nonaka & Takeuechi, 1995). Discussion on knowledge management explicitly highlights how the strategy evolved in an organizational context, in alliance with technological development. However, it is only the inclusive spirit with which contemporary digital technology is endowed that has the capacity to cultivate knowledge management to promote enhancement of knowledge capability of target groups. Contemporary *social technologies* and the connected spirit have enormous potential in ushering in social development by facilitating effective collaborations among diverse and scattered social agents. For this reason we have used the term *social technologies* to refer to such an empowering digital infrastructure.

Chapter 8 (*Social technology and knowledge management practices*) spells out the terminological usage and theoretical and practical reach of social technologies and how these attempt to build an inter-connected digital ecosystem by enabling every social member to participate in the digital network. *Social technology* is an umbrella term used to capture a wide variety of terminologies depicting internet-enabled communications, platforms and tools (for example, web 2.0, mobile 2.0, social media, social software, etc.) which have the potential to establish *collaborative connectivity* among billions of individuals around the globe (Chui et al., 2012). The inter-connected digital ecosystem, built by social technologies, serves as the implementing premise of our *social knowledge management framework*, which is detailed in Chapter 10. However, before the conceptual and implementational dynamics of our social knowledge management framework is articulated, we use Chapter 9 to discuss efforts undertaken to manage social knowledge and information for social benefit.

Chapter 9 (*Efforts undertaken to manage social knowledge and information for social benefit*) is dedicated to spelling out different attempts to manage social knowledge and information for social benefit, although the attempts cannot be formally categorized or recognized as *knowledge management* practices. While knowledge management as a formal strategy has gained popular recognition in an organizational context, it is seldom applied in social contexts. However, this does not imply that the activity of managing social knowledge for social benefit is an undone phenomenon. Historically, social functioning has been achieved as a result of informal knowledge collaboration, where social knowledge has been managed for social benefit. The chapter refers to historic attempts to manage social knowledge and information and how the efforts evolved with time and with the emergence of digital technologies. The chapter concludes by examining the inherent shortcomings of the discussed measures, paving the path for Chapter 10, which justifies the credibility and necessity of our social knowledge management framework in the context of holistic social empowerment.

Chapter 10 (*Social knowledge management: A social technology-enabled framework to bridge knowledge asymmetry of rural producers through virtual community formation*) is dedicated to spelling out in detail our social knowledge management framework, which we have devised to achieve rural empowerment from within. Our social knowledge management framework, by utilizing social technology as its backbone, attempts to establish effective collaboration between and across rural–urban communities. By facilitating effective intra- and inter-group knowledge exchange, the framework targets rural empowerment from within by developing rural actors' knowledge capabilities. The novelty of the framework rests in its motivation to facilitate collaboration by triggering virtual community formation. A social technology-supported social knowledge management framework attempts to mobilize crowd knowledge capital so that rural empowerment can be achieved by facilitating knowledge collaboration across rural–urban communities. Developing knowledge capabilities among rural participants by facilitating community formation and knowledge exchange endows our social knowledge management framework with the ability to mitigate the rural–urban information, knowledge and opportunity divide.

Part III of this book (*Social knowledge management in action: Some empirical studies in rural India*) shares some of our field experiences in rural India and spells out the effectivity of social knowledge management in terms of cultivating virtual communities. It is through the active and voluntary formation of such communities that rural members will develop knowledge capabilities via effective collaboration, which will attempt to realize a holistic vision of rural empowerment. This part is divided into three chapters. Chapter 11 (*Cultivating online communities of practice to facilitate practice-oriented rural–urban knowledge exchange through collaborative learning spaces*) builds on the aspect of achieving rural empowerment through community formation. The chapter offers empirical insights that highlight our research effort in cultivating *communities of practice* among rural producers and urban experts. An in-depth examination demonstrates how the cultivation of communities of practice through facilitation of collaborative learning spaces has a positive impact in enhancing knowledge capabilities of marginalized rural producers. Through the formation of communities of practice, rural producers get the provision to access and apply specialized knowledge with the help of expert guidance, thereby enhancing the quality of their skill set and awareness level. By virtue of collaboration, the members not only gain access to specialized knowledge but also develop the ability to internalize acquired and exchanged knowledge. This, in turn, enables the members to possess the credential and use the same in pursuit of personal benefits.

The theoretical formulation regarding the effectivity of cultivating communities of practice among rural members in the context of rural empowerment is practically justified in this chapter by citing instances from rural India. Two examples in the chapter show how collaborative knowledge exchange through cultivation of communities of practice creates an impact on rural members' skill set and awareness level.

While communities of practice have the potential to usher in a space for collaborative learning to cultivate a specific practice and subsequently enhance individual capability of rural members, *community of purpose* helps the members in translating their capability to improve their opportunity prospects. In Chapter 12 (*Cultivating communities of purpose to enhance market opportunities of rural producers through collaborative knowledge transaction*) we show how communities of purpose can be cultivated among rural–urban communities to mitigate the poor performance of rural economies. Communities of purpose refer to the formation of purposive communities, where the aim is to bridge the *market separation* experienced by rural producers (Singh et al., 2015). The chapter offers empirical evidence to show how we have attempted to build a community of purpose among rural–urban entities by using our social knowledge management platform. Purposive networking taking place across rural–urban entities paves the path for a collaborative supply-chain of the production process. The chapter explains the benefit of such collaborative production along a dual axes: collaboration with urban agents improves market performance of rural producers; and direct connection with urban consumers enables the rural producers to bypass exploitative middlemen, thereby addressing their issue of market separation. The chapter concludes with the prospects offered by community of purpose to enhance the opportunity scope for rural producers, thereby significantly contributing to the process of mitigating the rural–urban knowledge, information and opportunity divide.

While cultivating *communities of practice* and *purpose* using a social knowledge management framework yields positive outcomes in a rural context, it does not ensure creation of a *resilient community*, a community "that can withstand hazards, continue to operate under stress, adapt to adversity, and recover functionality after a crisis" (National Research Council, 2011). In order to do justice to our holistic vision of rural empowerment and mitigation of rural–urban divide on a sustainable basis, in Chapter 13 (*Cultivating communities of circumstance to enhance community resilience through knowledge sharing using collaboration and connections*) we have attempted to cultivate community of circumstance between rural–urban communities. Community of circumstance refers to mechanism towards building a *resilient community*, possessing a high rate of adaptive capacity on a collective level. However, *communities of practice* and *purpose* account to be mandatory prerequisites in building *communities of circumstance* among rural–urban communities. It is the cultivation of all three in amalgamation that has the potential to establish proposed social knowledge management frameworks as an effective strategy in mitigating rural–urban divide and subsequently ushering in holistic rural empowerment.

We conclude our book with **Part IV** (*What tomorrow may bring*), which is divided into two chapters. Chapter 14 (*Summary and discussions*) narrates in detail our research experience. While in this book we endorse a vision for holistic rural empowerment, the execution of the desired goal has often encountered local-operative hindrances. This chapter highlights our research journey, the obstacles faced on it and how we have attempted to overcome them in the process of chalking up a holistic strategy for rural empowerment.

Different types of virtual communities and the effective inter- and intra-group collaboration they support is conducive to the process of achieving holistic rural empowerment by mitigating rural–urban knowledge, information and opportunity divide. The credibility of the supported collaboration rests in positively influencing enhancement of agency, social capital and opportunity prospects of rural target group, thereby making our proposition crucial in achieving holistic rural empowerment. Capacity building for marginalized communities might be emergent (in endogenous community development) but it needs to be nurtured via external sources (by exogenous development) (Steiner & Farmer, 2017).

10 Introduction

This calls for developing an *empowering ecosystem* to foster *connection* and *collaboration* between external agencies and rural communities, leading to holistic development of the communities.

Chapter 15 (*Building a developmental ecosystem for rural empowerment*) focuses on the future prospects of our research. In doing so it endorses a vision towards building a developmental ecosystem that combines exogenous and endogenous development processes by connecting billions of individuals all over the globe as external agents (the *crowd capital*), including traditional development agencies for collaborative knowledge exchange. Democratization of science and technology, an increase in global connectivity using social technologies, and greater availability of data will facilitate a movement that will shift control from centralized development through a handful of traditional development agencies to decentralized development involving *crowd capital* – billions of development agents (Dehgan, 2012). Effective community formation and facilitation of inter- and intra-group collaboration happens to be a crucial prerequisite in the process of building an inter-connected developmental ecosystem. Such an ecosystem can only be formed once every member is equipped with sufficient knowledge and its operating abilities, thereby creating value out of knowledge exchange. Amidst this backdrop lies the possibility of a mitigated rural–urban knowledge, information and opportunity divide.

References

Alsop, R. & Heinsohn, N. (2005). Measuring Empowerment in Practice: Structuring Analysis and Framing Indicators. *World Bank Policy Research Working Paper* 3510. Available at: http://siteresources.worldbank.org/INTEMPOWERMENT/Resources/41307 _wps3510.pdf.

Bandyopadhyay, S., Bardhan, A., Dey, P., Banerjee, S., Das, S. & Mandal, K. (2017). A Social Knowledge Management Platform for Universal Primary Education Online. In *Harnessing Social Media as a Knowledge Management Tool*. Hershey, PA: IGI Global. doi:10.4018/978-1-5225-0495-5.ch005.

Chui, M., et al. (2012). The Social Economy: Unlocking Value and Productivity Through Social Technologies. *McKinsey Global Institute Report*. Retrieved from: https://www.mckinsey.com /industries/high-tech/our-insights/the-social-economy.

Dave, M., Dave, M. & Shishodia, Y. (2012). Emerging Trends and Technologies in Knowledge Management: A Holistic Vision. *International Journal of Recent Research and Review*, III, 60–67.

Dehgan, A. (2012). Creating the New Development Ecosystem. *Science*, 336(6087), 1397–1398. doi:10.1126/science.1224530.

Dellemijn, R.N.J.C. (2012). Knowledge Asymmetry in Inter-Firm Relationships (Master's thesis, University of Twente, Netherlands). Retrieved from: http://essay.utwente.nl/61982/.

Friedmann, J. (1992). *Empowerment: The Politics of Alternative Development*. Oxford: Wiley-Blackwell.

Lekoko, R.N. & Semali, L. (2011). *Cases on Developing Countries and ICT Integration: Rural Community Development*. Hershey, PA: IGI Global. doi:10.4018/978-1-60960-117-1.

National Research Council (2011). *Building Community Disaster Resilience Through Private-Public Collaboration.* Washington, DC: The National Academies Press. doi:10.17226/13028.

Ning, Y., Shu, P. & Feng, B. (2006). *Knowledge Capability: A Definition and Research Model.* Heidelberg: Springer. doi:330-340. 10.1007/11811220_28.

Nonaka, I. & Takeuchi, H. (1995). *The Knowledge Creating Company: How Japanese Companies Create the Dynamics of Innovation.* New York: Oxford University Press.

Samman, E. & Santos, M.E. (2009). *Agency and Empowerment: A review of concepts, indicators and empirical evidence.* Oxford: Oxford University Research Archive.

Singh, R., Agarwal, S. & Modi, P. (2015). Market Separations for BOP Producers: The Case of Market Development for the Chanderi Cluster Weavers in India. *International Journal of Rural Management*, 11(2), 175–193.

Steiner, A. & Farmer, J. (2017). Engage, participate, empower: Modelling power transfer in disadvantaged rural communities. *Environment and Planning C: Politics and Space*, 36(1), 118–138. doi:10.1177/2399654417701730.

UNESCO (2005). Towards Knowledge Societies. United Nations Educational, Scientific and Cultural Organization's World Report. Retrieved from: https://unesdoc.unesco.org/ark:/48223/pf0000141843.

World Bank (2001). *World Development Report 2000/2001: Attacking Poverty.* New York: Oxford University Press. Retrieved from: https://www.odi.org/sites/odi.org.uk/files/odi-assets/events-presentations/703.pdf.

Part I
Rural empowerment
Bridging rural–urban knowledge and information divide

2 Knowledge, knowledge divide and knowledge capability
A conceptual framework

1 Introduction

There have been multiple strands within academia that treat knowledge and define the resource in terms of respective disciplinarian ideologies. The quest for knowledge and to understand the same started in the philosophical tradition, with the pioneers being classical Greek theorists such as Aristotle and Plato. While the philosophical tradition dedicated itself to exploring the foundations of knowledge, it provided little account of how knowledge and knowledge exchange between different entities enable society to function on a daily basis. This chapter traces the multiple origins of knowledge within the formal parameters of study. In doing so the chapter eventually advocates for a sociological conception of knowledge, which focuses on the functionality of the asset in the context of social action, by considering knowledge to be a social product, constructed, shaped and transformed by social interactions.

This chapter is divided into four sections:

- The first part conceptualizes knowledge along sociological terms. Articulating knowledge as a social construct, the section bears reference to how social factors shape the acquisition and distribution of knowledge resource across society.
- The second part expands on the distribution ethics of knowledge resource and highlights how discriminatory social forces grant the privileged few with relevant knowledge and knowledge-operating capacities, while denying the marginalized the avenue to actively participate in knowledge transaction.
- The third part introduces and builds on the concept of knowledge capability, as furthered by capability theorists. In doing so the section fleshes out how enhancing knowledge capability (which accounts to be possession of knowledge asset along with knowledge-operating capacities) is crucial in the process of overcoming knowledge divide existing in society. The section concludes with the connecting spirit of contemporary information and communications technology (ICT) and its indispensability in enhancing knowledge capability of social members.

- The final section highlights the urgency of managing knowledge as a social strategy to sustainably enhance knowledge capability of social actors. Hinting at the importance of managing knowledge in ushering in efficient and effective distribution of knowledge resource throughout society, the section spells out the indispensability of the practice in enhancing knowledge capability of social actors, both at the individual and collective level.

2 Defining knowledge

Any effort dedicated to demystifying what knowledge is must, at the very beginning, chart the differences between knowledge, information and data. Davenport and Prusak (1998) define data to be a set of discrete, objective facts about an event. Following a similar thread, we can conceptualize data to be a collection of numbers and characters denoting values of qualitative or quantitative variables belonging to a set of items. Data becomes information when it is presented as a message that makes a difference to the receiver of the message. Data transforms into information when some meaning is added to it. Methods of adding meaning can be *contextualizing, categorizing, calculation, correction* and *condensation* (Dave et al., 2012). Information, therefore, refers to a sequence of symbols that can be recorded as a message (utterance or expression).

Knowledge, in contrast to information, refers to a holistic concept, which includes within its purview facts, information, description or skills acquired through experience and education. Knowledge refers to the theoretical and/or practical understanding of a subject. Brooking (1999) refers to knowledge as organized information, together with the understanding of what it means. The holistic notion of knowledge also gets reflected in Davenport and Prusak's (1998) definition of knowledge as a fluid mix of framed experience, values, contextual information and expert insights that provide a framework for evaluating and incorporating new experiences and information (Dave et al., 2012). In order to conceptualize knowledge in an organizational context, the authors formulated knowledge as being embedded not only in documents and repositories but also in organizational routines, processes, practices and norms. This marks the organic element of knowledge and further contributes in highlighting its difference in regard to the factual nature of information.

Knowledge is thought to derive its strength and application utility from its humane elements, which makes the same a curious compilation of information, coupled with skills, experiences and attitude (Dellemijn, 2012). The human elements (skills, experience and attitude) mark the supremacy of knowledge over information. Eminent classical sociologist Claude Levi-Strauss insightfully distinguished knowledge from information, where he identified the latter as raw and the former as cooked and processed (Burke, 2000). Knowledge attains its processing flavour over information through *verification, criticism, measurement, comparison* and *systemization*, all of which result from human interpretation of raw information.

Several scholars have conceptualized knowledge along dichotomous lines, with it comprised of two elements – *explicit* and *tacit* knowledge (Dave et al., 2012). Explicit knowledge refers to that element of knowledge which can be expressed in words and numbers. Explicit knowledge therefore refers to codified knowledge, which is well-defined, thereby making it easy to communicate via formal language. Tacit knowledge, on the other hand, is primarily expressed as insights, intuitions and hunches. It is highly personal and hard to formalize and imitate (Brie & Thomasberger, 2018). It is personal because it depends on individual actions, commitment and involvement, making it hard to formally communicate. Since it cannot be mechanically transferred, tacit knowledge needs to be accomplished (Dellemijn, 2012). Knowledge, in its holistic sense, is a curious compilation of both explicit and tacit elements.

3 Knowledge: A social product

The study of knowledge and how the asset can be utilized to boost social and organizational efficiency has gained significant importance in contemporary times with the inception of the notion of *knowledge society*. "The wealth of the nation no longer depends on its ability to acquire and convert raw materials, but on the abilities and intellects of all its citizens" (TFPL, 1999, p. 2). This emergent reality for organizations and nation states, facilitated by the concept of *knowledge society*, considers knowledge acquisition and processing to be the ultimate indicator of social advancement (Laszlo & Laszlo, 2002). The resultant emergence of the knowledge-centric approach has not only altered the way society and economy is managed in today's world, it has also offered redeeming possibilities in support of holistic developmental paradigms.

Human beings, being the premise of knowledge creation, assimilation and dissemination, are therefore identified as major drivers in knowledge-centric approaches. Knowledge-centric approaches, in contrast to conventional developmental paradigms, treat human beings as ends in themselves, instead of being means, or passive recipients, of social change (Sen, 2003). Conventional developmental paradigms trace growth and development in terms of economic opulence. They consider human beings as essentially productive means and propose models of economic growth by solely targeting income enhancement (Sen, 2003). In contrast to existing developmental paradigms, knowledge-centric approaches are developed on the concept that knowledge is power, and it is the possession and application of knowledge that has the capacity to enhance individual and collective credentials.

This approach has the capacity to offer redeeming possibilities because it does not consider knowledge to be inert and passive, rather as a resource constantly being created and modified in dialogue with social factors. Possession of knowledge has to be taken into account, along with an individual/group's social structuring and position, which shapes that particular entities' knowledge pool and transactional capacities. This sheds light on the social dynamics governing the pattern of knowledge production (Basu et al., 2016). Knowledge production mainly occurs along two lines: (a) institutional production, where specialized institutions, governed by social elites, are responsible for dissemination of "authentic" knowledge; and (b) a common-based peer production, a more recent knowledge production mode, where knowledge is produced by common mass. Although contemporary society has enabled common mass to contribute to the knowledge pool, often it is seen that the majority of contributors mostly come from affluent backgrounds. This sanctions knowledge's status as a social product. Not only the production logic of knowledge is governed by the social elites; the marginalized group also falls on the disadvantageous side of knowledge distribution. Social conventions, rules and regulations dictate the dynamics of both knowledge production and distribution. Amidst such a backdrop, knowledge becomes a social asset, the adequate possession and operation of which has compelling impact in shaping the users' social and economic credibility.

Although the inception and proliferation of knowledge-centric approaches can be traced to recent times, knowledge and its importance as an asset has been realized long back, where its epistemological origin can be traced to the time of classical Greek theorists Aristotle and Plato. The strand of knowledge conceptualized and furthered by classical Greek scholars has a philosophical premise and is mainly concerned with articulating the foundation of knowledge as an asset. The philosophical tradition interprets knowledge as residing in the mind of the object. This premise contributes in interpreting knowledge through a reductionist lens, which conceptualizes the asset in terms of the relationship between the individual subject, the knower, and the object or referent, the known (Adolf & Stehr, 2014). The urgency of the philosophical tradition to secure the foundations of knowledge disallows the strand to account for the social forces and factors that play a decisive role in the creation and transfer of knowledge between and across societies.

While knowledge is about the relationship between the subject and the object, the knower and the known, we need to remember that such a transactional relationship does not exist in a vacuum; it is mandatory to account for the social factors that enable realization or hinder such transaction of knowledge between interested parties. It is with an intention to account for the social factors in the process of production and distribution of knowledge across society that our research endeavour marks a departure from a philosophical conceptualization of knowledge. As an alternative, we embrace a sociological understanding of knowledge. Unlike its philosophical counterpart, sociological understanding of knowledge resists conceptualizing knowledge along articulate terms. A sociological understanding of knowledge treats the asset as the unpredictable product of diverse social forces operating and shaping the conditions of individual knowledge sources and recipients, where knowledge is identified as the product of unique socio-historical experiences (Meja & Stehr, 2005).

Sociological conceptualization of knowledge not only considers knowledge to be a social product constructed, shaped and transformed by social factors, but also focuses on the functionality of the resource in the context of social action. Unlike the philosophical tradition, which primarily dedicated itself to exploring the foundations of knowledge, a sociological understanding mainly focuses on the "work" knowledge performs in social action (Adolf & Stehr, 2014).

It was Max Scheler, in the early 1920s, who first used the term *Wissenssoziologie*, which can be translated as "sociology of knowledge" (Scheler, 1958). However, sociological understanding of knowledge gained a formal inception with Karl Mannheim. Scheler claimed that different "real factors" (*Realfaktoren*) condition thought in different historical periods and in different social and cultural systems in specific ways. Mannheim (1986) extended Scheler's formulation of human thought having social and cultural origins. Mannheim not only highlighted how human thought, rooted in socio-cultural dynamics, enables social functioning through relevant exchange between different social actors, but also recognized its importance in the context of social dispute resolution.

Mannheim identified human thought to be the ultimate factor triggering competition (Adolf & Stehr, 2014). This explains why knowledge-rich nations have better economic and social performance compared with the knowledge-impoverished ones (Weingart, 2015). Considering the role of human thought and perception in triggering competition has two implications. On the one hand, it makes the work of politics, society and economy knowledge-centric. On the other hand, knowledge is conceptualized to play a decisive role in the age of dissolution and conflict by providing sociological analysis of various competitive ideas, political philosophies, ideologies and diverse cultural products. The amalgamation of the above-stated implications makes sociology of knowledge a *diagnosis of its time*, a self-reflective practice which provides practical solutions in cases of dispute and disorientation by not only creating new knowledge but also by discarding and modifying the existing set (Adolf & Stehr, 2014).

The ability of knowledge in facilitating effective social functioning is premised on the theorization of knowledge as the generalized capacity to act on the world, to set something in motion (Stehr, 1994). Modern society is knowledge-based and the worlds of work, politics and everyday life are based on and transformed by knowledge. This credential of knowledge to usher in change by virtue of relevant exchange makes it urgent to analyse the role knowledge plays in society, instead of over-engaging with its foundations, as championed by philosophical tradition. The kind of work knowledge performs in the context of social action marks the inception and proliferation of a sociological understanding of the concept, which made explicit the role of social actors or individual knowledge sources in the process of knowledge creation and distribution. Knowledge as a social product is conceptualized to be rooted in social fabric, created, assimilated and distributed following social norms in which knowledge possession and knowledge operation of social actors are heavily guided by social dictates.

The fact that knowledge is a social construct and that social factors shape the distribution of knowledge acknowledges how the asset is embedded in social fabric; the logic of distribution guided by social factors also infers how knowledge distribution is shaped by discriminatory social forces. Society is intrinsically hierarchical and stratified. As a result, the ethics of knowledge distribution, shaped by social factors, also follow the logic of social stratification, which, although granting a privileged few access to knowledge and operating capacities, denies the marginalized such an opportunity. The resultant knowledge divide fractures our world, where scholars of knowledge-centric approaches have often equated inequality in knowledge with inequality in development. This leads Weingart (2015) to interpret the development status of urban conglomerates in terms of the knowledge access and acquisition ability of the sector, whereas the lack of it denies the rural hinterlands a similar status. Although knowledge divide is a social malady that has to be addressed following a democratic logic of knowledge distribution, we must remember that, since knowledge is intrinsically embedded in social fabric, such unequal distribution is to a great extent inevitable. Sociological conceptualization of knowledge has the potential to acknowledge the "impurity" of knowledge, its rootedness in all social institutions and cultural processes, its entanglement with power and interests, and its enormous variability. Our research therefore adopts a sociological understanding of knowledge to grasp the existing logic of knowledge creation and distribution following social forces and, in turn, provides prospective and contextual solutions to facilitate effective distribution of knowledge.

4 Knowledge divide

Knowledge can easily travel the world, thereby making the resource accessible to a wide array of social members. Yet, as the World Bank Development Report of 1998–99 suggests, the access to knowledge resource does not necessarily mean that users are empowered to operate the resource and achieve practical benefits. This can be explained using a simple example. "Knowledge about how to treat a simple ailment, such as diarrhea, has existed for centuries—but millions of children continue to die from it because their parents do not know how to save them" (World Bank, 1999). The World Bank differentiates between poor and rich countries, not only in terms of the former having less capital but also in terms of the former possessing less knowledge than the latter.

This opening sentence of the World Bank's Development Report, titled "Knowledge for Development", accurately grasps the unequal distribution of knowledge, even though the asset is generally present and flows throughout society. This highlights that availability, or even accessibility, to knowledge is not enough to guarantee the optimal usage of the asset in pursuit of practical gains. Since knowledge cannot be mechanically transferred, and instead has to be accomplished, development following knowledge acquisition and exchange is based on individual credentials. These individual credentials are in turn shaped by social factors, which ultimately govern the logic of knowledge acquisition, production and distribution.

A similar concern, echoing unequal distribution of knowledge, is articulated in UNESCO's World Science Declaration. "Most of the benefits of science are unevenly distributed as a result of structural asymmetries among countries, regions and social groups, and between sexes. What distinguishes the poor from the rich is not only they have fewer assets, but also they are largely excluded from the creation and benefits of scientific knowledge" (UNESCO, 1999). This highlights that providing access to knowledge remains redundant if the structural inequalities from which countries, regions and social groups suffer, and which mark their social positionings, are not accounted for.

UNESCO and the World Bank have jointly identified some factors that account for the knowledge divide existing between nations (World Bank, 1999). These are:

- **Absence of freedom** hindering knowledge possession and transactional capacities of individuals/group(s).
- **Lack of democracy** disallowing one and all to participate in knowledge transaction.
- **Constricted freedom of media** hindering dissemination of different strands of knowledge among the general mass.
- **Lack of quality infrastructure** to create, assimilate and democratically disseminate knowledge.
- **Lack of effective communication systems** to facilitate communication between different knowledge sources (individual/groups).
- **Lack of provision for primary and basic education** hindering the cognitive abilities required to possess and process knowledge.
- **Neglect on research and innovation**, which hinders creation of new knowledge and modification of that existing.
- **Lack of intellectual property rights**, which denies economic incentives for investing in new knowledge development.

The presence of the these factors in differential extents have serious implications in the study of knowledge divide between and across countries, regions and social groups. The emergent notions of knowledge society and globalization have given renewed importance to knowledge as an asset, and the dream of a boundary-less world has theoretically paved the path for unhindered knowledge exchange among different territorial spaces. However, Weingart (2015) insightfully conceptualizes how the notions have the capacity to accelerate knowledge divide, if not dealt with through a critical and investigative lens. The integrationist viewpoint of globalization often, instead of assimilating different knowledge sources within its parameters, favours the benchmarks and principals of *powerful* knowledge sources and tags them as essentially "global". The role of indigenous knowledge in ushering in development often remains obscure in the process. This leads to the formulation of developmental models premised on the ideology of the *powerful* West, which is externally thrust on other regions without incorporating any modifications in accordance to specificities of regional context. The domination of Western knowledge as "universal" knowledge has been facilitated by globalization through global institutionalization of mass education, through colonization, the nation-state and a global model of modernization. While this standardization creates and disseminates knowledge, the logic of distribution does not account for the social factors that are intrinsic to a particular location.

Dissemination of knowledge following this hierarchical distributive logic falls short in achieving "capacity building from below", which is a prerequisite in equitable distribution of knowledge. Knowledge is not an inert resource which can be mechanically possessed. Its value is only realized through active human participation in knowledge transaction. While these standardized sources make available "global" knowledge for all, the non-contextual nature of the distributed asset fails to achieve capacity building of individual knowledge users.

In contemporary society, where knowledge has renewed importance, the aspect of knowledge divide has attracted the attention of global policy-makers and developmental agents. The growth and dissemination of knowledge has increased exponentially, in proportion to the growth and development of scientific technologies (Laszlo & Laszlo, 2002). The role contemporary information and communications technology (ICT) plays in the dissemination of knowledge has enabled many to equate knowledge divide with digital divide. The premise of such an equation is informed by the fact that people having access to digital technologies will automatically become a part of the digital knowledge pool, which, through dialogue among different global knowledge sources, will improve knowledge-operating capacities of different users. Although theoretically such a causal relation can be drawn, several studies show that access to the internet does not necessarily ensure participation in production and distribution of knowledge (Rieu, 2005). Access to technology is not equivalent to overcoming knowledge divide, as the latter, in addition to technical access, requires the training, cognitive skills and regulatory frameworks crucial for translating knowledge resource for self-benefit. Knowledge encompasses different disciplines. The concept of knowledge, as analysed within different disciplinarian parameters, interacts in various settings, situations, within universities and organizations, between firms and government agencies, between media and population and between communities. These open interactions generate further knowledge. Contemporary ICT has immense potential in facilitating knowledge exchange among diverse and scattered groups by overcoming territorial limitations. However, such knowledge exchange retains a mechanical flavour if knowledge transaction following technology falls short in improving the capability set of individual knowledge contributors.

Hence a standardized model of knowledge dissemination with passive usage of technology for the purpose of mass-scale knowledge distribution falls short in realizing the true value of the resource. Knowledge is a constantly evolving dynamic concept, which is collective not unified, common not universal. In order to realize its full worth, knowledge has to be treated as a level of aggregation of interactions between different social sectors at a given moment, in a given place. This essence of knowledge denies any one particular strand of knowledge the status of "true knowledge". Rather, it acknowledges different strands of knowledge with equal weight, therefore considering knowledge to be plural. The implications of treating knowledge to be plural, following Foucault (1970), has serious spill-over effects in acknowledging the importance of indigenous and context-specific knowledge sources. Acknowledging different types of knowledge creates the provision "to connect" different knowledge sources, paving the path for effective collaboration (Burke, 2000). Bridging knowledge divide, therefore, is not about passive transmission of standardized knowledge to those who do not have it. Bridging knowledge divide entails connecting different strands of knowledge sources and allowing collaborative flows among multiple knowledge sources.

The ability to benefit from knowledge has two basic elements (Cohen & Levinthal, 1990): (a) the ability to acquire and apply knowledge that already exists; and (b) the ability to possess new knowledge. Knowledge can be realized in its fullest capacity following the dual axes if the authenticity and credential of different strands of knowledge, including indigenous knowledge, are acknowledged and encouraged to exchange. This emergent concern in favour of indigenous knowledge is manifested in the United Nations' agenda; in an attempt to strengthen international cooperation to solve the problems faced by indigenous people in areas such as human rights, environment, development, education and health, the international body declared the years 1994–2004 as the International Decade of the World's Indigenous People. This lays the premise for a developmental paradigm that will support active participation of indigenous communities in sustainable developmental strategies by recognizing the importance of local knowledge and participation in decision-making. Only such a developmental paradigm has the potential to facilitate democratic creation, assimilation and distribution of knowledge resource, by acknowledging the importance of indigenous knowledge sources and identifying them to be valuable in the enhancement of the collective knowledge pool. Technology, instead of being passively utilized, must be put to use in the pursuit of achieving optimal knowledge exchange between different knowledge sources. It is only when technology can be effectively used to cultivate knowledge capability of individual, as well as social groups, that a developmental paradigm can be envisioned that will target holistic empowerment of social actors from within.

5 Knowledge capability

It is not the mere possessing of knowledge resource but the ability to acquire, operate and exchange it that marks the knowledge capability of social actors as having a positive effect in mitigating extant knowledge divide. It is not inert possession of knowledge, but the knowledge capability of users, that makes knowledge acquisition and processing intrinsic to the process of boosting organizational and social performance. While there are multifarious ways to boost individual capability, we will briefly justify why we have chosen a knowledge-centric capability approach towards development, before delving into the detail of what knowledge capability is actually about and the possibilities it has to offer in the context of enhancing social and organizational benefits.

5.1 The importance of knowledge in capability theory

John Finnis and Martha Nussbaum have identified knowledge as remaining connected with the notion of human flourishing and development (Johnstone, 2005). Many contemporary philosophers have dedicated their academic quest into exploring how knowledge enables optimal social functioning. Bell (1989) has seen the African village and the prosperity of African civilization as the outcome of knowledge exchange, a way to "move a community from injustice to justice, from wrong to right, from brokenness to wholeness and from ignorance to truth" (Bell, 1989, p. 373). The resultant social upliftment is not simply derivative of passive knowledge possession, but, rather, active knowledge operation by community members, which has the potential to facilitate effective knowledge exchange by overcoming extant knowledge divide.

This marks the importance of *knowledge capability* over passive knowledge possession, in the context of *using* knowledge as an asset to yield positive outcome. A capability approach is premised on the idea that utility and access to resource are important, but they matter instrumentally rather than constitutively (Sen, 2003; Johnstone, 2005). In order to achieve a fully functional human life, access to relevant resources plays a crucial role. However, having access to resources, although a necessary criterion in the process, is not a sufficient condition to enable achievement of such a desired life. It is the systematic ability to acquire and use resource that makes human life fully functional.

The capability expansion of individual knowledge sources has the potential to yield effective socio-economic outcomes. This enables capability approach to transcend resource allocation. Emphasizing capability expansion of individual knowledge sources, capability theory paves the path for empowerment, the ensuring of freedoms and opportunities, and the securing of an environment in which human potential can be truly realized.

Knowledge has always acquired an important place in capability theories. The reason behind this has been aptly captured by Sen and Anand (1997). Their formulations of indices of poverty comprise three core dimensions, where *deprivation of education and knowledge* has been identified as one of the core dimensions. Apart from being a core dimension, the instrumentality of knowledge in overcoming the other two dimensions, of *survival deprivation* and *economic deprivation*, further marks the indispensability of knowledge in capability theories. Capability theories place knowledge in the larger context of human functioning, giving a new way of looking at knowledge processes in terms of freedoms and opportunities, thereby bringing out the ethical and progressive dimensions of the theory.

5.2 Dimensions of knowledge capability

While the earlier section of this segment discusses the importance that knowledge has in capability theories, we will now proceed to demystify the concept of knowledge capability. Although there is much research dealing with different dimensions of knowledge capability in the context of business organization to enhance organizational performance, there is no explicit specification on the dimensions of knowledge capabilities in the context of society at large where the objective is to improve social performance for social development. So we will first deal with the notion of knowledge capability in an organizational context.

5.2.1 Dimensions of knowledge capability in an organizational context

Conventional literatures define knowledge capability as the sum total of knowledge assets of organizations. This viewpoint becomes one-sided and partial as it neglects, to a great extent, the role individual knowledge sources play in the process (Dawson, 2000). Knowledge capability as a concept is not restricted to the sum total of knowledge assets; it denotes how knowledge sources of empowered individuals, through dialogue and exchange among themselves, collaboratively work for enhancing collective knowledge capability of the organization. Knowledge capability, in its very essence, incorporates both a macro- (organizational) and micro- (individual) level perspective on knowledge, intertwined along inseparable terms.

Several scholars have dedicated their academic quest into defining knowledge capability along accurate terms. Verna Allee defines core capability as "the sole speciality, knowledge and technology processed by an organization" (Allee, 1998, p. 53). Parashar and Singh define knowledge capability as the sum total of the knowledge assets (tacit and explicit) of the firm that determine its capability to absorb and create new knowledge (Parashar & Singh, 2005). The definitions, however, highlight a holistic perception of knowledge capability. The explicit importance of tacit knowledge assets, identifying the credential of knowledge capability in creating new knowledge and modifying extant set, implicitly highlights the importance of individual knowledge sources in enhancing organizational knowledge capability. Ning et al. (2006) also agree with this strand of conceptualization and subsequently conceptualize knowledge capability as collective learning, which is essential for organization to enhance competitive advantage.

According to Ning et al. (2006), knowledge capability includes *core knowledge resource,* which makes the organization competitive, and *knowledge-operating capabilities*, which make knowledge resource effective and profitable. While we are clear what knowledge resource entails, we will explain below what *knowledge-operating capabilities* constitute. *Knowledge-operating capabilities* include *learning capability, cultural capability* and *communication capability*, which in alliance enable *innovation capability*, which ultimately facilitates true manifestation of *knowledge capability* (Ning et al., 2006).

Learning capability not only refers to assimilation or acquisition of knowledge by organizations but also organizations' ability to exploit the same in pursuit of betterment. Learning, paving the path for creation of new knowledge, and modification of existing set are fundamental to organizations in marking their uniqueness in a knowledge economy era. The components of *learning capabilities* are: (i) *knowledge resources*, including tacit and explicit knowledge used by an organization; (ii) *absorptive capability*, which refers to capabilities towards assimilating, utilizing and creating knowledge; and (iii) *organizational learning system*, which enables individuals' learning activities within the organization.

Cultural capability "acts as an enabler in creating greater knowledge assets" (Ning et al., 2006). It is the organizational culture that either facilitates or destroys knowledge capability of organizations. The components of *cultural capability* are: (i) *openness*, which implies being open to new ideas, eagerness to come out of conventional practices and to experiment with new methods of doing things; (ii) *curiosity*, a quality related to inquisitive thinking, such as exploration, investigation, learning and a desire or aspiration towards gaining knowledge; and (iii) *cooperation and trust*, which enables peer-to-peer learning and trustful knowledge exchange.

Communication capability guarantees creation of new knowledge through exchange by not only promoting individual ability but by connecting those individual abilities in the generation of a collective whole. This reiterates that knowledge capability is simply not the sum of total knowledge assets, but that it has a broader significance, where the whole attains a heightened status rather than being just an amalgamation of its individual parts. The components of *communication capability* are: (i) *technique and tools*, which comprise the ICT communication infrastructure, including intra- and internet enabled applications to facilitate the process of knowledge sharing within and outside organizational boundaries; and (ii) *interacting ba*. The concept of *ba* offered by Nonaka and Noboru (1998) represents "a contextual place shared with others from which relationships emerge, and within which knowledge is exchanged or shared. This place may be physical, virtual, or mental or a combination of these." The *interacting ba* is a space where the conversion between tacit and explicit knowledge occurs through the sharing of knowledge and skills among peers.

Ning et al. (2006) conceptualize *innovation capability* as the reflection of all the above capabilities in dialogue with each other. It is through innovation capability, where the organization derives credentials to produce new knowledge assets by critically discarding the extant set, that the knowledge capability of an organization is manifested in its truest essence.

5.2.2 Dimensions of knowledge capability in social context

Since knowledge is a *social product*, it is to be noted that any discussion on knowledge capability in a social context needs to consider both the micro (individual context) and macro view (social context) simultaneously. An incorporation of both micro and macro perspectives in capability theories is articulated in Martha Nussbaum's works. She insightfully stated that "... developing an internal capability requires favorable external conditions. A child raised in an environment without freedom of speech/religion does not develop the same potential/religious capabilities as a child who is raised in a nation that protects these liberties ..." (Nussbaum, 2000, pp. 85–86). This statement highlights the urgency to accommodate a dual approach in the study of knowledge capability. The dual approach should involve, on one hand, direct nurturing of the capability of individual knowledge sources, and, on the other, indirect support through the creation of a generally empowering environment, which will enable individual members to realize the fruits of knowledge capability.

Following the conceptualization proposed by Ning et al. (2006) in an organizational context, we can conceptualize knowledge capability of individual within a social group as comprising two components: *core knowledge resource* that ensures availability and accessibility of knowledge; and *knowledge-operating capabilities* that make knowledge resource effective and actionable for societal benefit. As mentioned, even if we ensure availability of *core knowledge resources* to individual members of a social group (in the form of printed books or various forms of e-resources), the individual within a social group has to have *knowledge-operating capabilities* that include *learning capability, cultural capability* and *communication capability*, which in alliance enable *innovation capability*, which ultimately facilitates true manifestation of *knowledge capability*.

Learning capability of individual within a social group refers to capabilities towards acquisition, assimilation and exploitation of knowledge in pursuit of betterment. The components of *learning capabilities*, as discussed before, are: (i) *knowledge resources*; (ii) the *absorptive capability* of individual; and (iii) *availability of learning systems*, both formal (for example, schools) and informal (such as local communities) (Wenger, 1998), that enable individuals' learning activities within a social system.

Cultural capability is the culture of a social group that either facilitates or destroys knowledge capability of individual within a social group. For example, Mtega et al. (2013) have investigated how social-cultural practices hinder knowledge creation and sharing process among communities in rural areas in Tanzania. It has been observed that social-cultural practices limit some of the rural communities from accessing and nurturing some types of knowledge. The components of cultural capability, as discussed before, are: (i) *openness*, which implies being open to new ideas, eagerness to come out of conventional practices and to experiment with new methods of doing things; (ii) *curiosity*, a quality related to inquisitive thinking, such as exploration, investigation, learning and a desire or aspiration towards gaining knowledge; and (iii) *cooperation and trust*, which enable peer-to-peer learning and trustful knowledge exchange.

Communication capability within a social group is the capability of a social group to connect individuals, which, in turn, promotes the knowledge-sharing behaviour of individuals and helps create new knowledge through exchange. As discussed, the components of communication capability are: (i) *technique and tools*, which comprise the ICT communication infrastructure, including intra- and internet enabled applications to facilitate the process of knowledge sharing in a social context; and (ii) *interacting ba*, a space (physical, virtual, mental or a combination of these) where knowledge is exchanged or shared and the conversion between tacit and explicit knowledge occurs through the sharing of knowledge and skills among peers.

6 Managing knowledge resource to enhance knowledge capability

The importance that knowledge capability expansion has in ushering in holistic development enables us to interpret knowledge not as a resource, commodity or belief structure but, rather, as a core aspect of the way humans function in the world. Knowledge is instrumental as well as constitutive freedom (Johnstone, 2005). Knowledge interacts with the environment, feeding into society new ideas, methods, attitudes, resources and forms of activity and interaction, thereby altering social and material conditions. The constitutive and instrumental role of knowledge on capability and creating an empowering social and material environment makes knowledge capability a mandatory pre-requisite in the process of enhancing both organizational and social performance. A knowledge capability model, incorporating both micro- and macro-level perspective, enhances the ability of people to interact and communicate, thereby enhancing both individual and collective knowledge.

However, we need to remember that knowledge, both in organizational and social contexts, is highly distributed. In an attempt to expand knowledge capability on a macro and micro level along sustainable terms, it is crucial to connect the social actors to enable knowledge sharing. Both society and organizations are not simply a collection of individuals. Their effective functioning is governed by a network of social interactions, which makes viable knowledge and other resource exchange within the setting. It is to facilitate effective knowledge exchange among different actors, in an attempt to expand knowledge capability, that technology should be put to use.

Contemporary digital technologies have significantly altered the material basis of interaction and communication, thereby having significant influence in enabling and constraining processes crucial to communication. Contemporary ICT has the potential to enable changed patterns of interaction and knowledge exchange among individuals and groups that restructure some aspects of society (Johnstone, 2005). The importance technology has in fostering relevant knowledge exchange is reiterated by Hughes, who states "I see technology as a means to (re)shape the landscape ..." (Hughes, 2004, p. 3). In today's world, democratization of science and technology, the increase in global connectivity through the internet and mobile technologies and greater availability of data have the potential to support integration of billions of individuals. Such an effective integration ensures active participation of social members in processes related to innovation, wealth creation and social development in ways that were previously inconceivable. Effective collaboration between social actors has the capacity to advance the arts, culture, science, education, government and economy in surprising but ultimately profitable ways (Tapscott & Williams, 2006). Cell phones, for example, can bring the seed of transformation. Following rapid development of technology, cell phones have significantly altered the material and structural basis of communication in the modern era. Apart from enabling communication between dispersed social actors, the devices serve as platforms for services and learning, providing remote diagnostics for medical treatment, identifying centres of corruption, and serving as distributed sensors of communities and their ecosystems (Dehgan, 2012).

In order to facilitate capability expansion through optimal usage of current technologies, in an environment where knowledge is distributed, it becomes crucial to systematically *manage knowledge* using technology to foster efficient distribution and exchange of the same. *Management of knowledge resources* (Gao et al., 2018) can be seen as the process of enabling individuals to expand their knowledge capabilities and integrate different information resources to improve both social and organizational performance.

Knowledge and knowledge management have acquired such relevance in business contexts that knowledge management now occupies second position in corporate authorities' "must do" lists, ranking only after globalization (TFPL, 1999). Knowledge management (KM) is the process of applying a systematic approach to capture, structure, manage and disseminate knowledge throughout an organization in order to work faster, reuse best practices and reduce costly rework from project to project (Dalkir, 2005). With the growing popularity of the internet and mobile technologies and their applications (primarily web 2.0 and social media), the concept of "knowledge management 2.0 (KM 2.0)" has evolved to allow individuals to create and modify content collaboratively (Semple, 2012).

Knowledge management and the devising of effective managerial strategy to boost organizations' knowledge capability have received significant attention from social scientists, computer scientists, management schools, business experts, economists and developmental champions. However, in spite of its widespread significance in a business context, the concept has received little attention in the purview of holistic social development. Given the potential of managing knowledge in generating socio-economic outcome, it is important to analyse the prospects the concept has to offer in the context of society at large, where the objective will be to manage social knowledge for social development (Laszlo & Laszlo, 2002). The main aim of managing knowledge for social cause is to usher in social development and not only promote competitive advantage for companies. Managing knowledge for social cause refers to a framework for knowledge creation, assimilation and dissemination through social collaboration for societal benefits, enhanced by digital technologies (Bandyopadhyay et al., 2017). Such a framework paves the path for people to interact and collaborate with each other, establish community norms and values, share knowledge and information resources and build trustful relationships. Putnam identifies these factors as constituting the core values of social capital, which is defined as a relational resource comprising social networks, social norms, values, trust and shared physical resources (Bourdieu, 1992; Putnam, 2000).

A management approach with a holistic view has the capability to bring holistic social development. Knowledge capability of individual knowledge sources within a social setup plays a crucial role in facilitating effective management of knowledge resources. This chapter discusses the importance of knowledge, the extant knowledge divide, which cripples society, and the effectivity of knowledge capability in ushering in managerial tactics that will appropriately channelize knowledge resources for developmental concerns. In the following chapter we will take up in detail the intricacies of social context, which is the rural sphere in our case, and deal with the concept of rural empowerment. Theoretical understanding of empowerment, as furthered by us in the following chapter, attempts to vividly highlight the role that knowledge and knowledge-operating capacities, or knowledge capability, have in ushering in holistic rural empowerment. In-depth consideration of the social context (the rural sphere in this case) will shed light on how managerial tactics must be designed, which will attempt to enhance knowledge capability of rural actors on a sustainable basis.

Part I of the book spells out the importance of knowledge and knowledge management in enhancing knowledge capability of rural actors. After providing a conceptual framework of rural empowerment as a knowledge theoretic concept in the next chapter, Chapter 4 discusses contemporary efforts undertaken to empower marginalized rural population. Given the exogenous nature of contemporary attempts, Chapter 5 highlights how conventional developmental models, in an attempt to empower the rural marginalized, have mainly sought to achieve the goal by mitigating information asymmetry of rural participants. In this context, the difference between information and knowledge becomes pertinent. The rural marginalized can never be empowered by externally feeding them with information without inculcating the necessary experience and skills required to translate the information into knowledge. Chapter 6, the concluding chapter of Part I, explicitly builds upon the concern and highlights that the road to holistic rural empowerment lies in mitigating knowledge asymmetry of rural participants. It is by accrediting rural populations with access to knowledge, along with developing in them knowledge capability, that knowledge asymmetry of rural participants can be mitigated and their socio-economic prospects enhanced on a sustainable basis.

References

Adolf, M. & Stehr, N. (2014). *Knowledge*. New York: Routledge.
Allee, V. (1998). *The Knowledge Evolution*. Guangdong: Zhuhai Publishing House.
Bandyopadhyay, S., Bardhan, A., Dey, P., Banerjee, S., Das, S. & Mandal, K. (2017). A Social Knowledge Management Platform for Universal Primary Education Online. In *Harnessing Social Media as a Knowledge Management Tool*. Hershey, PA: IGI Global. doi:10.4018/978-1-5225-0495-5.ch005.

Basu, S. (2016). Knowledge Production, Agriculture and Commons: The Case of Generation Challenge Programme (Doctoral thesis, Wageningen University, Netherlands). ISBN: 978-9-462-57677-3.

Bell, R.H. (1989). Narrative in African Philosophy. *Philosophy*, 64(249), 363–379. doi:10.1017/s0031819100044715.

Bourdieu, P. (1992). *An Invitation to Reflexive Sociology* (1st ed.). Chicago, IL: University of Chicago Press.

Brie, M. & Thomasberger, C. (2018). Knowledge and Social Freedom. *Journal of Cultural Economy*, 12(4), 341–346. doi:10.1080/17530350.2019.1619613.

Brooking, A. (1999). *Corporate Memory: Strategies for Knowledge Management* (1st ed.). London: Cengage Learning EMEA.

Burke, P. (2000). *The Social History of Knowledge*. Cambridge: Polity Press.

Cohen, W.M. & Levinthal, D.A. (1990). Innovation and Learning: The Two Faces of R&D. *The Economic Journal*, 99, 569–596.

Dalkir, K. (2005). *Knowledge Management in Theory and Practice*. Boston, MA: Elsevier.

Dave, M., Dave, M. & Shishodia, Y. (2012). Emerging Trends and Technologies in Knowledge Management: A Holistic Vision. *International Journal of Recent Research and Review*, III, 60–67. Retrieved from: http://www.ijrrr.com/papers3/paper7.pdf.

Davenport, T.H. & Prusak, L. (1998). *Working Knowledge: How Organizations Manage What They Know*. Boston, MA: Harvard Business School Press.

Dawson, R. (2000). Knowledge capabilities as the focus of organisational development and strategy. *Journal of Knowledge Management*, 4(4), 320–327. doi:10.1108/13673270010379876.

Dehgan, A. (2012). Creating the New Development Ecosystem. *Science*, 336(6087), 1397–1398. doi:10.1126/science.1224530.

Dellemijn, R. (2012). Knowledge Asymmetry in Inter-Firm Relationships: A Suggestion for a Knowledge Sourcing Strategy for the Ministry of Oil of Iraq (Student thesis, University of Twente, Netherland). Retrieved from: http://essay.utwente.nl/61982/.

Foucault, M. (1970). The archaeology of knowledge. *Information (International Social Science Council)*, 9(1), 175–185. doi:10.1177/053901847000900108.

Gao, T., Chai, Y. & Liu, Y. (2018). A Review of Knowledge Management About Theoretical Conception and Designing Approaches. *International Journal of Crowd Science*, 2(1), 42–51. doi:10.1108/IJCS-08-2017-0023.

Hughes, T.P. (2004). *Human-Built World: How to Think about Technology and Culture*. Chicago, IL and London: University of Chicago Press.

Johnstone, J. (2005). Knowledge, development and technology: Internet use among voluntary-sector AIDS organizations in KwaZulu Natal (Doctoral thesis, Department of Information Systems, London School of Economics and Political Science, London). Retrieved from: http://etheses.lse.ac.uk/id/eprint/282.

Laszlo, K.C. & Laszlo, A. (2002). Evolving Knowledge for Development: The Role of Knowledge Management in a Changing World. *Journal of Knowledge Management*, 6(4), 400–412. doi:10.1108/13673270210440893.

Mannheim, K. (1986). *Conservatism. A Contribution to the Sociology of Knowledge*. London: Routledge and Kegan Paul.

Meja, V. & Stehr, N. (2005). *Society and Knowledge: Contemporary Perspectives on the Sociology of Knowledge and Science* (2nd ed.). New Brunswick, NJ: Transaction Publishers.

Mtega, W.P., Dulle, F. & Benard, R. (2013). Understanding the knowledge-sharing process among rural communities in Tanzania: A review of selected studies. *Knowledge Management & E-Learning*, 5(2), 205–217.

Ning, Y., Shu, P. & Feng, B. (2006). *Knowledge Capability: A Definition and Research Model*. Proceedings of the International Conference on Knowledge Science, Engineering and Management. Lecture notes in computer science, 4092, 330–340. doi:10.1007/11811220_28.

Nonaka, I. & Noboru, K. (1998). The concept of Ba: Building a Foundation for Knowledge Creation. *California Management Review*, 40(3). Retrieved from: http://home.business.utah.edu/actme/7410/Nonaka% 201998.pdf.

Nussbaum, M.C. (2000). *Women and Human Development: A Capabilities Approach*. Cambridge: Cambridge University Press.

OECD (2001). The Well-Being of Nations: The Role of Human and Social Capital. Retrieved from: http://www.oecd.org/site/worldforum/33703702.pdf.

Parashar, M. & Singh, S.K. (2005). Innovation Capability. *IIMB Management Review*, 17, 115–123. Retrieved from: https://www.iimb.ac.in/node/4321.

Putnam, R.D. (2000). *Bowling Alone: The Collapse and Revival of American Community*. New York: Touchstone.

Rieu, A.M. (2005). What is Knowledge Society? The epistemic turn. Retrieved from: https://halshs.archives-ouvertes.fr/halshs-00552293/document.

Scheler, M. (1958). *The forms of knowledge and culture: Philosophical Perspectives*. Boston, MA: Beacon Press.

Semple, E. (2012). *Organizations Don't Tweet, People Do: A Manager's Guide to the Social Web*. Chichester: John Wiley & Sons.

Sen, A. (2003). *Development as Capability Expansion*. New Delhi and New York: Oxford University Press.

Sen, A. & Anand, S. (1997). Concepts of Human Development and Poverty: A Multi-dimensional Perspective. *Poverty and Human Development: Human Development Papers 1997*, 1–20. Retrieved from: https://scholar.harvard.edu/sen/publications/concepts-human-development-and-poverty-multidimensional-perspective.

Stehr, N. (1994). *Knowledge Societies*. London: Sage Publications.

Tapscott, D. & Williams, A.D. (2006). *Wikinomics: How Mass Collaboration Changes Everything*. London: Portfolio.

TFPL (1999). Roles and skills for Knowledge Management. Retrieved from: https://kmeducationhub.de/skills-for-knowledge-management/.

UNESCO (1999). *Declaration on Science and the Use of Scientific Knowledge*. World Conference on Science. Retrieved from: www.unesco.org/science/wcs/eng/declaration_e.htm.

Weingart, P. (2015). Knowledge and Inequality. Retrieved from: https://www.researchgate.net/publication/238749535.

Wenger, E. (1998). *Communities of Practice: Learning, Meaning, and Identity*. Cambridge: Cambridge University Press.

Wenger, E. (2009). Social learning capability: four essays on innovation and learning in social systems. *Social Innovation, Sociedade e Trabalho*. Retrieved from: https://wenger-trayner.com/wp-content/uploads/2011/12/09-04-17-Social-learning-capability-v2.1.pdf.

Williams, B. (1978). *Descartes*. Hassocks: Harvester.

World Bank (1999). World Development Report 1998/1999: Knowledge for Development. Retrieved from: http://hdl.handle.net/10986/5981.

Xue, C. (2017). A Literature Review on Knowledge Management in Organizations. *Research in Business and Management*, 4(1). doi:10.5296/rbm.v4i1.10786.

3 Rural empowerment
A knowledge–theoretic approach

1 Introduction

The rural area or countryside is a territorial space located outside towns and cities. The rural sector owes its potential partly to its immense capacity in employment creation, and partly because production of indigenous items falls under its purview, which subsequently account to be native heritage. The importance of the sector has urged various public and non-governmental, as well as private, entities to undertake measures to reboost the sector. Yet how far such attempts have been successful in uplifting the status of the rural community, residing on the fringes, remains an essential aspect to investigate. If we do a quick survey across the world we will see how the production of indigenous items mostly comes from the rural fringes of nations. This chapter proposes mechanisms to empower rural economies' creative producers, both farm and non-farm, by equipping them with relevant information, knowledge and connection necessary for trade benefits. Across the globe, one of the key deficiencies in many rural communities is the lack of physical and/or virtual linkages to local, as well as larger, metropolitan areas' opportunity structures such as financial, technical, social and political resources. Subsequently, the communities have less access to various forms of knowledge resources, which inhibits them developing as active agents. This chapter conceptualizes empowerment as derivative of individual/group capabilities to possess adequate knowledge and apply the same in pursuit of self-betterment.

Alsop and Heinsohn (2005) define empowerment as "enhancing an individual/group's capacity to make choices and transform those choices into desired outcomes and actions". The capacity to make effective choices cannot be cultivated among rural marginalized populations if the target group is not agential to undertaking transformative action. And the ability to undertake transformative action is not only a manifestation of individual/group agency, but an enhanced social capital and opportunity scope, which, in alliance, contribute to translating intended actions to desired outcomes. Hence, in our developmental framework, we have attempted to simultaneously cultivate agency, opportunity structure (Alsop & Heinsohn, 2005) and social capital (Grootaert, 2003) of rural target group to achieve holistic rural empowerment. In the context of rural economy, it is indeed true that several empowering schemes – public, private as well as NGOs – have been undertaken to broaden the opportunity scopes of the creative producers. However, partly because of the sporadic nature of most of these initiatives and lack of follow-up guidelines, and partly due to the disadvantageous social position of the target group, attempts to broaden opportunity scopes have seldom translated themselves into an enhanced "opportunity structure". Cloward and Ohlin (1960) define *opportunity structure* as the opportunities available to people in a given society, which are shaped by respective social organization and structure of that entity. While the definition highlights the importance of social norms in framing opportunity structure, making the target group autonomous to bring self-induced changes negotiating with their restrictive social ambience – or, in other words, pronouncing their agency – becomes a mandatory prerequisite in the process of empowering the group.

Agency, defined as an individual/group's capacity to make purposeful choices, is a necessary condition, along with an enhanced opportunity structure to bring about empowerment of the target group (Samman & Santos, 2009). It is only when the rural marginalized population is equipped with sufficient knowledge crucial for self-betterment that will they develop the agency to choose among options and decide their own socio-economic course of empowerment. An enhanced agency, therefore, will not only open up new prospects of development for the rural marginalized but will also enable them to optimally utilize extant opportunity structures for self-betterment. In this context, social capital, which refers to strength of social ties and the norms governing social interactions among people in society (Grootaert, 2003), plays a crucial role in enhancing agency of rural participants. An enhanced social capital, referring to the strengthening of social networking ties at both global and local level and the removal of social barriers, enables individuals to take informed decisions through smooth and relevant exchange of knowledge.

While our definition of empowerment encompasses simultaneous cultivation of social capital, agency and the opportunity structure of rural target groups, equipping the marginalized population with knowledge becomes crucial in this framework to come up with strategies of self-development and self-sustenance of rural development. It is by making the rural population *knowledge capable* that we wish to bring rural empowerment from within, which will not only make the target group knowledge literate but inculcate in it evaluative capacities to process acquired knowledge for practical benefits. Hence our research endeavour conceptualizes rural empowerment as a knowledge–theoretic concept, which considers bringing the rural marginalized population within the knowledge network as a necessary and sufficient condition to achieve holistic rural empowerment.

The chapter is divided into three segments:

- The first part of the chapter focuses on significant works and the way they have conceptualized empowerment and the manifestation of the phenomenon in a rural context.

- The second segment discusses the essence of our conceptualization of empowerment as derivative of simultaneous cultivation of agency, opportunity structure and social capital among rural target groups. By fleshing out the theoretical relation between social capital, agency and opportunity structure, the section discusses how the three concepts are indispensable in the process of achieving community-driven rural empowerment.
- Finally, the third segment focuses on the relevance of equipping rural populations with knowledge in the process of achieving holistic rural empowerment. In due course the section focuses on how a rural marginalized community's agency, social capital and opportunity structure, being facilitators of empowerment, can get positively cultivated through effective knowledge sharing and management.

2 Empowerment and its manifestation in rural context

Achievement of holistic rural empowerment is one of the supreme global aims incorporated in the United Nations' agenda of Sustainable Development Goals. The aspect of poverty reduction features large in the rural developmental agenda because global poverty is essentially rural in nature. In order to aptly address the issues of global poverty, strategies have to be contextually framed that can take into consideration remoteness and potential of rural areas and provide targeted differentiated approaches. The United Nations' Sustainable Development Goals target rural empowerment via a bottom-up approach. The formulated policies therefore focus on livelihood enhancement of rural communities through fostering effective participation of local members in management of their own social, economic and environmental objectives.

A bottom-up approach to empowerment closely aligns with our developmental paradigm. By fostering effective participation of rural members in decision-making processes, the UN developmental agenda attempts to achieve close integration of rural areas with urban areas. The resultant integration is expected to narrow rural–urban disparities, expand opportunities and encourage the retention of skilled people, including youths, in rural areas. This will subsequently enable creation of job-market potential in rural economies (UNESCO, 2015). It is only when the rural population is empowered to transform their intended actions into desired outcomes by retaining their indigenous engagements that we can envisage a developmental paradigm which attempts to make individual national cultural heritage a global, sociocultural phenomenon by enabling the heritage to stay committed to its local roots. The UN's developmental charter insightfully maps out how extant marginalization of rural community becomes more acute in the case of developing nations, where the target group lacks access to basic services and economic opportunities. Therefore, in order to achieve sustainable rural development, the charter recommends promotions along the following axes to achieve sustainable rural development:

i Quality education to rural communities.
ii Providing them with access to basic services and information.
iii The formulation of pro-poor policy and providing social protection programmes.
iv Enhancing social capital and building resilience in rural community.
v Protecting and ensuring sustainable usage of traditional knowledge and assets.
vi Fostering and strengthening capacities of rural communities for self-organization for building social capital.
vii Inculcating processing abilities among rural members to interpret knowledge and use it for practical gains.

If we critically analyse the measures prescribed by the UN then we can see how the initiatives are framed in a way that encourages cultivation of self-sustenance and self-developmental strategies among rural communities; an attempt to empower the rural marginalized from within. It is by developing capabilities among rural communities that the UN developmental goals attempt to be sustainable, where, after the initial phase of external supervision, the rural members will develop the agency required to achieve desirable outcomes without the help of external monitoring.

While mitigation of rural–urban knowledge divide is one of the major agendas in the process of attaining holistic rural empowerment, we need to remember that what constitutes "rural" and "urban" has to be critically formulated, without premising the theorization on traditional rural–urban dichotomy. Conventional approaches conceptualize rural and urban in terms of population density and size, employment density, land cover, or a combination of these. However, such macro approaches are only capable of producing broadly similar spatial patterns for predominantly urban and predominantly rural areas, without providing adequate explanation for the zones and spheres where the boundary between the two blurs. Policy still treats urban and rural areas as polarized territorial spheres. The stringent division between rural and urban further contributes in making the opportunity structure of rural community more restrictive, thereby hindering their agency and networking capacities. However, the emerging concern to integrate urban and rural areas to achieve holistic empowerment of both communities through necessary exchange is primarily premised to challenge the existing dualism between urban and rural areas. The territorial and functional interdependencies between the two disallow us to read the operational dynamics of one without referring to the other.

Our distinction between the rural and the urban, instead of mimicking conventional categorization, seeks to challenge the same by adapting an integrationist approach instead of a separatist one. We wish to overcome the rural–urban knowledge divide by encouraging a two-way exchange of knowledge between these spatial entities. Conventional efforts premised on traditional rural–urban dichotomy adopt a compassion-driven approach, where they formulate measures to empower the rural marginalized by enabling one-way knowledge transmission from urban to rural entities without giving the latter scope to share their indigenous knowledge resources, which equally contribute to be a valuable intellectual capital. The integrationist approach we have adopted seeks to empower rural community by not only equipping them with relevant knowledge but also enabling them to share their own knowledge resources. It is through this two-way exchange that we wish to blur the rigid boundary between rural and urban and subsequently empower rural communities by enabling them to overcome their physical and informational isolation.

The framework of sustainable rural development, as devised by the UN developmental charter, precisely talks about this two-way exchange of knowledge between urban and rural areas. The provision to protect indigenous practices from the threat of extinction adds value to the indigenous knowledge resource of rural marginalized community. It is through the relevant two-way sharing, an attempt to empower the rural communities from within, that this can be undertaken. Jupp (2010) conceptualizes empowerment in Bangladesh's context as a contested concept, a moving target comprising complex interrelated elements and embracing values, knowledge, behaviour and relationships. This highlights that relevant exchange fostered to attain empowerment must have the potential to recognize difference and connect each informational node with the other, by enabling each to remain loyal to its local roots. The dynamic nature of exchange fostered by a two-way traffic therefore disallows empowerment to be a static concept. It is a dynamic manifestation of individual or group capabilities of taking informed decisions, networking effectively and transforming actions into desired outcomes by utilizing extant opportunity scopes along with venturing into newer prospects. The following section, by drawing theoretical co-relations, attempts to show how agency, social capital and opportunity structure facilitate empowerment from within by building on strategies of self-sustenance and self-development among rural target group.

3 Agency, opportunity structure and social capital: Facilitating empowerment

This section theoretically chalks out how agency, social capital and opportunity structure in amalgamation facilitate rural empowerment.

3.1 Empowerment and agency

Empowerment and agency are relational concepts (Samman & Santos, 2009). The conceptual interdependence becomes clearer in Ibrahim and Alkire (2007), where they draw a directly proportional relation between the two, thereby conceptualizing empowerment as an outcome of enhanced agency. In the process of measuring empowerment, three aspects need to be considered:

1   Existence of choice;
2   Use of choice; and
3   Achievement of choice.

Agency, combining direct control and effective power, therefore accounts to be primary in enhancing individual/group capacity to make purposeful choices and to successfully translate the choices into desired outcomes. The notion of cultivating agency directly opposes the top-down model of development. Instead of designing policies for specific groups, the development interventions need to be dedicated to attaining empowerment from within and consider individuals bringing about change through individual/collective activity (Sen, 1999). Equipping the rural marginalized to bring about self-induced transformation not only facilitates empowerment from within but is crucial in itself for sustaining the socio-economic wellbeing of the marginalized community. Thus agency in our rural developmental paradigm has been treated in terms of both its instrumental and intrinsic value; as a means to attain empowerment and also having value as an end in itself.

Ibrahim and Alkire (2007) define empowerment as a process in which people gain power over, power to (creating new possibilities), power with (acting in a group) and power from within. Effective cultivation of power among individuals/ groups is only possible when agency is treated as a multi-dimensional concept (Samman & Santos, 2009). Agency, being multi-dimensional, therefore comprises different spheres (the social structure in which people are embedded), domains (multiple areas of life in which a person may exercise agency) and levels (micro, meso and macro). This makes measuring agency along diverse socio-economic lines mandatory to derive a fairer idea on the multi-dimensional operationalization of the aspect. Jejeebhoy (2000) maps the common direct measures of autonomy as economic decision-making, freedom of movement, power relation within gendered groups, access to resources, and control over resources. In our research we have tried to track these among rural marginalized community to understand their extant hindrances and subsequently propose contextual measures to pronounce their autonomy by overcoming operative obstructions.

The impoverished knowledge base of the rural community features as one of the major factors restricting the agency of the members in taking informed decisions, thereby sustaining marginalization of the rural sector (Ali & Avdic, 2015). Our rural developmental framework is premised on enhancing the knowledge base of rural marginalized community in an attempt to enhance their agency and subsequently bring about rural empowerment from within. An enhanced knowledge base is not simply an outcome of providing members of marginalized community equal access to knowledge. Only when the rural marginalized become knowledge capable – that is, they develop evaluative capacities to process acquired knowledge for practical benefits – can they translate their enhanced knowledge base in pursuit of pronouncing individual and collective agency.

3.2 Empowerment and opportunity structure

One of the key deficiencies in many marginalized rural communities is the lack of linkage to local, as well as larger, metropolitan area opportunity structure, including financial, technical, social and political resources. Since marginalized rural communities are disconnected both physically and digitally from local as well as urban opportunity structures, they have: (i) less access to quality educational support, training and advisory services; (ii) less knowledge about the available local opportunities (community assets, sharable resources); (iii) less access to market links (buyer, seller, micro-credit, etc.); and (iv) less access to any forum to discuss their problems with relevant agencies. Widespread hindrances along the above-stated lines impoverish the knowledge base of the rural marginalized community. Lack of inter- and intra-communitarian linkage contributes in sustaining social, economic and civic isolation of rural community. As a result, the rural marginalized are not just deprived to venture in search of additional possibilities, but the lack of relevant knowledge alienates them from the extant welfare schemes devised for rural development. It is by equipping rural populations with relevant knowledge that we have not only attempted to enhance opportunity scopes for rural marginalized producers but have also made provision of optimal utilization of existing schemes to achieve holistic empowerment.

Alsop and Heinsohn (2005) insightfully chalk out the measurement criteria for degrees of empowerment into the following: "(i) whether the person has the opportunity to make a choice, (ii) whether the person uses the opportunity to choose, and (iii) once the choice is made, whether it brings desired outcome." This conceptualization highlights how opportunity structure, which refers to the formal and informal context within which actors operate, is equally mandatory, along with agency, in any developmental framework designed to achieve self-driven empowerment. Even though various formal laws have been undertaken, both along physical and digital lines, to improve socio-economic conditions of rural communities (Singh, 2009; Minkes, 1952), the informal and restrictive social structure often impedes them from utilizing the schemes designed for their benefit, thereby obstructing empowerment of the rural marginalized communities.

Out of its several schemes, the *Global Cottage Industry* initiative (Global Cottage Industry, 2012) undertaken in the Middle East to enable effective artistic exchange between Bedouin women of Tunisia and women of Abu Dhabi, as a part of Abu Dhabi's Ministry of Culture's Handicrafts Project, deserves special mention. The exchange has been fostered to cultivate and share indigenous artistic styles and patterns, thereby enabling rural indigenous producers to attain global recognition and identity. Similar initiatives have been undertaken in various nations to promote indigenous heritage and rural practitioners on the global platform. To promote the growth and improve the indigenous entrepreneurial journey of small and medium-sized enterprises (SMEs), the European Commission in 2008 adopted the Small Business Act, which demands specific initiatives and sustained efforts to enable SMEs to realize their true potential. It also encourages member states to implement measures in support of micro-enterprises (European Union, 2014). During the last decade, indigenous industries, both farm and non-farm, have increasingly become important components of modern post-industrial knowledge-based economies and have raised great interest about their effective economic value. Apart from this, the increasing penetration of online portals has created an opportunity for rural produce to gain global visibility, thereby creating enhanced market prospects for rural indigenous producers (IMARC, 2018). Several e-commerce initiatives, such as Etsy, Okhai, ArtFire and Supermarket, provide rural producers with subsidized prospects to create sellers accounts and sell their produce to a global market.

In spite of several initiatives taken both at global and local level, the welfarist agenda on which the initiatives have been premised have seldom been successful in addressing the issue at stake. In this context, we need to pay specific attention to the literacy level of the target group. While in the developed nations there can be provision for a decent literacy rate among rural practitioners, aspects of rural illiteracy loom large in the context of developing and Third World nations. As a result of low literacy rates, the rural population often does not have adequate knowledge regarding various schemes undertaken for their own benefit. Moreover, rural populations' physical and informational distance from urban transaction sites, due to weak inter- and intra-communitarian linkage, further aggravates their ignorance. Various national and international agencies have come up with a diverse range of skill-building training programmes for rural communities to enhance their skill sets, markets and entrepreneurial prospects. However, formulating training modules without addressing the specific nature of rural need and lack of provision to impart the curriculum in local language contributes to an alienation of the target group from the initiatives.

In order to provide members of rural communities with the capabilities needed for optimal usage of extant opportunity structures and cultivation of newer opportunities, knowledge capability among rural population needs to be enhanced. Development of operative capacities to process knowledge gained is a prior requisite if rural members are expected to benefit from the same. Only when the rural marginalized community develops evaluative capacities to process acquired knowledge by virtue of knowledge capability will they develop the credential to optimally utilize extant opportunity structure and venture out in search of newer possibilities of socio-economic betterment.

3.3 Empowerment and social capital

Along with agency and opportunity structure, social capital plays a crucial role in facilitating rural empowerment, as has been identified in the World Bank's Development Report 2000–2001. Social capital, referring to strength of social ties and norms governing social interactions, plays a crucial role, along with agency and opportunity structure, in translating intended actions into desired outcomes. Social capital refers to the network of relationships between people residing in society, purposive interaction between whom enables the society to function effectively (Putnam, 2000). Our attempt to improve the social capital of rural community in the process of empowering them attempts to enhance the target group's networking ties by fostering effective intra- and inter-communitarian knowledge and information exchange.

Smooth communication and relevant exchange of information enable people to interact and collaborate with each other, establish community norms and values, share resources and build trustful relationships, which are the core values of social capital (Putnam, 2000). An enhanced social capital often acts as an accelerating force to bring about empowerment for marginalized segments, by improving inter-connectedness and thereby enabling them to overcome geographical isolation. To strengthen the social capital of the rural community, this chapter proposes community empowerment schemes dedicated to eventually blurring the rural–urban knowledge divide.

Our integrationist view to overcome rural–urban knowledge divide by virtue of fostering two-way knowledge exchange between these spatial entities is undertaken to enhance inter-dependency of the two territorial units, instead of separating them further by conceptualizing them along polarizing terms. Fostering effective two-way networking between urban and rural communities is bound to have different, yet empowering, consequences for both. For example, by virtue of smooth communication and effective inter- and intra-communitarian exchange, rural communities will have improved access to various expert-mediated advisory services. Valuable advice from professional mentors will guide the rural target group to access quality resources based on their need, enable them to share their concerns on public forums and provide them necessary counselling wherever required. Smooth communications will enable mentors to interact with the rural community to identify problems and then let the mentors impart their knowledge to solve those problems, thereby enhancing the bridging social capital of the underprivileged community. Experts may also help rural marginalized community in assessing their community assets and competencies – such as traditional but extinct skills, arts, crafts, culture, and natural flora and fauna, wildlife, etc. – and help them translate these assets into opportunities. Access to such a knowledge pool derivative of effective rural–urban networking will not only enhance the social capital of rural community but will go beyond to mitigate their geographical isolation and enhance socio-economic prospects of the community. On the other hand, the two-way knowledge exchange making the dynamics of indigenous production known to urban crowd contributes in enhancing their intellectual capital. The indigenous knowledge assets of rural community shared in the process of two-way exchange will subsequently pave the path for contextual policy formulation by informing urban communities and policy-makers about the specific nature of rural need. It is through this symbiosis that our research framework targets rural empowerment specifically along dialogic terms.

In a digitally connected world it is important to use technology to strengthen the social capital of marginalized community by fostering effective exchange through the formation of virtual communities, which will enable underprivileged members of the rural community to be part of the global knowledge network. We will discuss these issues in greater details in Parts II and III. Strengthening social capital of rural communities by fostering purposive intra- and inter-communitarian networking will not only help in developing "bonding" social capital (social ties within homogenous groups) but also pave the path for "bridging" social capital (social ties within heterogeneous groups) by enabling interactions outside the purview of immediate closed community. Thus the cultivation of social capital and growth of purposive communities is not only required to enhance internal solidarity of rural community, it also contributes in placing the marginalized members within the global knowledge network. This accounts to be a precursory measure in securing empowerment for marginalized rural community along with an enhanced agency and opportunity structure of the target group, which will subsequently enable it to translate intended actions into desired outcomes.

4 Empowerment as a knowledge–theoretic concept

A vast body of literature has fleshed out the importance of managing knowledge, by facilitating effective knowledge exchange, as a mandatory requisite for improving living conditions in rural areas (Ali & Avdic, 2015; Vong et al., 2017). In this context, it needs to be remembered that management of knowledge can only yield a positive outcome in the context of rural empowerment if individual social actors within the social group are knowledge capable.

The previous section of the chapter chalks out the theoretical relationship between empowerment and agency, empowerment and opportunity structure, and empowerment and social capital, where agency, opportunity structure and social capital have been formulated as concepts facilitating empowerment of marginalized rural community. After discussing the facilitating agents, this section mainly chalks out the importance of managing knowledge in the context of achieving holistic rural empowerment. Our research initiative is designed to achieve rural empowerment by enhancing social capital, agency and opportunity structure of marginalized target group by equipping them with relevant knowledge required to pronounce life and livelihood prospects. Although attainment of rural empowerment through management of knowledge accounts to be our primary aim, such a developmental strategy will only be effective if the local community is knowledge capable to perform creation, storage and exchange of knowledge for communitarian betterment. This approach of ours to achieve holistic rural empowerment by making the rural community knowledge capable makes our conceptualization of empowerment a knowledge–theoretic one, where empowerment is considered as the end and ability to operate knowledge for benefit as the potential means to achieve empowerment.

4.1 Conceptualizing rural empowerment through management of knowledge

Knowledge, defined as theoretical and practical understanding of a subject, is considered the most crucial competitive asset in contemporary connected society

(Gao et al., 2018). Knowledge is a concept, skill, experience and vision providing a framework for creating, evaluating and using information (factual data) to achieve concrete benefits (Soltani & Navimipour, 2016). While knowledge is a valuable asset, its value is only realized by virtue of using and sharing it. Knowledge, being an intellectual capital, is capable of empowering people through relevant exchange in a connected environment. Since it is the sharing and using of knowledge that contributes in enhancing individual and collective empowerment, the concept of managing knowledge to boost performance outcomes is increasingly gaining importance in contemporary society. Management of knowledge refers to the simultaneous practice of capturing, documenting, retrieving and using this knowledge, along with creating, transferring and reusing it (Gao et al., 2018). The contemporary world and its connected nature have made the creation, assimilation and dissemination of knowledge an easy phenomenon, thereby enhancing the importance of managing knowledge to attain effective results. A vast body of literature highlights the importance of knowledge management from an organizational perspective (Daneshfard, 2006; Davenport & Prusak, 1998). Using innovative networking means to transfer knowledge has been effective in many contexts in improving organizational performance. However, if we can truly grasp the importance of knowledge as an asset we will identify the need to take the concept of knowledge management beyond organizational boundaries and attempt social development through optimal management of knowledge. The mechanisms are discussed in detail in Part II.

A valuable body of literature, which focuses on understanding the impact of knowledge management to improve organizational perspective, has primarily dealt with the dynamics of knowledge exchange in closed and homogenous organizational settings. Our research proposes to manage knowledge to facilitate social development in a heterogeneous social setting (Bandyopadhyay et al., 2015). Our proposed framework to manage knowledge for sustainable rural empowerment considers every actor as the possessor of knowledge, where we attempt to foster two-way knowledge transaction between urban and rural communities to mitigate extant knowledge divide. Although the physical and explicit knowledge isolation of rural community contributes to sustaining their marginalization, the implicit knowledge they possess through enculturation and experiences in their unique socio-cultural environment nevertheless accounts to be a valuable indigenous asset (Hess, 2006). Our adhered model of rural development thus premises on two-way knowledge exchange between urban and rural communities, where it considers both urban and rural communities as equal contributors to the knowledge pool, irrespective of their social location. Thus, by enabling the rural participants not only to acquire knowledge but also to share their own knowledge resources, our framework attempts to achieve rural empowerment from within by cultivating strategies of self-development and self-sustenance among the target group. We will discuss this framework in Part III of this book.

The contemporary era and the dream to have one integrated world devoid of territorial boundaries have immense potential in sustaining a symbiotic knowledge transaction, where both urban and rural communities contribute to the knowledge pool in the process of creating, assimilating and disseminating knowledge via effective exchange. Social networking ties enable people to connect, communicate and collaborate easily. The promise of connectedness has the capacity to create a complex knowledge infrastructure that enables easier, faster and more widespread exchange of knowledge (Hemsley & Mason, 2013). These affordances not only guarantee access to knowledge but, by fostering effective exchange, enable participants to develop evaluative capacities by virtue of which they gain the skill to process acquired knowledge for practical benefits. It is this knowledge capability of rural participants that contributes in enabling optimal management of knowledge to yield effective outcomes. It is the value of knowledge in its implementation mode, gained by virtue of relevant exchange, that leads to "developmental effectiveness". Developmental effectiveness contributes to reduced poverty and the building of capacity within communities, civil society and government to address their own developmental priorities (Stillman, 2013). This dynamic, two-way exchange of knowledge enables mutual differences in knowledge, skills, opportunity, culture and political power to complement, rather than contradict, each other. It is by realizing this spirit of inclusive knowledge management that we seek to deploy the concept in a heterogeneous social setting to attain holistic rural development.

4.2 Facilitating rural empowerment through management of knowledge

Having discussed what we mean by managing knowledge in the context of social development, this section will primarily talk about how such a strategy facilitates empowerment by enhancing agency, social capital and opportunity structure of rural marginalized community.

4.2.1 Management of knowledge and agency

In this section we will attempt to flesh out how possession and sharing of relevant knowledge pave the path for an enhanced agency among participants to take informed decisions, which subsequently pave the path for holistic empowerment. The role of managing knowledge in fostering empowerment can be traced to how management meets existing and emerging needs, identifies and exploits existing and acquired knowledge assets, and contributes in developing new opportunities (Quintas et al., 1997). Cultivation of the above-mentioned credentials is only possible when management of knowledge in social context is strategized in a way that contributes in enhancing individual and collective agency. Kockelman (2007), from an anthropological standpoint, tries to map the relation between knowledge and agency, where he insightfully conceptualizes agency as multi-dimensional, graduated and distributed and formulates knowledge as comprising "representational agency". It is the possession of knowledge that cultivates enhanced capacities to take informed decisions among individuals and groups and it is agency that cyclically determines how acquired knowledge can be optimally translated to achieve desired outcomes. However, while this work fleshes out the relation between knowledge and agency, its conceptualization of agency as a semiotic concept differs from the way we conceptualize agency in this work as both an end in itself and as a facilitating agent bringing empowerment.

In rural areas, management of knowledge serves to be a crucial strategy in preserving indigenous heritage, learning new things, solving new problems through effective collaboration, creating core competencies and creating new situations for individuals and organizations (Fernandez et al., 2004). Although management of knowledge improves explicit knowledge of rural target group by connecting them to advisory services and urban-based professional mentors through effective networking, implicit indigenous knowledge of rural community is cultivated by virtue of two-way knowledge exchange between urban and rural communities. In this context, it needs to be remembered that while granting access to knowledge is necessary, it does not suffice to be a sufficient condition in enhancing agency of rural marginalized community. It is only by fostering effective and dynamic two-way knowledge exchange through effective collaborations that attempts can be made to pronounce agency of a heterogeneous target group. Effective collaboration among individual knowledge sources within a social setup can only be realized when the individual actors are knowledge capable to perform optimal knowledge transaction. It is knowledge capability that contributes to enhancing agency of target group by facilitating management of knowledge for social empowerment.

Alsop and Heinsohn (2005) define agency in terms of asset endowments, which eventually enhance individual or group capacity to make effective choices. Asset endowments, being indicators of agency, thereby can be multi-faceted, such as psychological (capacity to envision), informational, organizational, social (social capital), financial and human (skills, literacy, etc.). Alsop and Heinsohn (2005) have been right in conceptualizing how one asset leads to endowment of other assets. If we want to ratify this conceptualization in terms of our research context, then we can see how our research initiative is oriented to attain rural empowerment by equipping rural marginalized community with relevant knowledge and the skill to exchange the asset. This has a direct influence in enhancing prospects of above-mentioned types of assets. We need to remember that specific action does not lead to empowerment. It is by cultivating different asset endowments by virtue of fostering relevant knowledge exchange between rural and urban communities that we can attempt to attain holistic rural empowerment by virtue of cultivating the implicit and explicit knowledge base of rural marginalized through effective collaboration.

Sen (1985), focusing on the intrinsic role (value as an end in itself) of agency, conceptualizes it as freedom to act, complemented with requisite means enabling successful translation of intended actions into desired outcomes. This considers both positive and negative views of freedom. While a positive view of freedom focuses on what a person can choose to do or achieve, instead of highlighting the absence of any particular type of constraint that prevents the person from achieving what he/she wants, a negative view of freedom precisely focuses on the absence of constraint and interference from external parties. An attempt to enhance agency of rural marginalized community through management of knowledge contributes in furthering both the above-mentioned notions of freedom. Knowledge exchanged through effective collaboration will not only enhance individual/group capacity to make effective choices (positive view), but easy communication fostered through symbiotic collaboration helps to mitigate hindrances, which are intrinsic to marginalized rural sector because of its physical and informational isolation. It is by blending both positive and negative views of freedom, of equipping rural marginalized with newer opportunities by simultaneously mitigating extant hindrances restricting smooth transition of their intended actions into desired outcomes, that our research framework attempts to envision holistic rural empowerment by pronouncing agency of marginalized target groups through effective management of knowledge.

4.2.2 Management of knowledge and social capital

Chaghouee and Mirakabad (2014) chalk out the intrinsic and directly proportional relation between knowledge management and enhanced social capital. Their work points out how knowledge management, positively enhancing social capital, contributes to enhancing intellectual capital of organizations. Other works similarly design the relation between these two concepts in terms of organizational performance (Styhre, 2008; Reijsen et al., 2014). However, our framework of holistic rural development attempts to enhance social capital of marginalized and isolated rural community by fostering inter- and intra-communitarian exchange through effective management of knowledge. It is through encouraging knowledge exchange via purposive collaboration that our developmental model attempts to cultivate social capital via management of knowledge in a heterogeneous social setting. This approach differs from the conventional practice of cultivating social capital via knowledge management in a homogenous organizational setting. Our approach of cultivating social capital of marginalized rural community in the process of empowering them from within following management of knowledge is in tune with UNESCO's research goal of an inter-connected knowledge society (UNESCO, 2005).

Knowledge society generates, shares and makes available to all members of society knowledge necessary for improving human conditions. It envisions an inter-connected social setup based on purposive knowledge exchange between communities. While knowledge society considers knowledge to be a valuable asset, its essence is premised on the culture of sharing knowledge to build an integrated society. The dream of having one world, premised on the motto of creating an integrated global community, has made the creation, assimilation and dissemination of knowledge an easy and smooth phenomenon in today's inter-connected age. It is because of this inter-connected spirit with which contemporary society is fused that we have attempted to use the symbiotic potential of knowledge sharing as a means to bring the isolated rural population within the purview of knowledge network. Purposive collaborations not only grant access to knowledge, but, by encouraging relevant sharing of knowledge, inculcate in members the evaluative capacities required to process acquired knowledge for practical benefits. Thus we can see how management of knowledge and social capital, instead of having a causal relation, share a cyclical bond in the process of attaining social empowerment.

A strengthened social capital enables knowledge acquisition, while exchange of relevant knowledge fostered via effective collaborations further contributes to the expansion of an individual/group's networking ties. It is through this cyclical relation between knowledge capital and social capital that the culture of sharing, on which knowledge society is premised, can be realized. Our research goal to attain rural empowerment through effective management of knowledge, part of which focuses on strengthening social capital of the target group, is designed with the ultimate aim to bring the isolated rural community within the knowledge network. It is by fostering effective collaboration and purposive knowledge transaction that we can devise schemes to empower rural marginalized community, by successfully mitigating extant rural–urban knowledge divide.

4.2.3 Management of knowledge and opportunity structure

Various international and national agencies have taken multiple initiatives to boost rural economies by providing upliftment schemes to indigenous producers. These include providing financial support, market access initiative assistance, international publicity by organizing fairs and exhibitions, the formation of farm and craft clusters and providing various skill development training to rural community members. However, the ideals promised by the policies are seldom realized in practical offerings. If we take the example of a Third World developing nation such as India, we can see how the inefficiency of extant support structures contributes significantly to sustaining the ignorance of rural community. The district-level government help-desks, District Industries Centres (DIC) and District Rural Development Cells (DRDC) serve as the primary information source of public schemes to rural community. Yet such governmental offices are seen as inefficient (Kumar & Rajeev, 2013) and this inefficiency directly affects the native communities. The communities often remain misinformed or uninformed about fairs held, government-sponsored allowances they are supposed to get, and other related aspects; all of which these government help-desks are expected to provide. Inefficiency in production in rural India largely owes its origin to such incompetent support structures.

Our proposed framework to attain rural empowerment through effective knowledge sharing fostered by purposive collaborations can serve to compensate for the inefficiency of extant global knowledge sources by granting rural community access to an alternative knowledge repository dynamically created through symbiotic knowledge transaction between urban and rural communities. Evaluative capacities inculcated among rural population through relevant and purposive knowledge transaction enable them to learn from shared experiences and ideas and apply their learning to improve their opportunity scopes. Social barriers, posed by restrictive social norms, can eventually be mitigated as a result of nurturing effective collaborations between rural and urban communities. Enhanced exchange, achieved by overcoming extant barriers, will enable the marginalized rural community to translate their opportunity scopes into enhanced opportunity structures. Social maladies, which bar the rural community from fully utilizing the welfare schemes devised for their betterment, can be mitigated to a great extent by fostering purposive inter- and intra-communitarian collaborations. Through knowledge acquisition and sharing, rural community, with an enhanced agency and social capital, will develop the credential to rise above the discriminatory social norms and practically utilize their opportunity scopes along with cultivating newer opportunities to enhance their overall opportunity structure.

5 Conclusion

This chapter, by drawing multiple cross-sectional theoretical relations, discusses in detail how holistic rural empowerment can be attained through effective knowledge transaction among urban and rural communities. It is implicit, combined with explicit, knowledge that together contribute to enhancing the knowledge pool of rural marginalized community. It is the simultaneous possession of processing abilities to use acquired knowledge to achieve desired outcome, along with knowledge possession, that together contribute to enhancing the knowledge pool of individuals on a holistic scale. The chapter is premised on the attempt to explore the potential of knowledge capability, or knowledge-operating abilities, in the overall context of rural empowerment.

While this chapter primarily draws upon the prospect of attaining rural empowerment through symbiotic knowledge exchange between urban and rural communities, the next chapter will talk about the practical efforts undertaken in developing nations to achieve rural empowerment. All the discussed schemes of the following chapter will shed light on the operational dynamics of undertaken projects and, in due course, attempt to outline their intrinsic drawbacks. Conventional schemes undertaken across the globe to empower the rural marginalized, although following multiple pathways, have attempted to deliver relevant information and knowledge to the rural community, but mainly do so without adequately involving the community members in their own developmental process. Neither the content of the information/knowledge to be disseminated nor the operational dynamics are known or decided by the community members for whom the schemes have been undertaken in the first place. As a result, the schemes often remain exogenous, or externally imposed, and fall short in delivering expected outcomes. The following chapter, which provides critical analysis of the schemes undertaken worldwide for rural empowerment, concludes with our conceptualization of a development ecosystem that attempts to bring rural empowerment from within, by making the rural community knowledge capable to process information and knowledge for communitarian betterment.

References

Ali, L. & Avdic, A. (2015). A Knowledge Management Framework for Sustainable Rural Development: The case of Gilgit-Baltistan, Pakistan. *The Electronic Journal of Knowledge Management*, 13(2), 103–165.

Alsop, R. & Heinsohn, N. (2005). Measuring Empowerment in Practice: Structuring Analysis and Framing Indicators. *World Bank Policy Research Working Paper* 3510. Available at: http://siteresources.worldbank.org/INTEMPOWERMENT/Resources/41307_wps3510.pdf.

Bandyopadhyay, S., Banerjee, S., Bardhan, A., Dey, P. & Das, S. (2015). *A Social Knowledge Management Framework for Harnessing Collective Knowledge Capital of Senior Citizens*. Proceedings of the 12th International Conference on Intellectual Capital, Knowledge Management & Organisational Learning. Retrieved from: http://toc.proceedings.com/28324webtoc.pdf.

Chaghouee, Y. & Mirakabad, M.R.Z. (2014). Knowledge management, social capital and intellectual capital relationships in process-oriented organizations. *Applied Mathematics in Engineering, Management and Technology*, 2(4), 298–303.

Cloward, R.A. & Ohlin, L.E. (1960). *Delinquency and Opportunity: A Theory of Delinquent Gangs*. New York: Free Press.

Daneshfard, A. (2006). Effective management of knowledge-centered organizations. *Tadbir Journal*, 174.

Davenport, T.H. & Prusak, L. (1998). *Working Knowledge: How organizations manage what they know*. Boston, MA: Harvard Business School Press.

European Union (2014). The Artistic Crafts Sector in Europe: Operative Plans and Strategic Visions. Interregional Cooperation Programme, European Union Regional Development. Retrieved from: https://issuu.com/ancitoscana/docs/3-eng.

Fernandez, B., Gonzalez, A. & Sabherwal, R. (2004). *Knowledge Management: Challenges Solutions and Technologies*. Upper Saddle River, NJ: Pearson Prentice Hall.

Gao, T., Chai, Y. & Liu, Y. (2018). A review of knowledge management about theoretical conception and designing approaches. *International Journal of Crowd Science*, 2(1), 42–51. doi:10.1108/IJCS-08-2017-0023.

Global Cottage Industry (2012). Retrieved from: http://handeyemagazine.com/content/global-cottage-industry.

Grootaert, C. (2003). *On the Relationship between Empowerment, Social Capital and Community-Driven Development*. Washington DC: World Bank. Retrieved from: http://documents.worldbank.org/curated/en/531651468780626484/On-the-relationship-between-empowerment-social-capital-and-community-driven-development.

Hemsley, J. & Mason, R. (2013). Knowledge and knowledge management in the social media age. *Journal of Organizational Computing and Electronic Commerce*, 23, 138–167. doi:10.1080/10919392.2013.748614.

Hess, C.G. (2006). Knowledge Management and Knowledge Systems for Rural Development. *GTZ Reader*. Retrieved from: http://www.fao.org/nr/com/gtzworkshop/Knowledge_Management_and_Systems.pdf.

Ibrahim, S. & Alkire, S. (2007). Empowerment and agency: A proposal for internationally-comparable indicators. *Oxford Development Studies*, 35(4), 379–403. doi:10.1080/13600810701701897.

IMARC (2018). Handicrafts Market: Global Industry Trends, Share, Size, Growth, Opportunity and Forecast 2018–2023. Report. ID: 4592343. Retrieved from: https://www.researchandmarkets.com/reports/4592343/handicrafts-market-global-industry-trends.

Jejeebhoy, S.J. (2000). *Women's Empowerment and Demographic Processes: moving beyond Cairo.* New York: Oxford University Press.

Jupp, D. (2010). Measuring Empowerment? Ask Them – Quantifying Qualitative Outcomes from People's Own Analysis: Insights for results-based management from the experience of a social movement in Bangladesh. *Sida Studies in Evaluation.* Retrieved from: https://www.oecd.org/countries/bangladesh/46146440.pdf.

Kockelman, P. (2007). Agency – The Relation between Meaning, Power and Knowledge. *Current Anthropology*, 48(3), 375–401.

Kumar, D. & Rajeev, P.V. (2013). Present Scenario of Indian Handicraft Products. *Asian Journal of Managerial Science*, 2(1), 21–27.

Minkes, A. (1952). A Note on Handicrafts in Underdeveloped Areas. *Economic Development and Cultural Change*, 1(2), 156–160.

Putnam, R.D. (2000). *Bowling Alone: The Collapse and Revival of American Community.* New York: Touchstone.

Quintas, P., Lefrere, P. & Jones, G. (1997). Knowledge management: a strategic agenda. *Long Range Planning Review*, 30(3), 385–391.

Reijsen, J., Helms, R., Batenburg, R. & Foorthuis, R. (2014). The impact of knowledge management and social capital on dynamic capability in organizations. *Knowledge Management Research & Practice*, 13(4), 401–417. doi:10.1057/kmrp.2013.59.

Samman, E. & Santos, M.E. (2009). *Agency and Empowerment: A review of concepts, indicators and empirical evidence.* Oxford: Oxford University Research Archive.

Sen, A. (1985). Well-Being, Agency and Freedom: The Dewey Lectures 1984. *The Journal of Philosophy*, 82(4), 169–221.

Sen, A. (1999). *Development as Freedom.* New York: Alfred A. Knopf.

Singh, K. (2009). *Rural Development: Principles, Policies and Management.* New Delhi: Sage Publications.

Soltani, Z. & Navimipour, N.J. (2016). Customer relationship management mechanisms: A systematic review of the state-of-the-art literature and recommendations for future research. *Computers in Human Behavior*, 61, 667–688.

Stillman, L. (2013). *Participatory action research & inclusive information and knowledge management for empowerment.* Proceedings of the ACM International Conference, Series 2, 163–166. doi:10.1145/2517899.2517903.

Styhre, A. (2008). The role of social capital in knowledge sharing: The case of a specialist rock construction company. *Construction Management and Economics*, 26(9), 941–951.

UNESCO (2005). Towards knowledge societies. United Nations Educational, Scientific and Cultural Organization World Report. Retrieved from: https://unesdoc.unesco.org/ark:/48223/pf0000141843.

United Nations (2015). Transforming our world: the 2030 Agenda for Sustainable Development. Retrieved from: https://unctad.org/en/PublicationsLibrary/ares70d213_en.pdf.

World Bank (2001). *World Development Report 2000/2001: Attacking Poverty.* New York: Oxford University Press. Retrieved from: https://www.odi.org/sites/odi.org.uk/files/odi-assets/events-presentations/703.pdf.

Vong, W., et al. (2017). Investigating the Roles of Knowledge Management Practices in Empowering Rural Youth to Bridge the Digital Divide in Rural Sarawak. *Journal of Integrated Design and Process Science*, 21(1), 61–79. doi:10.3233/jid-2017-0012.

4 Contemporary initiatives undertaken for rural empowerment

1 Introduction

Conventional rural developmental paradigms have primarily targeted the issue of rural empowerment through defined institutional structures and agencies created with such a "welfarist" mindset. However, though the rigor adopted to address the issue at stake deserves appreciation, we need to remember that institutional elitism inherently distances the schemes from the marginalized target group (Mansell, 2010). Instead of cultivating rural empowerment from within, the institutionally deployed schemes impose developmental parameters on the rural target group externally, without adequately considering the contextual specificities within which rural actors operate.

Denying the standardized institutional prescriptions, our alternative developmental paradigm shifts the focus to common mass, where each individual is considered to be an equal stakeholder and thereby indispensable to the developmental process. By transforming crowd to stakeholders, the proposed empowering ecosystem considers one and all to be potential contributors in the collective knowledge pool. It is by giving the rural community the provision to share their own indigenous knowledge assets, along with gaining new ones from outside, that the proposed empowering ecosystem targets rural development through cultivating individual and collective capacities of local members. Premising on cultivating strategies of self-sustenance and self-development among rural target group, our developmental framework identifies rural actors as potential agents bringing change, and thereby is in stark contrast to conventional developmental paradigms and their brand of institutionally driven rural empowerment.

The chapter is divided into four segments:

- The first part is dedicated to spelling out the promise and practice of "Rurbanization" mission. The mission premises on providing urban facilities to rural communities in order to enable these to overcome their marginalization. The initiative finds its place in the introductory section as one of the conventional developmental measures undertaken to achieve rural empowerment.

- Within the overall paradigm of rural empowerment, the second part traces the commitment of international agencies such as the United Nations in facilitating rural empowerment as an effective means to overcome marginalization of the rural sector. This section fleshes out the theoretical commitment of global institutions towards the motto of rural empowerment.
- The third part attempts to provide a practical glimpse of the schemes undertaken in developing nations with the motto of rural empowerment. Attempting to discuss how such schemes have targeted rural empowerment along diverse lines, this section explicitly brings out the exogenous nature of such schemes. Conceptualized primarily by developmental agents, the formulation of the schemes seldom involves the participation of local community.
- The fourth section expands on the exogenous nature of conventional rural empowerment models by individually pointing out the loopholes that most of the schemes suffer from. Departure from conventional exogenous rural empowerment models is only possible by attempting to cultivate strategies of self-sustenance and self-development among rural target group by facilitating effective collaboration within them. Only an alternative development framework enables rural stakeholders to enhance their networking capacities by connecting them both with members of their own group and across groups.

2 'Rurbanization': Promise and practice

The word "Rurban" (Rural + Urban) refers to a geographical territory, which by virtue of modernization acquires urban characteristics while retaining its indigenous roots and rural features. Sorokin and Zimmerman (1929) sociologically analyse the phenomenon following C.J. Galpin's terminological invention (Harms, 1939), where he interpreted the rural–urban integration and resultant rural transformation, in alliance with Talcott Parsons, as owing to urban expansion or rural migration (Parsons, 1954). While the scholars pioneered an entirely new paradigm to conduct research studies, we need to remember that in the period they were writing there were limited possibilities to practically translate their theorization to achieve rural–urban integration along concrete lines.

The contemporary era and its connecting spirit, boosting inter- and intra-communitarian linkage, have made geographical isolation almost a myth. Provision of easy exchange derived from improved communication has given innovative dimensions to the way collaborations can realize economic, social, political and civic activities. The smooth exchange has developed a socio-economic infrastructure, which makes possible a two-way effective exchange between rural–urban communities and setup. The result of enhanced communication therefore bears the potential to mark a decisive shift from conventional "Rurban" missions premised on value-loaded conceptualizations of what constitutes "rural" and "urban" and an implementation mode focusing on one-way knowledge transfer from urban to rural communities.

The European Parliament decided in 2010 to formally utilize the fruits of improved communication to trigger effective rural–urban cooperation in the continent (Urban–Rural Linkages, 2010). The following can be cited as the objectives of the European Rurban (Partnership for sustainable urban–rural development) Mission:

- Analysing territorial partnership practices between urban and rural areas.
- Achieving better cooperation between involved actors in rural–urban collaborations.
- Promoting territorial multi-level governance.
- Assessing tangible socio-economic gains resultant of effective rural–urban collaborations.
- Identifying the potential role of rural–urban collaborations in improving regional competitiveness and governance, thereby addressing the issue of rural empowerment.

Such nuanced public attempts to enhance rural–urban integration have not only been undertaken in developed parts of the world; developing nations such as India have also taken similar initiatives to foster rural–urban collaborations. The National Rurban Mission (NRuM), undertaken by the government of India in 2016, was launched with the aim to provide economic, social and physical infrastructural facilities to rural population in an attempt to uplift them and mitigate the marginalization of the country's rural sector (National Rurban Mission, 2016). The vision of NRuM focused on developing a cluster of villages that preserve and nurture the essence of rural community life, with emphasis on equity and inclusiveness, without compromising the facilities perceived to be essentially urban in nature. The cluster of "Rurban villages" as envisioned in the scheme is expected to stimulate local economic development, boost basic services and create well-planned clusters out of effective rural–urban integration. NRuM has been undertaken to trigger the following outcomes:

- Bridging rural–urban divide.
- Stimulating local economic development through employment generation and revenue creation.
- Triggering local and regional development.
- Attracting financial investments to boost the rural sector.

The above-mentioned initiatives, coupled with similar others undertaken across the globe, primarily rely on defined institutions and agencies to execute effective rural–urban integration. Dependence on institutions and agencies to usher in rural development essentially means these formal infrastructures are viewed as indispensable to the developmental framework, thereby shifting the focus from the marginalized target group for whom the policies have been framed. Moreover, the physical and informational distance urban-based policymakers share from rural stakeholders further contributes to the formulation of non-contextual policies, without keeping in mind the specific nature of rural need. Although rural development is a crucial aspect, which needs to be immediately addressed, agency/institution-based standardized developmental measures have fallen far short in addressing the issues persistent in specific rural contexts in which the actors operate.

The linear dissemination of information and resources from urban to rural communities adhered to by agency-based developmental models essentially views the rural segment as inferior, thereby denying the communities the scope to exchange their indigenous assets. There is an immense need to create an alternative and dynamic developmental paradigm, which will modify its course in accordance with the specific cultural contexts in which the framework is applied. This will shift the focus from standardized institutional practices to the rural community, who will thereby become determinants of their own course of socio-economic empowerment. Cultivating agency, social capital and enhancing the opportunity structure of rural target group will make the community active initiators of transformation, instead of being passive recipients of externally imposed changes. This will throw open the door to effective rural–urban symbiosis, characterized by two-way exchange between the two territorial sects. Developing the strategies of self-sustenance and self-development of the rural target group will thereby attempt to bring rural empowerment from within, following a reverse trajectory to that favoured by the normative institution-induced developmental models (Basak et al., 2016).

3 United Nations' initiatives towards rural empowerment

Sporadic attempts over a long period have been undertaken across the world to empower the rural sector. However, collaborative efforts on a global level to address the issue of region-wise development can be traced to the unanimous effort undertaken by the United Nations and its 191 member states in 2000. The subsequent formulation of Millennium Development Goals (MDGs) was done with an international commitment to combat poverty, hunger, disease, illiteracy, environmental degradation and discrimination against women (Millennium Development Goals, 2000).

Apart from the formulated MDGs undertaken to address discrepancies in the above-mentioned sectors, other selected indicators of development, not related to specific targets, were also incorporated. These additional indicators included population, fertility rate, life expectancy at birth, adult literacy rate and gross national income per capita. These relevant indicators were decided to be calculated at sub-national levels: by rural and urban area (region-wise), by socio-economic group, and by age and gender. The explanation of the MDGs makes it clear how the UN formulated developmental goals targeted at rural development primarily along a poverty eradication axis. While it is true that the primary attribute of global poverty is rural in nature, we must not forget that there are other, equally crucial, aspects apart from poverty which need attention for sustainable growth of the rural sector. Moreover, the MDGs had been formulated with a few stakeholders, without adequately involving developing countries. The standardized MDGs, not adapted to specific national needs, thus fell far short in specifying accountable parties, and thereby ended up reinforcing vertical interventions (Fehling et al., 2013).

Gibbs (2015) traces the failure of the MDGs to the inability of the measures to bring the entire world under its developmental purview. The fact that the success of the goals was not experienced equally across the globe becomes explicit if we take into consideration the Asian and African scenarios. Southeast Asia could only exceed the goal of poverty reduction by 16%, south Asia by 12.5% and northern Africa by 1.2%; Sub-Saharan Africa, witnessing the worst consequences, was 12.5% away from the goal of extreme poverty reduction (Gibbs, 2015). The disappointing results highlight that while the MDGs made considerable progress along the above-stated axes in developed parts of the world, the exclusion of the developing regions prevented the measures offering hope to the majority of the global marginalized. Gender inequality was a primary focus of the MDGs. However, the noble intention of mitigating the same could not practically translate to enhanced gender equality because the measures primarily relied on securing formal representational seats for women to address the inequality issue. Formal legal measures are not sufficient to bring a more just gendered distribution where gender inequality persists in spite of added representation of women in formal civic, educational, economic and other related spheres. While the MDGs' aim to address gender inequality primarily focused on formal education, the measures also remained mostly redundant in enhancing the global literacy rate. In countries affected by conflict, the proportion of out-of-school children increased from 30% in 1999 to 36% in 2012 (Gibbs, 2015). Primarily to address these loopholes, the United Nations attempted in 2015 to reformulate MDGs to more holistic Sustainable Development Goals (SDGs).

With a revisionary approach, the SDGs have a target of simultaneously addressing poverty reduction, inequality, sustainability and economic growth with job creation (Clarke, 2015). The SDGs include in total 17 targeted goals, and have emerged as a bold commitment to provide sustainable solutions to the most pressing challenges faced by the world today (United Nations, 2018).

In order to have a deeper penetration of undertaken measures in the remotest sectors of the world, the SDGs attempted to use the inclusive potential of contemporary digital technologies and encouraged public–private partnerships to facilitate development of marginalized sectors. Deploying technology for the purpose of social development has been incorporated as a primary resolution in the Rio+20 Agenda (Dehgan, 2012), which attempted to expand on the UN Millennium Development Goals. The new Sustainable Development Goals attempted to include a mechanism for international scientific cooperation and coordinated research to address the major sustainable developmental challenges (United Nations, 2018). In order to effectively functionalize the undertaken measures, the implementing agencies were directed to follow close interconnections and synergies between goals, trade-offs, indicators and target. Rooted in human rights, the framework of the SDGs provides opportunities for civil society engagement by encouraging local action and partnership. The reformulated developmental model therefore encourages community participation, which is expected to increase stakeholders' involvement in their own decision-making process, thereby paving the path for a more democratic and responsive governance. But although the undertaken SDGs are embedded in a symbiotic provision, enabling close interconnection between policy formulators and stakeholders, the primary reliance of the model on formal institutions to carry out the implementation restricts to a great extent the measures' ability to foster effective dialogue.

Rural empowerment, under the aegis of the SDGs, has witnessed innovative turns. The reformulated developmental framework has been an evolutionary step in integrating the world along redefined terms, by democratizing the use of science and technology in enhancing global connections. The resultant interconnection not only attempts to address the issues faced due to territorial isolation, it also cultivates collective concerns pertaining to severe social maladies such as poverty, inequality, sustainability, consumption and discrimination. Although the SDGs are also reliant on institutional execution, the revised vision of the developmental framework contains the formal provision for inclusive development, where inter-connection between policy formulators and rural stakeholders throws open the space for dialogue. In the following section we will discuss different rural empowerment schemes undertaken in developing countries, following both physical and digital lines. An in-depth analysis of the measures undertaken, in the context of the territorial specificities in which they have been adopted, will shed light on how far the initiatives have been successful in making the rural target group true stakeholders in determining their own course of socio-economic development.

4 Rural empowerment: Some measures taken in developing nations

Rural empowerment does not unfold in linear fashion. Giving access to advanced urbanized services to rural community may not successfully translate in mitigating the marginalization of the sector. It is about cultivating both individual and collective capacity among rural community in a sustainable fashion, by virtue of which the marginalized community will gain the competency to utilize developmental measures designed for their benefit. This will enable the marginalized rural community to empower themselves from within, where they have the provision of applying welfare measures formulated for them following their local pace and needs, instead of following standardized institutional prescriptions (Veen, 2017).

The conventional agency/institution-based developmental measures followed across the globe have been undertaken along multiple facets. The multi-faceted intervention actions include fostering dialogue, conflict resolution, livelihood, human rights, relief and rehabilitation, health, advocacy, democracy, reforms, primary health care, child and gender protection, basic and secondary education (both formal and vocational), water and environmental sanitation, national resource management and human and institutional development in rural community. Out of the diverse facets, education has been one of the primary areas to have received significant attention as it has been identified as a sector facilitating improvement in other related domains. The widespread illiteracy of the rural community further contributes in sustaining the socio-economic maladies intrinsic to the rural sector.

If we go back to the inception of a global education system, then we can see how historically the sector and the educational institutions mainly accommodated the elite sections of society. Spurred on mostly in urban city spaces, these educational institutions often had a negligent view towards educating the marginalized rural segment, scarcely focusing on genres of rural interest/concern. If we look into the traditional educational framework of Europe in the 19th century we can trace how British and French universities, being connoisseurs of knowledge dissemination, mostly focused on preserving knowledge instead of producing it (Cole, 2009). This approach made the orientation of the universities mostly theoretical, with little focus on vocational or practical education.

It is the North American legislative framework that first made an attempt to shift the elitist focus of education and made provision for public higher education, thereby policy-wise sanctioning equal access to specialized knowledge for all (Blackie, 2016). The welfarist position was formalized in the Morrill Act of 1862, which enabled widespread access to technical education, thereby allowing the American rural sector to transform its agricultural industries (Christy & Williamson, 1992). This new approach to education, in stark contrast to the European model, contained a broader base to address a comprehensive range of community priorities. Similar universities cropped up in Europe in the 20th century, with a vocational orientation. Provisions to boost the educational sector in the developed parts of the world, enabling easy access to specialized information and knowledge to all, considerably contributed to sustainable growth of the marginalized sector. Moreover, incorporation of vocational courses in the curriculum enabled intensive research on those genres, leading to a subsequent boost for sectors such as agricultural production, etc.

The process of creating higher educational institutions with a focus on transformational systems in agriculture and other related issues of rural concern have not transplanted successfully in developing nations. After considering the European and American context, if we turn our attention to the continent of Africa we can see how the educational system of the latter, suffering from the hangover of colonial education for a significant span of time, gave less importance to training of agricultural scientists and indigenous practitioners.

Eicher and Haggblade (2013) show in their work how very few African universities were adequately linked to national and regional priorities and social support. In economies such as those in Africa, which derive significant revenue from indigenous practices and production, such a negligent approach towards indigenous practices further contributes to sustained marginalization of the continent. Muhammed (2007) traces the reasons why rural development has been neglected in the continent. He identified the following as causal factors: (i) poor commitment and capacities in partner countries; (ii) poor financial commitment extended to the poor; and (iii) lack of adequate educational infrastructure to nurture the awareness level of the marginalized and others. Olayiwola and Adeleye (2005) have rightly identified such negligence to be one of the major contributors in widening the rural–urban gap and sustaining rural isolation.

It is only recently that the African continent has witnessed sporadic attempts to achieve rural development by addressing community priorities. With the undertaking of the SDGs and the attention on the world's developing sectors, the continent has seen a structural reorientation in its educational sector, where public policies have directed higher educational institutions to produce "job creators" instead of "job seekers" (Blackie, 2016). Several attempts have also been undertaken, following SDG dictates, along technical lines to target a more inclusive development. The rapid penetration of smartphones has opened up new prospects for the rural poor, through which they can explore commodity and input prices easily, thereby giving them better power in the marketplace. Kenya has witnessed various initiatives to provide easy access to financial resources to citizens. Of the multiple initiatives undertaken, the M-PESA initiative deserves special mention for its attempts to include those previously excluded from the banking system.

In 2014, the Barefoot College, committed to scaling up its successful Barefoot Approach of Community, extended its welfarist approach in Africa, primarily concentrating on Senegal, Burkina Faso, Tanzania, Liberia, South Sudan and Zanzibar (Kummitha, 2017). Six rural centres were developed in the countries aimed at enabling local women to electrify their villages through solar power. The Barefoot Approach, which provides training to illiterate target groups, attempts to boost communicational and entrepreneurial prospects of rural African women through both humane and technical intervention.

The Brazilian state of Amazonas has taken similar efforts following digital lines to achieve social development. The state's government, in order to boost its education sector and create a cohort of literate and informed citizens, founded the Amazonas Media Center in the largest city, Manaus, to disseminate educatory and advisory services to its population. Although the centre was founded in 2007, it received a boost under the aegis of the SDGs and witnessed the engagement and enrolment of more than 30,000 students in 1,500 Amazonas communities (Pelsue, 2014).

The above-mentioned measures, although in early stages, targeted rural development along sustainable paths because they promised benefits to local communities by making them stakeholders in determining their own socio-economic course of empowerment. It is the processual evolution of rural communities' standards of living and wellbeing, by the community itself, which we have identified as empowerment in our developmental framework. Hence empowerment becomes a dynamic concept, an unpredictable outcome of a confluence of various factors whose simultaneous cultivation enables rural target groups to develop their individual/collective potential as contributing members of society.

The impact of technological advances, coupled with internationally coordinated efforts to spread technology in an inclusive way to poor countries, has had an important impact on quality of life for billions of poor people (Dehgan, 2012). Targeting social development along digital axes has received further impetus under the SDGs, which tried to democratize the usage of science and technology in pursuit of social development. Having a closer commitment to human rights than the MDGs, the developmental framework followed by the SDGs have a more flexible approach to enable measures to adapt in accordance with national needs. The above-mentioned examples of Europe and Africa, juxtaposed against one another, explicitly reflect how empowering infrastructure, their ideology, nature, scope and method of implementation, varies from place to place. This reiterates the urgency to formulate developmental measures suited to specific cultural needs. A significant number of empowering measures for rural development have been taken in developing countries, following both physical and digital paths and keeping in mind community concerns. Following, we will provide snippets of rural development measures undertaken in developing nations, specifically focusing on developing nations of south-east Asia, and conduct an in-depth analysis of their operationalization processes, exposing the limitations of extant schemes in making rural populations true stakeholders.

4.1 Indonesia

Indonesia, a south-east Asian nation, has been home to hundreds of ethnic groups and their indigenous heritage. The country's commitment to preserve its cultural heritage and indigenous practices has resulted in adoption of several welfare initiatives aimed at achieving rural development. These initiatives included support from the International Fund for Agricultural Development (IFAD) for the Rural Empowerment and Agricultural Development Programme Scaling Up Initiative (READ SI) undertaken by Indonesia (READ SI, 2016). Before going into the intricacies of the programme, it is important to briefly articulate the roles and responsibilities of IFAD, the supporting agency. IFAD helps communities plan activities and manage their development needs, improve agricultural production and develop rural enterprises. It also provides access to markets and enables infrastructural development by facilitating improvements in roads, water supply, irrigation facilities, etc. The objectives of IFAD have significantly shaped the mission and vision of rural empowerment measures undertaken in Indonesia.

Supported by IFAD from 2008–2014, READ attempted to empower smallholder farmers to improve income and production and strengthen village-level institutions by integrating community-driven development and agricultural productivity. Various private, public and non-governmental agencies have been entrusted with the responsibility of conducting practical actions to bring about transformation in Indonesia's rural economy. The programme primarily targeted three rural sectors in Indonesia: Sulawesi, West Kalimantan and NTT (East Nusa Tenggara). In these rural locales developmental policies attempted communitarian empowerment by boosting individual and collective skills, as well as confidence and resources, thereby enabling rural members to sustainably improve their farm and non-farm production, income and livelihoods. The developmental strategies targeted inclusion of Indonesian ethnic groups and indigenous people by adopting policies along three axes:

- *Village agriculture and livelihood development,* which includes community mobilization, improvement of agriculture and livelihoods, savings, loan and financial literacy and nutrition of rural population.
- *Services, inputs and market linkages,* including agricultural extension services, financial services, seed supply markets and systems, cocoa farmer support services and markets, livestock production, health services and market.
- *Policy and strategy development* to strengthen public schemes and institutional framework to improve indigenous production and enhance the livelihoods of the practitioners.

The above-mentioned welfare measures undertaken for rural empowerment clearly reflect Indonesia's policy-wise commitment towards a community-driven developmental model. However, primary reliance on agency-based dissemination of incentives for rural community failed to mobilize the local community effectively. Inadequate involvement of local administration to a great extent contributed to keeping the measures distant from the target group, where external imposition of measures could hardly achieve rural empowerment from within. In order to have a deeper penetration, the scaling-up initiative of READ attempted to shift the focus from project to programmatic action with the intention to influence future public and private investment in the domain of rural development. The scaling-up initiative identified the territorial incapacitation of physical intervention and deployed a knowledge management solution to the issue of rural marginalization. Deploying technology for rural cause, the scaling-up initiative of READ premised the initiative on a strong knowledge management and evidence-based policy dialogue framework and institutional capacity building. Similar efforts have been undertaken in Jakarta, the capital city of Indonesia, whose conceptualization of achieving empowerment is premised on an informational and knowledge–theoretic perspective. The Internews Center for Innovation and Learning, in alliance with the Rockefeller Foundation, conducted in 2011 a nine-month research project named "Embracing Change: The Critical Role of Information". The initiative attempted to disseminate practical guidelines to marginalized populations of Jakarta on how to navigate the digital medium and use the acquired information to promote community resilience (Frohardt & Jones, 2018). Even though the efforts remained more committed to community concerns, we must remember the importance formal institutions have been granted in practically executing the measures.

4.2 Iran

Iran, located in western Asia and commonly referred to as the Islamic Republic of Iran, is primarily at a developing stage; although the national economy is considerably supported by the industrial sector, its rural developmental policies need more precision. The country has a rich repository of natural resources, which make it mandatory to devise nuanced schemes in support of sustainable prosperity for its agricultural sector (Aref & Aref, 2011). The Iranian government has formulated various public policies to boost national agricultural production. The sector has received significant attention because of the following credentials:

- Agriculture provides food, which is of utmost importance to Iran's growing economy.
- Agricultural exports generate foreign exchange, which significantly contributes to the national revenue.
- Agriculture generates savings that the non-agricultural sector requires for capital accumulation, therefore ensuring balanced growth of the rural economy.
- The growing agricultural sector creates a local market for non-agricultural goods.

Several public schemes have targeted sustainable agricultural development by integrating the efforts of rural agricultural organizations, rural communities and farmers in rural areas. However, their institutional reliance has to a great extent distanced these schemes from the rural target group, where the schemes have remained largely incapacitated in organizing farmers into structured developmental paradigm (Aref & Aref, 2011). Aref and Aref rightly identify rural empowerment as an enabling quotient, facilitating self-induced development of individual/collective capacities as contributing members of society. Rural empowerment should cultivate the abilities of individuals, organizations, businesses and government and facilitate interconnections among these entities; it must enable creation of a collaborative working environment (Aref & Aref, 2011). It is the ability of rural communities to mobilize resources from within by virtue of an enhanced inter- and intra-communitarian linkage, coupled with their negotiating power, that paves the path for developing the skills and community structures necessary for development.

The Iranian government has taken several measures to boost its rural sector by entering into alliance with various private and non-governmental organizations to successfully execute the undertaken measures. The measures include increased public investment in rural infrastructure and agriculture, reorientation of safety nets to create better job prospects in rural areas and the strengthening of the human resource base through education, nutrition, empowerment of women and building physical infrastructure. Although the measures taken are multi-faceted and may seem theoretically effective, the initiatives have fallen well short in addressing the pressing problem Iran's rural economy faces in the context of efficient production and marketing of high-value livestock, fruit, vegetables and fishery output (Aref & Aref, 2011). The alienation of policy-makers from the specific nature of rural needs contributes to formulation of policies ineffective in addressing the issues at stake. In order to develop a more community-centric rural developmental perspective by optimally utilizing the natural resource repository, the Iranian government must liberalize its stringent marketing and trade policies (Aref & Araf, 2011). Resultant relaxation will encourage effective vertical co-ordination between its farm and non-farm sectors, between policy formulators and the target group. Enhanced communication across different groups is expected to facilitate increased flow of rural credit through non-banking financial intermediaries.

Apart from taking measures along physical lines, the Iranian government has also deployed technology for deeper penetration of its rural developmental efforts. Rapid development of information and communications technology (ICT), followed by easy and affordable availability of telecommunication infrastructures, have offered promising prospects to developing nations, giving them the provision to establish purposive connections across the world (Lekoko & Semali, 2011). The Iranian government has utilized the inclusive potential of contemporary digital technologies to bring positive outcomes in the following domains:

- Agriculture and health.
- Infrastructure, communication and community informatics/knowledge.
- Economic empowerment and small-scale entrepreneurship.
- Policies, strategies and e-governance.

There are public attempts to boost the rural sector through provision for digital inclusion and the building of an informational ecosystem, where each social actor is considered to be a potential contributor to the collective knowledge pool. Much of the "ICT promise" for rural transformation has been expressed in terms of the power of information and knowledge. However, information and knowledge transactions, especially with disempowered people and groups, are a complex process (Basak et al., 2016) and not generally amenable to across-the-counter productization and monetization. Only some kinds of information – such as agriculture price information, health-related information, etc. – can be delivered usefully through a rural kiosk-based model. Most other information and knowledge transactions are much more human interaction intensive and need to be done in an altruistic and community-minded spirit. The Iranian government's attempt to deploy technology in pursuit of social development deserves appreciation, but the initiatives often fail to make considerable impact in the absence of an empowering ecosystem to guide the marginalized target group on optimal usage of digital platforms.

4.3 India

India, one of the largest developing nations, has 640,000 villages, with 68.84% of the total population residing in the rural fringes (Pangannavar, 2015). The national government has taken various rural developmental measures to boost the country's rural sector, with the comprehensive range of activities including agricultural growth, development of social and economic infrastructure, fair wages, housing, public health, education, village planning, nutrition and communication. The public means to implement the measures are primarily premised on having an integrated view of resources available and optimally utilizing the same in pursuit of concrete benefits.

A self-reliant village community has been the mission of the nation since the time of the British Raj. Even the foreign government could identify how the rural sector serves as the backbone of the economy and implemented measures – such as the Marthandam Project, the Gurgaon Experiment, the Baroda Rural Reconstruction Movement, the Firka Development Project, etc. – to enable the sector to attain workable levels of self-sufficiency through introducing community development schemes (Pangannavar, 2015). However, the distance of the governing apparatus from the rural target group significantly contributed to making the measures ineffective in attaining a self-sustaining rural economy.

The main challenge for empowering rural India post-independence was in managing transition of 80% of the rural population from a village-centric agricultural based economy to an industry-based rural economy. The structural transformation contributed to negligence towards indigenous practices, where significant numbers of indigenous practitioners left their traditional practices to earn better wages. This negligence towards indigenous practices at the cost of increasing national revenue through industry-based production was a serious threat to the emerging nation. In order to preserve its cultural supremacy, the post-independence Indian government took measures to increase efficiency in rural production. The measures undertaken included:

- Maximization of agricultural production and growth of rural industries (both village and cottage industries).
- Generating employment opportunities, thereby creating job prospects in the rural economy to attract younger generations to engage in rural production.
- Providing basic infrastructural amenities to rural sectors, such as drinking water, electricity, subsidized credit facilities.
- Enhancing local communities' control over the rural economy and participation in decision-making process.

Although the measures taken by the Indian government for rural empowerment are multi-faceted, they have largely been committed to fighting poverty. The Self-Help Group (SHG) scheme undertaken by the government with the purpose of providing micro-credit facilities to rural Indian women primarily had a poverty eradication mindset. The measure attempted to develop the entrepreneurial capacities of rural women, thereby enabling them to become independent "bread-winners" (Kamaraj, 2009). However, although the measure had a transformatory potential, it fell short in fully utilizing the potential of the scheme for the betterment of rural community. While vocational training given to the rural women as a part of this scheme successfully imparted skills of market value to rural community, it seldom helped the community to utilize the schemes to enhance individual and collective socio-economic prospects. Moreover, non-availability of training modules in local languages often barred the target group, the majority of whom are illiterate, to fully grasp the knowledge imparted. Although the SHG scheme had a well-articulated anti-poverty mission, its non-contextual application prevented it from being an effective instrument for rural rejuvenation for poor rural households.

Apart from undertaking measures along physical lines, the Indian government also introduced rural developmental initiatives along digital lines, to have a deeper penetration. The Common Service Centre (CSC) scheme has been undertaken to align with the Indian government's mandate of a socially, financially and digitally inclusive society (Dass & Bhattacherjee, 2011). Undertaken as a part of the Digital India Programme, the CSC scheme attempted to construct 100,000 service centres in remote rural areas to serve as the access points for delivery of essential public utility services, social welfare schemes, health care and financial, education and agriculture services, apart from hosting G2C (Government to Citizen) services for citizens in rural and remote areas of the country. The scheme to set up digitally enabled service centres across rural India was planned with the intention to provide rural communities access to digital infrastructure, to be used by the community for the benefit of the community. However, entrusting rolling out responsibilities to private entities led to non-involvement of local administrations and failure to attain concrete benefits. The private players, external to the setting, remained largely ineffective in mobilizing local community to utilize the digital infrastructure implanted for community benefit.

In order to have a deeper penetration, the revised version of the CSC scheme was formulated, keeping in mind community concerns (IT for Change, 2009). Although the scheme's reformulation witnessed the incorporation of some local agencies, it could not completely distance itself from the bureaucratic nepotism intrinsic to organizational dissemination. Sporadic digital literacy training, although bringing basic technical knowledge to certain segments of the target group, was not enough to sustain the motivation of rural non-users. Lack of knowledge on how to conduct purposive activities through the digital forum prevented the rural community from reaping the fruits of digitization. Although the CSC scheme has enormous potential in ushering in rural development by digitally empowering the local community, the standardized developmental paradigm it follows restricts the scope of the scheme. Primary reliance on agency-based execution, coupled with non-contextual formulation of training modules and lack of application guidelines on how to use the digital medium to produce concrete benefits, blocked the CSC scheme from achieving holistic success.

4.4 Pakistan

In Pakistan, the rural economy also serves as the primary revenue generator. Pakistan has also adopted an institutional developmental model to boost its rural sector, a formal commitment taken as a part of the Social Welfare Act in 1961 (REPID, 2018). The nation saw the successive emergence of various non-profit and private institutions committed to achieving rural empowerment. To have a grassroot impact, the public schemes encouraged collaboration between these agencies and various community-based organizations (CBOs), which employ local, rural members to bring community-driven transformation. In this context, the emergence and proliferation of a non-profit organization, Rural Empowerment and Institutional Development (REPID), since 2007 serves as a perfect example to reflect the practical operationalization of rural development in the nation. In its attempt to promote sustainable development, REPID has made alliances with several CBOs to secure deeper penetration and impact.

This alliance with more than 40 CBOs across Pakistan enabled the creation of an Economic Development Network (EDN), which targeted rural development along multi-faceted axes. The intervention genres include fostering dialogue among rural–urban communities, both inter- and intra-communitarian conflict resolution, enhancing livelihoods and human rights in local community, and promoting relief, rehabilitation, democracy and reforms. Measures have given considerable attention to the rejuvenation of primary and secondary education, protection of child and gender rights, and provisions for shelters, safe drinking water and environmental sanitation. The initiatives, while identified rural transformation as the end result, recognize national resource management and sustained human and institutional development as potential means to achieve the end. While the Pakistani scenario reflects adoption of formal attempts to initiate community-driven development by deploying several CBOs in the process of rural development, we need to remember that even such CBOs are not completely devoid of the bureaucracy organizations come with. The bureaucratic structure intrinsic to organizations fails to realize the merits of informal crowd-sourced transactions. The resultant hierarchy largely bars the crowd from being true stakeholders, thereby restricting local community participation in the process of determining the course of rural socio-economic empowerment.

Since 2011 the Internews Center for Innovation and Learning has made considerable efforts in developing nations such as Pakistan and Myanmar to improve socio-economic prospects of marginalized segments of the population by deploying technology. The initiative has attempted to build a virtual ecosystem framework, which will facilitate deeper appreciation for the dynamics, flows, networks, and communication behaviours that characterize information ecosystems in environments of change and disruption (Frohardt & Jones, 2018). The effort to create an informational ecosystem in pursuit of social development acknowledges the importance of multi-dimensional information need; its creation, distribution and ability to adapt and regenerate according to the specific context of a given situation and community.

Although the effort to achieve social development by utilizing technology in appropriate ways to develop an informational ecosystem happens to be theoretically sound, undertaking such initiatives without disseminating prior digital literacy training to the under-privileged and illiterate target group restricts the scope of such measures. Moreover, it needs to be remembered in this context that technological interventions for social transformation are more than just making people "literate" in ICT and making it accessible. Björn-Sören (2011) shows that there is a gap between information and communications technologies and socio-economic development. He argues that, if information is critical to development, then ICT, as a means of sharing information, is not simply a connection between people but a link in the chain of the development process itself. ICTs can enhance the functioning of markets because they can properly integrate and bind the floating market components into static contents in order to provide a sustainable model. Björn-Sören's conceptualization therefore advocates in favour of the empowering credentials that the technology-induced information ecosystems should have, which is not simply derivative of providing the non-users with "access" to technology. Any technology-mediated initiative, apart from providing access to the digital medium, must also target building evaluative capacities among the target group to enable them to use the information acquired through the digital medium in pursuit of self-betterment.

5 Limitations of current institution-based rural empowerment paradigms

A brief glimpse of the rural empowerment paradigm undertaken across the globe presented above sheds light on the operational dynamics and specific ideology behind undertaking the initiatives. Although the measures have mitigated the anomalies of a selected few from the rural community, they fall far short of addressing rural empowerment on a holistic level (Aref & Aref, 2011). The following can be broadly cited as significant factors hindering mass-scale rural empowerment following the institution-based developmental model:

- Institutional prescriptions and the executional policies following organizational stringency happen to be a mismatch to the informal rural setting, which has a territorial and cultural pace which cannot be addressed by standardized models.

- The elite policy formulators share a considerable physical, informational and cultural gap from the rural stakeholders. Insufficient knowledge about the specific nature of rural need and the hindrances faced by the community compels the policy formulators to design policies not contextually suited for rural community (Mansell, 2010).
- Various training and capacity-building programmes for rural community adopted as a part of facilitating rural development are often available in non-local languages. Non-availability of learning modules in local language often prevents the rural community from utilizing the programmes for their benefit.
- Although the rural community has received various skill-development training from public, private and non-governmental parties, lack of application guidelines on how to utilize acquired skills in pursuit of concrete benefits have prevented the rural community reaping the fruits of such measures.
- In cases where measures have been undertaken for providing equal market opportunities via the digital channel to marginalized rural community, doing so without prior dissemination of contextual digital literacy training has obstructed practical realization of such efforts.
- In instances where measures have been undertaken to digitally empower rural community, we need to remember that imparting digital literacy training to rural non-users is not enough to guarantee their digital participation. The training has to be supplemented by guidance on purposive usage of the digital medium, through which the rural community can derive concrete benefits, thereby ensuring their motivation to use the platform.

Conventional efforts taken to usher in rural development inevitably attract the above-stated loopholes. Their primary reliance on structured organizations to carry out successful implementation suffers from the bureaucratic nepotism which any institutional setup unconditionally attracts. The hierarchy, derivative of the bureaucratic structure, further contributes in preventing a close alliance between elite policy formulators and marginalized target groups. Lack of necessary dialogue between the two entities results in the formulation of standardized welfare measures not designed to address the specific nature of rural needs.

6 Conclusion

It is indeed true that the various initiatives undertaken across the developing nations, along multiple axes, have attempted to mitigate rural isolation by providing rural community with access to important information crucial for pronouncing prospects of self-development. However, we need to remember that information does not have any intrinsic value; its entire worth rests in its use, and its value is derived out of purposive sharing and exchange of informational resource. The extant schemes, while making available valuable information to rural community, do not give them the ability to process the acquired information. As a result, the acquired information remains at the level of factual data to the rural community, where lack of processing abilities and opportunities prevent the community benefiting from purposive sharing of information. In the next chapter we will discuss how the sporadic attempts of extant measures to feed the rural community with information, along with application of standardized techniques for information dissemination/execution, together contribute in making the schemes exogenous. They impose the measures externally on rural target group, without involving the local community in the process of attaining rural development (Mansell, 2010). Non-involvement of local community in the decision-making process further contributes in non-contextual formulation of rural welfare schemes. In order to effectively facilitate rural empowerment from within, it is crucial to design an integrated and inter-connected developmental ecosystem, where the task of carrying out successful execution of welfare schemes rests on optimal mobilization of local bodies and informal crowd sources, instead of external institutional mechanisms (Dehgan, 2012; Basak et al., 2016). Our solution rests in proposing an alternative developmental framework for rural empowerment freed from the stringency of institutional prescriptions and organizational execution. While the extant policies externally impose the measures on rural target group, in our decentralized developmental model we have identified local rural actors as well as various urban actors as agents of change. This will be presented in the latter part of this book.

References

Aref, A. & Aref, K. (2011). Rural Empowerment for Sustainable Agricultural Development in Iran. *Journal of American Science*, 7(11). Retrieved from: http://www.jofamericanscience.org/journals/am-sci/am0711/042_7032am0711_350_353.pdf.

Blackie, M. (2016). Higher Education and Rural Development in Africa: Building a new Institutional Framework. *African Journal of Rural Development*, 1(2), 115–125.

Basak, J., Parthiban, R., Roy, S. & Bandyopadhyay, S. (2016). *A Community-driven Information System to Develop Next Generation Collaborative and Responsive Rural Community (NCoRe)*. Proceedings of the ITU Kaleidoscope Academic Conference: ICTs for a Sustainable World (ITU WT), Bangkok, 1–8. doi:10.1109/ITU-WT.2016.7805727.

Björn-Sören, G. (2011). Informational capabilities – the missing link for the impact of ICT on development (English). E-Transform knowledge platform working paper; no. 1. Washington, DC; World Bank Group. Available at: http://documents.worldbank.org/curated/en/227571468182366091/Informational-capabilities-the-missing-link-for-the-impact-of-ICT-on-development.

Christy, R. & Williamson, L. (1992). *A Century of Service: Land-Grant Colleges and Universities, 1890–1990*. New Brunswick, NJ: Transaction Publishers.

Clarke, J. (2015). Seven Reasons the SDGs will be better than the MDGs. *The Guardian*. Retrieved from: https://www.theguardian.com/global-development-professionals-network/2015/sep/26/7-reasons-sdgs-will-be-better-than-the-mdgs.

Cole, J. (2009). *The Great American University*. Philadelphia, PA: Perseus.
Dass, R. & Bhattacherjee, A. (2011). *Status of Common Service Center Program in India: Issues, Challenges and Emerging Practices for Rollout* (W.P. No. 2011-2002-03). Indian Institute of Management Ahmedabad. Retrieved from: https://core.ac.uk/download/pdf/6455060.pdf.
Dehgan, A. (2012). Creating the New Development Ecosystem. *Science*, 336(6087), 1397–1398. doi:10.1126/science.1224530.
Eicher, C. & Haggblade, S. (2013). The Evolution of Agricultural Education and Training: Global Insights of Relevance for Africa (Working Paper Series 183417). Michigan State University, Department of Agricultural, Food, and Resource Economics.
Fehling, M., Nelson, B. & Venkatapuram, S. (2013). Limitations of the Millennium Development Goals: A Literature Review. *Global Public Health*, 8(10), 1109–1122.
Frohardt, M. & Jones, S.B. (2018). Why Information Matters. The Rockefeller Foundation. Retrieved from: https://assets.rockefellerfoundation.org/app/uploads/20141118163158/5e90168a-3f48-4bb3-af69-1a565a218281.pdf.
Gibbs, D. (2015). MDGs Failure. *The Borgen Project*. Retrieved from: https://borgenproject.org/mdg-failures/.
Harms, E. (1939). Rural Attitudes in Modern Urban Life. *Social Forces*, 17(4), 486–489.
IT for Change (2009). ICTs for community development in India: Going beyond the basic CSC model. Retrieved from: https://itforchange.net/sites/default/files/ITfC/Note_on_ICTs_for_CD-ITfC.pdf.
Kamaraj, K. (2009). *Performance of Self-Help Group in Tamil Nadu*. Bangalore: Southern Economist.
Kummitha, R.K.R. (2017). Barefoot Approach and Its Practice. In *Social Entrepreneurship and Social Inclusion*. Singapore: Palgrave Macmillan. doi:10.1007/978-981-10-1615-8_4.
Lekoko, R.N. & Semali, L. (2011). *Cases on Developing Countries and ICT Integration: Rural Community Development*. Hershey, PA: IGI Global.
Mansell, R. (2010). Power and interests in developing knowledge societies: exogenous and endogenous discourses in contention. *Journal of International Development*, 26(1), 109–127. doi:10.1002/jid.1805.
Millennium Development Goals (2000). Retrieved from: www.who.int/topics/millennium_development_goals/about/en/.
Muhammed, M.A.S. (2007). *Rural Development and Enterprise Development*. Alexandria: Sustainable Development Association.
National Rurban Mission (2016). Retrieved from: http://vikaspedia.in/social-welfare/rural-poverty-alleviation-1/schemes/national-rurban-mission-nrum.
Olayiwola, L.M. & Adeleye, A.O. (2005). Rural Development and Agro-Industrial Production in Nigeria: Concepts, Strategies and Challenges. *Journal of Social Sciences*, 11(1), 57–61.
Pangannavar, A. (2015). A Research Study on Rural Empowerment Through Women Empowerment: Self-Help Groups, A New Experiment in India. *International Journal of Law, Education, Social and Sports Studies (IJLESS)*, 2(1), 51–56.
Parsons, T. (1954). *Essays in Sociological Theory*. New York: Collier-Macmillan.
Pelsue, B. (2014). A Radical Idea in the Rainforest. Retrieved from: https://www.gse.harvard.edu/news/ed/14/ 09/radical-idea-rainforest.
READ SI (2016). Rural Empowerment and Agricultural Development Programme Scaling Up Initiative. Final programme design report, IFAD, Indonesia. Retrieved from: https://webapps.ifad.org/members/eb/120/docs/EB-2017-120-R-11-Programme-design-report.pdf.

REPID (2018). Retrieved from: https://www.icermediation.org/organizations/rural-empowerment-and-institutional-development-repid/.

Sorokin, P. & Zimmerman, C. (1929). *Principles of Rural–Urban Sociology*. New York: Holt.

United Nations (2018). Global indicator framework for the Sustainable Development Goals and targets of the 2030 Agenda for Sustainable Development. Retrieved from: https://unstats.un.org/sdgs/indicators/Global%20Indicator%20Framework%20after%20refinement_Eng.pdf.

Urban-Rural Linkages (2010). Retrieved from: https://ec.europa.eu/regional_policy/en/policy/what/territorial-cohesion/urban-rural-linkages/.

Veen, E. (2017). Development as an Ecosystem. Retrieved from: https://www.clingendael.org/publication/development-ecosystem.

5 Information asymmetry and rural producers

1 Introduction

This chapter spells out the hindrances intrinsic to rural producers in developing nations due to extant information asymmetry and proposes prospective solutions for mitigating the same. The rural communities in developing nations owe their marginalization to a great extent to their information deficit pertaining to multi-faceted socio-economic factors. Lack of adequate information often disempowers them from actively participating in market transaction (David, 2012). Information asymmetry of rural producers has witnessed the emergence of several schemes to eradicate the issue at hand and empower rural producers. However, an in-depth description of the schemes reveals how information dissemination alone is not sufficient in uplifting the status of the rural marginalized. It is necessary to inculcate skills and experience among rural target group, by virtue of which they will develop the credentials to process acquired information for benefit.

The chapter is divided into three segments:

- The first section of the chapter, after providing a brief account of the way existing works conceptualize informational asymmetry, tries to locate informational asymmetry within different entities in the context of rural economy. Subsequently the section analyses the impact of such asymmetry in contributing and sustaining market inefficiency of rural production.
- In the second section the chapter provides a brief idea of the existing schemes undertaken both at the global and local level to mitigate information asymmetry and how such schemes remain inadequate in achieving holistic rural empowerment.
- Finally, the chapter concludes by hinting at the urgency to move beyond equipping rural producers with the informational resource and simultaneously inculcating in them evaluative capacities to process the information acquired. It is information literacy coupled with processing abilities that in combination attempt to enhance the knowledge base of the rural target group; a precursory measure to achieving holistic rural empowerment.

2 The need for information and the effect of information asymmetry

Information about something or someone is a much-prized possession. Hence asymmetrical or unequal distribution of such information is bound to put those in possession of less information in a precarious position (Arrow, 1963). Studying the consequences of information asymmetry in the domain of market is indeed a heavily researched area. Researchers from diverse domains, such as economists and financial experts, have dedicated themselves to chalking out strategies to deal with asymmetrical information. Information asymmetry is thought to arise when buyers and sellers, at the time of the economic transaction, possess differential information. This differential information, disturbing the equilibrium, further influences the trade. Most of the works in mainstream economics read informational asymmetry with the assumption that sellers have greater knowledge about their products, which enables them to sell their produce along terms and conditions beneficial to them. Such power enables the sellers to remain on the advantageous side of opportunism and adverse selection (Auronen, 2003) and manipulate the trade, essentially by hiding important information (Akerlof, 1970). Reading informational asymmetry along such lines is useful in studying large-scale business transactions. However, such an assumption falls short in explaining a plethora of small-scale informal transactions happening in the rural economy, where urban buyers are at a more advantageous position and the rural sellers (the producers) have far less knowledge about the value of their products in both the global and local market contexts in which they operate. Organized in an informal structure, the rural producers, due to multi-faceted hindrances, find it difficult to hold a prominent place in the urban market (Khan & Amir, 2013). This persistent isolation of the rural producers often results in inefficient production, which fails to meet the growing demand for rural produce (Choudhury, 2004). In this context we can also trace the origin of resultant market failure in information asymmetry.

So, following mainstream economic theorization, we would not be correct in articulating this informational gap as placing the sellers or rural producers in a comparatively advantageous position. It is true that the rural producers have more knowledge about their produce than anyone else does in the market. However, their disadvantageous market position and rural orientation prevent them utilizing the additional information they have in pursuit of profitable returns. The resultant production inefficiency and constricted freedom of rural producers hint at how information is not just an economic resource but a social necessity as well (Arrow, 1963). Thus, possessing relevant information is not just required from an economic standpoint but is also mandatory for the growth of a self-sustaining rural economy. It is because of this differential nature of informational asymmetry at play in rural economy that the sector demands exclusive attention, which will enable us to come up with innovative and unique strategies pertaining to the mitigation of such asymmetrical information.

3 Information asymmetry of rural producers in developing nations

This section focuses on demystifying the information asymmetry faced by rural producers. By discussing the agents with whom the rural community experiences informational asymmetry, the section focuses on analysing the impact of such asymmetrical information aggravating rural market inefficiency.

The word "asymmetry", by definition, resonates the spirit of bilateral disequilibrium. In the asymmetrical relation prevalent in rural economy, if we consider the rural producers to be at one end of the spectrum, then the other end is necessarily occupied by another entity or organization. We will chalk out the nature and intricacy of asymmetrical relation rural producers experience with different entities, who are integral to the process of rural production and consumption.

3.1 Information asymmetry between producers themselves

Rural producers, primarily residing in rural pockets across the globe, are a scattered community. Their physical distance from each other, as well as from urban markets, has considerably hampered their information pool. Lack of information about fellow producers impedes community development and the formation of an integrated community of rural producers. Since these rural producers are already isolated, a sense of belonging to a community composed of the likes is crucial in sustaining the motivation of these already marginalized producers. For example, we are all aware of the importance handicrafts have in the global context. Apart from the share it contributes to the global economy, the handicrafts sector also has a major role to play in sustaining indigenous artistic heritage (Bhat & Yadav, 2016). An integrated artisan community is thus required from the standpoint of sustaining the global handicrafts sector, which will enable each artisan to benefit from collective support and guidance.

An enhanced inter-communitarian communication paves the path for prominent economic benefits. Exchange of information pertaining to important aspects of production – such as designing, pricing, availability of raw materials, logistics of production and other related issues between rural producers – ensures a more optimal and ethical production. A rural Indian producer residing in Kandi, a village located in the Murshidabad district of West Bengal, narrated the problems of asymmetric informational relationship within a community and how it affects production. In a qualitative interview conducted by our research group at Kandi in October, 2017, she said, "We do not know what others in our locality are producing, from where they are procuring raw materials or getting easy finance, what are the marketing channels they are using, and so on. That means we cannot learn from others, or discuss with them aspects which are common to our production process." The experiential narration of the rural Indian producer highlighted the dissatisfaction derivative of an obstructed peer-to-peer learning scope resultant of weak intra-communitarian communication. The asymmetric informational relationship among rural producers could have been handled to some extent through peer-to-peer knowledge exchange. But lack of inter- and inter-communitarian linkage restricts the possibility.

3.2 Information asymmetry between producers and their prospective buyers

The distance the rural producers share from their prospective buyers is not just a physical one, but also virtual in nature, which significantly derives its nourishment from rural–urban knowledge divide. The asymmetrical information between these two entities results in an unbridgeable gap between the nature of urban demand and rural product, thereby restricting profitable convergence of rural supply with urban demand. Moreover, lack of information about the producers and the nature of their engagements disallows the wholesale buyers from optimally utilizing the potential of rural producers. Bartels (1968) posited that the facilitation of market development in any industry required the bridging of separations between the producers and the consumers that existed on multiple dimensions. He added that these separations may be of four types: "spatial (physical distances), temporal (time difference between production & consumption), informational (concerned parties having different/unequal knowledge about products and market conditions), and financial (buyers not possessing purchasing power at the time they have willingness or buy)" (Bartels, 1968, p. 6). So one of the major reasons for market separation between rural producer and urban consumer is the information asymmetry that exists between them. Limited use of communication platforms coupled with the spatial separation of rural producers from the customers inhibit the producers from gauging market demand, both in terms of quantity and type of produce. Accordingly, it makes it difficult for the producers to plan their production schedules (Singh et al., 2015). The intermediation by different agents also leaves them with little opportunity to know the feedback about their products and to know about the wants of customers (Ghouse, 2012).

The rural Indian producer residing in Kandi traced the reason for her poor sales to the distance she shares with her buyers. In the qualitative interview conducted by our research group in October, 2017, she said, "We are rural producers. Most of the urban buyers are unaware of what we are producing. Hence they simply buy from urban markets … Since we do not have proper linkage with urban crowd, we, the rural producers, often produce designs, some of which are considered outdated by urban tastes." This personal narration of a rural producer highlights the practical hindrances rural community faces due to the information asymmetry they experience with urban consumers; lack of information about the rural producers and the nature of their engagements prevents the wholesale buyers optimally utilizing the potential of rural creative force. Ignorance about the exact skill set of the producer, the working conditions in which the producer produces and the exact amount of time the producer has the discretion to invest for the purpose of production disallows the buyers to tap the indigenous pool in its full capacity. All these factors, in alliance, contribute to poor market performance of rural produce, in spite of the same having enormous demand in urban context.

3.3 The information asymmetry between rural producers and middlemen

Middlemen are crucial conjunctive elements in rural–urban divide. Most of the rural producers' market performances are heavily reliant on these intermediaries, who connect the small-scale producers to respective retail units. Apart from market linkage, these middlemen also enjoy immense significance in fiscal matters. They often lend cash with exorbitant interest rates to the rural producers in times of need. Though the relationship between the producers and middlemen essentially thrives on exploitation, we can cite multiple instances where the rural producers continue their reliance on these oppressive entities even after being aware of the exploitative nature of this informal bond. It is with the middlemen that the rural producers have direct contact. The physical, informational and communicational distance rural producers share with each other, urban consumers and government and international agencies makes the situation more acute, as the middlemen essentially thrive by capitalizing on rural producers' lack of knowledge. Helplessness resulting from ignorance and compulsive trust due to lack of easily accessible transparent platforms on the part of the rural producers have been cited by many as primary reasons fostering the parasitic bond between producers and middlemen (Mitra et al., 2018).

The exploitative nature of the bond is reflected in the personal narration of an Indian tribal rural producer located in the district of Birbhum. The rural producer recorded selling mostly in state- organized fairs, which occur seasonally. In order to have minimal cash-flow throughout the year, she told how she sold her produce to local middlemen, who in turn sold the products to urban retail units. Although the rural producer during the interview expressed awareness regarding the increased price with which the middleman resells her products, she simultaneously expressed her helplessness in the scenario. Lack of information regarding selling or supporting channels compels rural producers like her to stick to existing channels, even after becoming aware of their exploitative nature. The middlemen chalk out their strategic economic moves precisely by capitalizing on rural producers' ignorance and lack of necessary information.

Concerns over the isolation of rural producers have also given rise to various non-governmental organizations (NGOs) who act as ethical intermediaries between rural producers and urban consumers (Jadhav, 2015). Working closely with local community, the NGOs often have direct contact with rural producers, where the effectivity of the former rests in directly communicating relevant information to the latter. Many circumstances can be cited where the NGOs act as intermediaries in relaying market-related information to rural producers. These efforts, while dedicated to eradicating the extant information gap, often remain insufficient in achieving their desired goal. Cultivating extreme dependence of rural communities on the NGOs, these efforts seldom empower rural communities to develop self-credentials in the process of mitigating their overall information asymmetry.

3.4 The information asymmetry between rural producers and government agencies

The importance of the rural producers (both farm and non-farm goods) in terms of revenue-generation and employment creation has meant various national government bodies and international agencies cannot remain indifferent to the needs and challenges faced by the rural producers. Different national-level governing bodies have undertaken multiple initiatives for the betterment of these rural producers, which, in turn, would benefit the rural economy. Such initiatives primarily include: financial support, development and adoption of the more target-oriented legislative framework, capacity-building programmes, market linkages and better provision for physical infrastructure. The government-sponsored initiatives are primarily aimed at remediating the current and acute unemployment problem, transformation in the national economy, poverty alleviation and business growth (David, 2012). But inadequate information and the physical and virtual distance urban-based policy formulators share with the rural target group have disallowed optimal utilization of these welfare schemes. Lack of information about the rural producers has hindered the national governments and international agencies in coming up with strategies best suited for the rural sectors. Moreover, ignorance about public policies and welfare schemes on the part of the rural producers has further distanced them from the arena of such welfare schemes, which are precisely aimed at achieving rural community well-being. If we take India as an example, then we can see that the government has come up with district-level support structures such as District Industries Centres (DIC) and District Rural Development Cells (DRDC) to provide local-level assistance to rural community. However, the majority of the artisans across rural Bengal, with whom our research team interacted, explicitly stated the inefficiency of such public support structures. A Bankura-based terracotta artist in his interview narrated the limited assistance of public bodies, apart from providing a minimal daily allowance of Rs75 to rural producers by virtue of their participation in state fairs. He also stated how local level government help-desks, on top of being inefficient in delivering adequate information to the local community, also resort to partiality. Favouritism practised by public bodies only enables a particular group of relatively privileged rural producers to participate in state exhibiting forums and fairs. The practised discrimination further disallows the public schemes to implement empowering measures for overall rural community.

4 Impact of information asymmetry on market efficiency: An Indian case study

In the context of rural economy, it is indeed true that the rural producers are owners of unique knowledge pertaining to their produce. But their physical and virtual distance from the market has prevented them from using their informational resource for profitable returns. It is only after the producers have become marketable actors – by gaining access to the adequate informational resource and developing skills to process acquired informational resources for practical benefits – that market efficiencies can be enhanced through improved transaction patterns in a market. In this context, it is important to articulate that we are not reading informational asymmetry solely along theoretical lines. We have tried to substantiate our theoretical propositions by citing a qualitative case study conducted among Indian rural producers. The hindrances faced by them due to the information asymmetry they experience with different agents have been practically validated in this section by justifying the theoretical formulations with the experiential accounts of rural producers. The reality of rural producers has been captured by conducting a qualitative survey among 70 such producers located across the Indian state of West Bengal.

4.1 Methodology

The following study, undertaken to assess rural producers from the angle of information asymmetry, is based on in-depth qualitative interactions with selected crafts producers coming from Birbhum, Bankura, Coochbehar, Dinajpur (Uttar and Dakshin), Medinipur (Purba and Paschim), Bishnupur, 24 Parganas (Uttar and Dakshin), Bardhaman, Murshidabad, Alipurduar and Hooghly districts of West Bengal. The number of respondents interviewed totalled 70 rural crafts producers or rural artisans. With the help of the qualitative survey we have tried to record and subsequently analyse the experiential accounts of the rural Indian artisans to understand the hindrances they face in the course of production.

In the qualitative research conducted, artisans interviewed from different locales recorded different types of hindrances they face in the course of their production. Though each one of their experiential accounts considerably differed from the others, by critically and contextually reading individual experience in relation to the group experience we have tried to arrive at an understanding of collective reality. A contextual reading of the experience has been particularly insightful from our research standpoint. Although mainstream economics' reading of asymmetrical information primarily assumes sellers to be in a privileged position, the differential situation among the Indian crafts producers compels us to read information asymmetry recorded by the community as mainly leading to market inefficiency, instead of providing market opportunities to rural artisans. It is through the contextual reading of experiential accounts of rural artisans that we can trace the role of informational asymmetry and subsequently analyse how it impacts the process of rural production.

4.2 Observation

In the following sections we will break up the entire production process into multiple levels and talk about the challenges artisans face in each level due to asymmetric informational relationship with other agents. We will conclude this section by illustrating a way forward to address this issue by inducing purposive intra- and inter-communitarian exchange within rural community.

4.2.1 Inability to produce in accordance with market demands

The majority of the artisans with whom we interacted can be categorized as non-farm producers; crafts producers to be specific. In the process of making aesthetic craft items they stated that they conceptualize or innovate newer designs. But the rural orientation of the artisans prevents them coming up with appropriate items to satisfy the hunger of the ever-changing urban market. The example of the works of a Birbhum-based kantha artist can shed light in this context. Although the stitching done by the artisan is intricate and flawless, the colour combination opted for is often considered to be a mismatch for urban tastes and preferences, thereby reducing the market value of the product. In some cases, design catalogues and the internet act as bridging mediums, feeding the artisans with relevant information, which subsequently results in improved production. This additional exposure, initiated by some NGOs, has thrown open the door to information to some selected artisans, whose knowledge-wise upliftment and empowerment have helped secure a stable position in the market for these artisans. However, most of the artisans are unaware of the urban fashion trends and demands due to lack of formal/informal communication channels. The impact of disrupted communication in aggravating inefficiency in rural production is manifested in the remark of a Murshidabad-based self-help group producer specializing in stitching. In an interview conducted at Kandi, Murshidabad, in October 2017, she said, "… Since we do not have proper linkage with urban crowd, we, the rural producers, often produce designs, some of which are considered outdated by urban tastes." The experiential account of our respondent suggests how informational poverty plays a decisive role in determining the market performance of rural producers. Although, in most of the cases, the skill set of the rural producers is intricate, their lack of necessary market-related information often demerits their position and performance in the urban economy.

4.2.2 Issues pertaining to agents dealing with raw materials

Unavailability of appropriate and affordable raw materials both in quality and quantity often poses a hindrance in the rural production process. However, in some places, where there are a considerable number of artisans engaged in the production of similar objects, some of the raw materials required are available locally. For instance, artisans from Birbhum and Pingla, who engage in the production of similar art forms in bulk, such as Kantha stitching and Potochitro painting respectively, reported local availability of essential raw materials. However, in most other cases rural producers stated multi-faceted obstructions limiting availability of affordable raw materials. A Dinajpur-based rural producer engaged in woodwork recorded the hindrance pertaining to availability of raw materials. He narrated travelling to three locations, namely Siliguri, Khairibari and Khidirpur dock in Kolkata, to procure raw wood. Since wood is a heavy material, transporting it from such far locations incurred additional travelling cost, which the rural producer is compelled to bear. Travelling long distances not only incurs additional cost but also demands time investment, which can be immensely problematic for the rural producers. Artisans' lack of information regarding alternative raw material procuring channels make the hindrances pertaining to procurement of raw materials more pronounced. Since the rural producers lack information about region-wise availability of raw materials at affordable prices, they are not motivated or equipped to search for newer channels. Some of the rural producers we interacted with explicitly stated the reasons behind preferring known shops to buy the raw materials. Since financial crunch is a perennial problem faced by the Indian artisans, a Birbhum-based artisan, who passionately helps his mother on her self-help group-related activities, recorded the reason for such a preference. He said that most of the time, though they buy the raw materials with their own investment, purchasing it from known shops fosters trust and keeps open the provision for buying on credit, if need be. It is precisely because of the lack of information that such micro-level benefits assume greater status and direct the rural production process by demotivating producers to venture out for better opportunities, thereby restricting them to the already-known parasitic channels.

4.2.3 Issues pertaining to agents dealing with logistics support

Both procurement of raw materials and delivery of finished products to buyers require transportation of goods at bulk. Though most of the artisans with whom we interacted stated how such logistics are handled mostly via informal personal contacts, lack of information often impedes the upgrading of such *crowd-sharing* activities to an organized activity. For example, the majority of the self-help group women residing in the countryside of Bengal with whom our research group interacted recorded a preference for sharing rides with other producers to go to nearby urban sites, both for procurement of raw materials and delivery of finished products. Such activities allow them to save time and money. But since, in some cases, location and other details of people having similar procurement and delivery requirements remain unknown, they at times are compelled to bear the whole transportation cost, which often is a burden, given their financially insecure status. An elderly self-help group producer recorded immense difficulty in sustaining her small-scale jute business due to the additional factors intrinsic to rural production. Having no one to help her in her business, the rural producer narrated how transporting the produced good to urban customers is problematic at her age. In this context, even though the rural producer showed artistic capability, issues pertaining to logistics and her lack of alternative channels to transport her goods to urban customers primarily contribute to poor sale.

4.2.4 Issues pertaining to procurement of orders and sale of products

Sixty-five of the 70 rural non-farm producers (even the micro-entrepreneurs) interviewed identified state fairs as the primary site for selling their produce.

Most of them said they received their major orders from the contacts obtained by attending such fairs. However, since these marginalized producers are completely isolated from the market, they are compelled to rely on local-level government offices to obtain necessary and relevant information pertaining to such fairs. A considerable number of artisans, while complaining about the inefficiency of local government agencies, stated that because of the resultant discrimination they often miss out on important dates pertaining to the fairs. Even in cases where they are successful in acquiring the relevant information, we must remember that fairs are seasonal in nature and hence these fairs offer little scope for financial stability throughout the year. However, even though the supply pattern in the Indian crafts sector is more often than not erratic in nature, it undoubtedly has a perennial market demand. Hence it is necessary, amidst the backdrop of asymmetrical information, to investigate the alternate avenues of sale and study how rural producers can strike business in those avenues.

Although the Indian government has come up with multiple retail brands – such as Bangasree, Manjusha, Khadi, Biswabangla, etc. – who buy directly from the rural producers, an in-depth interaction with the rural target group revealed how such an exposure offers opportunity to only a select few. Just eight artisans out of the 70 interviewed recorded sales to such government organizations. A Bankura-based terracotta artist recorded how these governmental units, on grounds of artistic inferiority, never buy his works and how these public units only provide exposure to a selected few in the rural community. Such partiality severely affects the rural producers, because lack of information has confined most of them to only the known sales channels.

4.2.5 Issues pertaining to financial aspects

Sixty out of the 70 artisans with whom we interacted stated that they receive payment only after the completion of placed order. But the production process, from its very initiation, requires cash – for procurement of raw materials, for example – without which the production process cannot start. A Birbhum-based rural Kantha producer reported how the nature of receiving payments post-production makes a financial crunch inevitable at the time of procurement of raw materials. Capitalizing precisely on this need, a class of rural money-lenders or middlemen have gradually evolved and prospered, thriving on lending money to these rural producers at high rates of interest.

There are multiple government-sponsored schemes providing loans at subsidized rates to rural producers. However, the difficulty of going through the lengthy official procedure and, in some instances, lack of adequate financial information have confined a considerable number of rural producers to the locally available money-lenders. This points to the urgent need to devise a more target-oriented and contextual rural credit market, suited to mitigate production-related challenges in the Indian crafts sector (Choudhury, 2004). Another Birbhum-base Kantha producer's narrative clearly reflects the inefficiency of public financial structures, which has compelled him to take monetary help from informal sources such as friends and local money-lenders. Although he is aware of the lack of transparency inherent in such informal transaction domains, the difficulty in getting subsidized loans sanctioned has left him with no alternative.

Moreover, lack of financial information and assistive platforms further prevents these rural producers coming up with adequate strategies to cope up with the loss incurred due to change of government fiscal policies.

4.2.6 Alienation from the digital world

Sixty-two out of the 70 artisans reported nil or minimal digital literacy. Lack of basic education and access to digital technologies (especially the internet) has kept them unable to utilize the fruits of digitization. Contemporary ICT has heightened itself to such a status that information has become the most important and accessible resources in this era. Yet our in-depth interaction with the artisans revealed quite a disappointing result; only 2% of all the artisans interviewed recorded resorting to a digital medium for the purpose of their trade. Digital ignorance of the majority has disallowed them to access and use the information available online for the betterment of their business. Not only is the digital adherence rate of rural producers alarming, their ignorance as to how the medium can boost sales by encouraging virtual collaboration is additionally disappointing. When asked by our research group, one of our rural respondents, although recording poor sales, explicitly expressed distrust of the digital medium's ability to boost her sales. This response has to be interpreted as the mindset of a person who has never had the privilege to experience the digital medium's effectivity. Widespread digital illiteracy and alienation from the operative dynamics of the e-channels thereby contribute in sustaining the ignorance of rural producers regarding newer designs of products, multiple online selling outlets and other relevant information. Only 2% of the total rural producers interviewed said they resorted to smartphones for communicating with customers.

4.2.7 Issues related to skill-building opportunities

Even if the artisans feel that they want to upgrade their skills or learn a new skill, they do not have adequate information regarding the availability of potential trainers and/or informational sources which they can tap into to enhance the skills required to translate acquired informational resource into holistic knowledge pool.

During our interventions we showed some of them YouTube videos on the design of soft toys and the making of low-cost jewellery. They not only tried to learn from the new digital informational source but also used the information, with the help of contextual training, to enhance their application sense and knowledge pool. However, skill-providing channels, which lead to the successful translation of information to knowledge resources, are seldom available. Even in contexts where provisions of such contextual training facilities are made for artisans, the sporadic nature of the initiatives, coupled with lack of application guidelines on how to utilize acquired skills for profitable returns, have largely rendered the measures inadequate in practically realizing mass-scale rural empowerment.

A rural self-help group producer residing in the village of Kandi stated having received government-sponsored stitching training, where the rural members were paid a minimal amount in lieu of their participation in the training programme. However, our respondent also recorded how such training, though inculcating stitching skills among rural participants, provided no subsequent guidance on how to use the acquired skills to enhance market prospects. As a result, our respondent insightfully remarked, "We are a set of skilled women. But we do not know what to produce and where to sell."

4.3 The impact of information asymmetry on Indian rural producers: Findings

The impact of information asymmetry on Indian rural producers has been summarized in Table 5.1. The multi-faceted hindrances, as shown in Table 5.1, which arise in different levels of the production and marketing process due to asymmetrical information, become further acute due to the lack of basic literacy among most of the Indian artisans. The resultant asymmetry in information, or possession of insufficient information, not only hampers artisans' trade from an economic perspective but also acts as a psychologically demotivating force. This reiterates our conceptualization of information, not just as an economically accelerating force but as a social phenomenon ensuring overall welfare of the artisan community.

If the intention is to address market inefficiency in the crafts sector arising out of rural artisans' lack of information and knowledge, then it becomes mandatory to devise ways to improve the communicational aspect. Enhanced inter- and intra-communitarian linkage will foster purposive informational exchange between actors relevant to the process of rural production. Purposive exchange will subsequently contribute in inculcating skills among the rural community to utilize the information gained in pursuit of achieving practical benefits. Now, as the Indian case study highlights, we can see how the different actors who experience information asymmetry, though interlinked, are geographically scattered. In such a scenario it becomes almost impossible to bridge the gap physically. Being informal, inefficient and mostly manual in nature (Reddy et al., 2016), production procedure in the crafts sector often suffers from the stigma of inferiority and backwardness. In an attempt to generate renewed market possibilities for craft items, it is necessary to contemporize traditional craft practices (Kumar & Rajeev, 2013; Jena, 2010). The first step to contemporizing traditional practices is to make the artisans aware of the advantages of organized production (KPMG, 2016). And organized production essentially demands well-connectedness within its different actors. Thus we can

Table 5.1 Impact of information asymmetry on Indian rural producers: Findings

Findings of the study	Supporting testimonials (first order concepts)	Resultant obstructions (Second order/derivative of first-order testimonials)
Information asymmetry within rural community obstructing peer-to-peer learning	"We do not know what others in our locality are producing and how. That means we cannot learn from others, or discuss with them aspects which are common to our production process."	• Social – lack of intra-communitarian linkage obstructs collaborative creation and growth of communitarian solidarity. • Economic – obstructs economic growth by preventing rural community learning from each other's market performances.
Information asymmetry between rural and urban communities due to weak communication between rural producers and urban consumers	• "We face difficulty to replicate designs suited to urban fashion markets because of weak communication with our urban customers." • "We are rural producers. Most of the urban buyers are unaware of what we are producing. Hence they simply buy from urban markets. ... Since we do not have proper linkage with urban crowd, we, the rural producers, often produce designs, some of which are considered outdated by urban tastes."	• Social – distance from urban mainstream transaction sites and consumers contributes to social isolation of rural community • Economic – mismatch between rural supply and urban market trends contribute to poor sale of rural goods
Information asymmetry between rural producers and other agents in the supply-chain	• "I have to travel far away to buy raw materials. It takes up additional time and cost, which I could have used to boost my production." • "I have no option other than delivering my products to the doorstep of my urban customers myself because I do not know reliable logistics providers." • "We mostly sell in fairs. We do not have much knowledge about alternative selling channels. ... The fairs do not happen all throughout the year, it hampers our sale."	Economic: • Lack of information about alternatives and ethical raw material procurement sources and logistic channels aggravate inefficiency in rural production • Lack of information about alternative selling channels (both physical and digital) restrict the rural producers to using only known channels of sale

Findings of the study	Supporting testimonials (first order concepts)	Resultant obstructions (Second order/derivative of first-order testimonials)
Information asymmetry between rural community and fiscal agents leading to financial instability of rural community	• "Banks take a lot of time to sanction loans. We are compelled to take loans from friends or money-lenders, paying high interest rates." • "Some artisans receive *shilpi-bhata* (monetary allowance given to rural producers by the government). However, all of us are not aware of mechanisms to get such monetary allowance for artisans in our locality."	Economic: • Lack of fiscal knowledge disallows them to utilize public schemes, especially subsidy to help rural community • Lack of government-sponsored financial advisory services restricts ability of rural community to enhance their entrepreneurial prospects • Prevalence of exploitative middlemen and the high rate of interest they charge from rural community further impoverishes them economically
Information asymmetry between rural producers and government and non-government agencies, including urban NGOs	• "Government bodies, like Bangasree and Manjusha only buy from selected artisans who have good infrastructures. Products of poor artisans like us never get selected." • "Apart from providing Rs75 as a participation fee for attending state fairs, the government has not helped us in any production-related aspects." • "We have received skill-building trainings from government and NGOs. But they have not given us any market linkage or guidance on how to use the skills to gain profit." • "Most of the times the local DIC office does not give us adequate information about new schemes, upcoming fairs, etc."	• Social – differential treatments of rural producers by government and non-government agencies further marginalizes the already marginalized • Economic – lack of public support and application guidelines regarding supply chain of rural production process and how to boost existing production processes contribute in enhancing inefficiency in rural economy

Source: All tables, figures and photographs in this book are by the authors.

see how easy and smooth communicational exchange is an indispensable prerequisite in the process of equipping rural artisans with the information and skills required for self-betterment. This theoretical formulation has been postulated by gaining insight from the qualitative research conducted among rural Indian artisans. We need to understand that artisans' lack of adequate information is not a region-specific issue. It features prominently in the overall context of developing nations, where insights gained from the empirical study conducted in India can be a true representation of the hindrances faced by artisans in developing countries.

It is only through the simultaneous acquisition of informational resources and skills that artisans will develop an enhanced knowledge pool, which is essential in bringing holistic rural empowerment. In the following section we will discuss the extant measures undertaken in the context of developing nations to mitigate informational asymmetry experienced by rural artisans and other agents, and the reason why such measures have proven themselves inadequate in achieving concrete rural empowerment.

5 Contemporary measures undertaken to reduce information asymmetry

Several measures for rural marginalized community have been undertaken to provide access to various physical and digital informational sources. Several NGOs have also attempted to provide the role of ethical intermediary, feeding relevant information to marginalized rural communities. However, the sporadic and non-contextual framing of these measures, without keeping in mind the specific orientation and nature of rural need, has heavily rendered these measures inadequate in achieving mass-scale rural empowerment. These initiatives have undoubtedly provided rural community with access to informational resources. However, we need to understand that access alone cannot bring positive outcomes, if it is not coupled with optimal usage of such acquired information in pursuit of practical benefits. Most of the extant initiatives exhibit an exogenous approach to rural empowerment. For example, various academic and vocational skill training programmes have been organized by various public, private and international bodies to cultivate and upgrade the skill set of rural producers, thereby enhancing their market prospects. However, the training modules, often formulated in non-local languages, are not contextually framed for rural audience, both in terms of their nature and content. Scrase (2003) rightly identifies this issue by highlighting how well-intentioned government policies, undertaken in different countries to preserve "traditional" and indigenous practices, lack on-the-ground local knowledge, neglect marginal workers and display all the failures associated with top-down developmental policies. As a result of micro-level discrimination and non-contextual formulation, the schemes remain exogenous in approach, externally imposed, which, though destined to provide rural community with access to information, fail to bring about empowerment from within on a large scale.

Following, we will discuss various national and international schemes undertaken to improve informational asymmetry between rural producers and other agents in the system. Under similar categorization we will also enlist efforts of NGOs to act as information intermediaries in the process of mitigating information asymmetry. The chapter, after providing detailed insight into undertaken initiatives, concludes with an analysis to show how such measures have remained mostly inadequate in addressing the issue of rural empowerment on a holistic scale.

Rural marginalization significantly owes its origin to the lack of quality education, where widespread illiteracy often denies rural community the ability to access, understand and utilize crucial information necessary for self-benefit. Several initiatives have been undertaken, at the global and local level, to promote quality education among marginalized rural community. A Colombian government initiative – leading to the formation of Craft Revival Trust, *Artesanías de Colombia South America* – in alliance with UNESCO came up with specific objectives to boost the nation's cottage sector (CRT and UNESCO, 2005) by empowering the practitioners with necessary information and connection. The measures included:

- Provisions for counselling and technical assistance and training in the crafts sector, specifically in the areas of design and technology.
- Enabling the national crafts target group to compile, process and disseminate technical information related to capital, raw materials, environmental conservation, processes, products and services for crafts.

The intervention subsequently conducted a creativity workshop, computer-aided design workshop, design counselling, specialized counselling, workshop courses, technical assistance, mobile workshops and seminars.

If we take into consideration the impact of the interventions initiated by the Colombian government to boost the nation's crafts sector, then we can see that the measures undertaken along digital lines were equipped to seep into the remotest sectors. However, the findings show that the intervention, in spite of being rigorous, could only expose 50% of the target group to the tastes and trends of the global market economy (CRT and UNESCO, 2005). In the case of *guadua* (a variety of bamboo native to Colombia, Ecuador and Venezuela), activities such as design intervention and costing structure could achieve an annual average sales growth rate of 22%. The partial percolation of the measures shows how non-contextual application of these schemes alienates a significant portion of the target group from the purview of these initiatives.

Efforts to empower rural community using digital lines can also be traced in India. The Indian Farmers' Fertiliser Cooperative (IFFCO) is the largest organization in India responsible for the production and distribution of fertilizers for farmers through a cooperative network. IFFCO Kisan first launched Green SIM in 2007, a packaged service available exclusively on the Bharti Airtel network, which provides agricultural information through Outbound Dialling messages (OBD), SMS and a farmer helpline to support rural customers improve their farming practices. Subsequently, IFFCO came up with "IFFCO Kisan – Agriculture App", a content-centric app marketed as a complementary product to the Green SIM service. It is a mobile data-driven service, providing a "one-stop shop" information portal to Indian farmers with access to agriculture content. The app includes modules such as weather news, market rates, expert advice, news, a crop information library, loan request and other such relevant information.

The IFFCO Kisan app undoubtedly contains important information. But the farmers, who are mostly illiterate, seldom possess capacities to operate and benefit from digital solutions. Lack of context-specific training in this regard further contributes to distancing such initiatives from the actual stakeholders. It is only when the adaptive guidelines are premised on practical coping mechanisms that they possess the potential to empower the target group to avail the facilities by overcoming the hurdles intrinsic to their social location. In cases where measures have been undertaken to educate rural mass through information dissemination, it has been done without inculcating necessary digital literacy training to the rural non-users. As a result, the rural community could not develop the credentials to translate the information gained along digital paths into desired outcomes.

Apart from these initiatives, multiple initiatives have been undertaken both at global and local level to boost rural production (both farm and non-farm) by providing necessary information. This includes providing information regarding finance, the market, mechanisms to enhance public visibility of local producers at the global level, the formation of craft clusters, provision of various skill-development training to art practitioners and so on. The initiatives include a Colombian scheme to advise regional organizations on the interpretation and application of design policies and to formulate joint strategies, programmes and projects for the crafts sector by engaging in a dialogic exchange with the rural crafts community (CRT and UNESCO, 2005).

The South African government, on realizing the potential of small, medium and micro enterprises (SMMEs) in revenue generation and employment creation, authorized the Department of Trade and Industry (DTI) to undertake measures to boost the sector (David, 2012). Formation of the Small Enterprise Developmental Agency (SEDA) under the public aegis, together with the DTI, led to measures, along the following lines, to boost indigenous production: developing a business plan, training, coaching and mentoring and utilizing marketing materials. The measures were aimed at providing South Africa's rural crafts community with necessary information and market connections essential for self-betterment.

The self-help group (SHG) programme has been undertaken by the government of India to provide an enabling environment to address poverty and sustainability of rural community through the creation of micro-finance facilities (VOICE, 2008). As part of the programme, several academic and vocational training schemes are being provided to the rural marginalized SHG members to upgrade their skill set and market prospects. However, lack of follow-up guidelines on how to translate information gained in pursuit of practical returns has rendered these training schemes less meaningful in generating self-employability for rural women.

The inefficiency of Indian district-level government help-desks, the DIC and DRDC, has already been highlighted through the case study presented above. As a result, the Indian rural community often remains misinformed or uninformed about the news of fairs held, government-sponsored allowances they are supposed to get, and other related aspects, which these government help-desks are expected to provide to the artisans. The inadequacy of public measures has often been tackled by entrusting local NGOs with the responsibility of building a self-reliant rural community. Incorporating NGOs in the process of rural empowerment, where the assigned bodies are expected to act as information intermediaries delivering necessary services to rural community, has been in the five-year plan agendas of Indian governments since the early 1980s (Jadav, 2015). The reason why NGOs are considered to be prospective information intermediaries is because of their reputational ability to work closely with the rural communities. Working with the local community at ground level gives the NGOs the leverage to feed contextual information to the rural communities by keeping in mind the local context of specificities and needs. The NGOs' potential in this context has made creation of a network of NGOs working at ground level an immediate and important public agenda priority. However, we need to remember that, while the NGOs can be identified as potential information intermediaries working to mitigate rural isolation, their physical mode of implementation restricts their scope. Along with this, the focus of NGOs on specific aspects to bring positive change can seldom be extended to the cause of holistic empowerment.

Redundancy of public initiatives in the purview of achieving holistic rural empowerment can also be traced in the South African context. A qualitative study, conducted among SMMEs in Uthungulu district, in the province of KwaZulu Natal, highlights how 73.8% of total rural artisans interviewed recorded ignorance about government schemes (David, 2012). Inefficiency in production in the rural sector largely owes its origin to inefficient support structures. Lack of proper guidance prevents the marginalized rural community transforming their intended actions into desired outcomes.

Most indigenous producers are located in scattered rural pockets. Lack of communication between them, coupled with their physical distance from the market, not only prevents the rural producers establishing themselves as an integrated community; it also virtually isolates them by denying them the relevant information essential for production. Various public as well as non-governmental and private initiatives have actively worked for placing the rural producers in the mainstream market by bringing their unheard stories to the surface. However, our primary interaction with Indian artisans and secondary academic interpretations of the Colombian and South African crafts sectors' experiences reflected scant percolation of such welfarist initiatives to bring about positive change on a large scale.

If we look into the Indian context, our case study highlights how the physical and virtual isolation disallows more than 80% of the interviewed artisans to produce in accordance with market demands. Their isolation contributes to the widespread ignorance pertaining to the nature of contemporary market trends. Several channels operating within the country – namely non-governmental agencies such as Banglanatak, governmental agencies like Bangasree and the Manjusha operative in Bengal, as well as private actors such as Fabindia – act as potential exhibiting and selling forums for rural skills and produce. However, it needs to be remembered that only a handful of artisans out of the overall community have such privileged linkages. It is indeed true that the efforts taken positively contribute to overcoming the isolation faced by rural artisans by feeding them with contextual market information and advertising scopes. However, these initiatives are restricted to only a select target group, thereby excluding the majority of the artisan community from their empowering purview. As a result, most of the Indian artisans are compelled to adhere to exploitative intermediaries for market-connect and sustenance.

Contemporary rural producers have also witnessed a rapid increase in digital forums dedicated to directly engaging artisans in the market transaction process. Multiple e-commerce sites such as ArtFire, Supermarket and Okhai, among several others, have sprung up to give artisans across the globe direct-selling access to international consumers. However, our primary case study conducted in India highlighted that as few as 2% of the total artisans interviewed recorded the ability to resort to such channels for trade benefits. A major problem is logistic support, including knowledge of proper packaging required for order fulfilment. Moreover, digital ignorance, widespread among rural artisan community, disallows these artisans to optimally utilize the digital medium for self-betterment. It is only when provisions of contextual digital literacy have been made for the rural target group that we can expect positive outcomes from emerging digital selling channels.

The emergence and prospering of e-commerce sites is not just restricted to rural craft practitioners. Several e-commerce sites have cropped up with the aim to provide unrestricted market opportunities to agrarian practitioners. Farmer's Club in Turkey was launched with this aim under the joint initiative of Vodafone Turkey and TABİT, a Turkish social enterprise focusing on ICT enablement for smallholder farmers. Farmer's Club attempted to provide to smallholder Turkish farmers packaged offerings, which included market information and market connect. The club used Vodafone Turkey's network to disseminate information related to land, products, meteorology data, information regarding market prices and direct connection to buyers. The initiative, although noble, had shallow percolation because farmers often did not have the technological infrastructure and expertise to make use of the initiative.

If we try to critically demystify the public welfare schemes and intentions framing them, then we can see how these schemes premise themselves on a one-way informational transaction between the policy formulators and stakeholders. Even in the case of Farmer's Club, which attempted to provide information to smallholder Turkish farmers, neither the content of the information nor the operational dynamics of the initiative were decided by the local community. It is the policy formulators who designed the initiative and imposed it on the rural community. The non-participation of the local community therefore makes disseminated information an external imposition in the absence of a local community's ability to process the same. Moreover, the physical and informational distance between policy formulators and rural stakeholders has contributed to non-contextual framing of developmental policies. Existing developmental schemes are formulated with the aim to just feed information to the rural target group, without giving them the scope to share the informational assets they already possess and are acquiring in the process. This one-way feeding of information disallows the entities to engage in dialogue, thereby sustaining the alienation of policy formulators from the rural target group. In this context we need to remember that it is only through relevant sharing of information that the true value of the informational asset can be realized to develop the skills necessary to translate the informational resource to the holistic knowledge pool. While the feeding of factual information is crucial to improve informational poverty of marginalized rural community, we need to remember that access to informational resource alone cannot achieve any positive outcome. It is only when the rural target group, through effective exchange, develops evaluative capacities to process information gained in pursuit of practical returns that the resultant experience can enhance their knowledge pool. It is an enhanced knowledge pool that is a precursor to achieving holistic rural empowerment.

6 Conclusion

The chapter concludes by highlighting the difference between "information" and "knowledge", where the latter is conceptualized as a holistic concept, comprising a capability to process, internalize and utilize factual information, leading to skills and competency development. The difference between information and knowledge has been brought in to remind readers of the urgency to transcend from the former to the latter, in the context of achieving rural empowerment from within. Sharma (1997) argued that reducing information asymmetry by providing complete information is not a sufficient condition to reduce problems arising from information asymmetry. The recipient of information may "either have little knowledge to interpret the information supplied or gathered or when the recipient is not knowledgeable to determine which information should be gathered, is missing or is invalid.... Without the experience, skills and attitude elements of knowledge, the information cannot be interpreted" (Dellemijn, 2012).

In our context of rural producers, along with providing access to factual information, it is also essential to impart knowledge, which will enable them to convert their acquired informational resource into a more holistic knowledge pool (Hess, 2006). While the flow of information or factual data takes a uni-directional course, knowledge comprising information, skills and experience is more of a communicable asset, whose value rests in relevant exchange. It is the knowledge pool that we attempt to enhance in our research framework, by relying on the spirit of inter-connectedness and sharing ushered in by contemporary information and communications technology.

The following chapter goes a step beyond informational asymmetry and introduces Dellemijn's conceptualization of "knowledge asymmetry". This is defined as "lack of equality or equivalence of a combination of information, experience, skills, and attitude between two participants in a transactional relationship" (Dellemijn, 2012). Knowledge asymmetry consists of the already-known construct information asymmetry, as well as experience, skills and attitude asymmetry. The chapter, by explaining the concept of knowledge asymmetry, tries to explain rural marginalization in light of the concept. Rural marginalization owes its existence not only to the information gap of a rural community but also to the communitarian inability to process information for concrete benefit, thereby further relegating the rural community to the underprivileged fringes. The approach traces knowledge asymmetry as a source towards cultivating and sustaining rural inequality.

References

Akerlof, G.A. (1970). The Market for Lemons: Quality Uncertainty and the Market Mechanism. *The Quarterly Journal of Economics*, 84(3), 488–500.

Arrow, K. (1963). Uncertainty and the Welfare Economics of Medical Care. *The American Economic Review*, 53(5), 941–973.

Auronen, L. (2003). Asymmetric Information: Theory and Applications. Proceedings of the Seminar in Strategy and International Business, 1–35.

Bartels, R. (1968). The General Theory of Marketing. *Journal of Marketing*, 32(1), 29–33.

Bhat, J. & Yadav, P. (2016). The Sector of Handicrafts and its Share in Indian Economy. *Arabian Journal of Business and Management Review*.

Choudhury, S. (2004). Transaction Cost and Asymmetry of Information – The Twin Odds of Indian Commercial Banks in Rural Credit Market: Theoretical Fragility. *Social Change and Development*, 2(1), 157–174.

CRT & UNESCO (2005). *Designers Meet Artisans: A Practical Guide*. Published jointly by Crafts Revival Trust and UNESCO. Retrieved from: https://www.worldcat.org/title/designers-meet-artisans-a-practical-guide/oclc/406005443.

David, N.S. (2012). Information Asymmetry and Obstacles on SMMEs growth in the Rural Areas of uThungulu District Municipality of KwaZulu-Natal. University of Zululand. Retrieved from: http://hdl.handle.net/10530/1227.

Dellemijn, R.N.J.C. (2012). *Knowledge Asymmetry in Inter-Firm Relationships* (Master's thesis, University of Twente, Netherlands). Retrieved from: http://essay.utwente.nl/61982/.

Ghouse, S. (2012). Indian Handicraft Industry: Problems and Strategies. *International Journal of Management Research and Review*, 2(2), 345–353.

Hess, C.G. (2006). Knowledge Management and Knowledge Systems for Rural Development. *GTZ Reader*. Retrieved from: http://www.fao.org/nr/com/gtzworkshop/Knowledge_Management_and_Systems.pdf.

Jadhav, D. (2015). *Role of NGO in Rural Development*. Sangli: IMRDA. Retrieved from: http://imrda.bharatividyapeeth.edu/media/pdf/page_no_114_to_220.pdf.

Jena, P.K. (2010). Indian Handicrafts in Globalisation Times: An Analysis of Global Local Dynamics. *Interdisciplinary Description of Complex Systems*, 8(2), 119–137.

Khan, W. & Amir, Z. (2013). Study of Handicraft Marketing Strategies of Artisans in Uttar Pradesh and its Implications. *Research Journal of Management Sciences*, 2(2), 23–26.

KPMG (2016). *Innovation through Craft: Opportunities for Growth: A Report for the Crafts Council*. London: Crafts Council.

Kumar, D. & Rajeev, P.V. (2013). Present Scenario of Indian Handicraft Products. *Asian Journal of Managerial Science*, 2(1), 21–27.

Mitra, S., Mookherjee, D., Torero, M. & Visaria, S. (2018). Asymmetric Information and Middleman Margins: An Experiment with Indian Potato Farmers. *Review of Economics and Statistics*, 100(1), 1–57. doi:10.1162/REST_a_00699.

Reddy, K.P., Reddy, M.D., Rao, L.J., Reddy, M.N. & Reddy, T.N. (2016). Report on Pilot Action Research Project on Forgotten Category Rural Artisans' Transformation into Rural Entrepreneurs. Retrieved from: https://www.panchayatgyan.gov.in/documents/30336/0/Final+Report+full.pdf/4cd4ef01-fcfb-43e4-b16d-d189cf6da275.

Scrase, T. (2003). Precarious Production: Globalisation and Artisan Labour in the Third World. *Third World Quarterly*, 24(3), 449–461.

Sharma, A. (1997). Professional as an Agent: Knowledge Asymmetry in Agency Exchange. *Academy of Management Review*, 22(3), 758–798.

Singh, R., Agarwal, S. & Modi, P. (2015). Market Separations for BOP Producers: The Case of Market Development for the Chanderi Cluster Weavers in India. *International Journal of Rural Management*, 11(2), 175–193.

VOICE (2008). A Report on the Success and Failure of SHGs in India: Impediments and Paradigm of Success. Submitted to the Planning Commission, Government of India. Retrieved from: http://planningcommission.nic.in/reports/sereport/ser/ser_shg3006.pdf.

6 Knowledge asymmetry and its mitigation through enhancement of knowledge capability

1 Introduction

The preceding chapter marks the importance of information as a valuable asset in the context of rural empowerment. In doing so, with the help of primary and secondary case studies, it highlights the hindrances faced by the rural community of developing nations due to the information asymmetry they share with urban-based market and civic bodies. It also discusses efforts taken in developing countries to target rural empowerment by mitigating information asymmetry of rural community. However, the chapter ends with a very important concern: the urgency to move beyond providing mere factual information and concentrating on enhancing the knowledge pool of rural community. The limitations of extant measures primarily rest in their attempt to equip rural community with information without inculcating or developing the experience, skills and attitude required to interpret acquired information. Dellemijn (2012) conceptualized experience, skills and attitude together as comprising knowledge, which has in turn been defined by him as the credential that enables interpretation of factual information. While the preceding chapter has briefly touched upon the difference between information and knowledge, in this chapter we will provide an epistemological analysis of the difference and articulate why mitigating information asymmetry, although necessary, is not a sufficient condition for achieving holistic rural empowerment.

This chapter introduces the concept of knowledge asymmetry (Dellemijn, 2012; Sharma, 1997) and chalks out the importance of enhancing experience, skills and attitudes of rural community, along with equipping them with relevant information, in any attempt to bring holistic empowerment in the context of developing nations. While the chapter highlights the effectivity of knowledge over information and targets mitigation of knowledge asymmetry instead of information asymmetry as a means to achieving rural empowerment, it does not identify possession of knowledge as the end in itself. It is through purposive use and sharing that knowledge turns into a valuable asset with the potential to overcome rural marginalization by enhancing agency, social capital and opportunity structure of target group. It is only when rural community derive *knowledge capability*, which constitutes *knowledge assets* coupled with *knowledge-operating capabilities*, that the rural sector will develop the capacity to compete with other developed sectors. Development of knowledge capability of individual rural members has to be followed by purposive exchange of knowledge through community formation, which only in amalgamation has the prospect of mitigating knowledge asymmetry of rural members. Mitigation of knowledge asymmetry, channelizing knowledge capability of rural members into generating enhanced opportunity prospects, can be identified as a mandatory prerequisite in the process of attaining holistic rural empowerment.

The question that needs to be addressed in this context is how should knowledge be distributed? A lot of effort and government policy have gone into ensuring "equal" distribution of knowledge assets by guaranteeing equality of knowledge access. However, in recent years significant research interest has been shown in the concept of "equity", which would guarantee distribution of knowledge resources according to individual need to ensure development of individual knowledge capability.

At the most basic level, a system based on the principle of *equality* propagates that all individuals should be eligible to access an equal number of resources. An *equitable system*, on the other hand, focuses more on the distribution according to individual needs, such that certain individuals are given more attention and resources than others. Both equity and equality are strategies towards providing fairness. *Equality* is treating everyone the same and trying to provide equal access to resources. This strategy can promote fairness if everyone starts from the same place and has the same need. On the other hand, *equity* is giving everyone what they need. In some sense, equity *appears* unfair, since it assumes unequal distribution of resources. But it actively attempts to bring everyone equal by "levelling the playing field". A growing number of observers, influenced by thinkers such as Amartya Sen and John Rawls (Sen, 1973), argue that the fairness or equity of access and use, rather than equal distribution of information goods, may be a more useful foundation for formulating appropriate social policies (Lievrouw & Farb, 2003).

"Equity" is derived from the Greek word *epiky*, which means principles of reasonableness and moderation in the exercise of one's rights. Unlike equality, it is difficult to specify universal criteria for "reasonableness and moderation" because the concepts forming the premise of equity necessarily have a contextual base. The contextual focus of equity, by negating the standardization offered by equality, therefore embodies the idea of justice according to natural law or right, quite contrary to equality, which means identical in value (Doctor, 1992). In order to empower the already marginalized and enable them to be agential participants in social, economic, and civic activities, the concept of inequity, or fairness in justice, becomes more pertinent than inequality (Young, 2001). While efforts undertaken to address inequity provide contextual benefits to communities in respect of their socio-economic locations, efforts addressing inequality apply a more generalized notion and make available opportunities for all, irrespective of socio-economic background. The equality principle, by its very premise, attempts to achieve identical value for every social actor (Doctor, 1992, p. 52). As a result, rich and poor getting benefits alike leads to persistence and widening of the socio-economic gap present between the two groups.

In our context, it needs to be reiterated that the difference between information and knowledge, as we have seen earlier, primarily lies in terms of the human elements (experience, attitudes and skills), which are intrinsic to knowledge. Information being factual in nature, its need can, to a great extent, be satiated by enabling equality in informational access. On the other hand, as far as knowledge is concerned, very few situations exist in which knowledge resources can be characterized as identical in value (Lievrouw & Farb, 2003). The human elements intrinsic to knowledge disallow its categorization following universalized logic. Hence, in the context of knowledge, equity or fairness and reasonable distribution of knowledge among individuals, groups, regions, categories or other social units become crucial to enable people to avail the opportunity to achieve whatever is important or meaningful to them in their lives. Knowledge is unfairly distributed, where equality of access alone cannot guarantee the mitigation of knowledge divide. It is by designing policies of equitable knowledge access and use that attempts can be undertaken to mitigate knowledge asymmetry of marginalized social sectors.

Addressing inequity has the capacity to target holistic empowerment by contextually addressing the needs of the marginalized. Extant measures to overcome information asymmetry of rural sector essentially fail because they attempt to address the inequality issue. Although the undertaken measures enable equal access to empowering schemes to all from the rural community, their standardized prescriptions often fall short in addressing issues specific to rural context. Lack of contextual adoption of the measures makes them rigid in their nature and significantly restricts their scope in bringing mass-scale effects. Equity or fairness of access to knowledge assets across individuals and groups has redeeming prospects, whereas strict equality of access falls short in ensuring such prospects (Gorman, 2000).

A shift towards knowledge and mitigation of knowledge asymmetry through development of knowledge capability of rural target group accounts to be the brand of rural empowerment we are vouching for. Mitigation of knowledge asymmetry and the process of developing knowledge capacity ensure enhancement of social, economic, cognitive and civic abilities of rural community, thereby transforming them from crowd to stakeholders in their own empowerment process. Strategies of self-sustenance and self-development nurtured by such an empowering model facilitate steady growth of agency among the marginalized target group. This approach contradicts the conventional developmental models, which base themselves on uni-directional informational flow from specialized agencies to the marginalized, without equipping the target group with the ability to process disseminated information.

This chapter is divided into four segments:

- The chapter begins by differentiating information from knowledge and subsequently conducts a comparative analysis of the two, to justify its advocacy for knowledge over information in the context of rural empowerment. Premising on the difference, the first segment progresses on to highlight how mitigation of information asymmetry, although necessary, is not a sufficient condition to attain holistic rural empowerment. Mitigation of information asymmetry can be crucial for addressing the issue of inequality, but falls short in building on the experiences, skills and attitudes of target group necessary to interpret the acquired information. The segment concludes by introducing and justifying the concept of knowledge asymmetry and its relevance in sustainable enhancement of individual and collective abilities of marginalized rural community.

- The second segment, following the trajectory of the preceding section, while focusing on the relevance of knowledge, traces the importance of knowledge as an asset primarily to the knowledge-operating capacities. Knowledge asset combined with knowledge-operating capacity, known as "knowledge capability", is identified in this segment as the crucial factor which has the potential to cultivate strategies of self-sustenance and self-development among marginalized rural community.
- The third segment continues to examine the importance of knowledge capability in the context of mitigating overall knowledge asymmetry and theoretically fleshes out its potential in ensuring wellbeing and freedom of marginalized target group. Through the enhancement of knowledge capability, avenues for effective knowledge collaboration and community formation will be triggered, which has the potential to help mitigate knowledge asymmetry of rural members – the final and mandatory prerequisite to achieving holistic rural empowerment.
- Finally, the fourth segment builds on the concept of equity and establishes the potential of knowledge capability in addressing persistent and pressing issues of rural inequity. In stark contrast to conventional developmental paradigms dedicated to target rural inequality through standardized means, our attempt to cultivate knowledge capability among rural target group attempts to enhance credentials of rural members following local pace and need. Additionally, enhancement of knowledge capability builds the path for effective knowledge transaction and community formation, thereby attempting to mitigate knowledge asymmetry of rural members. Amidst the backdrop of mitigated knowledge asymmetry, rural members develop the potential to nurture their capability in generating opportunity prospects. The chapter concludes by highlighting the effectivity of such an empowering paradigm in building a developmental ecosystem, which has the capacity to empower the mass in engaging in their own developmental and decision-making process.

2 From information asymmetry to knowledge asymmetry

2.1 Information and knowledge: A comparative analysis

The answer to what is information and how it is different from knowledge is discussed in Chapter 1. In our context, information refers to objective factual data, possession of which enhances individual and group capacities to take informed decisions. It is a commodity, the acquiring of which requires fixed cost and potential channels (Grant, 1996; Sharma, 1997). The importance of information as an intellectual resource has enabled many organizations to take action to manage their informational assets to boost performance (Stinchcombe, 1990). However, although various firms have undertaken the strategy of information management with the expectation of positive outcomes, we need to remember that equipping an individual/group with information does not necessarily guarantee interpreting abilities to process the information for practical benefits. From being possessors of information to interpreters of information, the process essentially entails following certain steps chronologically. In the initial phase an individual/group gains information, followed by developing skills to interpret the information, which subsequently leads to gaining experience and deriving capacities to use and disseminate created and acquired information on a large scale. It is when the target group derives evaluative abilities to process acquired information that their information repository is transformed into a dynamic knowledge pool.

Knowledge comprises factual information coupled with experiences, skills and attitude (Dellemijn, 2012). While the factual information, which can be codified and expressed numerically, accounts to be *explicit knowledge* (Polanyi, 1966), *tacit knowledge* is composed of human elements such as experience, skills and attitudes (Dellemijn, 2012). It is the human elements that mark the difference between information and knowledge, where the latter is no longer restricted to being a commodity, like the former. Lack of human element in information enables the same to get transferred mechanically between agents having the desired affordability power. Knowledge, on the other hand, cannot be mechanically transferred and has to be accomplished through collaborative creation and dissemination.

Access to relevant information addresses the inequality issue by ensuring availability of a standardized set of factual data to all who seek it. While it is possible to acquire information with desired affordability, acquiring knowledge is not simply about purchasing power and, instead, requires negotiation with one's immediate social surrounding and a sound understanding of the same to develop a comprehensive knowledge pool. The human elements, which give a social flavour to knowledge, make it a concept more pertinent in the context of social development. The objective and factual nature of information, without the incorporation of human elements, remains an external imposition if the individual/group does not develop self-induced capacities to process the same in pursuit of benefit. While the discussion so far fleshes out the importance of knowledge over information as a resource in the context of holistic development, following we will try to articulate how and why sole target to mitigate information asymmetry falls short in addressing the real issue at stake.

2.2 *From information asymmetry to knowledge asymmetry*

In a social setup, where information has gained value as an asset, measures to mitigate information asymmetry and the striving for effective information management have been undertaken along multifarious axes. Various organizations have sought to use information management to boost performance by building transparent and informed relationships with related agencies. Interdependence, being intrinsic to production and distribution processes, urges organizations to collaborate with related agencies, where contracted agencies acquire and supply products and services among themselves, through increased interaction. However, in the context of such contract-bound formal collaborations, disputes arise with difference of interests. The resultant misalignment of goals between a principal and agent in a contract-bound relationship leads to loss of efficiency (Eisenhardt, 1989). Baiman (1982) identified information asymmetry as the root cause of agency problems in a contractual relationship when goals are incongruent. An agency relationship exists when one or more individuals (called principals) hire others (called agents) in order to delegate responsibilities to them (Baiman, 1990). Lack of information prevents the principal from discovering the true abilities and competencies of the agent (Akerlof, 1970). It is to address this problem that firms have undertaken informational management as a strategy for improving professional performance.

Information asymmetry can be defined as a "situation where the agent has private information that is relevant to the contractual agreements with, and is not revealed/available to the principal" (Dellemijn, 2012). The positive outcome derived from making available relevant information to concerned parties has been justified both by theoretical and practical evidences. The effectivity of information management in boosting efficiency has enabled social actors to invest the potential of the asset beyond organizational boundaries, and utilize it in pursuit of social development. The measures undertaken worldwide to address information divide have made serious attempts along multiple axes – such as civic, market and social domains – to address the issue of information asymmetry. As discussed in detail in the earlier chapter, the efforts have attempted to give access to diverse and relevant information to the target group, with a vision to enhance the latter's awareness level by overcoming the marginalization they face owing to a dearth of information. It is nonetheless true that efforts undertaken to mitigate information asymmetry, both within and outside organizations, have been inspired to achieve effective management through addressing the inequality issue. Efforts with such an orientation make equal provision for all to access factual data. However, inculcating skills and creating opportunities to utilize the acquired information rest on cultivation of particular individual/collective credentials. Granting transforming abilities to process the information does not fall within the purview of the schemes dedicated to mitigating informational asymmetry. Keeping these limitations in mind, now the question becomes how far the measures dedicated to mitigating information asymmetry have proven successful in bringing effective outcomes; to what extent is the factual and objective nature of information solely capable in improving performance by enhancing individual/collective credentials?

Significant numbers of scholars, who have researched the impact of efforts undertaken to mitigate information asymmetry in the organizational sector, have concluded that possession of relevant information by the principal does not necessarily guarantee understanding of the behaviours and actions/results of agents (Dellemijn, 2012). The principal, in a contractual relationship, might possess relevant information about the agents. However, possessing such information is not tantamount to understanding the same (Sharma, 1997). It is here that knowledge comes into context, where the human elements (experience, skills and attitudes) play a crucial part in translating possession of information to understanding of information. The principal can have little knowledge to interpret the information supplied by the agent or gathered by the principal, or the principal can lack adequate knowledge to assess which information should be gathered or is missing/invalid. This proves that the principal is subjected to agency problems, even when formally no information asymmetry exists (Sharma, 1997).

In the case of efforts undertaken to mitigate information asymmetry for the cause of social development, similar limitations are witnessed owing to the factual nature of information. Following a uni-directional dissemination mode from formal institutions to citizens in need, the measures, while imparting important information to target group, have also fallen far short in nurturing the supplementary human elements necessary to translate acquired information in pursuit of practical benefits. In the context of social development, concentrating simply on mitigation of information asymmetry brings additional challenges than those experienced by firms. Organizations are primarily homogenous, comprising members with similar affiliations and interests. Bridging information asymmetry can only be effective if parties sharing equal footing get access to relevant information and use it to attain desired results. Possession of similar credentials enables them to process the acquired factual data following a similar pace, thereby enabling mitigation of information divide to yield effective outcomes. However, in a social context, the formal institutions (for example, government or development agents) who are entrusted to mitigate extant information divide, and the marginalized target group who are expected to benefit from the resultant mitigation, are inherently placed in different social footing. Linear dissemination of information from formal institutions, although targeting multiple domains, remains externally imposed on the target group and is only theoretically capable of addressing the issue of inequality. Non-alignment of the measures with the requirements of the target group thereby thrusts factual data on the latter without enabling them to develop the knowledge pool necessary to interpret acquired information. This proves that bridging information asymmetry is not enough, because even if the target groups are equipped with necessary information they need to simultaneously develop the human elements (experience, skills and attitudes) to process the same and derive benefits.

Our primary goal is attaining rural empowerment from within, where members of our target group are already placed in a disadvantageous location because of the hindrances intrinsic to their territorial and social location. As we have mentioned earlier, our research context has primarily urged us to advocate for knowledge over information. Our advocacy for equipping marginalized rural community with necessary knowledge instead of information is followed by attempting to mitigate knowledge asymmetry (Dellemijn, 2012) of rural community, instead of information asymmetry, to enhance individual and collective capacities of rural members. Our formulation of knowledge asymmetry is a realistic and useful evaluation of information asymmetry, which is thought to allow for more accurate modelling and analysis of persistent social isolation. The Oxford dictionary defines asymmetry as "lack of equality or equivalence of a combination of information, experience, skills and attitude between two entities in a relationship". This holistic vision compels attempts to address issues of knowledge asymmetry with a dual target; addressing informational issues along with nurturing human elements (experiences, skills, attitudes).

Mitigation of knowledge asymmetry not only yields benefits along individual lines but also cultivates collective opportunities. Knowledge asymmetry can only be mitigated through effective inter- and intra-group knowledge transaction. In other words, community formation and communitarian knowledge exchange are intrinsic to the process of mitigating knowledge asymmetry. It is only through mitigation of knowledge asymmetry that rural members will develop the credentials to nurture their capability in pursuit of generating concrete opportunity.

While this section highlights the importance of knowledge over information and justifies the importance of mitigating knowledge asymmetry, instead of information asymmetry in the context of rural empowerment, we need to remember that possessing knowledge is not the end in itself. The following section will flesh out that it is not just the possession, but the usability, of knowledge that grants individuals/groups the power to take informed decisions, one of the crucial prerequisites in the process of mitigating overall knowledge asymmetry of rural target group.

3 Knowledge capability: From knowledge possession to knowledge operation

If we take into consideration the credentials of knowledge, it becomes clear that human abilities transform information to knowledge. Knowledge creation is therefore social in nature and is embedded in social relations and the way people and systems organize themselves (Young, 2012). Polanyi (1966) argued that individual capacity to "know more than one can tell" is the critical feature of knowledge. Knowledge thereby transcends tangibility, which is intrinsic to information, and associates itself with abstract human elements. The human capacity enables the possessors to use information and transform it into individual knowledge that is bound to oneself. Several works have directly attributed knowledge possession with paving the path for enhanced living conditions (Ballon & Krishnakumar, 2011). While it is undoubtedly true that knowledge plays a crucial role in enhancing individual and collective living conditions, it needs to be remembered that it is not mere possession of knowledge, but its operating abilities, that has the potential to enhance individual and collective capabilities.

It is the possession of knowledge asset along with knowledge-operating capacities, and together constituting "knowledge capability", that ensures successful translation and utilization of information in pursuit of practical gains (Ning et al., 2006). Knowledge capability primarily refers to the dynamic aspect of knowledge asset, which endows the possessors with the ability to reconstruct with the changing of environment. Knowledge capability significantly constitutes *learning capability, cultural capability* and *communication capability*, aspects which have been detailed in Section 5 of Chapter 2. Ning et al. (2006) have correctly identified that, in a contemporary knowledge economy with technological innovation, resources are not the key elements in competition. The core capability determines both individual and collective performance. Ning et al. (2006) have defined core capability in terms of organizational context, referred to as the knowledge embedded in different abilities within the organization. It is the specific knowledge resources that make core capabilities hard to imitate by competitors and make the organization/individual/group competitive. This is the essence of core capability and is defined as knowledge-operating capability. Knowledge-operating capabilities include *learning capability, cultural capability* and *communication capability*, which in alliance enable *innovation capability*, which ultimately facilitates true manifestation of *knowledge capability* (Ning et al., 2006). This is discussed in detail in Chapter 2 (Section 5.2).

The definition itself makes explicit the distance knowledge capability shares from information possession. While information can be mechanically transmitted from one owner to another, knowledge, and more so knowledge capability, has to be accomplished through sustained cultivation of external and internal (human) factors. The outcome it achieves has led several firms to implement knowledge management by attempting to enhance knowledge capability of individual knowledge workers as a strategy to boost efficiency and company performance on a sustainable basis (Chiu & Chen, 2016).

Knowledge management strategy entails steady and simultaneous growth of knowledge infrastructure capability, coupled with knowledge process capability. The firms that have undertaken knowledge management capability have done so by identifying knowledge process capability as the accelerating force leading to optimal utilization of knowledge infrastructural capability, thereby determining organizational effectiveness (Chiu & Chen, 2016). Organizational commitment plays a crucial role in this context. Undertaking knowledge management capability as a strategy requires proactive authorities who are willing to engage knowledge workers in peer-to-peer sharing across organizational boundaries by focusing on development of social media tools, along with construction of knowledge infrastructure. In this context it needs to be remembered that, even in the context of strategy, value of knowledge rests in knowledge processing and operating abilities and not in passive possession of knowledge asset (Freeze & Kulkarni, 2007).

With the development of theory of capabilities, knowledge-related features have received extensive attention. The enhancement of freedom, which is an intrinsic goal of capability approach, is formulated to derive from the knowledge operating and processing abilities individuals/groups possess (Ballon & Krishnakumar, 2011). The fact that knowledge cannot be mechanically transferred and instead has to be accomplished makes development of knowledge capability a processual act. A knowledge system is formulated to include four dimensions: technique and knowledge, technology system, management system and value system (Ning et al., 2006). Knowledge capability is dynamically formulated as an outcome of interaction between these different dimensions.

Although knowledge capability is a processual activity and develops over time, an individual/group is accepted as knowledge capable if the entity can successfully pass through all the mentioned levels of knowledge capability. A simultaneous ability to tell, do, teach and innovate ushers in knowledge capability among possessors, which endows in them the ability to understand information and utilize it profitably. It is this dynamic knowledge capability that not only ensures optimal utilization of factual data, but, by enhancing individual/collective awareness level, paves the path for informed decision-making by positively impacting individual and collective agency. Although the majority of works conceptualize the importance of knowledge capability in an organizational context, strategies of self-development and self-sustenance cultivated by knowledge capability ensure redeeming prospects for the concept in the context of social development. The following section fleshes out how this dynamic knowledge capability has the potential to enhance living conditions and freedom of human subjects in rural setting by positively contributing to the process of mitigating their knowledge asymmetry.

4 Knowledge capability of rural members in mitigating knowledge asymmetry

This section is dedicated to highlighting the role of knowledge capability in enhancing living conditions of marginalized members of rural community. The rural empowerment framework we are advocating is premised on mitigating knowledge asymmetry of rural participants. However, mitigation of knowledge asymmetry of rural community remains a far-fetched dream if the individual members are not knowledge capable. This calls for making the rural producers knowledge capable, by virtue of which they are expected to nurture strategies of self-development and subsequently enhance their living conditions. While our framework makes cultivation of knowledge capability among rural producers mandatory in the process of mitigating their knowledge asymmetry and subsequently achieving rural empowerment from within, why we have premised our solution on a capability approach requires clarification.

Capability approach refers to a framework where assessment of human wellbeing relies on real opportunities that people face (Ballon & Krishnakumar, 2011). A focus on social achievements, by tracking the means adhered to and hindrances operative in the process of achieving the goals, enables capability approach to offer important and alternative dimensions in the study of poverty beyond traditional income-based measures. While income-based measures primarily premise their analysis on individual/group productive capacities, capability approach traces social functioning as a dynamic manifestation of individual/group action amidst a restrictive social setting. Capability approach therefore takes into account the contextual hindrances social actors face while translating their intended actions into desired outcomes. This approach, instead of providing equal provision to all, attempts to develop the capability set of target group in accordance with the specific social setting the individual actors or the group is subjected to.

The following section is divided into two sub-sections:

- The first sub-section highlights the importance of capability approach in our research context.
- The second sub-section, building on the premise of the first, discusses our research strategy of enhancing the capability set of rural members by equipping them with knowledge and knowledge-operating capacities.

4.1 The capability approach: Building capability set of target group

Dr Amartya Sen, an eminent economist, has brilliantly articulated the importance of cultivating capability set of target group in order to achieve holistic development (Sen, 1988; Sen, 2003). The essence of capability approach rests in its attempt to provide unconventional parameters to evaluate social change in terms of the richness of human life resulting from it. Capability approach sees human lives as sets of "doings and beings" (functionings), and relates the evaluation of quality of life to the assessment of the quality to function (Sen, 1988). Functionings are defined as the achievements of a person, where any functioning reflects part of the state of that person. Capability, reflecting various combinations of functionings a person can achieve, is a derived notion, manifesting in a person's freedom to choose between different ways of living. Capability approach, in considering people as active rather than passive agents, formulates the claim that the functionings are constitutive of a person's being, and evaluation of a person's wellbeing has to take into consideration a detailed assessment of the constituent elements. Enhancing overall conditions of human lives being the premise of the paradigm distances it from standardized traditional developmental paradigms, which attempt to achieve development primarily through economic opulence. Although the capability approach formally came to exist as a developmental paradigm largely following Sen's articulation, its theoretical foundations date back to Aristotle.

In investigating the problem of "political distribution", Aristotle saw quality of life in terms of valued activities and the capabilities to achieve those activities (Ross, 1980). The word *"eudaimonia"* used by Aristotle has often been mistakenly interpreted as "happiness". But in its broader sense the term transcends a utilitarian viewpoint of happiness, conceived as derivative of material prosperity; it refers to fulfilment of lives and explores the dimensions of human nature beyond mere economic intentions (Nussbaurn, 1988). Influenced by Aristotle, Karl Marx's formulation of political economy resonated with a similar concern. Marx related reformulation of the foundation of political economy to the success of human lives in terms of fulfilment needed for human activity (Marx, 1959). The importance of functionings and capabilities to function as determinants of wellbeing has also been articulated by Adam Smith (Smith, 1776). Although these classical theorists, in their political and economic formulations, have given significant importance to the overall quality of human life, beyond mere economic prospects, the premise of this brand of thought has been brilliantly captured by Immanuel Kant in his *Grundlegung zur Metaphysik der Sitten* (Abbot, 1909).

Kant highlighted the urgency to move beyond economic or strictly utilitarian prospects of human life by conceptualizing human beings as ends in themselves, rather than being a means to other ends. This principle has broader relevance and can render alternative dimensions in different respect, such as analysing poverty, progress and planning (Sen, 1988; Sen, 2003). Human beings are agents, beneficiaries and adjudicators of progress. However, their indispensable role in production often leaves them viewed as primary means of production. This dual nature creates confusion in positioning human beings as means or ends in a developmental framework, thereby making policy formulation a debatable act with varying targets. Traditional income-based models focus on real income and economic growth as characteristics of development and conceptualize human beings as productive means (Sen, 1988; Sen, 2003). Kant insightfully highlights the inherent fallacy in such an approach. To justify Kant's formulations, Sen cited the context of South Africa and Sri Lanka as examples, where the former, in spite of witnessing a higher rate of Gross National Product (GNP) than the latter, has low achievements in quality of life when compared to Sri Lanka (Sen, 2003). Because economic prosperity does not necessarily translate into enriching the lives of the people, it falls short in being an end in itself, indicative of enhanced individual and collective living standards. Even as a means, merely enhancing average economic opulence can be inefficient in pursuit of holistic and valuable ends. Therefore, in order to ensure responsive developmental planning and policy-making, we have to face the issue of identification of appropriate ends, in accordance to which the effectiveness of the means can systematically be assessed.

The underlying philosophy that distinguishes capability approach from traditional developmental models dedicated to addressing the issue of inequality becomes explicit in Aristotle's statement that, "the life of money making is one undertaken under compulsion, and the wealth is evidently not the good we are seeking; for it is merely useful and for sake of something else" (Ross, 1980). The statement highlights an aspect of human nature that profit-driven ideations of utilitarianism fall short in providing an explanation for. Deriving inspiration from all these classicists, Sen identified going beyond commodity-mindedness, and evaluating various functionings of human life, as an alternative that offers the possibility of achieving holistic development. A focus on examinations of functionings and the capability of the person to achieve them frees capability approach from the stringencies of conventional developmental paradigms and targets development by enhancing the capability set of target group.

Many theorists have considered the "basic needs" approach as offering compelling pathways to addressing the issue of global inequality. Defining needs in terms of food, clothing and shelter, the approach attempts to eradicate inequality and develop the under-privileged by enabling equal access to basic needs. However, this commodity-centric approach can only provide solutions to material needs of human beings, whose mental capacities are expected to improve as a result of satisfaction of commoditized need. The mechanical articulation of human needs prevents this approach from promising holistic social development. Sen criticizes the commodity-centric view of the "basic needs" approach and highlights its shortcomings by conducting a relational study between access to basic commodities and its spill-over effect in enhancing the capability set of target group (Sen, 2003). He attempts to translate commoditized need of food and nutrients and analyses the capability of being well-nourished as different from the standardized need for food and nutrients. This difference makes it viable that, while equal access to basic amenities can be provided across communities, the capability of being well nourished varies from person to person and gets differentially formulated in accordance to diverse factors such as metabolic rates, gender, age, climatic variations, ailments, etc. This points out the difference between commodity and capability, where the former, granting equal access to basic material amenities, may not, in effect, get translated into an enhanced capability set due to operative social issues. As a result, although the target group is granted access to valuable physical assets, their lack of capability often impedes them in using the assets to function effectively.

After having discussed the theoretical foundations of capability approach and the distance it shares from traditional developmental models, it is now time to demystify the approach and chalk out its redeeming uniqueness. The potential of capability approach in enhancing individual and collective freedom distinguishes it from other conventional developmental initiatives (Sen, 2003) which, unlike the former, externally thrust welfare measures on the target group. It is the ability of the approach in cultivating strategies of self-sustenance and self-development among the target group that makes capability approach intrinsic to the process of attaining holistic social development, where transformation is achieved and is manifested proactively by social actors. An enhanced capability set, subsequently expanding individual and collective freedom, empowers the target group to transcend from being crowd to stakeholders in their own developmental process. Instead of viewing the target group as passive puppets of change, the capability approach enables the target group to take informed decisions and attempt to attain development from within.

Marx identified expansion of freedom as a collective and conscious effort to "replace the domination of circumstances and chance over individuals by the domination of individuals over chance and circumstances" (McLellan, 1977). Capability approach has the potential to provide justice to Marx's insightful formulation because the expansion of individual and collective freedom targeted by the approach is premised on conceptualization of freedom in terms of both its instrumental and intrinsic value. The instrumental view of freedom conceptualizes freedom as a means to attain valuable ends of higher degree and social relevance. The instrumental aspect of freedom, which capability approach incorporates, recognizes and values the capability set as the best alternative available. It is the fulfilment of the desired outcome that matters most in this context, where freedom acts as an enabler in selecting the most appropriate alternative for achieving the end. The intrinsic view of freedom, on the other hand, treats freedom and the expansion of it as an end in itself. As a result, the entire process of assessing profit and the selection of pathways to attain the same become important. Opportunities available to social actors to choose other alternatives achieve significance of their own. It is both the practical fulfilment derived out of freedom (instrumental) and the end act of exercising one's power to choose (intrinsic) that, in alliance, accredit capability approach to pronounce human subjects as agential actors, endowing them with the capacity to shape their own social fabric rather than being shaped by it. It is these criteria of capability approach that make it intrinsic to any social developmental initiative in general, and to our rural developmental framework in particular. Amidst a social setting that is already ostracized and discriminated against, empowering the rural target group from within must ensure enhancement of their capability set, which will subsequently expand both intrinsic and instrumental freedom of the marginalized community.

The importance and indispensability of capability approach in a social developmental context has been discussed in detail in this sub-section. The following sub-section explains our research initiative to enhance the capability set of the rural target group by equipping them with knowledge and knowledge-operating capacities. The sub-section aims to clarify why we have chosen knowledge as a means to enhance the capability set of our marginalized rural target group.

4.2 A knowledge-centric capability approach for mitigating knowledge asymmetry

In order to fully convey the essence of the rural empowerment framework we are advocating, it is necessary to provide clarifications along double axes. While justifying the importance and potential of capability approach in the process of achieving social development accounts to be one part, the other part relates to clarifying why we have attempted to equip the rural target group with knowledge and knowledge-operating capacities in an effort to empower them. The theoretical formulations of knowledge as a holistic concept, as discussed in the earlier parts of this chapter, enable it to be a potential means in sustainable enhancement of capability set of marginalized rural community. While the social and human aspects of knowledge mark its importance as an asset, cultivation of knowledge-operating capacities, commonly referred to as knowledge capability, accounts to be a crucial strategy undertaken in our empowering paradigm.

Attempting to cultivate both external (information) and internal (experiences, skills and attitude) factors, knowledge as a resource is inherently individual bound and facilitates sustainable growth of individual and collective strategies of self-development. Having access to knowledge and possessing operating abilities therefore enable members of the target group to be potential contributors to the global knowledge pool. The agency derived as a result is conducive to the growth of an inter-connected developmental ecosystem. Possession of knowledge and capability to operate the asset enable the successful transition of common people from being "passive" crowd to "active" stakeholders in their own developmental process. This shows the congruency that knowledge possession and knowledge-operating capacities, or knowledge capability, have in mitigating overall knowledge asymmetry of marginalized target group. Knowledge capability, reflective of enhanced individual credentials, is a prerequisite in initiating effective inter- and intra-group knowledge collaboration, which offers potential prospects in mitigating knowledge asymmetry of marginalized members. Amidst the backdrop of mitigated knowledge asymmetry, the target group will have the provision to exploit their knowledge capability into generating concrete opportunity prospects.

Most of the works focusing on the effectivity of knowledge management in achieving benefits, both within and outside an organizational context, have used the terms "capability" and "knowledge capability" interchangeably (Ning et al., 2006). A similar co-relation between the two can be found in classical works focusing on capability approach, which bears explicit mention of knowledge and its effectivity in enhancing capability set of target group (Sen, 2003). Sen's formulation of capability approach insightfully identifies the role educational development plays in enhancing individual and collective capability set. Reference to educational infrastructure in capability approach highlights the decisive role played by the exposure to specialized knowledge in the act of enhancing capability set of marginalized community.

Ballon and Krishnakumar (2011) have formulated a similar research ideation, which draws a positive relation between knowledge and living conditions capability, implying that they mutually enhance each other. Premising his research in Bolivia, Ballon intended to highlight the role of social factors in shaping individual/group capability set. Identifying the deprived capability level of the rural poor as the major factor sustaining marginalization of the members, Ballon contrasts it to the enhanced living conditions of privileged urban residents. The discrepancy in the living standards of the two territorial groups in Bolivia enabled Ballon to trace the knowledge asymmetry existent between the groups to be one of the primary factors differentially shaping the capability sets of the two communities. Ballon's work identifies knowledge and its operating capacities as important indicators of individual/group capability set, thereby justifying the importance of knowledge as an asset in enhancing capability, and the cultivation of knowledge capability as precursory to development of the marginalized.

We have attempted, in premising and building onto this strand of research ideation, to enhance the capability set of rural community by equipping them with relevant knowledge and knowledge-operating capacities. The issues resulting from rural populations' knowledge asymmetry cannot be addressed fully by only giving them access to knowledge asset. Endowing knowledge-operating abilities, or, in other words, making the rural population knowledge capable, offers the possibility of overcoming the isolation faced by the community and establishing them as agential contributors to the global knowledge pool. Only when the rural members become knowledge capable will they bear the ability to initiate effective inter- and intra-group knowledge transaction. As we have mentioned in the first chapter, knowledge capability of rural actors will manifest in their *learning, cultural* and *communicational* capability, which in amalgamation will develop *innovative* capability of individual knowledge sources. When the individual knowledge sources develop learning capacities through knowledge exchange amidst a favourable social culture or ambience, they develop capacities to innovate on existing knowledge sources through effective communication. This highlights that it is not mere possession of knowledge, but its operative abilities, through which individual knowledge sources develop the power to innovate, that has the potential to mitigate knowledge asymmetry faced by marginalized communities. The redeeming possibilities that both knowledge and capability offer in context of mitigating knowledge asymmetry has urged us to identify the same as a potential strategy in our rural empowerment framework through the creation of an inter-connected developmental ecosystem.

5 Conclusion

The chapter logically breaks down and marks the indispensability of knowledge and knowledge capability in context of mitigating knowledge asymmetry of marginalized rural community. It clearly distinguishes knowledge from information, in terms of the theoretical foundations and practical manifestations of the concepts, and advocates for a knowledge-driven approach to rural empowerment. The chapter justifies the importance of empowering the rural target group with knowledge resource and operating capabilities by shifting the focus from information asymmetry to knowledge asymmetry. Such a shift in focus is accompanied by an academic suggestion furthered in the chapter which advocates for mitigation of knowledge asymmetry of the target group as a potential strategy to overcome rural marginalization. Eradication of knowledge asymmetry reflective of enhanced inter- and intra-group knowledge exchange creates a conducive environment that enables rural members to translate their knowledge capability in pursuit of generating lucrative opportunity prospects.

Knowledge asymmetry and its mitigation 109

The factual nature of information makes mitigation of information asymmetry a simple procedure. The asymmetry can be mitigated by supplying the target group with access to adequate information. However, the social dimension of knowledge makes knowledge acquisition a complex and time-consuming procedure, which cannot be purchased but has to be accomplished. Therefore, knowledge asymmetry cannot be mitigated by ensuring access to adequate knowledge resources only; endowing the target group with knowledge-operating capabilities serves to be equally important in the process of empowering the rural target group with knowledge resources. Only when rural members are knowledge capable will they develop the credentials to initiate inter- and intra-group knowledge transaction, which is reflective of mitigated knowledge asymmetry. In this context, the following questions arise:

a How to develop a systematic approach to capture, structure, manage and disseminate knowledge to empower rural target group with knowledge resources and knowledge-operating capabilities?
b How can we create a framework for managing knowledge that allows rural participants to create and modify content collaboratively to bridge the rural–urban information and knowledge divide?
c How the inclusive potential of contemporary digital technology, comprising internet-enabled communications, platforms and tools (for example, web 2.0, mobile 2.0, social media, social software, etc.), can be exploited to establish *collaborative connectivity* among billions of individuals across the globe, to help cultivate knowledge and knowledge capabilities of rural population?
d How a digital space for engagement and development of rural population can be created to manage social knowledge so that the rural users are provided with a multi-community connectivity, making it quicker and easier for members to connect, communicate, collaborate and learn by getting connected to relevant people and information in one integrated workspace?

Part II of this book attempts to answer all these questions by proposing knowledge management as an effective strategy in enhancing knowledge capability of social actors. It is the development of knowledge capability of social actors that actually marks their credentials in initiating and sustaining knowledge collaboration across the globe, thereby paving the path for an ambience characterized by mitigated knowledge asymmetry. Amidst the backdrop of reduced knowledge asymmetry, rural members will not only be knowledge capable but will also gain the ability to exploit their capability in generating lucrative opportunity prospects. Part II starts by narrating in Chapter 7 what knowledge management is and how it evolved gradually over time in organizational context to incorporate exchange of both tacit and explicit knowledge within its purview. Discussion of knowledge management explicitly highlights how the strategy evolved in organizational context, in alliance with technological development. However, it is only the inclusive spirit with which contemporary digital technology is endowed that has the capacity to cultivate knowledge management to promote enhancement of knowledge capability of target group. Our research attempt, after analysing knowledge management and its evolution in a business context, explores how the strategy can be optimally put to use for the cause of social development. Taking it outside organizational parameters, our research quest attempts to invest the potential of contemporary digital technologies to realize the effectivity of *social knowledge management* in bringing holistic rural empowerment.

Contemporary digital technology and its connected spirit have enormous potential in ushering in social development by facilitating collaborations among diverse and scattered social agents. For this reason we have reserved the term "social technologies" to refer to such an empowering digital infrastructure. Chapter 8 in Part II spells out the terminological usage and theoretical and practical reach of social technologies alongside the attempts to build an interconnected digital ecosystem by enabling every social member to participate in the digital network.

While knowledge management in organizational context has been taken up in detail in Chapter 7, we have reserved Chapter 9 to discuss the multifarious ways to manage social knowledge and information for social benefit. The chapter offers in-depth references to efforts undertaken to manage social knowledge and information, where managerial attempts have been adopted for social cause. Although the efforts, undertaken both along physical and digital lines, have an innovative premise and offer respite from traditional developmental measures, the chapter highlights the inherent loopholes that most of these initiatives suffer from. A critical examination of efforts undertaken to manage social knowledge and information for social benefit paves the path for Chapter 9, where we articulate the effectivity of our *social knowledge management framework* to satiate the given cause.

The interconnected digital ecosystem, built by social technologies, serves as the implementing premise of our social knowledge management framework, which we will take up in detail in Chapter 10 of Part II. Our *social knowledge management framework*, designed to serve social cause, is more holistic in its approach, as compared to organizational knowledge management models. Our framework attempts to usher in holistic rural empowerment by investing the potential of social technologies. Using social technology to manage social knowledge for social development, we have referred to our framework as social knowledge management, which is distinct, more contextual and emancipatory from extant efforts undertaken to manage social knowledge and information for social cause. Our social knowledge management framework, by utilizing social technologies as a medium, attempts to establish effective collaboration between and across rural–urban communities. By facilitating effective intra- and inter-group knowledge exchange, the framework targets rural empowerment from within by successfully mitigating knowledge asymmetry of rural actors.

References

Abbot, T. (1909). *Fundamental Principles of the Metaphysics of Morals, in Kant's Critique of Practical Reason and Other Works on the Theory of Ethics* (6th ed.). London: Longmans.
Akerlof, G. (1970). The Market for Lemons: Quality Uncertainty and the Market Mechanism. *The Quarterly Journal of Economics*, 84(3), 488–500.
Baiman, S. (1982). Agency Research in Managerial Accounting: A Survey. *Journal of Accounting Literature*, 1, 154–213.
Baiman, S. (1990). Agency Research in Managerial Accounting: A Second Look. *Accounting, Organizations and Society*, 15(4), 341–371.
Ballon, P. & Krishnakumar, J. (2011). Measuring Capability Poverty: A Multi-dimensional Model-based Approach (PhD thesis, University of Oxford). doi:10.13140/2.1.1022.2884.
Chiu, C. & Chen, H. (2016). The Study of Knowledge Management Capability and Organizational Effectiveness in Taiwanese Public Utility: The Mediator Role of Organizational Commitment. *SpringerPlus* 5(1), 1520. doi:10.1186/s40064-016-3173-6.
Dellemijn, R. (2012). Knowledge Asymmetry in Inter-Firm Relationships: A Suggestion for a Knowledge Sourcing Strategy for the Ministry of Oil of Iraq (Student thesis, University of Twente, Netherland). Retrieved from: http://essay.utwente.nl/61982/.
Doctor, R.D. (1992). Social Equity and Information Technologies: Moving toward Information Democracy. *Annual Review of Information Science and Technology*, 2, 43–96.
Eisenhardt, K. (1989). Agency Theory: An Assessment and Review. *Academy of Management Review*, 14(1), 57–74.
Freeze, R. & Kulkarni, U. (2007). Knowledge Management Capability: Defining Knowledge Assets. *Journal of Knowledge Management*, 11(6), 94–109. doi:10.1108/13673270710832190.
Gorman, M. (2000). *Our enduring values: Librarianship in the 21st century*. Chicago, IL: American Library Association.
Grant, R. (1996). Toward a Knowledge-Based Theory of the Firm. *Strategic Management Journal*, 17 (Winter Issue), 109–122.
Lievrouw, L. & Farb, S. (2003). Information and Equity. *Annual Review of Information Science and Technology (ARIST)*, 37, 499–540.
Marx, K. (1959). *Economic & Philosophic Manuscripts of 1844*. Moscow: Progress Publishers.
McLellan, D. (1977). *Karl Marx: Selected Writings*. Oxford: Oxford University Press.
Ning, Y., Shu, P. & Feng, B. (2006). *Knowledge Capability: A Definition and Research Model*. Proceedings of the International Conference on Knowledge Science, Engineering and Management, Lecture Notes in Computer Science, 4092, 330–340. doi:10.1007/11811220_28.
Nussbaurn, M. (1988). Nature, function and capability: Aristotle on political distribution. *Oxford Studies in Ancient Greek Philosophy*. Retrieved from: https://www.wider.unu.edu/sites/default/files/WP31.pdf.
Polanyi, M. (1966). *The Tacit Dimension*. Magnolia, MA: Peter Smith.
Ross, D. (1980). *Aristotle: The Nicomachean Ethics*. Oxford: Oxford University Press.
Sen, A. (1973). *On economic inequality*. Oxford: Clarendon Press.
Sen, A. (1988). *Capability and well-being*. Proceedings of the World Institute for Development Economics Research conference.

Sen, A. (2003). *Development as Capability Expansion*. New Delhi and New York: Oxford University Press.
Sharma, A. (1997). Professional as an agent: Knowledge asymmetry in agency exchange. *Academy of Management Review*, 22(3), 758–798.
Smith, A. (1776). *An Inquiry into the Nature and Causes of the Wealth of Nations*. London: Methuen & Co.
Stinchcombe, A. (1990). *Information and Organizations*. Berkeley, CA: University of California Press.
Young, I.M. (2001). Equality of Whom? Social Groups and Judgments of Injustice. *Journal of Political Philosophy*, 9(1), 1–18.
Young, J. (2012). *Personal Knowledge Capital*. Oxford: Chandos Publishing.

Part II
Social knowledge management and social technologies
Conceptual foundations

7 Knowledge management and its evolution in organizational context

1 Introduction

The preceding chapters have differentiated knowledge from information, highlighted the value of knowledge as resource and discussed the extant knowledge divide which cripples society. Subsequently, we have proposed management of knowledge as a strategy to usher in knowledge capability expansion of organizational and/or social members. Our research framework defines information as factual data having a purpose. On the other hand, our reliance on knowledge as an asset to generate socio-economic value rests on interpreting the credential of the concept in terms of its potential to transform information into experience, values, contextual information and personal insight in pursuit of generating new information and experience (Limaye et al., 2017). Although knowledge as an asset has secured a considerable position in the context of contemporary society, both at the institutional and social level (Laszlo & Laszlo, 2002), passive possession of the asset seldom has the capacity to realize the value of the resource in attainment of positive outcome. Achieving both individual and collective performance enhancement requires knowledge capability of social actors to be enhanced, so that knowledge can be used, shared, brokered and managed throughout a diverse and distributed global setting (Limaye et al., 2017).

The importance of knowledge and the urgency to manage it to achieve optimal and efficient social functioning has existed since civilization emerged, as a result of effective collaboration among different social actors (Pizziconi & Wiig, 1997). However, the study of knowledge and knowledge management on a formal level is of recent origin and first emerged in the context of business organizations. First instances of the term "knowledge management" appeared in the year 1975, in articles written by Goel, Henry and McCaffery (Serenko & Bontis, 2004), where knowledge management emerged "as an ultimate view to transform information (= description) to knowledge (= action)" (Tzortzaki & Mihiotis, 2014). Since the time of its inception, several scholars from diverse disciplines have devoted their academic quest to define and explore the dimensions of knowledge management as a formal strategy to boost competitive advantage. While no unanimity could be achieved among the diverse definitions of knowledge management as conceptualized by different scholars from diverse disciplines, knowledge management can be generally referred to as the process of enabling individuals to improve their learning efficiency and integrate different knowledge resources to improve competitive advantage (Gao et al., 2018). Knowledge management is generally viewed as a process, where related activities are formed to carry out key elements of strategies and operations. Knowledge management refers to the cumulative process of *creating, storing, transferring* and *applying* knowledge to improve individual and collective efficiency (Xue, 2017).

This chapter locates the trajectory of knowledge management as a strategy to boost organizational performance. The chapter is divided into the following segments:

- The chapter starts by providing the historical background of knowledge management as was practised in pre-industrial society, long before the concept attained formal recognition.
- The second section fleshes out the social and structural architecture that paved the path for formal adoption of knowledge management as a strategy in organizations.
- The third and fourth sections are reserved to discuss the research around defining knowledge management, and the processes and strategies intrinsic to the concept. By discussing the definitions and conceptualizations pertaining to knowledge management, as has been furthered by different strands of study, these sections are dedicated to highlighting the intricacy of knowledge management as a strategy to boost competitive advantage within an organization in all its complexity.
- The fifth section highlights the relationship between knowledge capability of organizations and knowledge management. In doing so it chalks out how organizational knowledge capability can be positively impacted through optimal knowledge management, where management of tacit and explicit knowledge in amalgamation paves the path for expansion of knowledge capability of organizations.
- The sixth section traces the evolution of knowledge management in a business context after its formal inception as a strategy to boost organizational performance. The section is divided into three sub-sections, each sub-section pertaining to the three generations of knowledge management, as has been periodically practised by firms to achieve heightened efficiency. The chapter concludes by highlighting how third-generation knowledge management practices, based on peer-to-peer and collaborative knowledge exchange in alliance with contemporary digital technologies, have the potential to expand knowledge capability of organizations on a holistic level.

2 How society used to manage knowledge: A historical perspective

Knowledge management, as a formal discipline, has many recognized origins (Wiig, 2000). The diverse origins, chronologically, include:

- Abstract philosophical thinking.
- Concrete concerns for requirements of expertise in the workplace.
- Perspectives of educators and business leaders.
- Recent perspective coming from efforts to explain economic driving forces in the "knowledge era" and 20th century efforts to increase social and organizational effectiveness.

While we have mentioned only four, there exist other multiple strands which conceptualize knowledge management following their own disciplinarian thread. It is with dialogue and debate among its different strands that knowledge management is viewed in the 21st century as among the most effective apparatus in boosting competitive advantage and social positioning of an organization. Although knowledge and knowledge management have secured a formal position in contemporary society, it is necessary to question whether the concepts only enjoy relevance in the context of contemporary setup.

The idea of knowledge in pre-industrial society was primarily guided and informed by the philosophical foundation of the notion (Adolf & Stehr, 2014). The traditional philosophical view treated knowledge in stringent terms, and reduced it to the relationship between individual subject, the knower, and the object/referent, the known. While the tenets of the philosophical tradition have been dealt with in detail in the first chapter, we reserve this section to highlight how philosophical foundations of knowledge were confined to ascertaining the "validation" of warrants of knowledge claims. This reductionist idea, in heralding an abstract conception of "true" knowledge, distanced it from the "impurities" of social forces, which equally contribute in shaping, sustaining and transferring knowledge. Knowledge and knowledge management are embedded in the social fabric – even in the pre-industrial phase, when not formally recognized as a managerial and functioning strategy.

The relevance of managing knowledge to achieve social functioning and subsequently boost social efficiency dates back to hunter–gatherer societies. Effective collaboration and exchange of expertise between different social members resulted in the inception and growth of human civilization, even though the social actors were not managing knowledge in ways we refer to the notion in today's world. If we take the instance of first hunters, we can see how their sustenance was dependent on using collective skills to hunt their prey. In order to carry out the task collectively and effectively it was necessary for each member of the hunting group to possess knowledge about the skills and expertise of other members to ensure optimal coordination between group members. Awareness of each member regarding the skills of the others, and subsequently devising coordination strategies to capture the prey, in a way resonate the essence of knowledge management and its effectivity in enhancing efficiency. This was not only limited to creation of knowledge in early societies; it also incorporated knowledge transfer, where acquired skills and expertise were systematically taught and transferred to up-coming hunters to ensure long-term viability of the group. Society, since its inception, has been able to function because knowledge has been created, stored, applied and transferred, be it informally, through generations, prior to the time when "knowledge management" emerged as a formal strategy.

We will also highlight Phoenician civilization to further explain how management of knowledge served to be the premise of society even in pre-industrial times. Phoenicia was a civilization that originated in the eastern Mediterranean, specifically in modern-day Lebanon. It was organized into city-states, where the early traces of civilization were manifested when Phoenicians, in order to sustain their community, started trading among themselves. This has been historically seen as one of the early examples of modern trade, which includes economic transactions among geographically dispersed places. Even with the absence of technology and smooth communication channels, Phoenicians conducted successful trade by optimally managing knowledge and expertise of different community members. As one of the pioneers of modern trade, Phoenicians were concerned about how knowledge and trade logistics and merchant practices were built and transferred to members to make operations successful. This early trade model, based on knowledge sharing between members of dispersed locations, happens to be one of the early examples showing the effectivity of managing knowledge in driving economic activities (Pizziconi & Wiig, 1997).

Since pre-industrial times, knowledge and knowledge management have traversed a long path towards acquiring their contemporary essence. Although the above-mentioned examples highlight how knowledge and knowledge management had implicit importance in early society, their explicit recognition as formal assets capable of generating socio-economic value was made possible as the concepts began their gradual entries within different disciplinarian parameters. The importance of knowledge and knowledge management in boosting competitive advantage of business organizations was acknowledged only after the notions had been acclaimed by specialists as important in the context of generating economic value. Noble Prize-winning scholar Paul Romer's seminal work on "economics of ideas" can be identified as one of the key driving forces marking the importance of knowledge in an economic context. While traditional economic models were grappling with inefficiency resulting from scarcity of physical resources, available labour, capital, etc., Romer's conceptualization advocating the ability of knowledge-based products to generate economic growth and innovation served as a ray of hope (Pizziconi & Wiig, 1997). Romer postulated how making people knowledgeable brought innovation and continued ability to create and deliver products and services of highest quality. Knowledge has a sustainable dimension to it, which not only enhances the awareness level of its users but also enables them to innovate by capitalizing on their existing knowledge base. This role that knowledge plays makes its more important than exhaustible tangible resources in generating socio-economic benefit. Romer premised on this credential of knowledge and therefore inferred that economic efficiency is directly related to effective knowledge capture, reuse and building upon prior knowledge.

Romer's postulation informed how knowledge can function as a driver of long-term economic growth. He devised his "economics of ideas" as an attempt to answer the question, *Why was progress speeding over time?* Romer conceptualized progress to be arising "... because of the special characteristic of an idea, which is if [a million people try] to discover something, if one person finds it, everybody can use the idea" (Kiernan & Sugden, 2018). Romer's conceptualization not only marked the relevance of knowledge in an economic context, but it also related efficiency to the sharing attribute of the asset in boosting collective competence. It is perhaps the formal acknowledgement of this credential of knowledge in the economic domain that acted as an accelerating force in marking the relevance of the concept and the urgency to manage it in the business context. Although formal recognition of knowledge in the economic domain can be considered as a major driver in formalizing knowledge management as a strategy, other allied aspects, such as technological development and globalization, also contributed generously in shaping managerial tactics and charting the importance it shares at present in organizational and social settings.

3 Information systems and globalization: Impetus to knowledge management

Knowledge management has been established as a discipline since 1991. The emergence of knowledge management as a formal intellectual discipline was primarily triggered by the importance of sharing knowledge resources among individuals, corporations and nations in the context of boosting competitive advantage. The driving force behind adoption of knowledge management as a formal strategy was the need to utilize knowledge effectively and efficiently. Optimal knowledge management was seen as having the potential to maximize an enterprise's knowledge-related effectiveness and returns from its knowledge assets, by renewing them constantly in the process (Pizziconi & Wiig, 1997). Core components of knowledge management, as we refer to the term today, include people/culture, processes/structure and technology. In this context it must be remembered that knowledge and the urgency to manage it did not emerge in organizational and social contexts in vacuum; the development of technology, coupled with allied social forces, can be considered as determining factors, in alliance with which knowledge management emerged and evolved as a strategy. Although knowledge management in today's world can be considered to a great extent as technologically driven, we need to remember that neither the managerial tactics nor the technical intricacies have remained constant over the years. The evolution of knowledge management from a mechanical to a more organic approach in recent times, recognizing the importance of human elements in the process of managing knowledge, has been achieved in tandem with the way technology has evolved over the years and supported the practice of knowledge management. While technology in its earlier phase supported uni-directional or, at the most, bi-directional knowledge transmission from expert to stakeholders, contemporary digital technology, with its interconnected spirit, has the potential to facilitate effective collaboration between diverse agents by supporting multi-directional knowledge exchange. It is the power of contemporary digital technologies that has the ability to appropriately recognize human elements in the process of managing knowledge, by enabling one and all to participate in the process of knowledge creation, acquisition and dissemination.

The very first move towards a knowledge-centric business approach started with information management (Stenberg & Thi, 2017). Back then, information was considered to be the key in management, research and development, and hence considered to be of primary interest in a business context. Any organization was considered to be an information processing unit, which made information management critical to organizations. The *information system* prevailing at the time enabled creation and storage of relevant information to boost organizational efficiency. Information systems refer to formal organizational systems, designed to collect, process, store and distribute information. Information systems incorporate specific reference to information and the complementary networks of hardware and software that people and organizations use to collect, filter, process, create and distribute data. Information management was practised by firms implementing information systems to maintain digital repositories of organizational data, which were considered to be an organizational asset. This phase shared chronological similarity to some extent with the managerial tactics, as practised in first-generation knowledge management, which we will explain in the later sections of this chapter.

The notion of knowledge management gained importance over information management following publication in 1995 of Nonaka's and Takeuchi's book, *The Knowledge Creating Company* (Nonaka & Takeuchi, 1995), which made explicit the dynamic nature of knowledge through introduction of the Socialization-Externalization-Combination-Internalization (SECI) model. Several scholars realized the value of organizational knowledge creation as a primary factor enhancing competitive advantage of the organization (Wong & Aspinwall, 2005). This shift resulted in significant alterations in existing managerial tactics adopted by firms. The shift implied that businesses that can capture knowledge and deploy it into operations, production and services will have an advantage over their competitors. As a result, the key focus of information systems transformed from management of information to that of knowledge (Wong & Aspinwall, 2005). A class of information systems thus evolved, which are referred to as knowledge management systems (KMS), dedicated to effectively managing knowledge, which is intangible, dynamic, boundaryless and context-specific, unlike static and tangible information. Alavi and Leidner (1998) traced the reason behind the emergence of KMS as evolving from the "… need to enable systematic organizational learning and memory by facilitating coding and sharing knowledge across organizational entities that previously may have had little occasion for interacting" (Alavi & Leidner, 1998, p. 2).

Several scholars have defined and interpreted KMS following multiple lenses. Damodaran and Olphert referred to KMS as information systems that are perceived as facilitating organizational learning by capturing important (content and processes) "knowledge" and making it available to employees as necessary (Stenberg & Thi, 2017). Alavi and Leidner defined KMS as "Information Technology (IT) based systems, designed to support and enhance the organizational process of knowledge creation, storage/retrieval, transfer and application" (Alavi & Leidner, 2001, p. 14). The above definitions highlight the effectivity of KMS in creating an identity associated and loyal to the company, while at the same time making people in the organization promote trust, social norms, expectations and obligations (Sherif et al., 2006). Encouraging engagement of organizational members, KMS transcended information management and enabled knowledge management to enter its second generation. Comprising knowledge repositories, knowledge maps and collaborative tools (Alavi & Leidner, 1999; Bernard, 2006), KMS are a curious amalgamation of tools and practices, of IT-based systems coupled with methods and techniques crucial to deploying the information system in pursuit of optimal knowledge management. It is with the ultimate aim of achieving and enhancing the effectiveness and efficiency of knowledge management practices that KMS have been adopted and utilized by many organizations.

However, apart from the technical factor, another aspect – globalization – looms large in shaping and evolving knowledge management as a strategy. Globalization, by nullifying geographical boundaries, plays a crucial role in altering the way business practices are conducted globally. By throwing open national firms to international markets, in a globalized setting, only those firms with a competitive advantage over others could survive. The importance of knowledge and knowledge management in enhancing competitive advantage became the primary resort for several organizations seeking to sustain their existence in a highly competitive globalized setting. However, information management alone was no longer sufficient in boosting competitive advantage of firms because it largely neglects the human elements of the organizations. To sustain and succeed in a globalized setting, it became mandatory to cultivate explicit knowledge of organizations, along with tacit elements embedded in a firm's organizational members. It is the dual acknowledgement of explicit knowledge infrastructure, along with the tacit or human elements on a formal level, that primarily marked the initiation of knowledge management in its truest terms.

4 Knowledge management: Definitions

With the formal emergence of knowledge management as a discipline, different scholars from diverse fields undertook to define the concept and to comprehensively conceptualize its nature, scope and characteristics. The emerging and diverse strands, although attempting to highlight the effectivity of knowledge management in boosting business performance following various pathways, unanimously agreed upon the importance and potential that knowledge has in altering economic practices. Knowledge, in this context, was conceptualized as a dynamic human resource that justifies personal belief to obtain the truth (Nonaka, 1994). It is indicative of an intangible asset, acquisition of which requires complex cognitive processes of perception, learning, communication, association and reasoning (Epetimehin & Ekundayo, 2011).

It is the acquisition of knowledge that makes mechanical transferring of knowledge almost an impossibility. Knowledge needs to be accomplished, learned, which ties it to social units. It became important to address the intangibility and dynamic aspect of knowledge in any managerial tactics dedicated to systematically integrating knowledge into a collective pool. This dynamic quotient of knowledge is not universal, structured and rigid. The human elements present in knowledge make it crucial to manage the resource in accordance with specific contexts, by considering the specificities intrinsic to a particular context. This explains the reason why strategies of knowledge management adopted in varied contexts to boost socio-economic performance are not uniform in nature.

Several scholars, from diverse fields of study, have tried to define knowledge management through varied lenses. Following, we will provide the multiple definitions of knowledge management, as furthered by many scholars over the years, to highlight the debate surrounding the concept, as well as give the reader a fair idea as to how the conceptualization of knowledge management evolved over time.

One of the early definitions came from Horwitch and Armacost (2002), who saw knowledge management as the creation, extraction, transformation and storage of the correct knowledge and information in order to design better policy, modify action and deliver results (Gao et al., 2018). Skyrme conceptualized knowledge management (Skyrme, 2002) as the explicit and systematic management of vital knowledge and its associated processes of creating, gathering, organizing, diffusion, use and exploitation. While these definitions highlight the supreme importance of knowledge and the urgency to manage it, they explicitly reserve some sentiments regarding what constitutes "correct" or "vital" knowledge. It is the organizational politics and viewpoints that determine which knowledge can be considered "correct" and/or "vital" for creation and distribution in the context of a particular business entity.

A decisive turn in the study of knowledge management can be traced to the year 2004, following April and Izadi's definition of knowledge management (Gao et al., 2018). They defined knowledge management as a philosophy made up of both the collect function (data and information dimensions) and the connect function (knowledge and wisdom function). This definition can be seen as one of the earliest instances marking the shift from knowledge to wisdom, following the hierarchy as depicted in the D-I-K-W Pyramid model. This model conceptualizes Data, Information, Knowledge and Wisdom in a hierarchical fashion, where data, referring to nothing but "factoids", a number out of context, occupies the lowest rung, followed by information, knowledge and, finally, topped by wisdom (Laszlo & Laszlo, 2002). Wisdom has been defined as the ultimate step, which uses knowledge for the creation of understanding. The shift from knowledge to wisdom not only marks "the shift from knowledge acquisition to knowledge meaning creation", it also reiterates the importance and indispensability of human agency in realizing the fruits of knowledge management (Laszlo & Laszlo, 2002). It is the human elements like experience, skill and attitude that translate passive possession of knowledge to active understanding, by virtue of which knowledge management bears the potential to enhance overall efficiency.

It is during this time that the concept of *personal knowledge management* emerged, referring to management of knowledge at an individual level (Kirby, 2005). The crucial fact that cultural norms, which influence human behaviours, are the most critical elements for successful knowledge creation and distribution entered the popular academic domain at this time. This new mindset implied that cognitive, social and organizational learning processes are essential to the success of a knowledge management strategy. This enabled knowledge management as a strategy to have a dual aim, that is simultaneous cultivation of explicit and tacit knowledge resources, to usher in holistic effect.

The importance of human or tacit elements of knowledge in the paradigm of knowledge management has only increased since 2004. Wang's definition of knowledge management in the year 2007 explicitly bears reference to such a shift. He defined knowledge management as knowledge transfers, between explicit and tacit, between individual and collective (Wang et al., 2015). The importance of human elements in the process of knowledge management is further reiterated in Pauleen and Gorman's definition of the notion as formulated in 2011 (Pauleen & Gorman, 2011). They defined knowledge management as the application of managerial tactics through individual strategies, based on experience and skills, to create maximum value for individuals. The importance of people in the process of knowledge management has also been chalked out by Rouse. According to Rouse (2013), knowledge management refers to an enterprises' conscious and comprehensive efforts to gather, organize, share and analyse its knowledge in terms of resources, documents and people skills. The latter and more recent definitions therefore explicitly focus on the management of tacit knowledge and thereby define knowledge management in their respective ways, which to them enables the cultivation of implicit knowledge. This shift in knowledge management shows how over the years, along with the importance of explicit knowledge, tacit knowledge comprising human elements has gained considerable recognition; firms realized that competitive advantage cannot be achieved if the knowledge credentials of individual organizational members are not improved. Moreover, with the inception and growth of globalization, territorial isolation has almost become a myth in contemporary times. Effective collaborations, facilitated by globalization, have altered the way business is conducted in today's world. Instead of focusing knowledge management within single, independent business entities, globalized society has thrown open the door to increased networking among different entities. In order to sustain effective collaboration, knowledge management both within and across business entities became mandatory in the process of achieving competitive advantage. This level of knowledge management can be neither reached nor realized if individual organizational members are not encouraged to participate collaboratively in the process of creation, storage, distribution and application of knowledge.

5 Knowledge management: Processes and strategies

While the earlier section has given some insights regarding the multiple definitions of knowledge management, this section discusses the different processes and strategies that are intrinsically linked to knowledge management. Various scholars have viewed knowledge management as a process having the following areas of emphasis (Pizziconi & Wiig, 1997):

- Top-down monitoring and facilitation of knowledge-related activities.
- Creation and maintenance of knowledge infrastructure.
- Renewing, organizing and transforming knowledge.
- Leveraging knowledge assets to realize their value.

5.1 Processes of knowledge management

In order to achieve the above-stated functions, knowledge management as a process includes knowledge creation, storage, transfer and application (Kayworth & Leidner, 2003; Zaim, 2006; Fong & Choi, 2009; Turner et al., 2012). Although there exists considerable difference in the way different scholars have conceptualized the processes related to knowledge management, knowledge creation, storage, transfer and application feature in almost every strand dedicated to the study of knowledge management and its processes.

The development of *knowledge management process capabilities* is congruent with managing knowledge resource, not within, but across, organizations. Process capabilities determine collection of two types of knowledge: to seek and acquire new knowledge, and to create new knowledge out of existing knowledge through collaborations between individuals and business partners. There exists considerable difference among scholars regarding their conceptualizations of knowledge processes. However, conceptualization of knowledge process by Gold et al., (2001) appropriately captures the twin motive of process capabilities of acquiring new knowledge and creating new knowledge from an existing knowledge set.

Gold et al., (2001) conceptualize process capabilities as comprising knowledge **acquisition, conversion, application and protection. Acquisition** refers to processes oriented towards obtaining knowledge. Many terms, such as *acquire, seek, generate, create, capture*, have been interchangeably used in different contexts, all of which refer to accumulation of knowledge. **Knowledge conversion**, triggered by knowledge management activities, makes firms' existing knowledge useful. Firms' ability to organize, integrate, combine, structure, coordinate or distribute knowledge enables knowledge conversion. ***Knowledge application*** refers to the actual use of knowledge. Storage, retrieval, contribution and sharing enable optimal application of knowledge (Appleyard, 1996). Finally, ***knowledge protection*** refers to the security-oriented knowledge management processes designed to protect the knowledge within an organization from illegal or inappropriate use and theft (Liebskind, 1996).

The SECI model, proposed by Nonaka and Takeuchi (1995), best embraces the twin motive of process capabilities of acquiring new knowledge and creating new knowledge from an existing knowledge set. This model uses four processes of knowledge conversion – socialization, externalization, combination and internalization – to create knowledge in organizations.

The SECI model (Figure 7.1) is premised on the notion that knowledge is continuously converted and created, as users practise, collaborate, interact and learn. Nonaka and Takeuchi explain this continuous dynamic swirl of knowledge through the SECI model, denoting the flow of tacit and explicit knowledge within a firm.

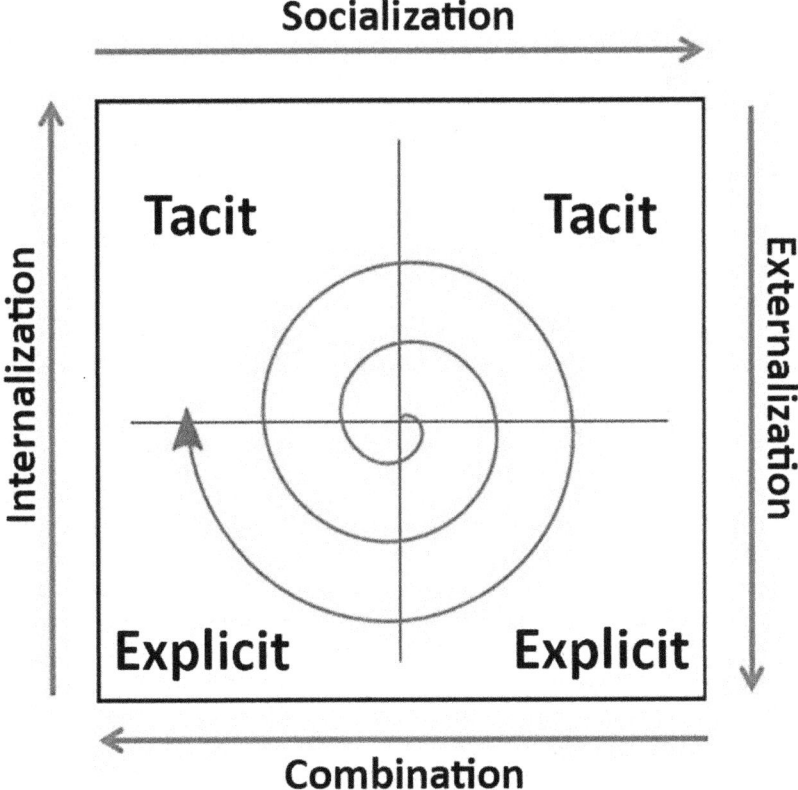

Figure 7.1 SECI model of Nonaka and Takeuchi

Socialization refers to the conversion of tacit to tacit knowledge through collaborative exchange of knowledge among peers. It occurs when tacit knowledge is transferred through practice, guidance, imitation and observation.

Externalization occurs when tacit knowledge is converted to explicit knowledge. It gets reflected when tacit knowledge is codified into documents, manuals, etc., so that it can spread more easily within the organization.

Combination takes place when explicit knowledge is converted to explicit knowledge. It is the simplest form, where codified knowledge sources are combined to create new knowledge.

Internalization occurs when explicit knowledge is converted to tacit knowledge. It can be achieved by enabling the learner to improve his/her explicit knowledge, by means of which the extant tacit knowledge of the entity is enhanced.

The SECI model remains at the core of knowledge conversion theory within knowledge management, and almost universal adherence to the model may itself serve to be an indication that some aspects of it appeal to virtually all cultures (Andreeva & Ikhilchik, 2011). The commitment to an interactive knowledge management phase is explicitly reiterated in comments of international groups such as the Organization for Economic Co-operation and Development (OECD). The OECD's commitment to knowledge management was formally postulated in 1996 in *The Knowledge-based Economy*, where the organization stated that "the OECD economies are more strongly dependent on the production, distribution, and use of knowledge than ever before" (Tzortzaki & Mihiotis, 2014).

The above-stated processes and the functions they offer have been almost unanimously agreed upon as essential to optimal knowledge management. However, the specific ways in which different scholars have conceptualized knowledge management as a process differ, if not in terms of conceptualization but in terms of terminology (Gao et al., 2018). However, with the passage of time, evolution of the processes of knowledge management into a holistic framework highlights efforts aimed at managing both the explicit and tacit dimensions of knowledge within the paradigm of knowledge management.

5.2 Strategies of knowledge management in organizational context

One of the main purposes behind the introduction and evolution of knowledge management in organizations has been to boost the positive impact and outcomes on organizational performance (Rasula et al., 2012; Ahmed et al., 2015). The recent acknowledgement of tacit knowledge, as having an equal resourceful value like explicit knowledge, has significantly altered the extant practice of knowledge management. The emerging strand of knowledge management, emphasizing the human elements of the firm, marked the importance of social actors and their capability set in the process of enhancing the competitive advantage of an organization (Liao & Wu, 2009).

Such an effective knowledge management practice is expected to provide opportunities to organizations to explore tacit and explicit knowledge of individuals, groups and organizations, and convert this knowledge into organizational assets for use towards responsive decision-making. Optimal knowledge management, with a twin focus on management of explicit and tacit knowledge assets, helps in enhancing the overall effectiveness and efficiency of an organization on a sustainable basis (Dahiya et al., 2012; Byukusenge et al., 2016). Xue (2017) has also identified effective and holistic knowledge management as the key factor in enhancing an organization's operational activities by reducing the lead time, product-to-market time and design-cycle time, as well as improving product quality.

This makes it clear that effective knowledge management requires a proper strategy, which must be capable of creating, storing, transferring and applying both tacit and explicit knowledge assets to generate competitive advantage. One of the major challenges in practising knowledge management on an effective scale is to derive a fair and practical understanding of how knowledge sharing can be promoted among relevant human agents. Effective knowledge management rests on development of a successful knowledge-sharing strategy (Swacha, 2015). Knowledge sharing (both tacit and explicit) can be broadly defined as "the exchange of knowledge between and among individuals, [aimed] at bringing knowledge sources together and manipulating it into new knowledge structures" (Gao et al., 2018).

Many scholars have identified optimal sharing of knowledge (both tacit and explicit) as the leading strategy to practise effective knowledge management. It is only though successful knowledge sharing that knowledge management systems will be able to develop an in-built reputation feedback, which will subsequently make the practice a self-reflective one (Hung et al., 2011). In order to facilitate successful knowledge sharing, attention needs to be given to a multitude of factors which shape the sharing abilities of individual knowledge sources. Tohidinia and Mosakhani (2010) evaluated the influence of potential factors on knowledge-sharing behaviour and subsequently advocated in favour of considering relevant factors from diverse perspectives in a knowledge management framework in order to facilitate systematic knowledge sharing within and across organizations.

5.2.1 Codification strategy vs. personalization strategy

An effective knowledge management system, in order to provide competitive advantage for the organization, must be tightly related to objectives and business strategies of organizations (Zack, 1999). The strategic direction of the organization, to a great extent, determines the direction of knowledge management activity. Greiner et al., (2007) rightly identify two main objectives, following which the organizations design their knowledge management activity:

- Knowledge management initiative undertaken to improve organizational efficiency.
- Knowledge management initiative undertaken to improve organizational innovation.

128 *Conceptual foundations*

These two types of knowledge management strategy differ in their objective, strategy and knowledge type. Research shows that companies that use knowledge management to improve efficiency of operational processes use database and information systems to disseminate the desired practices independently from the "human knowledge carrier". Firms dedicated to process efficiency primarily target their goal through management of explicit knowledge resources. Codification strategy pertains to management of explicit knowledge resource (Greiner et al., 2007; Saito et al., 2007). This strategy aims to collect codified knowledge, store it in databases and provide available knowledge in explicit and codified form. Codification strategy enables knowledge to get externalized and attempts to enhance organizational efficiency by relying on reuse of existing codified knowledge (Hansen et al., 1999; Malhotra, 2004). Design of database, document management and workflow management accounts are examples of knowledge management activities following codification strategy.

Companies which undertake knowledge management activities to improve organizational innovation rely more on *personalization strategy*, instead of *codification strategy*. The focus of personalization strategy is not only to store knowledge, but to use information technology to help people *communicate* their knowledge. Personalization strategy is premised on *socialization* (Nonaka & Takeuchi, 1995; Nonaka & Noboru, 1998) as it enables and supports sharing of tacit knowledge. The objective of this strategy is to transfer, communicate and exchange knowledge via knowledge networks, such as intranet-/internet-enabled discussion forums and/or social networking. The personalization approach is premised on complex, unstructured and unique processes, chosen to solve new problems, create customer-specific solutions and develop product innovation (Hansen et al., 1999). Personalization strategy encourages creation and exchange of knowledge by enabling communication and collaboration in a person-to-person approach. "Treasures hidden in employees' minds" accounts to be the key to personalization strategy (Greiner et al., 2007). Informal sharing of tacit knowledge enabled by personalization strategy through socialization has been viewed as critical for knowledge creation and innovation (Leonard & Sensiper, 1998). Discussion forums, video conferences, online chat, etc. can be cited as exemplary tools supporting personalization strategy.

In this brief discussion, codification and personalization shed light on how technology acts as an enabling force in the context of both the strategies. In the codification approach, technology and digital repositories become directly important in storing explicit knowledge, while, in personalization strategy, technology acts as a facilitating force in connecting different organizational and/or social members. In spite of the importance of technology in both the contexts, conventional approaches have primarily linked technology to codification approach. Given its obvious importance, codification approach has often been synonymous with a "technology-oriented approach" (Saito et al., 2007). Such utilization of technology to create, store and reuse explicit knowledge does not support those knowledge processes, which are engaged with the sharing, transfer and application of knowledge. We will discuss technologies that support *personalization strategy* in the next chapter under "social technologies and knowledge management practices". We will show how, with the growing popularity of the internet and mobile technologies and their applications (primarily web 2.0 and social media), the concept of "knowledge management 2.0 (KM 2.0)" has evolved to allow individuals to create and modify content collaboratively (Semple, 2012), which, in turn, promotes *technology-driven* sharing of both explicit and tacit knowledge.

Technology has become a new weapon to realize modern-day socialization (Saito et al., 2007). In order to reach a balance between the information system-oriented knowledge management approach (codification strategy) and the human-centred knowledge management approach (personalization strategy) it is deemed that technology must facilitate both by encouraging effective collaborations. Many scholars (Umemoto, 2002; Umemoto et al., 2004) have interpreted a balance between both these strategies to be effective in boosting organizational performance on a sustainable and holistic scale.

5.2.2 Expanding knowledge capability through knowledge management

As it has been illustrated in the preceding chapter, effectiveness of knowledge sharing is heavily dependent on the knowledge capability of individual actors. Defined as knowledge possession, coupled with knowledge-operating abilities, it is the ultimate aim of expanding firms' knowledge capability that governs the recent attempts at knowledge management within organizations. Explicit recognition of firms' human elements in the process of knowledge management makes it mandatory to investigate how knowledge capability of organizational members impact and inform knowledge management practices and how optimal knowledge management practices lead to expansion of knowledge capability of knowledge workers, in particular, and the organization in general.

Following Ning et al. (2006), knowledge capability of organizations is determined by the dual effect of knowledge possession and knowledge operation. Chapter 1, following Ning's trajectory, has explicitly marked out how knowledge operation is facilitated by the learning, cultural and communicational capability of organizations (Ning et al., 2006). This highlights that management of knowledge resources to expand organizational capability is not just restricted to knowledge acquisition, sharing and exchange within organizational boundaries. In order to mobilize knowledge management practices in pursuit of knowledge capability expansion on both a micro (individual) and macro (organizational) level, it is equally mandatory to establish inter-organizational collaborations, along with intra-organizational networking, which will facilitate collaborative creation and exchange of knowledge on a wider scale and setting. It is with this dual lens of managing knowledge along both micro and macro perspectives that firms can utilize their knowledge management practices to enhance, over time, their capabilities for creating value (Bohn, 1994; Dutton & Thomas, 1985). Inkpen and Dinur (1998) also explore how a collaborative learning process, paving the path for peer-to-peer interaction, positively impacts knowledge capability of organization, which, in turn, enhances the organizational capability.

Gold et al. (2001) identify organizational capability as derivative of infrastructural capability and process capabilities. While infrastructural capability enables firms to manage knowledge resources internally, process capabilities attempt to enhance organizational capability by optimally managing knowledge resources with both internal and external entities. With the passage of time, knowledge management has moved from managing knowledge within individual organizational units to managing knowledge in a network of organizations, and society at large. Therefore, not only intra-organizational knowledge management but inter-organizational knowledge management have become crucial in the process of enhancing organizational capability. This dual perspective boosts organizational capability by enhancing knowledge-operating ability of both the organization and individual members embedded in an organization or a social group. It is only when knowledge management can target capability expansion following both a micro and macro lens that it marks its effectivity in boosting the competitive advantage of companies. Facilitating both intra- and inter-organizational knowledge management requires effective collaboration within and across organizations.

5.2.3 Cultivating social capital to expand knowledge capability

In order to facilitate knowledge capability by optimally managing knowledge resource, both within and across organizations, it is necessary to cultivate social capital (Gold et al., 2001; Nahapiet & Ghoshal, 1998), through which effective collaboration, both within and across organizations, can be realized and sustained. Cultivation of social capital accounts to be the base in enhancing knowledge capability by building on both knowledge possession and knowledge-operation capabilities. At the same time, a strengthened social capital not only enhances core knowledge resource and knowledge-operating abilities of individual members within an organization but also enriches the grounds of external collaboration for the overall organization.

Social capital can be defined as resources embedded in a social structure. It is purposive actions that lead to optimal access and mobilization of such resources in the process of achieving organizational/social benefits. In this context, the social resources theory (Lin, 1982) has insightfully explored how access to and use of social resources (resources embedded in social networks) positively contribute to improving socio-economic statuses. The theory goes a step beyond to identify how social conventions play a major role in granting access and usability of these resources. Access to and usage of social resources are largely determined by the positions in the hierarchical structure (the strength of position proposition) and the use of weaker ties (the strength of tie proposition). Bourdieu (1986) defines the volume of social capital as a "function of the size of the network and the volume of capital (economic, cultural and symbolic) possessed by networked individuals". Flap (2004) defines social capital as a combination of network size, the relationship strength, and the resources possessed by those in the network. Similar focus on social relations and networks in the process of analysing social capital has also been provided by Portes (1998).

Many researchers working in the field of social capital conceptualized the concept as a collective rather than an individual property and as a relatively immutable endowment, an inherited asset from a distant past (Putnam, 1993; Putnam, 2000). A different group of scholars conceptualizes social capital primarily as an individual asset, embedded in individual networking capacities, which can enable achievement of individual goals, in conjunction with or instead of personal resources (Bourdieu, 1986; Flap, 2004; Portes, 1998). In this context, social capital no longer becomes an ascriptive asset and possible to cultivate by creating and building it (Krishna, 2002). The conceptualization of social capital as an individual asset traces its origin to social network research in the early 1970s. The main research questions which eventually crop up from such a conceptualization are two-fold: first, how individuals invest in social relations and create effective networking ties (social capital); and, second, how individuals utilize their social capital to pronounce prospects of self-betterment – how they make it productive (Lin, 1999).

From a social network perspective, social capital can be classified along two axes:

Bonding social capital: This refers to ties between individuals in a closed homogenous social setting. Bonding social capital is often associated with enhancing intra-communitarian linkage between local communities, enabling increased exchange in a closed networking setup.

Bridging social capital: This refers to ties between individuals in a heterogeneous social setting which crosses social divides or generates networking possibilities between social groups. From a network perspective, bridging social capital places the actors within a structured and inter-connected framework, where each is able to tap into the social network resources of other social groups. It is with the intention to benefit from shared repository of knowledge and other resources that bridging social capital enables creation of vertical ties, often operating across formal hierarchical structures.

Flap (2004) explores how people equipped with better social capital possess enhanced potential in attaining goals. Enhanced networking ties will enable the members to learn from others' failures and successes through effective sharing. The resources of others are helpful in goal attainment because they add to personal skills and experiences, or because they help individuals to develop credentials required to realize otherwise unrealizable goals. An enhanced social capital has been seen as facilitating positive outcomes in diverse domains related to academic performance, intellectual development, health status, occupational attainment, employment opportunities, entrepreneurial success or failure, and even juvenile delinquency, among other things (Cook, 2014).

Following these conceptualizations, it can be said that the notion of social capital in the context of knowledge management contains three ingredients: knowledge resources embedded in a social structure; accessibility to such knowledge resources by individuals; and the capacity to use or mobilize such knowledge resources to conduct purposive actions. Thus conceived social capital contains three intersecting elements: the structural (embeddedness), opportunity (accessibility) and action-oriented (use) aspects (Lin, 1999).

McElroy (2003) suggests that "social capital points to the *value of relationships* between people in firms, and between firms and other firms inclusive of *trust, reciprocity, shared values, networking and norms*" (Putnam, 2000). McElroy uses the term *social innovation capital* to illustrate how firms, as a social system, organise themselves and execute the process of creation and integration of new knowledge. Knowledge creation is therefore social in nature and is embedded in social relations and the way people and systems organise themselves (Young, 2012). In order to improve organizational efficiency, both intra- and inter-organizational social tie-ups can be exploited as a strategy to enhance knowledge capability both at the individual and organizational level.

Internet-enabled web tools, including tools for creation of online communities and virtual space, are now facilitating social aspects of networking. Virtual communities enable individuals to get connected with people and groups, sharing common interests. Purposive and contextual sharing of information, as a result, open up new possibilities for individuals to generate value and knowledge through such effective exchange. Research has shown that virtual community plays an important role in knowledge creation, assimilation and exchange. In the words of Rheingold (1993): "A virtual community is a group of people who may or may not meet one another physically and who exchange words and ideas through the mediation of computer bulletin boards and networks."

The inclusive potential with which today's ICT is infused contributes to ushering in a new era of connectedness, which makes knowledge creation, assimilation and dissemination, both within and across groups, feasible. Making online knowledge acquisition easy, contemporary digital media have immense capacities in boosting social capital (Gur, 2012). Rather than relying on a single "community" or source for information, advice and resources, people do better when they actively venture out in search of opportunity scopes applicable to them, following digital media and web sources for different situations (Hopkins & Thomas, 2004). Hence cultivating social capital within organizations facilitated by web technologies and tools is a major step forward in terms of innovative ways of learning in contemporary organisations.

The credential of knowledge management processes in ushering in effective collaboration will not be realized in the absence of a strengthened base of social capital. Organizational structure, culture and technology must encourage effective exchange, both within and across organizations, to improve social capital of organizational members. Strengthening of social capital happens to be the building premise of the dynamic collaboration we are trying to articulate in this context. A strengthened base of social capital is crucial in not only initiating effective collaborations, both within and across organizations, but also mandatory in sustaining such ties.

6 Three generations of knowledge management in organizational context

The earlier sections explicitly highlight how the conceptualization of knowledge management, its processes and strategies, have considerably altered over time. This is indicative of the fact that the nature of management has also not remained consistent over the years. In this regard, we need to remember that knowledge as an asset, unlike information, is not fixed and objective. It is highly dependent on human elements – such as experiences, skills and attitude – that make it individual bound and unpredictable. Lack of static and tangible elements makes the process of knowledge creation and exchange uncertain and heavily reliant on individual and social factors. While this indicates the dynamic quotient of knowledge, which happens to be its characterizing feature, it subsequently has a spill-over effect in devising strategies for optimal knowledge management.

The fact that knowledge is not static calls for a management approach that is neither universal nor structured and rigid. The human element present in knowledge makes it crucial to manage the resource in accordance with specific contexts, by considering the specificities intrinsic to a particular context. This explains the reason why strategies of knowledge management adopted in varied context to boost organizational performance are not uniform in nature. However, it needs to be remembered that acknowledgement of tacit elements of knowledge and its role in the enhancement of organizational capability was not embraced within the parameters of knowledge management until recently. When knowledge management emerged as a discipline, increasing economic efficiency of firms by storing and reusing codified knowledge accounted to be its primary objective. Over time, not only determining what kind of knowledge is relevant to the development and maintenance of a firm's competitive edge has changed; tactics to manage this dynamic knowledge have also considerably altered with time and with change in social structuring.

Following, we will explain in detail the different generations of knowledge management (KM), in relation to the ethics of knowledge exchange as practised in different temporal spans, in order to provide a trajectory of the way KM has evolved as a practice. Considerable debate exists among scholars regarding the chronological categorization of KM in respect of different generations. In order to evade confusion, we have categorized the generations of KM by following Nonaka and Takeuchi's seminal conceptualization in their work, *The Knowledge Creating Company* (Nonaka & Takeuchi, 1995). The authors conceptualized knowledge creation and transfer in organizations following four processes – socialization, externalization, combination, and internalization. **Socialization** takes place when tacit knowledge gets converted to tacit knowledge. Conversion of tacit knowledge to explicit knowledge leads to

externalization, while **combination** refers to conversion of explicit knowledge into explicit knowledge. Finally, **internalization** takes place when individuals imbibe explicit knowledge and convert that to tacit knowledge. We have categorized generations of knowledge management following the four knowledge exchange processes as furthered by Nonaka and Takeuchi.

Our chronological categorization of three generations of knowledge management practice starts with first-generation KM, where KM practices primarily focused on **combination**. Premising on the conversion of explicit knowledge to explicit knowledge, this generation of KM primarily relied on *codification strategy*.

Second-generation knowledge management, in alliance with technological development, attempted a shift from digital repositories, as maintained in the first generation, towards a more interactive knowledge management system-oriented practice. At this temporal phase, with the effort to create a collective knowledge pool, KM practices started recognizing the importance of organizational members as "knowledge workers". This phase mainly relied on **externalization**, where individual knowledge workers were encouraged to convert their tacit knowledge resources into explicit knowledge assets with a techno-management approach, realized through knowledge management systems (KMS).

Third-generation KM marks a shift from the *collective* focus of its preceding generation and instead encourages development of a *collaborative* knowledge pool. At this generation, KM practice becomes more human-centred and based on tacit knowledge exchange between individual knowledge workers. Contemporary digital technologies (web 2.0 and social media in particular) and its connecting spirit enable **socialization**, which makes KM a collaborative practice, following a personalization strategy (realizing the concept of *ba* [Nonaka & Noboru, 1998], as discussed in Chapter 2 (section 5.2.1)).

While Nonaka and Takeuchi conceptualized **internalization** as conversion of explicit knowledge resource to tacit knowledge, we think internalization is a more all-encompassing aspect and even incorporates conversion of tacit knowledge to tacit knowledge. It is internalization of any knowledge asset, be it tacit or explicit or both, that marks and reflects the knowledge capability of individual knowledge workers. This ethic of knowledge exchange has resided throughout different generations of KM, where the internalizing credentials of knowledge workers have ascertained the success of KM as a practice.

6.1 First-generation knowledge management

The first generation of KM was about applying information technology to accomplish knowledge sharing and coordination across the enterprise. The KM initiatives in this generation emphasized the explicit nature of knowledge and tended to interpret it as an object that can be stored in repositories, manipulated, combined and transferred using technology. These approaches are described as codification strategies for KM (Hansen et al., 1999), or technocratic schools of KM (Earl, 2001). Access to explicit (or codified) knowledge was provided via a centralized electronic repository, providing many an opportunity to search for and retrieve codified knowledge as and when needed. This technology and codification-focused approached was intended to increase efficiency through sharing of knowledge via central repositories of knowledge already existing within organizations. This generation of knowledge management relied on "information portals, a period dominated by explicit representation of information necessary to support back and front office integration" (Snowden et al., 2003). So, during this phase, knowledge was shared via centralized repositories.

This sort of knowledge management helped firms to devise a substitutive strategy in case any member resigned, where organizational knowledge bore evidence of the knowledge resource in possession of the member, which can be easily imparted to the one who newly joins the position of the resigned member. This generation of knowledge management treated human entities of firms as mere instruments or means, thereby easily replaceable.

This brand of knowledge management, while over-engaged with the cultivation of a collective and codified (or explicit) knowledge pool as organizational knowledge (*combination*, as in Nonaka's SECI model), paid little attention to improving the credentials of individual knowledge sources (organizational members). A focus on a centralized organizational knowledge repository, without making avenues for the members to interact and share knowledge among themselves, marks the limitations of this approach. Negligence in nurturing the credentials of individual knowledge sources makes circulation of organizational knowledge highly mechanical, where the resultant exchange fails to bring about any organic growth and innovation.

To summarize, the focus of first-generation KM (FGKM) can be termed as supply-side KM (McElroy, 2003) and its primary characteristic is its overwhelming emphasis on the distribution of existing codified knowledge throughout an organization using information technologies (for example, information indexing and retrieval systems, knowledge repositories, data warehousing, document management systems, etc.).

6.2 Second-generation knowledge management

Unlike first-generation KM, second-generation knowledge management (SGKM) practices are more focused on human resource and KM process in general. Also characterized as demand-side KM (McElroy, 2003), the initiatives in this generation of KM practices focused on production of *new* knowledge. One of the major problems of FGKM was its failure to differentiate between individual and organizational knowledge. SGKM recognizes the importance of individual learning, since all organizational knowledge begins with learning and innovation by individuals. Then only the knowledge held by individuals can be *externalized* (following SECI terminology) to create organizational knowledge.

As implied above, SGKM schemes take a life cycle view (process view) of knowledge in human organizations. FGKM schemes begin by stressing codification and *combination* issues, in the process of which they invariably turn to technology. SGKM, by contrast, starts by invoking a life cycle view of the subject (McElroy, 2003). New knowledge is created and is then subjected to a natural process of validation. Knowledge that survives the validation process is subsequently operationalized, including codification and transfer, following supply-side tradition. Invariably, the adoption of new knowledge leads to the displacement of old, thereby completing the cycle (McElroy, 2003).

Thus SGKM moved the focus to interaction between learning and technology use, because firms gradually realized that access to technology alone cannot deliver comprehensive knowledge management. The initial inception of SGKM can be traced to 1993, when Peter Drucker developed the idea of "knowledge worker and the knowledge-intensive firm" (Tzortzaki & Mihiotis, 2014). This era, however, was given a formal birth in 1995, following publication of Nonaka and Takeuchi's book, *The Knowledge Creating Company* (Nonaka & Takeuchi, 1995). This made explicit the dynamic nature of knowledge through the introduction of the Socialization-Externalization-Combination-Internalization (SECI) model.

As indicated earlier, this generation of knowledge management gives more importance to human resource and KM process; consequently, the focus is shifted from mechanical enhancement of an organizational knowledge pool to eventually developing credentials of individual knowledge sources. Organizational members, from being mere employees, are transcended to the status of knowledge workers in this phase. SGKM recognizes the ability of individual knowledge sources to share their own knowledge asset, thereby contributing to the organic enhancement of a collective knowledge pool through *externalization*. Emphasis on individual knowledge sources in an attempt to enrich the collective knowledge pool enables SGKM to overcome the limitations of FGKM.

6.3 Third-generation knowledge management

KM practices in the second generation primarily emphasized capturing, accumulating and disseminating knowledge through knowledge management systems (KMS) (Boughzala & Dudezert, 2011). KMS refer to IT-based systems developed to support and enhance the organizational processes of knowledge creation, storage/retrieval, transfer and application (Alavi & Leidner, 2001). Yet for many organizations, KMS became enormous repositories whose use was hindered by the sheer volume of data and the associated difficulties of keeping the knowledge accurate and up to date (Alavi et al., 2005).

Moreover, the "socialization" component, as proposed in Nonaka's SECI model, to facilitate conversion of tacit to tacit knowledge through collaborative exchange of knowledge among peers was missing from second-generation initiatives. Several scholars therefore identified the need for a third-generation knowledge management, which should be closer to democratization and personalization of work and focus more on heuristic or tacit knowledge (Snowden,

2002; Sveiby, 1997). Knowledge management at third generation has been increasingly identified as a collaborative social process, instead of being an engineered method of management. In this era the focus of knowledge management shifted to creation of new knowledge, through voluntary sharing of knowledge within organizations, between organizations and with external partners (Tzortzaki & Mihiotis, 2014).

The technological innovations that trigger third-generation knowledge management are the internet and internet-enabled applications in general and web 2.0 and mobile applications (for example, social media) in particular. These enable pervasiveness of virtual communication, which is enhanced by ubiquitous computerization and advanced networking technology (Dutta & Mia, 2007). Web 2.0 has come into vogue in the last couple of years, following the concept of collaborative and interactive communications through internet-based virtual communities (O'Reilly, 2005). Through the web 2.0 platform, traditional knowledge management with a centralized knowledge repository has shifted into a more interactive conversational approach. That is why third-generation knowledge management practices are also referred to as KM 2.0. We will discuss this aspect in detail in the next chapter.

By fostering relevant exchange and effective virtual collaborations, contemporary technology has opened up new possibilities for human agency. It is this human agency in third-generation knowledge management that facilitates innovative ways of collaborative knowledge creation, assimilation and dissemination within firms. Focusing on people, collaboration and cooperation, methods of knowledge management as followed in the third generation primarily include action-reviews, peer-assists and knowledge cafes as a means to increase mass-scale knowledge exchange. The increased globalized setting of the 21st century spelt out the urgency to take knowledge management and apply it in a social setting. This highlighted the need to evolve knowledge management as a practice to deal directly with how people and organizations create and utilize knowledge and understanding on a daily basis (Limaye et al., 2017). Knowledge management, following this essence, cannot be practised if organizational knowledge is treated as a passive repository.

Third-generation knowledge management uses interactive tools enabling synchronous (for example, online chat using text, audio and/or video) and asynchronous (for example, instant messaging, discussion forums) communication to enable conversation towards knowledge exchange and the generation of new ideas for innovation in an interactive online environment (referred to as *ba* by Nonaka and Noboru [1998]). Social capital is cultivated online as members interact with each other, disregarding geographic boundaries to gain ideas and insight (Young, 2012). These features would support what Von Krogh et al. (2000) call conversation and dialogue at the heart of the knowledge-creation processes, and what Laurillard (2007) calls a conversational framework at the heart of learning. In this way it is possible to see the development of third-generation knowledge management with an emphasis on valuing conversation and dialogue. The exploitation of conversation in the interactive space within the virtual environment is a key component of human and social capital development (Young, 2012).

This transition from conventional to *conversational* knowledge management was made possible by contemporary digital technologies and social media, which facilitated informal knowledge sharing among social actors across social spaces (Lee & Lan, 2007). With increasing emphasis on human interaction, coupled with a connecting digital infrastructure, the foundations of knowledge management shifted from knowledge repositories to conversational collaborative premise. The conventional approach to knowledge management primarily focused on collection of knowledge in a centralized repository and its accessibility, whereas a *conversational approach* to knowledge management emphasizes integration and collaboration of knowledge creation among knowledge workers. In its conversational sense, knowledge management became increasingly associated with management of tacit knowledge resources of knowledge workers with the help of contemporary digital technologies. In facilitating effective collaboration, knowledge management practices followed in the third generation, with the aid of digital infrastructure, attempted to harness *collaborative* intelligence (Lee & Lan, 2007).

Collaborative intelligence as a concept, facilitated by internet-enabled interactive networking technologies such as web 2.0 (O'Reilly, 2005), gains precedence in our research context, as compared to collective intelligence. Although human interaction accounts to be the premise of collective intelligence, the concept retains its inclination for a centralized authority determining which knowledge is to be packaged as "collective" intelligence. Knowledge management practice undertaken to boost collective intelligence, as has been to some extent followed in the second generation of knowledge management, follows entirely a macro perspective, which inevitably favours organizational interest or interest of the whole over the interest of individual parts or knowledge workers employed by an organization. It is nonetheless true that capability expansion of individual knowledge workers seems to be useless unless they are embedded in an organizational/social fabric. However, it needs to be remembered that these individual members must be recognized as potential knowledge sources in order to usher in democratic and efficient knowledge exchange, mandatory for boosting overall organizational capability.

Collaborative intelligence, being intrinsic to third-generation knowledge management, has the potential to bring out the power of networked knowledge. Networked knowledge, derived from active participation and knowledge transaction between individual knowledge workers, in the absence of a centralized authority, fosters knowledge exchange voluntarily by individual knowledge workers in an attempt to boost organizational capability. Managerial practice dedicated to cultivating collaborative intelligence has the optimum capacity to usher in knowledge management following both macro and micro dimensions.

In an attempt to cultivate collaborative intelligence, the objective of knowledge management following web 2.0 can be listed as the following (Lee & Lan, 2007):

- Contribution – knowledge management practices must support contribution from one and all, thereby identifying every human agent as a potential knowledge source.
- Sharing – knowledge management must facilitate sharing of both tacit and explicit knowledge resources so that knowledge content is made freely available.
- Collaboration – knowledge management practices must facilitate collaboration by encouraging collaborative creation and maintenance of knowledge content by knowledge providers.
- Dynamic – knowledge management practice must adopt a flexible approach, which will enable the practice to remain dynamic and in tune with changing socio-economic environment.
- Reliance – knowledge contribution, undertaken as a knowledge management measure, must be based on trust between knowledge providers and domain experts. Knowledge exchange based on reliable bonds can to a great extent limit inappropriate use of knowledge.

Acknowledgement of the above-mentioned dimensions within knowledge management practice has only been recently attempted and is distinctive of the managerial tactics as followed in its third generation. It is only in the third generation that knowledge management became a social process, by not only enabling management of tacit and explicit knowledge resources, both within and across organizations, but also by enabling firms to exploit the potential of connecting with external agents (*crowd knowledge*) in boosting its competitive advantage. Only such a holistic approach towards knowledge management, coupled with the aid of contemporary digital infrastructure, has the potential to enhance the knowledge capability of organizations.

7 Conclusion

While this chapter has focused intensively on the evolution of knowledge management as a concept and practice, the next chapter discusses the intricacies of contemporary digital technologies, which have made possible the evolution of knowledge management in such a way. As we have seen in this chapter, emergence of knowledge management as a concept dates back a long way. However, the inclusive and *conversational* way in which it is encouraged to practice today, giving equal importance to explicit and tacit knowledge resources, have only been possible because of the connecting spirit with which contemporary digital technologies are infused. The detailed description regarding the technicalities and functionalities of contemporary technologies, as postulated in the following chapter, will illuminate and justify the evolution of knowledge management in accordance to technical development along relational terms.

References

Adolf, M. & Stehr, N. (2014). *Knowledge*. New York: Routledge.

Ahmed, S., Fiaz, M. & Shoaib, M. (2015). Impact of Knowledge Management Practices on Organizational Performance: An Empirical Study of Banking Sector in Pakistan. *FWU Journal of Social Sciences*, 9(2), 147–167.

Alavi, M. & Leidner, D.E. (1998). Knowledge Management and Knowledge Management Systems: Conceptual Foundations and an Agenda for Research. INSEAD Working Paper 98/57/TM Retrieved from: https://flora.insead.edu/fichiersti_wp/inseadwp1998/98-57.pdf.

Alavi, M. & Leidner, D.E. (1999). Knowledge Management Systems: Issues, Challenges, and Benefits. *Communications of the AIS*, 1(7). Retrieved from: http://blog.ub.ac.id/izuaf/files/2013/11/Knowledge-Management-Systems-ISSUES-CHALLENGES-AND-BENEFITS.pdf.

Alavi, M. & Leidner, D.E. (2001). Review: Knowledge Management and Knowledge Management Systems: Conceptual Foundations and Research Issues. *MIS Quarterly*, 25(1), 107–136. Retrieved from: http://www.jstor.org/stable/3250961.

Alavi, M., Kayworth, T.R. & Leidner, D.E. (2005). An empirical examination of the influence of organizational culture on knowledge management practices. *Journal of Management Information Systems*, 22(3), 191–224.

Andreeva, T. & Ikhilchik, I. (2011). Application of the SECI Model of Knowledge Creation in Russian Cultural Context: Theoretical Analysis. *Knowledge and Process Management*, 18, 56–66. doi:10.1002/kpm.351.

Appleyard, M. (1996). How Does Knowledge Flow? Interfirm Patterns in the Semiconductor Industry. *Strategic Management Journal*, 17, 137–154.

Bernard, J.G. (2006). *A typology of knowledge management system use by teams*. In proceeding of the 39th Hawaii International Conference on System Science. doi:10.1109/HICSS.2006.34.

Bohn, R. (1994). Measuring and Managing Technological Knowledge. *Sloan Management Review*, 61–72.

Boughzala, I. & Dudezert, A. (2011). *Knowledge Management 2.0: Organizational Models and Enterprise Strategies* (pp. 1–282). Hershey, PA: IGI Global. doi:10.4018/978-1-61350-195-5.

Bourdieu, P. (1986). "The Forms of Capital," in G. John Richardson (Ed.), *Handbook of Theory and Research for the Sociology of Education* (pp. 241–258). Westport, CT: Greenwood Press.

Brown, J.S. & Duguid, P. (1998). Organizing Knowledge. *California Management Review*, 40(3), 90–111.

Byukusenge, E., Munene, J. & Orobia, L. (2016). Knowledge Management and Business Performance: Mediating Effect of Innovation. *Journal of Business and Management Sciences*, 4(4), 82–92.

Cook, K.S. (2014). Social Capital and Inequality: The Significance of Social Connections. *Handbook of the Social Psychology of Inequality*. Retrieved from: https://www.springer.com/gp/book/9789401790017.

Dahiya, D., Gupta, M. & Jain, P. (2012). Enterprise Knowledge Management System: A Multi Agent Perspective. *Information Systems, Technology and Management*, 285(4), 271–281.

Dutta, S. & Mia, I. (2007). *Global Information Technology Report 2006–2007*. Retrieved from: https://digitalscholarship.unlv.edu/cgi/viewcontent.cgi?article=1275&context=lib_articles.

Dutton, J. & Thomas, A. (1985). "A Relating Technological Change and Learning by Doing," in R. Rosenbloom (Ed.), *Research on Technological Innovation, Management and Policy* (pp. 187–224). Greenwich, CT: Jai Press.

Earl, M.J. (2001). Knowledge management strategies: Toward taxonomy. *Journal of Management Information Systems*, 18(1), 215–233.

Epetimehin, F.M. & Ekundayo, O. (2011). Organisational knowledge management: survival strategy for Nigeria insurance industry. *Interdisciplinary Review of Economics and Management*, 1(2), 9–15.

Flap, H.D. (2004). *Creation and Returns of Social Capital*. London: Routledge.

Fong, P.S.W. & Choi, S.K.Y. (2009). The Processes of Knowledge Management in Professional Service Firms in the Construction Industry: A Critical Assessment of Both Theory and Practice. *Journal of Knowledge Management*, 13(2), 110–126.

Gao, T., Chai, Y. & Liu, Y. (2018). A Review of Knowledge Management about Theoretical Conception and Designing Approaches. *International Journal of Crowd Science*, 2(1), 42–51. doi:10.1108/IJCS-08-2017-0023.

Gold, A., Malhotra, A. & Segars, A. (2001). Knowledge Management: An Organizational Capabilities Perspective. *Journal of Management Information Systems*, 18, 185–214. doi:10.1080/07421222.2001.11045669.

Greiner, M., Bohmann, T. & Krcmar, H. (2007). A Strategy for Knowledge Management. *Journal of Knowledge Management*. doi:10.1108/13673270710832127.

Gur, A. (2012). Bowling Online: Examining Social Capital and the Impact of Internet-Generated Interactions. *College Undergraduate Research Electronic Journal, University of Pennsylvania*. Retrieved from: http://repository.upenn.edu/curej/152.

Hansen, M.T., Nohria, N. & Tierney, T. (1999). What's Your Strategy For Managing Knowledge? *Harvard Business Review*, 77(2), 106–116.

Hopkins, L. & Thomas, J. (2004). e-social capital: Building community through electronic networks. Institute for Social Research, Swinburne University. Retrieved from: https://pdfs.semanticscholar.org/c0c0/c05c16b93089abe11b568893b9e76314598f.pdf.

Horwitch, M. & Armacost, R. (2002). Be all it can be: Helping knowledge management. *Journal of Business Strategy*, 26. doi:10.1108/eb040247.

Hung, S.Y., Durcikova, A., Lai, H.M. & Lin, W.M. (2011). The influence of intrinsic and extrinsic motivation on individuals' knowledge sharing behaviour. *International Journal of Human-Computer Studies*, 69(6), 415–427.

Inkpen, A.C. & A. Dinur. (1998). Knowledge Management Processes and International Joint Ventures. *Organization Science*, 9, 454–468.

Kayworth, T. & Leidner, D. (2003). *Organizational Culture as a Knowledge Resource* (1st ed.). Heidilberg: Springer-Verlag.

Kiernan, P. & Sugden, J. (2018). Two Top US Economists Win Nobel for Work on Growth and Climate. *The Wall Street Journal*. Retrieved from: https://www.wsj.com/articles/nobel-in-economics-goes-to-american-pair-1538992672.

Kirby, W. (2005). Personal knowledge management: supporting individual knowledge worker performance. *Knowledge Management Research and Practice*, 3(3), 156–165. doi:10.1057/palgrave.kmrp.8500061.

Krishna, A. (2002). *Active Social Capital: Tracing the Roots of Development and Democracy*. New York: Columbia University Press.

Laszlo, K.C. & Laszlo, A. (2002). Evolving Knowledge for Development: The Role of Knowledge Management in a Changing World. *Journal of Knowledge Management*, 6(4), 400–412. doi:10. 1108/13673270210440893.

Laurillard, D. (2007). "Pedagogical forms for mobile learning," in N. Pachler (Ed.), *Mobile learning: towards a research agenda*. London: WLE Centre, IoE.

Lee, M. & Lan, Y. (2007). From Web 2.0 to Conversational Knowledge Management. Towards Collaborative Intelligence. *Journal of Entrepreneurship Research*, 2(2), 47–62.

Leonard, D. & Sensiper, S. (1998). The Role of Tacit Knowledge in Group Innovation. *California Management Review*, 40(3), 112–132. doi:10.1142/9789814295505_0013.

Liao, S.-h. & Wu, C.-c. (2009). The Relationship Among Knowledge Management, Organizational Learning and Organizational Performance. *International Journal of Business and Management*, 4(4), 64–76. Retrieved from: https://pdfs.semanticscholar.org/f998/8b009e07ac73d30091e8fadf471aa5de74d5.pdf.

Liebskind, J. (1996). Knowledge Strategy and the Theory of the Firm. *Strategic Management Journal*, 17, 93–107.

Limaye, R., Sullivan, T., Dalessandro, S. & Jenkins, A. (2017). Looking through a Social Lens: Conceptualizing Social Aspects of Knowledge Management for Global Health Practitioners. *Journal of Public Health Research*. 6(761). doi:10.4081/jphr.2017.761.

Lin, N. (1999). Building a network theory of social capital. *Connections*, 22, 28–51.

Lin, N. (1982). "Social resources and instrumental action," in P.V. Marsden and N. Lin (Eds.), *Social structure and network analysis* (pp. 131–145). Beverly Hills, CA: Sage.

Malhotra, Y. (2004). "Why Knowledge Management Systems Fail? Enablers and Constraints Of Knowledge Management in Human Enterprises," in M.E.D. Koenig and T.K. Srikantaiah (Eds.), *Knowledge Management Lessons Learned: What Works and What Doesn't* (pp. 87–112). Medford: NJ: Information Today.

McElroy, M.W. (2003). *The New Knowledge Management: Complexity, Learning, and Sustainable Innovation*. Boston, MA: Butterworth-Heinemann.

Nahapiet, J. & Ghoshal, S. (1998). Social Capital, Intellectual Capital and the Organizational Advantage. *Academy of Management Review*, 23(2), 242–258.

Ning, Y., Shu, P. & Feng, B. (2006). *Knowledge Capability: A Definition and Research Model*. Proceedings of the International Conference on Knowledge Science, Engineering and Management, Lecture Notes in Computer Science, 4092, 330–340. doi:10.1007/11811220_28.

Nonaka, I. (1994). A dynamic theory of organizational knowledge creation. *Organization Science*, 5(1), 14–37.

Nonaka, I. & Noboru, K. (1998). The concept of Ba: Building a Foundation for Knowledge Creation. *California Management Review*, 40(3). Retrieved from: http://home.business.utah.edu/actme/7410/Nonaka%201998.pdf.

Nonaka, I. & Takeuchi, H. (1995). *The Knowledge Creating Company: How Japanese Companies Create the Dynamics of Innovation*. New York: Oxford University Press.

O'Reilly, T. (2005). What is Web 2.0. Retrieved from: http://www.oreillynet.com/pub/a/oreilly/tim/news/2005/09/30/what-is-web-20.html.

Pauleen, D.J. & Gorman, G.E. (2011). *Personal Knowledge Management: Individual, Organizational and Social Perspectives*. Farnham: Gower Publishing Limited.

Pizziconi, V. & Wiig, K. (1997). Knowledge Management: Where did it come from and where will it go? *Journal of Expert Systems with Applications*, 13(1), 1–14.

Portes, A. (1998). Social capital: its origins and applications in modern sociology. *Annual Review of Sociology*, 24, 1–24.

Putnam, R. (1993). *Making democracy work: civic traditions in modern Italy*. Princeton, NJ: Princeton University Press. doi:10.2307/j.ctt7s8r7.

Putnam, R.D. (2000). *Bowling Alone: The Collapse and Revival of American Community*. New York: Touchstone.

Rasula, J., Vuksic, V.B. & Stemberger, M.I. (2012). The Impact of Knowledge Management on Organizational Performance. *Economic and Business Review*, 14(2), 147–168.

Rheingold, H. (1993). *The Virtual Community: Homesteading on the Electronic Frontier*. Cambridge, MA: MIT Press.

Rouse, M. (2013). Knowledge Management. Retrieved from: https://searchdomino.techtarget.com/definition/knowledge-management.

Saito, A., Umemoto, K. & Ikeda, M. (2007). A Strategy-Based Ontology of Knowledge Management Technologies. *Journal of Knowledge Management*, 11(1), 97–114. doi:10.1108/13673270710728268.

Semple, E. (2012). *Organizations Don't Tweet, People Do: A Manager's Guide to the Social Web*. Chichester: John Wiley & Sons.

Serenko, A. & Bontis, N. (2004). Meta-review of Knowledge Management and Intellectual Capital Literature. *Knowledge and Process Management*, 11(3), 185–198.

Sherif, K., Hoffman, J. & Thomas, B. (2006). Can technology build organizational social capital? The case of a global IT consulting firm. *Information & Management*, 43(7), 795–804. Retrieved from: http://www.sciencedirect.com/science/article/pii/S0378720606000681.

Skyrme, D.J. (2002). The 3Cs of Knowledge Sharing: Culture, Co-opetition and Commitment. Retrieved from: http://www.skyrme.com/updates/u64_f1.htm.

Snowden, D. (2002). Complex acts of knowing: paradox and descriptive self-awareness. *Journal of Knowledge Management*, 6(2), 35–56.

Snowden, D., Stanbridge P., Shelton R. & Sage J. (2003). Study on market prospects, business needs and technological trends for business knowledge management-KMME study. European Commission DG Information Society, Pre-Final Report. Retrieved from: https://ec.europa.eu/information_society/doc/library/business_knowledge_management.pdf.

Stenberg, E. & Thi, X. (2017). *A Literature Review of the Field of Knowledge Management Systems* (Master's thesis on research design and methods, Halmstad University, Sweden). Retrieved from: http://urn.kb.se/resolve?urn=urn:nbn:se:hh:diva-33247.

Sveiby, K.E. (1997). *The New Organisational Wealth: Managing and Measuring Knowledge-Based Assets*. San Francisco, CA: Berrett-Koehler Publishers.

Swacha, J. (2015). Gamification in knowledge management: motivating for knowledge sharing. *Polish Journal of Management Studies*, Czestochowa Technical University, Department of Management, 12(2), 150–160. Retrieved from: https://ideas.repec.org/a/pcz/journl/v12y2015i2p150-160.html.

Tohidinia, Z. & Mosakhani, M. (2010). Knowledge sharing behavior and its predictors. *Industrial Management & Data Systems*, 110(4), 611–631.

Turner, J. R., Zimmerman, T. & Allen, J. (2012). Teams as a Sub-Process for Knowledge Management. *Journal of Knowledge Management*, 16(6), 963–977.

Tzortzaki, A. & Mihiotis, A. (2014). A Review of Knowledge Management Theory and Future Directions. *Knowledge and Process Management*, 21(1), 29–41. doi:10.1002/kpm.1429.

Umemoto, K. (2002). "Managing Existing Knowledge Is Not Enough: Recent Developments In Knowledge Management Theory And Practice," in C.W. Choo and N. Bontis (Eds.), *The Strategic Management of Intellectual Capital and Organizational Knowledge* (pp. 463–476). Oxford: Oxford University Press.

Umemoto, K., Endo, A. & Machado, M. (2004). From Sashimi to Zen-In: The Evolution of Concurrent Engineering at Fuji Xerox. *Journal of Knowledge Management*, 8(4), 89–99.

Von Krogh, G., Ichijo, K. & Nonaka, I. (2000). *Enabling Knowledge Creation: How to Unlock the Mystery of Tacit Knowledge and Release the Power of Innovation*. Oxford: Oxford University Press. doi:10.1093/acprof:oso/9780195126167.001.0001.

Wang, K.Y., Tan, L.P., Cheng, S.L. & Wong, W.P. (2015). Knowledge Management Performance Measurement: Measures, Approaches, Trends and Future Directions. *Information Development*, 31(3).

Wiig, K. (2000). Knowledge Management: An Emerging Discipline Rooted in a Long History. *Knowledge Horizons: The Present and the Promise of Knowledge Management*. doi:10.1016/B978-0-7506-7247-4.50004-5.

Wong, Y.K. & Aspinwall, E. (2005). An empirical study of the important factors for knowledge-management adoption in the SME sector. *Journal of Knowledge Management*, 9(3), 64–82. doi:10.1108/13673270510602773.

Xue, C. (2017). A Literature Review on Knowledge Management in Organizations. *Research in Business and Management*, 4(1). doi:10.5296/rbm.v4i1.10786.

Young, J. (2012). *Personal Knowledge Capital* (1st ed.). Amsterdam: Elsevier.

Zack, M.H. (1999). Developing a knowledge strategy. *California Management Review*, 41(3), 125–145.

Zaim, H. (2006). Knowledge Management Implementation in IZGAZ. *Journal of Economic and Social Research*, 8(2), 1–25.

8 Social technology and knowledge management practices

1 Introduction

The preceding chapter highlighted how knowledge management as a practice evolved in a business context in tandem with technological development. This chapter takes a reverse strand and attempts to show how contemporary technology, apart from being a potential knowledge-exchange medium, has significantly contributed to making knowledge management a social process in its current form. We have reserved the term *social technology* to refer to this contemporary digital technology. While we will provide formal definitions to justify the terminology usage, social technology in this context is an umbrella term used to capture a wide variety of terminologies depicting internet-enabled communications, platforms and tools – for example, web 2.0, mobile 2.0, social media, social software, etc. – which have the potential to establish *collaborative connectivity* among billions of individuals over the globe.

The inclusive spirit of social technology, in facilitating effective networking between and across social groups, has given new dimensions to the practice of knowledge management. Contemporary social technology not only supports organizations to create and exchange their explicit knowledge resources, but its potential to foster informal communication enables organizations to use social technology to encourage exchange of the tacit knowledge resource of organizational knowledge workers. In addition to this, social technology has the potential to optimally capture and apply crowd knowledge in the process of boosting competitive advantage of organizations. Its credentials allow social technology not only to qualify to be a potential medium in fostering knowledge management practice, but, rather, the transition of knowledge management practice to a social process in its current form has largely been made possible with the aid of these contemporary digital technologies.

The ability of social technology to facilitate effective collaboration has made *sharing* the premise of contemporary social and economic transactions. The emergence of a sharing economy in the 21st century, guided by the principal of using social technology to foster effective collaboration, has significantly altered extant and traditional economic practices. This emergent economy identifies every human entity as a potential producer/consumer of knowledge, therefore

146 *Conceptual foundations*

an able contributor to the collaborative economic framework. It is the connecting spirit of contemporary social technologies that has paved the path for optimal capturing and application of crowd knowledge to generate socio-economic benefits. This chapter explicitly articulates how the enlisted credentials of social technologies can be harnessed to create an inclusive knowledge management framework.

The chapter is divided into two main sections: the first, after providing definitions of social technology and its associated components, attempts to characterize the same to arrive at the prospects it has to offer in both the economic and social domain. The latter section discusses practical instances of organizations utilizing social technology as a medium to facilitate knowledge management practices. The practical evidence placed amidst theoretical characterization of social technologies will enable the reader to analyse the role contemporary digital technologies play in transforming knowledge management practice into a social process.

2 Social technology: A conceptual perspective

We have entered into a new *networked world*. Technology has enabled us to interact, innovate and share knowledge in ways previously unthinkable. We call this the Networked Society (Castells, 2004), facilitated by internet-enabled communications, platforms and tools that include regular personal computers, embedded computers and mobile personal devices (cell phones, PDAs, tablets), connected together using computer networking technologies. We call them *social technology*, an umbrella term used to capture a wide variety of terminologies depicting internet-enabled communications, platforms and tools – for example, web 2.0, mobile 2.0, social media, social software, etc. – which have the potential to establish *collaborative connectivity* among billions of individuals across the globe. This digital revolution is giving rise to a new economy – a "digital network economy" (Brousseau & Nicolas, 2007). When two persons connect, their lives change. With everything connected, our world changes.

This concept of a connected world using social technology has the potential to transform the way we innovate, produce, govern and sustain ourselves (Fitzgerald et al., 2013; Greenstein et al., 2013). This internet-enabled digital economy has already started transforming the organization of firms, industries, markets and commerce (OECD, 2008). Some of these impacts can be exemplified as follows:

- Billions of people now use social media for learning, marketing, shopping and decision-making. Internet-based social media sites enable us to create and consume multi-modal user-generated content; and facilitate us to stay connected with friends, family, colleagues, customers and clients. Social networking can have a social purpose, a business purpose, or both, through sites such as Facebook, Twitter, LinkedIn and Instagram, among others.

Social networking has become a significant base for the marketing and advertising sectors seeking to engage customers. Increasing use of social media platforms – including social networking sites, blogs, video sharing sites, etc. – now allows consumers to seamlessly share their consumption behaviours online. Such *socially shared consumption* (Kunst & Ravi, 2014) can range from electronic word-of-mouth to formal online reviews, as well as automated product mentions facilitated by social media applications.

- The rapid development of social technology has enabled the development of what we call the new *platform economy* (Parker et al., 2016; Parker et al., 2017), an emerging economic arrangement which brings together strangers in one forum and fosters effective exchange of goods and services among them (for example, Airbnb, Lyft, LendingClub, etc.). In this digitally driven platform economy, consumers and service providers form a collaborative network using the platform. Platform is the foundation of the entire ecosystem, providing a space for the exchange of information, trading, logistics and other facilities to consumers and service providers. They perform various economic activities on the platform, including information exchange, demand matching, payment and receipt and delivery of goods. The participants of the platform economy interact and cooperate with each other, which enables creation of greater value.

- The notion of platform economy, being a digital facilitator in economic and social transaction, is premised on the ideological and operative dynamics of sharing/collaborative economy (Sundararajan, 2016). This nascent form of economic arrangement encourages shared creation, production, distribution, trade and consumption of goods, services and ideas by *crowd* (for example, YouTube, Airbnb, Etsy, BlaBlaCar, etc.), and hence is termed *crowd-based capitalism* (Sundararajan, 2016). This attempt to build an integrated economy through effective sharing of goods (both informational goods and physical goods) and services is premised on the motivational and philosophical foundation of "sharism". The collaborative culture cultivated by a sharing economy has enabled billions of people across the globe to get connected and actively participate in the process of achieving social development and developing collectively capacities to solve social atrocities (Tapscott & Williams, 2006).

- The notion of *crowd collaboration* in a business context is an extension of what is known as outsourcing: operationalizing some of the internal business functions using external business entities. However, instead of an organized business body with a centralized governing apparatus, crowd collaboration has a decentralized premise and relies on free individual agents (the *crowd*) to collaborate to perform a given operation or to find solutions for a given problem using social technologies (Tapscott & Williams, 2006). This kind of outsourcing is also referred to as *crowd-sourcing* (Horton & Chilton, 2010), to reflect this difference. These crowd-based operations may be incentivized by monetary or equivalent reward, though it is not always mandatory.

- Benkler (2006) uses the term "networked information economy" and "commons-based peer production" to describe a "system of production, distribution, and consumption of information goods characterized by decentralized individual action carried out through widely distributed, non-market means that do not depend on market strategies". The examples of such collaborative efforts are creation of free and open source software and Wikipedia.

Today, an increasing proliferation of social technologies – which include broadband connectivity, web technologies, mobile devices, social media and cloud services – enables us to share the infrastructure and resources available anywhere in the world. We are seeing manifestations of this phenomenon in the creation of flourishing business models (Airbnb, Uber, Kickstarter, etc.) that rely heavily on the principles of collaborative consumption and sharing economy (Sundararajan, 2016). People are now living in a "digitally-connected global society" where each individual in a crowd of people has the potential and opportunity to collaborate for a social mission and share their expertise and knowledge to help others in the community. As depicted by Tapscott (2014), "For over a century humanity has been taking steps to realize (Nathaniel) Hawthorne's vision of a world where human intelligence could be networked. That age has arrived.... The Age of Networked Intelligence is an age of promise. It is not simply about the networking of technology but about the networking of humans through technology. It is not an age of smart machines but of humans who, through networks, can combine their intelligence, knowledge, and creativity for breakthroughs in the creation of wealth and social development. It is an age of vast new promise and unimaginable opportunity."

2.1 Defining social technology

Historically, "social technology" has two meanings (Li & Bernoff, 2012): a term related to "social engineering", a concept developed in the 19th century (Pelikan, 2003; Nelson, 2002; Nelson & Sampat, 2001; North & Wallis, 1994; Sugden, 1989; Schotter, 1981); and a term to depict "internet-enabled *social software*", a concept that evolved in the early 21st century (Duarte, 2011; Andersen, 2011; Derksen et al., 2012; Chui et al., 2012).

As the conceptualization of social technologies varies from "social engineering" to "social software", for our purpose we will be focusing on the second depiction of social technology and try to derive the meaning of social technologies in terms of "digital technologies used by people to interact socially and together to create, enhance, and exchange content" (Duarte, 2011; Andersen, 2011; Derksen et al., 2012; Chui et al., 2012). Social technologies are defined as any digital technology used for social purposes or on a social basis, and include social hardware (traditional communication tools such as PCs or smart mobile devices), social software (operating platforms such as web 2.0 or mobile 2.0) and socially enabled applications (tools and services such as social media) (Alberghini et al., 2010).

Social technologies are instantly comprehensible via some kind of media. Koo et al. (2011) describe several new-generation media types: "telephone is a traditional medium; video conferencing, email and instant messenger representing computer media; and blog and social networks representing new social media." Communication technologies such as telephone, voicemail, email, video conferencing and instant messaging all help virtual team or group members stay in touch and share information with each other.

Chui et al. (2012) define social technologies as digital technologies that people use to interact with each other socially to create, enhance and exchange content. The following three characteristics distinguish social technologies from other technologies:

- Social technology is a derivative of information technology.
- Social technology provides rights to communicate with anyone and create and/or modify content in a distributed fashion.
- Social technology provides distributed access to communication tools and digital content.

2.2 Components of social technologies

As indicated earlier, social technology in our context is an umbrella term used to capture a wide variety of terminologies depicting internet-enabled communications, platforms and tools – such as web 2.0, mobile 2.0, social media tools, social software, etc. – which have the potential to establish *collaborative connectivity* among billions of individuals across the globe. In the following sub-sections we will illustrate these components of social technology.

2.2.1 Web 2.0: From mass communication to communication by the masses

As per the World Wide Web Consortium (W3C), "The World Wide Web is the universe of network-accessible information, an embodiment of human knowledge." Web 1.0 was the first generation, facilitating the static web presence of several companies, e-commerce and information repositories. Generally, websites in the web 1.0 era are known as *Read-Only Web*, since they are engineered, designed, developed and maintained by professional web developers or content experts. Users can only view them, without any provision to contribute.

Web 2.0 – also termed "Read-Write Web", Participative (or Participatory) web (Blank & Reisdorf, 2012) or Social Web – is the second generation of the World Wide Web that enables and encourages users' contributions and interactions. Web 2.0 technologies allow for many common web applications, such as social networking, blogs, wikis and many other tools for real-time collaboration (Zyl, 2009). O'Reilly (2005) originally coined the term web 2.0 to

150 *Conceptual foundations*

differentiate the dynamic, collaborative and interactive features of web 2.0 from the static, non-interactive features of web 1.0. Web 2.0 has shifted the directionality of the flow of content over the internet from a purely producer-centred model to a more multi-directional model enabling participation of any individual and generation of online content by the masses (Kim et al., 2009).

Thus web 2.0 has opened opportunities for participation by ordinary users in content generation. Any user can produce and consume content over the internet using any application on the web 2.0 platform, be it user-generated videos in YouTube, product reviews in Amazon or status updates in Facebook, etc. Blank and Reisdorf (2012) describe web 2.0 as an "antithesis of the mass society model (Rosenberg & White, 1957) of mass media that has dominated Western societies for the past 150 years". The production and distribution of content by mass media require large amounts of investment, which is available only to large organizations such as radio and television networks, newspapers, book publishers, etc. With the emergence of the web 2.0 platform, we notice a huge shift from a "mass society model" to a personalized production and distribution model (Benkler, 2006).

According to Blank and Reisdorf (2012), success of web 2.0 depends on two primary features. First, the "network effects", indicating that the value of product or service increases with increasing numbers of users. On the internet, network effects are easier to achieve, since users' participation can grow very easily on the web 2.0 platform. For example, the value of video-sharing platforms such as YouTube or social networking sites such as Facebook is high because of the network effects that have facilitated user growth. The second feature of web 2.0 is the "platform" itself, which creates simple and reliable environments where users can participate and interact. Examples of web 2.0-enabled platforms include social networking sites (Facebook, for example), video-sharing sites (YouTube), hosted services, blogs, wikis and collaborative consumption platforms (such as Airbnb, Lyft, etc.). The two components are intimately linked: the platform provides the structure that helps network effects to emerge, provided large numbers of users believe that the platform is valuable. Based on this analysis, Blank and Reisdorf (2012) define web 2.0 as: "Using the internet to provide platforms through which network effects can emerge."

2.2.2 Mobile 2.0: The social web meets mobility

Web 2.0 is primarily a collection of browser-based internet technologies that enable anyone with a computer and internet connection to participate in any web 2.0 platform. Mobile 2.0 is a successor to web 2.0, leveraging the strength and capabilities of web 2.0-supported applications and extending them to the mobile platform, making them more powerful and usable through mobile apps. Mobile web 2.0, or simply mobile 2.0, is used to improve and enrich mobile computing, enabling users to access the advanced features of the web anytime, anywhere, on the go using mobile apps.

The way people interact with mobile phones and the way they conduct their daily lives are changing. Users are exposed, via a mobile phone, to services that just a few years ago could not have been imagined (Boyera, 2007). These services encompass web applications including social media services that integrate GPS, camera, maps, mobile wallet; the list continues. In today's world, mobile devices act as complex carriers for receiving and providing multi-modal information, and, at the same time, as platforms for novel services. The mobile applications are also generating newer possibilities that enable the mobile devices to act as a powerful interface to communicate with the external world through ubiquitous access to the internet.

In the near future we may assume that the web 2.0 services will mainly be accessed from mobile devices. One obvious reason for using mobile web is that users can access web 2.0 and related internet-enabled services anywhere, anytime, on the go with an internet-connected smartphone. Smartphones enable us not only to gain access to internet on the go, but also to combine functions of the device (GPS, camera, etc.) with the capabilities of the internet. Many mobile apps draw information from the web or are run almost entirely from the web. At the same time, mobile web uses the context aware services that probe the location, state of user (walking/sitting), availability of user (from calendar), weather, etc. to personalize the service provisioning.

2.2.3 Socially enabled applications: Social media

Traditionally, internet, in the age of web 1.0, used to be only a content provider and users were passive consumers of content. Increasingly, consumers are utilizing applications on web 2.0-enabled platforms – social networking, blogs and wikis, etc. – to interact by producing and consuming content. These socially enabled applications on web 2.0 platforms can be described as *social media*, which can now significantly impact the dynamics of interactions within informal social groups and formal organizations. These applications – such as blogs, video sharing (for example, YouTube), presentation sharing (e.g., SlideShare), social networking (e.g., Facebook, LinkedIn), instant messaging (e.g., Skype) and groupware (e.g., Google Docs) – facilitate the active participation of users, thereby promoting a more socially connected digital platform (Anderson, 2007). According to Kietzmann et al. (2011), "Social media employ mobile and web-based technologies to create highly interactive platforms via which individuals and communities share, co-create, discuss, and modify user-generated content."

There is a general agreement as to what digital tools may be *classified* under social media, but there is no single definition of social media, especially across disciplines (Carr & Hayes, 2015). Social media have often been conceptualized techno-centrically, often considered to be synonymous with web 2.0 (O'Reilly, 2005). Additionally, most of the time the term "social media" and "social networking sites (SNS)" are used interchangeably. Although SNS (for example, Facebook, Twitter, etc.) by their nature are typically social media tools, not all social media are inherently social networking sites (Carr & Hayes, 2015).

Some existing definitions focus on the nature of message exchange pattern in social media. For example, Russo et al. (2008, p. 22) defined social media as "those that facilitate online communication, networking, and/or collaboration", and Lewis (2010, p. 2) described it as a "label for digital technologies that allow people to connect, interact, produce and share content". However, according to Carr and Hayes (2015), "these definitions are problematic in that they could easily be applied to other communication technologies such as email, missing the unique technological and social affordances that distinguish social media".

We will follow the definition by Carr and Hayes (2015), who define social media as: "*Internet-based channels* that allow users to *opportunistically interact and selectively self-present*, either in *real-time or asynchronously*, with both *broad and narrow audiences* who derive *value from user-generated content* and the *perception of interaction* with others." The clarifications of the terms are given below (based on Carr and Hayes (2015)):

Internet-based: Social media are a set of online tools operating on the internet. Web 2.0 may be sufficient, but not necessary, for developing social media tools.

Opportunistically interact and selectively self-present (also known as *channel dis-entrainment*): In a face-to-face communication, both the participating agents in the communication dyad need to present simultaneously. However, in social media the user participates as and when he or she is willing to do that (Walther, 1996).

Either in real-time or asynchronously: Although social media support real-time chat functionalities (synchronous communication), social media predominantly provide asynchronous communication tools that do not require simultaneous presence of interacting participants, making temporal commitments discretionary; the user can participate whenever he/she wants to participate in a social media channel (Walther, 1995; 1996).

Broad and narrow audiences (also termed masspersonal communication): Masspersonal communication refers to situations when "mass communication channels are used for interpersonal communication, interpersonal channels are used for mass communication, and when individuals simultaneously engage in mass and interpersonal communication" (O'Sullivan & Carr, 2018). Social networking sites such as Facebook and Twitter, for example, are ideal venues to explore masspersonal communication, where users are allowed to broadcast messages to a mass audience, or multicast messages to a group or audience, or unicast messages to a single audience; while, on the other hand, receivers may reply either interpersonally to the individual or group or through mass messages of their own (Walther et al., 2010).

User-generated value: According to Carr and Hayes (2015), "the value (i.e., benefit or enjoyment) of using social media is derived from the contributions from or interactions with other users rather than content generated by organization or individual hosting the medium". The value of the social medium may be different from its content, generated by an individual user/organization. For example, a broadcast message on a product or service may be promoted in a social media channel by an organization, but individuals may derive greater utility and value not from the message itself but from the user-generated comments about that message. Their perception about the product or service may be less influenced by the organization-generated message than by the peer feedback (Walther et al., 2010).

Perception of interaction with others: With the proliferation of digital agents, algorithms and other artificial intelligence-based mechanistic features operating online, it is possible that users *perceive* an interactive element while operating on a social media channel, even if that interaction is not with other human users. In other words, a social media channel provides a sense of interactive engagement with others, even when the interaction is not with human users. Additionally, geocentric services such as Foursquare (a local search-and-discovery mobile app) and Tinder (a location-based social search mobile app) may "allow an individual to perceive herself or himself as interacting with others in a specific location (e.g., airport terminal, city park) even without message exchange—merely acknowledging the presence of others may facilitate perceptions of interaction" (Lindqvist et al., 2011).

Vuori (2011) characterizes and categorizes social media applications from the perspective of 5C – *communication, collaboration, connecting, completing* and *combining* – as illustrated below:

Communication: Social media tools provide opportunities to publish content, express opinions and create influence through sharing content and/or opinion. Communication is executed through blogs and microblogs (for example, Twitter), media-sharing systems (e.g., YouTube, SlideShare, etc.) and instant messaging (e.g., WhatsApp), etc.

Collaboration: Social media enables users to create and edit content collectively without location and time constraints. Wikis (for example, Wikipedia) are examples of social media applications supporting collaborative creation and updating of content.

Connecting: Social networking sites enable users to form online virtual communities by connecting people with similar interests and creating communities around these interests.

Completing: Social media tools are used to augment content or connect content with other content. Examples are Pinterest, Google Reader and Digg.

Combining: Combined social media sites are typically called mashups, meaning "a coherent combination of pre-existing web services that allow a certain user within a platform to use another application, in a specific window, without the need to get out of the initial website" (Bonson & Flores, 2011). Google Maps, for example, allows users to pinpoint geographically the locations of hotels and restaurants, and so on.

This categorisation of the 5Cs is only suggestive. There are social media tools that support two or more functionalities (Jalonen, 2014). For example, Facebook and Twitter can embed videos and photographs from another location on the web; similarly, wikis can provide RSS feeds to keep up with updates on a certain article (Vuori, 2011).

Social media have had a significant impact on patterns of communication between organizations, communities and individuals. Organizations have now started using social tools to improve internal collaboration, interact with customers, solve problems in a distributed fashion using *crowd* knowledge, etc. In this age, leaders of consumer-facing companies in particular have started using co-creation both to solve problems and engage their customers. This creates an immensely challenging environment for firms, as many established management practices are not well-suited to deal with customers who no longer want to listen to organization-generated content; instead, they want organizations to listen to their voice and want to get appropriately engaged with the organization.

3 Social technology and knowledge management

3.1 Networking and collaboration

Organizational knowledge management is currently undergoing a positive transformation due to the proliferation of social technology usage, both at personal and organizational level. This trend is changing the traditional knowledge management implementations (monolithic, centralized and controlled) to implementations based on digital networking and collaborative sharing (Krogh, 2012; Mujadi et al., 2006). In this section we will show how social technologies alter knowledge management practices within an organization (Faraj et al., 2011). As pointed out by Chatti et al. (2007): "In the modern media and knowledge-intensive era of collaboration culture, the one-size-fits-all, centralized, static, top-down, and knowledge-push models of traditional learning initiatives need to be replaced with a more social, personalized, open, dynamic, emergent, and knowledge-pull model for learning."

Social media are fundamentally disrupting the way employees deal with knowledge. Bebensee et al. (2011) argue that social media and other socially enabled applications have three layers of relevance to knowledge management. First, they are based on socially oriented principles, including peer production and unbounded collaboration. Second, these applications, such as social networking, media sharing, blogs, wikis, etc., are easy to use. Third, they are based on open platforms and enabling services that rely on network effects. Many of the social media platforms offer significant benefits to users (for example, YouTube) because of network effects.

In a case study of knowledge management in a multinational firm (Krogh, 2012), Paroutis and Saleh (2009) show that employee-generated content through blogging and other socially enabled applications helped people to share knowledge to perform their job more effectively and efficiently. It also enhanced management of personal knowledge using intelligent search techniques that helped employees find answers to important questions and stay informed about the relevant news, etc. In such a learning context, technology not only connects individuals to digital repositories of knowledge but also to other people, thereby creating a peer-to-peer learning environment. Such an environment enables people to share ideas, collaboratively creating new content and getting effective support to learn with and from peers (Chatti et al., 2007).

The knowledge management models in this context focus on the social aspect of managing knowledge and place a strong emphasis on community building through knowledge networking that would help to use, share and sustain knowledge in a collaborative way. Such communities and networks can only be created if the members of the organization can transcend organizational boundaries to involve all stakeholders, including peers, customers, partners, suppliers and various types of formal and informal communities relevant for that organization. This requires a participatory culture with relatively low barriers to self- expression and a strong support for an open culture, enabling 360-degree knowledge sharing. In a participatory culture, members feel socially connected with each other and feel encouraged to contribute, since they believe that their contributions matter (Chatti et al., 2007).

3.2 The social technology and SECI model-based knowledge processes

Nonaka and Takeuchi (1995) adopt a dynamic model of knowledge management, known as the SECI model, with a focus on knowledge creation, collaboration and practice (discussed in Chapter 7). The model represents four modes of knowledge conversion: socialization (tacit to tacit), externalization (tacit to explicit), combination (explicit to explicit) and internalization (explicit to tacit). Chatti et al. (2007) have shown how social media and other web 2.0 technologies are ideal tools to implement Nonaka's SECI knowledge-creation theory, facilitating all *socialization, externalization, combination* and *internalization* processes. This is illustrated below:

Socialization: Following the concept of *ba*, as proposed by Nonaka and Noboru (1998), the *socialization* process starts with building a "field" or "space" of social interaction. The knowledge within individuals, or the *tacit* knowledge, is sometimes difficult to codify but can be shared through social interaction. This interaction in an online virtual space can enable sharing of tacit knowledge through collaborative participation using both informal and formal networks. Social media greatly facilitate building of such virtual spaces and transfer tacit knowledge from one person to another through text-audio-video chat, social networking sites (for example, Twitter or Facebook), etc. Community-based features of social media coupled with ease of use, informality and openness create an environment in which social interactions and tacit knowledge sharing are better facilitated (Gordeyeva, 2010; Zheng et al., 2010). Social media support the sharing of tacit knowledge by encouraging social connections and informal communication among experts and non-experts by providing a collaborative as well as a brainstorming space for new knowledge creation via open participation, dialogue and discussion using online communication tools such as audio–video conferencing and instant messaging systems. This also helps to reduce the time and effort needed for knowledge sharing (Gordeyeva, 2010).

Social networking sites (SNS) promote building of social community of practices (CoP), enabling tacit knowledge flow within community members having similar learning interests (Chatti et al., 2007; Hildrum, 2009). Embedded instant messaging and discussion forums in purposive social networking sites support users to exchange tacit practical knowledge among participants (Raisanen & Oinas-Kukkonen, 2008). In addition, SNS tend to increase interpersonal trust through closer social connectivity and more frequent communication among members that, in turn, helps to transfer tacit knowledge more effectively (Gordeyeva, 2010).

Externalization: This refers to the process of knowledge conversion from tacit to explicit knowledge, thus creating new, codified knowledge from tacit knowledge. Social media in general provide unique opportunities to capture context-rich knowledge through content creation and exchange. Blogs, for example, facilitate the externalization process by allowing the users to create and distribute content, thus providing a space not only to capture personal knowledge but also to distribute the reflection of others on that knowledge through contextualized discussions across blogs. Wikis, for example, can influence both externalization (codification of personal knowledge) and internalization of tacit knowledge (integrating the information provided by wiki with an individual's knowledge base) (Cress & Kimmerle, 2008). It helps knowledge sharing by providing a space for collaborative knowledge capturing and sharing through social interactions (Chatti et al., 2007; Gordeyeva, 2010). In wikis, encyclopedic-style knowledge repositories may evolve through the iterative integration of user-generated content. In this context it is important to note that knowledge can be expressed and captured in social media through multi-modal representation and expression, which include text, audio, graphics and images, video, etc. Each mode of representation has its own affordances and its own strategies for representing knowledge (Kress, 2003). Hence users need to be familiar with a range of different modes of expressions to determine most effective mode(s) in representing and communicating their knowledge in social media.

Combination: This is the process of integrating different bodies of explicit knowledge. Knowledge can only be stored and accessed once it has become codified, or *explicit*. Blogs and wikis combine context-rich and searchable explicit knowledge assets using distributed, community-driven knowledge repositories. During the combination process, new knowledge is created through reconfiguration and reorganization of existing explicit knowledge. Other examples are mashups (Fichter, 2013) that can be used to combine content from more than one source, remixing and assembling it to form a new service.

Internalization: This is the process of personalizing explicit knowledge into tacit knowledge. Internalization is a process of *personal knowledge management* (PKM), which enables an individual to manage his or her personal knowledge and augment it with newly acquired tacit knowledge, obtained through conversion of explicit knowledge (Razmerita et al., 2009; Jarche, 2013).

Social media tools also facilitate internalization through PKM through tacit knowledge sharing.

3.3 Social media analytics and customer knowledge management

Social media are widely used in business today to grab the attention of consumers and influence them to make purchase decisions (He et al., 2018). At the same time, consumers also use social media platforms to share information and express opinions, experiences and evaluations about various products and services. Such "socially shared consumption" (Kunst & Ravi, 2014) can range from electronic word-of-mouth in personal social networking circles to online reviews and reflections on those reviews in designated online forums, all facilitated by social media applications. The pervasive use of social media platforms has generated massive consumer-generated content. Before taking a purchase decision, millions of consumers now depend on consumer-generated reviews on social media to evaluate products and services (Laroche et al., 2013).

To extract knowledge about their customers' likes and preferences from the customer-generated content, organizations need to develop capability to collect, store and analyse social media data to derive actionable insights for decision-making and forecasting (Duan et al., 2013; Schoen et al., 2013; He et al., 2016). As an outcome of this requirement, *social media analytics* has emerged as an important area of study. Numerous companies have now devised social media analytics tools (for example, Hoodsuite, Sprout Social, Google Analytics, Radian 6, etc.) that help organizations "to collect, monitor, analyze, summarize, and visualize social media data to facilitate conversations and interactions to extract useful patterns and intelligence" (Fan & Gordon, 2014).

Customer knowledge has three components: *knowledge for customer, knowledge about customers* and *knowledge from customers* (Gebert et al., 2002; He et al., 2018).

1. *Knowledge for customers*: This is a uni-directional flow of product/service knowledge from organizations to customers to advertise their products/service offering and activities of organizations. Nowadays, organizations are using social media extensively not only to advertise their products/service offering but also to demonstrate their offerings using audio–visual aids (such as an organization's own Facebook pages, online advertisements in selected social media channels, discussions about their offerings in designated blogs/forums, YouTube for product demonstration, etc.). At the same time, organizations can analyse the effectiveness of any marketing campaign by monitoring customer feedback using social media analytics tools.
2. *Knowledge about the customer:* Organizations are always trying to understand the needs of customers in order to satisfy them. At the same time, organizations are also trying to track the customers' preferences and motivations, as well as their demographic and psychographic characteristics

(Zembik, 2014). Organizations are adopting different analytics tools to trace the digital footprints of customers in order to gain knowledge about the customers.

3   *Knowledge from the customer:* Organizations are always concerned about customers' impressions, expectations, experiences and insights regarding a product or service. This valuable knowledge from the customer can be used for service and/or product improvement. The knowledge gathered from customers can also be used by organizations towards reputation and brand management, quality monitoring, sales and marketing, etc. For example, an organization can use such knowledge to predict a crisis situation (Jin et al., 2014). Additionally, a company could analyse the customer reviews of its products on its Facebook or Twitter pages to gain critical business insight and knowledge about customer satisfaction regarding its products or services, such as identifying product flaws, improving product quality and maximizing product differentiation.

In summary, social media analytics has had a strong impact, and implications for the management and use of online information suggest great potential to generate new knowledge and business value (He & Xu, 2016).

3.4 Management of crowd knowledge for organizational benefits

In a connected world, organizational knowledge need not be cultivated within the organizational boundary. Using social technologies, organizations can leverage the knowledge of people outside company borders (Krogh, 2012), such as external experts, consumers and a host of *unidentifiable outsiders* who could be potential contributors to the organizational knowledge pool. These *unidentifiable outsiders* may be termed as *crowd*. An evolving knowledge management practice driven by social media is a *crowd-based* approach to managing knowledge (Newell, 2014). Traditionally, the word "crowd" is used to designate an unorganized or self-organized group of people around a common purpose or experience. Today, organizations try to exploit the knowledge of "crowd" for organizational benefits. Crowd-sourcing, defined as outsourcing business responsibilities to crowds using information technology, can significantly influence the ability of an organization to build competitive advantage, leveraging *crowd* knowledge. As a result, firms build *crowd capital*, which is "a heterogeneous knowledge resource generated by an organization through its use of crowd capability, which is defined by the structure, content, and process by which an organization engages with the dispersed knowledge of the *crowd*" (Prpic & Shukla, 2013).

Many organizations have successfully exploited the potential of crowdsourcing as a productive tool. According to Benkler and Nissenbaum (2006), "Commons-based peer production is a socio-economic system of production that is emerging in the digitally networked environment. Facilitated by the technical infrastructure of the Internet, the hallmark of this socio-technical system is collaboration among large groups of individuals who cooperate effectively to provide information, knowledge or cultural goods without relying on either market pricing or managerial hierarchies to coordinate their common enterprise."

Wikipedia and similar cyber-knowledge resources are good examples of how wisdom of crowd can be exploited for community benefit. Numerous e-learning platforms connect knowledge seekers with knowledge providers over the internet. In this context, crowd knowledge capital may be conceived as a heterogeneous knowledge resource, derived from dispersed knowledge of the *crowd*, and it can become a key resource (a form of capital) to facilitate distributed knowledge transfer.

Two fundamental challenges can be identified with this new approach (Krogh, 2012). The first is the problem of knowledge spill-over outside the organization's boundaries. Traditionally, organizational knowledge is considered to be a valuable resource that needs to be protected. However, through the use of social media, proprietary knowledge could be spilled-over outside the organization. A second problem is the risk of diluting the organization's proprietary knowledge. This problem arises because of easy accessibility to knowledge outside the organizational boundary through the use of social media tools. Hence employees might tend to use knowledge from publicly available resources that are also available to competitors. Thus there is a chance of dilution of proprietary knowledge. Another related issue is the reliability of external, unreliable knowledge sources that may find their way into the organizational knowledge repositories.

3.5 *Enterprise social software:* Social *tools for knowledge management*

Enterprise social software (ESS) is a class of socially enabled applications used within an organization and usually integrated with other enterprise-wide software platforms (for example, ERP). ESS is a general term that describes social networking and collaboration tools used in large organizations (Enterprise Social Software, (n.d.).) Usually ESS can be accessed from computers or mobile devices and it provides an organization with real-time communication channels and a flexible and dynamic social platform. An organization uses ESS to improve transparency across the organization and to make relevant information easily accessible, irrespective of location and the organization's hierarchy.

ESS offers user-friendly and flexible tools that facilitate natural and active engagement between all stakeholders – including employees, suppliers, distributors, partners and other business entities – by allowing them to get connected and interact anytime, anywhere. It not only encourages employee engagement but also enables real-time knowledge sharing and innovation, thus improving organizational efficiency and promoting collaborative culture. At the same time, ESS helps the utilizing and showcasing of internal experts and knowledge, promotes informal learning and enhances employee satisfaction and performance. Some ESS tools are described below:

IBM Connections [https://www.ibm.com/in-en/marketplace/ibm-connections-engagement-center] IBM Connections is a leading social software platform that helps people to get engaged in critical business processes with networks of experts. Along with complete social analytics tools and metrics to analyse characteristics of networks and communities, it integrates *social* platforms with IBM software and third-party applications including Microsoft applications, such as Microsoft's Office, SharePoint, Outlook and Windows Explorer.

Nuclino [https://www.nuclino.com/] Nuclino is the easiest way for teams to organize and share knowledge. It creates collaborative documents in real time and instantly connects them as a wiki. It uses tree, board, and graph view to explore and organize knowledge visually.

eXo Platform [https://www.exoplatform.com/] eXo Platform is an open-source collaboration platform that delivers knowledge, document and content management, project collaboration tools and social engagement, integrated into the applications for an enterprise. eXo Platform helps to build bridges between employees, tools and information, transforming organizational practices through improved collaboration.

Yammer [https://www.yammer.com/] Yammer is termed as a corporate-friendly platform for business networking with *social* features that helps businesses manage all forms of internal communications. The software facilitates communication using many different channels and includes a large repository of documents with provision to create collaborative documents. It can easily be integrated with many other platforms and is accessible from all mobile devices. Yammer is an intelligent system that not only gathers stores and evaluates information but also protects critical information and uses a robust set of analytic tools to generate reports that can provide actionable insights.

Slack [https://slackhq.com/] Slack is a messaging app that offers one platform for providing real-time messaging, file sharing, archiving and searching. Slack enables communities, groups or teams to join via a specific URL or invitation sent by a team administrator or owner. Slack is not only an organizational communication tool but also a community engagement platform. With a large number of third-party services, Slack supports integration with Trello, Google Drive, Dropbox, etc.

Workplace by Facebook [https://work.facebook.com/] Workplace by Facebook is a social network solution that is designed to cater to businesses and employees. It offers users a host of benefits to promote better communication and improved collaboration. It provides tools that are very similar to Facebook tools and can be used, among other applications, to join groups, share information and organize events. The platform can be used for employees to create profiles, connect with others via instant messaging and create groups for individuals who share interests with each other or those from common departments.

Zoho Connect [https://www.zoho.com/connect/] Zoho Connect is a software application for enterprise social networking that allows people to connect, share ideas and disseminate information with their colleagues. Users can also post messages, leave comments, share files and hold discussions in real time. Zoho Connect basically functions as a private social network of businesses enabling collaboration and realization of concepts.

4 Conclusion

So far we have discussed the potential of social technology in realizing a holistic vision of knowledge management within an organization, leading to organizational benefits. Some researchers refer to these initiatives as "social knowledge management" in organizational context (for example, Helmes et al., 2017). Although there is a plethora of research dealing with application of social technologies for knowledge management within a business organization to enhance the organizational performance, there is no explicit proposal for knowledge management in the context of society at large where the objective is to manage knowledge for social development.

Therefore, *social knowledge management* can also be defined as the management of knowledge for social development. Knowledge management, as practised in a contemporary phase (third generation) uses crowd knowledge to boost the competitive advantage of firms. This emergent emphasis to facilitate both intra- and inter-organizational knowledge management reflects how knowledge management as a practice has already expanded beyond the boundaries of particular organizations. The task now becomes to assess how the strategy can be effectively used not just to boost organizational performance but also to achieve overall social benefit. Utilizing knowledge management for social cause happens to be the primary accelerating force behind our research drive.

The inter-connected digital ecosystem, built by social technologies, serves to be the implementing premise of our *social knowledge management framework*, which has been detailed in Chapter 10. However, before the conceptual and implementational dynamics of our social knowledge management framework is articulated, we have reserved the following chapter to discuss the efforts undertaken to manage social knowledge and information for social benefit. While knowledge management as a formal strategy has gained popular recognition in an organizational context, it is seldom applied in a social context. However, this should not imply that the activity of managing social knowledge for social benefit is an undone phenomenon. Historically, social functioning has been achieved as a result of informal knowledge collaboration, where social knowledge has been managed for social benefit. The following chapter bears reference to attempts undertaken to manage social knowledge and information and how the efforts evolved over time and with the emergence of digital technologies.

References

Alberghini, E., et al. (2010). *Implementing knowledge management through IT opportunities: definition of a theoretical model based on tools and processes classification.* Proceedings of the 2nd European Conference on Intellectual Capital, Lisbon, Portugal, 22–33.

Andersen, K.N. (2011). *Social Technologies and Health Care: Public Sector Receding, Patients at the Steering Wheel?* Conference proceedings of Social Technologies 11: ICT for Social Transformations, 17–18.

Anderson, P. (2007). *What is Web 2.0? Ideas, technologies and implications for education.* JISC reports. Retrieved from: http://www.jisc.ac.uk/media/documents/techwatch/tsw0701b.pdf.

Bandyopadhyay, S., Banerjee, S., Bardhan, A., Dey, P. & Das, S. (2015). *A Social Knowledge Management Framework for Harnessing Collective Knowledge Capital of Senior Citizens.* Proceedings of the 12th International Conference on Intellectual Capital, Knowledge Management & Organisational Learning. Retrieved from: http://toc.proceedings.com/28324webtoc.pdf.

Bebensee, T., Helms, R. & Spruit, M. (2011). Exploring Web 2.0 applications as a means of bolstering up knowledge management. *Electronic Journal of Knowledge Management*, 9, 1–9.

Benkler, Y. (2006). *Wealth of Networks: How Social Production Transforms Markets and Freedom.* New Haven, CT: Yale University Press.

Benkler, Y. & Nissenbaum, H. (2006). Commons-based peer production and virtue. *Journal of Political Philosophy*, 14, 394–419.

Blank, G. & Reisdorf, B. (2012). The Participatory Web. *Information, Communication and Society*, 15(4), 537–554. doi:10.1080/1369118X.2012.665935.

Bonson, E. & Flores, F. (2011). Social media and corporate dialogue: the response of the global financial institutions. *Online Information Review*, 35(1), 34–49.

Boyera, S. (2007). *Opportunities and Challenges of Web Technologies on Mobile Platform.* Proceedings of the Datamatix Gitex Conference, Dubai, UAE. Retrieved from: http://www.w3.org/2007/08/sb_gitex/all.html.

Brousseau, E. & Nicolas, C. (2007). *Internet and Digital Economics: Principles, Methods and Applications.* Cambridge: Cambridge University Press.

Carr, C.T. & Hayes, R.A. (2015). Social media: Defining, developing, and divining. *Atlantic Journal of Communication*, 23(1). doi:10.1080/15456870.2015.972282.

Castells, M. (2004). *The network society: a cross-cultural perspective.* Northampton, MA: Edward Elgar Publishing.

Chatti, M.A., Klamma, R., Jarke, M. & Naeve, A. (2007). *The Web 2.0 driven SECI model-based learning process.* Proceedings of the 7th IEEE International Conference on Advanced Learning Technologies. Retrieved from: http://kmr.nada.kth.se/papers/TEL/CKJN_ICALT07.pdf.

Chui, M., et al. (2012). *The Social Economy: Unlocking Value and Productivity Through Social Technologies. McKinsey Global Institute Report.* Retrieved from: https://www.mckinsey.com/industries/high-tech/our-insights/the-social-economy.

Cress, U. & Kimmerle, J. (2008). A systemic and cognitive view on collaborative knowledge building with wikis. *International Journal of Computer-Supported Collaborative Learning*, 3, 105–122.

Derksen, M., et al. (2012). Social technologies: Cross-disciplinary reflections on technologies in and from the social sciences. *Theory Psychology*, 22(2), 139–147.

Duan, W., Cao, Q., Yu, Y. & Levy, S. (2013). *Mining online user-generated content: using sentiment analysis technique to study hotel service quality.* Proceedings of the 46th Hawaii International Conference on System Sciences, 3119–3128. doi:10.1109/HICSS.2013.400.

Duarte, A.T. (2011). *Privacy and Health System Solution Case.* Conference proceedings of Social Technologies 11: ICT for Social Transformations, 17–18.

Enterprise Social Software (n.d.). Retrieved from: https://www.techopedia.com/definition/30928/enterprise-social-software-ess.

Fan, W. & Gordon, M.D. (2014). The power of social media analytics. *Communications of the ACM*, 57(6), 74–81.

Faraj, S., Jarvenpaa, S.L. & Majchrzak, A. (2011). Knowledge collaboration in online communities. *Organization Science*, 22, 1224–1239.

Fichter D. (2013). What Is a Mashup? Retrieved from: http://books.infotoday.com/books/Engard/Engard-Sample-Chapter.pdf.

Fitzgerald, M., Kruschwitz, N., Bonnet, D. & Welch, M. (2013). Embracing Digital Technology: A New Strategic Imperative. *MIT Sloan Management Review*.

Gebert, H., Geib, M., Kolbe, L. & Riempp, G. (2002). *Towards customer knowledge management: integrating customer relationship management and knowledge management concepts.* Proceedings of the 2nd International Conference on Electronic Business, 296–298. Retrieved from: https://pdfs.semanticscholar.org/7368/257ce51d96a8cb0cde68b6f1c5efad179205.pdf.

Greenstein, S., Goldfarb, A. & Tucker, C. (2013). *Economics of Digitization*, International Library of Critical Writings in Economics series. Northampton, MA: Edward Elgar Publishing.

Gordeyeva, I. (2010). Enterprise 2.0: Theoretical foundations of social media tools' influence on knowledge sharing practices in organizations. (Master's thesis, University of Twente, Netherlands). Retrieved from: http://essay.utwente.nl/59921/1/MA_thesis_I_Gordeyeva.pdf.

He, W. & Xu, G. (2016). Social media analytics: unveiling the value, impact and implications of social media analytics for the management and use of online information. *Online Information Review*, 40(1). doi:1108/OIR-12-2015-0393.

He, W., Tian, X., Chen, Y. & Chong, D. (2016). Actionable social media competitive analytics for understanding customer experiences. *Journal of Computer Information Systems*, 56(2), 145–155.

He, W., Weidong, Z., Xin, T., Ran, T. & Vasudeva, A. (2018). Identifying customer knowledge on social media through data analytics. *Journal of Enterprise Information Management*, 32(1), 152–169. doi:10.1108/JEIM-02-2018-0031.

Helmes, R., Cranefield, J. & Reijsen, J. (2017). *Social Knowledge Management in Action – Applications and Challenges.* Heidelberg: Springer.

Hildrum, J.M. (2009). Sharing tacit knowledge online: A case study of e-learning in Cisco's network of system integrator partner firms. *Industry & Innovation*, 16, 197–218.

Horton, J.J. & Chilton, L.B. (2010). *The Labor Economics of Paid Crowdsourcing.* Proceedings of the 11th ACM Conference on Electronic Commerce, 209–218. doi:10.1145/1807342.1807376.

Jalonen, H. (2014). *Social Media and Emotions in Organisational Knowledge Creation.* Proceedings of the Federated Conference on Computer Science and Information Systems, Warsaw. Retrieved from: https://annals-csis.org/Volume_2/pliks/39.pdf.

Jarche, H. (2013). Personal Knowledge Management. Retrieved from: http://www.jarche.com/wp-content/uploads/2013/03/PKM-2013.pdf.

Jin, Y., Liu, B.F. & Austin, L.L. (2014). Examining the role of social media in effective crisis management: the effects of crisis origin, information form, and source on publics crisis responses. *Communication Research*, 41(1), 74–94.

Kietzmann, J.H., Hermkens, K., McCarthy, I.P. & Silvestre, B.S. (2011). Social media? Get serious! Understanding the functional building blocks of social media. *Business Horizons*, 54(3), 241–251. doi:10.1016/j.bushor.2011.01.005.

Kim, D.J., Hall, S.P. & Gates, T. (2009). Global diffusion of the Internet XV: Web 2.0 technologies, principles, and applications: A conceptual framework from technology push and demand pull perspective. *Communications of the Association for Information Systems*, 24, 657–672.

Koo, C., et al. (2011). Examination of how social aspects moderate the relationship between task characteristics and usage of social communication technologies (SCTs) in organizations. *International Journal of Information Management*, 31, 445–449.

Kress, G. (2003). *Literacy in the New Media Age*. New York: Routledge.

Krogh, G.V. (2012). How does social software change knowledge management? Toward a strategic research agenda. *The Journal of Strategic Information Systems*, 21(2), 154–164. doi:10.1016/j.jsis.2012.04.003.

Kunst, K. & Ravi, V. (2014). *Towards a Theory of Socially Shared Consumption: Literature Review, Taxonomy, and Research Agenda*. Proceedings of the 22nd European Conference on Information Systems. Retrieved from: https://pdfs.semanticscholar.org/b722/b0ed3cce8093514c8b7946478d3bdbbf71c8.pdf.

Laroche, M., Habibi, M.R. & Richard, M.O. (2013). To be or not to be in social media: how brand loyalty is affected by social media. *International Journal of Information Management*, 33(1), 76–82.

Lewis, B.K. (2010). Social media and strategic communication: Attitudes and perceptions among college students. *Public Relations Journal*, 4(3), 1–23.

Li, C. & Bernoff, J. (2012). *Groundswell: Winning in a World Transformed by Social Technologies*. Cambridge, MA: Harvard Business School Press Books.

Lindqvist, J., Cranshaw, J., Wiese, J., Hong, J. & Zimmerman, J. (2011). *I'm the mayor of my house: Examining why people use foursquare-a social-driven location sharing application*. Proceedings of SIGCHI Conference on Human Factors in Computing Systems, Vancouver. doi:10.1145/1978942.1979295.

Mujadi, H., Takeda, H., Shakya, A., Kawamoto, S., Kobayashi, S., Fujiyama, A. & Ando, K. (2006). *Semantic Wiki as a lightweight knowledge management system*. Conference proceedings of Semantic Web, 4185, 65–71. Retrieved from: http://www-kasm.nii.ac.jp/papers/takeda/06/muljadi06aswc.pdf.

Nelson, R.R. (2002). Bringing institutions into evolutionary growth theory. *Journal of Evolutionary Economics*, 12, 17–28.

Nelson, R.R. & Sampat, B.N. (2001). Making Sense of Institutions as a Factor Shaping Economic Performance. *Journal of Economic Behavior and Organization*, 44, 31–54.

Newell, S. (2014). Managing knowledge and managing knowledge work: What we know and what the future holds. *Journal of Information Technology*, 30(1), 1–17.

Nonaka, I. & Noboru, K. (1998). The concept of Ba: Building a Foundation for Knowledge Creation. *California Management Review*, 40(3), 40–54. doi:10.2307/41165942.

Nonaka, I. & Takeuchi, H. (1995). *The Knowledge Creating Company: How Japanese Companies Create the Dynamics of Innovation*. New York: Oxford University Press.

North, D. & Wallis, J. (1994). Integrating institutional change and technological change in economic history: a transaction cost approach. *Journal of Institutional and Theoretical Economics*, 150, 609–624.

OECD (2008). The Future of the Internet Economy. Policy brief. Retrieved from: www.oecdministerialseoul2008.org.

O'Reilly, T. (2005). What is Web 2.0? Design patterns and business models for the next generation of software. *International Journal of Digital Economics*, 65, 17–37.

O'Sullivan, P.B. & Carr, C.T. (2018). Masspersonal communication: A model bridging the mass-interpersonal divide. *New Media & Society*, 20(3), 1161–1180. doi:10.1177/1461444816686104.

Parker, G., Alstyne, M.V. & Choudary, S. (2016). *Platform Revolution: How Networked Markets are Transforming the Economy, and How to Make Them Work for You.* New York: W.W. Norton.

Parker, G., Van Alstyne, M.V. & Jiang, X. (2017). Platform Ecosystems: How Developers Invert the Firm. *MIS Quarterly*, 41(1), 255–266.

Paroutis, S. & Al Saleh, A. (2009). Determinants of knowledge sharing using Web 2.0 technologies. *Journal of Knowledge Management*, 13(4), 52–63. doi:10.1108/13673270910971824.

Pelikan, P. (2003). Bringing institutions into evolutionary economics: another view with links to changes in physical and social technologies. *Journal of Evolutionary Economy.* 13, 237–258.

Prpic, J. & Shukla, P. (2013). *The theory of crowd capital.* Proceedings of the 46th Annual Hawaii International Conference on Systems Sciences. Retrieved from: http s://arxiv.org/ftp/arxiv/papers/1210/1210.2013.pdf.

Raisanen, T. & Oinas-Kukkonen, H. (2008). *A system architecture for the 7C knowledge environment.* Proceedings of the 17th European- Japanese Conference on Information Modelling and Knowledge Bases, Pori, Finland. 217–236.

Razmerita, L., Kirchner, K. & Sudzina, F. (2009). Personal Knowledge Management: The Role of Web 2.0 tools for managing knowledge at individual and organisational levels. *Online Information Review*, 33(6), 1021–1039.

Rosenberg, B. & White, D.M. (1957). *Mass Culture: The Popular Arts in America.* Glencoe, IL: Free Press.

Russo, A., Watkins, J., Kelly, L. & Chan, S. (2008). Participatory communication with social media. *Curator: The Museum Journal*, 51, 21–31. doi:10.1111/j.2151-6952.2008.tb00292.x.

Schoen, H., Gayo-Avello, D., Metaxas, P.T., Mustafaraj, E., Strohmaier, M. & Gloor, P. (2013). The power of prediction with social media. *Internet Research*, 23(5), 528–543.

Schotter, A. (1981). *The economic theory of social institutions.* Cambridge: Cambridge University Press.

Sugden, R. (1989). Spontaneous order. *Journal of Economic Perspectives*, 3(4), 85–97.

Sundararajan, A. (2016). *The Sharing Economy – The End of Employment and the Rise of Crowd-Based Captitalism.* Cambridge, MA: MIT Press.

Tapscott, D. (2014). *The Digital Economy.* New York: McGraw-Hill.

Tapscott, D. & Williams, A.D. (2006). *Wikinomics: How Mass Collaboration Changes Everything.* London: Portfolio.

Vuori, V. (2011). Social Media Changing the Competitive Intelligence Process: Elicitation of Employees' Competitive Knowledge. (Doctoral thesis). Retrieved from: https://www.researchgate.net/publication/309637579_Social_media_changing_the_competitive_intel ligence_process_Elicitation_of_employees'_competitive_knowledge.

Walther, J.B. (1995). Relational aspects of computer-mediated communication: Experimental observations over time. *Organizational Science*, 6, 186–203. doi:10.1287/orsc.6.2.186.

Walther, J.B. (1996). Computer-mediated communication: Impersonal, interpersonal, and hyperpersonal interaction. *Communication Research*, 23, 3–43. doi:10.1177/009365096023001001.

Walther, J.B., DeAndrea, D., Kim, J. & Anthony, J.C. (2010). The influence of online comments on perceptions of antimarijuana public service announcements on YouTube. *Human Communication Research*, 36, 469–492. doi:10.1111/j.1468-2958.2010.01384.x.

Walther, J.B., Carr, C.T., Choi, S., DeAndrea, D., Kim, J., Tong, S. & Heide, V.D.B. (2010). "Interaction of interpersonal, peer, and media influence sources online: A research agenda for technology convergence," in Z. Papacharissi (Ed.), *The Networked Self* (pp. 17–38). New York: Routledge.

Zembik, M. (2014). Social media as a source of knowledge for customers and enterprises. *Journal of Applied Knowledge Management*, 2(2), 132–148.

Zheng, Y., Li, L. & Zeng, F. (2010). *Social media support for knowledge management*. Proceedings of the International Conference on Management and Service Science, Wuhan, China. doi:10.1109/ICMSS.2010.5576725.

Zyl, A.S.V. (2009). The impact of Social Networking 2.0 on organisations. *The Electronic Library*, 27(6), 906–918. doi:10.1108/02640470911004020.

9 Efforts undertaken to manage social knowledge and information for social benefit

1 Introduction

We started Part II of this book by highlighting the importance of knowledge management as a practice in organizational context. We devoted Chapter 7 to discussing the positive contributions knowledge management has to offer in enhancing business performance, if contemporary digital technologies are used as a medium to disseminate knowledge as a managerial strategy. Given the importance of the digital medium as a disseminating tool, we devoted Chapter 8 to discussing the credentials contemporary social technology is endowed with, which have the capacity to accredit renewed possibilities to the practice of knowledge management. It is the collaborative spirit of social technologies that has the capacity to extend knowledge management as a practice from organizational to social domain.

It is true that knowledge management as a formal practice seldom made a presence in the social context. However, this does not imply that the activity of managing social knowledge for social benefit is an undone phenomenon. Several attempts have been made over different time periods to manage social knowledge for social benefit. Such efforts have altered over time and with changing social structuring in a way similar to organizational knowledge management practices. Managing social knowledge to achieve social functioning was an accepted practice even in prehistoric days. In the absence of basic technology, human sustenance was primarily dependent on purposive knowledge exchange, where social functioning was derivative of optimal management of social knowledge for social benefit. With the advent of civilization and development of science and technology, several innovative ways emerged to optimally manage knowledge for society. Subsequently the development of digital technologies offered redeeming possibilities in the said field. This chapter tries to trace, following digital paths, the evolution of initiatives undertaken to manage social knowledge for social cause.

Many of the developmental initiatives undertaken for social transformation using digital technologies are exogenous in nature. They push or impose developmental policies without considering the nature and problems of an individual member of the social community. These conventionally followed exogenous developmental models assume that technology (hardware, software and services) already exists in the world, as does the experience of its use. Therefore the developmental task is to encourage acquisition and application of technology, support training of its use and promote the type of regulatory changes as needed (International Telecommunication Union, 2011). This approach is based on the traditional theories of modernization, which articulate development in terms of transfer of technological infrastructure from developed to developing nations.

Although these exogenous developmental approaches are not formulated with the local pace and context in which they are applied in mind, nonetheless these efforts have led to development along certain axes; for example, ICTs are increasingly acquired and used, telecommunication infrastructure is improved and its costs are reduced. Widespread adherence to ICT because of the above-mentioned favourable factors enabled connection with the outside world, beyond an immediate local context. These exogenous models targeted development in developing regions along the following dimensions: agriculture and health, infrastructure, communication and community informatics, economic empowerment, policy, strategy and e-governance (Lekoko & Semali, 2011; International Telecommunication Union, 2005).

Following this exogenous model, initial attempts to deploy ICT for managing social knowledge can be traced to the formulation of community information systems (CIS). Instead of focusing on managing social knowledge, the initial efforts attempted uni-directional dissemination of specialized information to social groups using ICT. An information system designed to serve community is rightly identified as a community information system. Similar to the nature of organizational knowledge management as practised in the first generation, CIS did not attempt to make the information dissemination interactive. They mainly attempted to realize a *combination* of knowledge resources, where explicit knowledge is converted to explicit knowledge and transferred via a uni-directional pattern. Specialized information was distributed to or externally imposed on social groups following an exogenous approach, where the content of disseminated information was decided by policy formulators and developmental agents, including government agencies, instead of being devised in line with local requirements.

This phase led to a second generation, which saw the emergence of social managerial initiatives with an interactive premise. The efforts undertaken during this phase attempted to support interaction from stakeholders in relation to disseminated knowledge. Attempts undertaken at this phase relied on *externalization* strategy, where experts' tacit knowledge is converted to explicit form to provide contextual solutions to stakeholders. Although interaction happens to be the premise of second generation, it needs to be remembered that the efforts only made provision for the stakeholders to interact in terms of disseminated information. Hence stakeholders, even at this phase, remained passive consumers of information, without having the opportunity to create new knowledge and modify existing set.

While the evolution of organizational knowledge management over three generations has been analysed by several scholars, such structured chronological demarcation is absent in the case of activities undertaken to manage social knowledge for developmental purposes. Here we have identified those practices as belonging to second generation, which reflected an inclination to facilitate stakeholders' involvement within the process of managing social knowledge. Managerial practices adopted in this phase incorporate a bi-directional mode of knowledge transmission, from an expert to target group. Although the interactive premise enabled the target group to pose queries regarding disseminated information, this generation attempted neither targeted community formation nor to make the target group "producers" of information. Similar to second-generation organizational knowledge management, initiatives adopted for social cause, at this phase, were only limited in initiating collective efforts. With a bi-directional information transaction mode, while the allied technology supported collection of information from diverse sources, the technological infrastructure of that time lacked the reach and extent to support multi-agent collaboration and exchange, as will be shown later.

The practice of managing knowledge, which taps the potential of social technology in enabling social participants to acquire skills and experience crucial to process acquired information and knowledge, accounts to be the characteristic of the most recent, or third, generation. It is the inclusive spirit of contemporary social technology that has the potential to facilitate effective multi-agent collaboration and exchange of knowledge in social context. Social technology, as we have seen in the preceding chapter, has opened up new social and economic dimensions premised on effective sharing and collaboration. Similar to its organizational counterpart, management of social knowledge practised at this phase has the capacity to optimally exploit crowd resources and facilitate effective collaboration among them in the process of empowering social actors. Facilitation of multi-agent collaboration accredits these practices with a networking spirit, which, apart from empowering individual social actors, attempts to create an environment conducive to generating and sustaining collaboration. The collaborative premise of the third generation is heavily reliant on *socialization* strategy; it is the conversion of tacit knowledge into tacit knowledge through informal collaborations that makes third-generation attempts self-sustainable in nature. Facilitating intra- and inter-group socialization with the help of social technologies, efforts of third generation can be identified as appropriately equipped to dynamically manage social knowledge.

This chapter will discuss the different temporal phases through which efforts to manage social knowledge for social cause evolved over time. The chapter is divided into four sections:

- The introductory part narrates efforts undertaken to manage social knowledge in historic times. In the absence of technology, these practices mostly relied on physical means to manage social knowledge, where the

170 *Conceptual foundations*

  activity of managing social knowledge was mostly premised on informal knowledge transaction between social actors.
- After discussing the historical initiatives, we have reserved the second section of this chapter to describe the change in the practice of managing social knowledge following the advent of digital technology. In the first generation, efforts to manage social knowledge resorted to the digital medium to disseminate information to target groups from specialized agents following a linear pattern.
- In the third section, second-generation management of social knowledge following digital paths is discussed. Following the change in nature of digital technology, efforts to manage social knowledge at this phase attempted to discard the uni-directional information flow of the preceding generation and endorse an interactive premise.
- The chapter concludes with the third-generation managerial practices undertaken for social cause. In this phase, managing social knowledge transcends the bi-directional mode of its preceding generation and supports multi-agent knowledge collaboration by using the connecting spirit of contemporary digital technologies as the disseminating medium.

2 Managing social knowledge: A historical perspective

Contemporary efforts to manage knowledge, as has been undertaken in its third generation, coupled with the application of social technology, have only recently operationalized the importance of tacit knowledge, thereby encouraging its exchange. However, we need to remember that socialization, which promotes exchange of tacit knowledge (Nonaka & Takeuchi, 1995), not only builds the premise for contemporary knowledge management efforts; rather, socialization has enabled social functioning since time immemorial. We will return to the examples of hunters in ancient society, referred to in Chapter 7, to highlight how early men ensured the sustenance of their community by managing knowledge of social relevance.

In ancient days, in the absence of basic technology, human sustenance was primarily dependent on optimal utilization of natural resources. In the absence of basic technology, early man relied on crude tools to hunt animals as a means to sustain life. In order to successfully hunt their prey, men's knowledge about each other's hunting skills played a crucial role. Hunting in early society was a collective act, where men of ancient communities participated together. In order to defeat and hunt the wild beast it was mandatory that the activities of hunters be coordinated, which would ultimately lead to a successful hunt. Being aware of other's hunting skills is a procedure, which mainly took place through socialization and exchange of tacit knowledge among social actors. This time period, marking the dawn of early civilization, had not yet witnessed the wave of formal education. Specialized knowledge then was mainly of tacit form, created and exchanged across generations through informal communication. It is the advent of formal education (birth of language), and revolutionary efforts to document or codify specialized knowledge, that led to the growth and emergence of explicit knowledge. Before that, social functioning was primarily achieved, as the example of the early hunters proves, through socialization, or exchange of tacit knowledge, which co-incidentally also accounts to be one of the primary strategies of contemporary formalized knowledge management efforts in organizational context.

Following the inception of formal education, the revolutionary development of the printing press can be seen as one of the earliest examples of efforts undertaken to codify knowledge. The emergence of printing presses gifted knowledge with the potential to be circulated easily from one user to another. Printed materials in the form of books, newspapers, pamphlets and magazines enabled literate users to access specialized and codified knowledge. It is because of the ease with which explicit knowledge can be transferred from one human entity to another that efforts to manage knowledge mostly focused on exchange of explicit knowledge. When knowledge management entered the business world as a formal strategy, we can see how the practice primarily relied on *combination*, where explicit knowledge resources were stored in digital repositories for future use. That generation of knowledge management not only failed to recognize the potential that socialization has to offer in the domain of knowledge management; existent technology was also incapable of facilitating widespread informal communication and tacit knowledge exchange.

Exchange of tacit knowledge resource, gaining equal importance to that of explicit knowledge in contemporary knowledge management practices, has been made possible with the help of a supportive technological infrastructure. While, in earlier societies, having simple social structure meant that socialization could be achieved through face-to-face settings, in modern complex society this tacit knowledge exchange can only be facilitated through the virtual community formation using social technologies. The preceding chapter focused on how the widespread reach and connecting spirit of social technology enables the technological infrastructure to achieve sustainable and effective collaboration by facilitating formal and informal communication within and across social groups. This credential of social technology, when put to use in the domain of knowledge management, highlights the potential of the practice outside organizational boundaries. As a result, knowledge management practices started to be implemented gradually in attempts to harness social technology's potential to yield social benefit.

However, it must be remembered that, even before technology acquired its present form, there had been practices aimed at managing social knowledge for social cause. In reality, and in a way similar to the evolution of knowledge management as a practice within organizations, efforts to manage social knowledge for social benefit also evolved in tandem with technological development. While the evolution of knowledge management and of technology has been dealt with in preceding chapters, we will now trace the evolution of practices undertaken to manage social knowledge in social context following a digital path.

172 *Conceptual foundations*

3 The first generation: Facilitating information dissemination through community information systems

With the advent of digital technology, managing knowledge took a decisive shift. First-generation deployment of digital services to manage social knowledge can be traced to the formulation of community information systems (CIS); an aptly named information system designed to serve the community (Venkatappaiah, 1999). The emergence of CIS can be traced to the growing concern that disempowered groups largely owe their marginalization to the lack of adequate information crucial to undertake informed decisions. CIS emerged as a digital infrastructure that attempted social development by feeding relevant information to socially marginalized people.

The initial attempts to implement ICT practices for developmental purposes started with CIS, which sought to facilitate community improvement in Third World countries through effective information dissemination (Childers, 1975). CIS attempted to provide information to mitigate problems and crises encountered by individuals in their everyday lives, and to facilitate self-reliance and self-determination: information in the community for the community.

The content of the information to be provided by CIS was determined by developmental agents and welfare pioneers. Bunch (1982) first attempted to articulate a systematization of CIS by dividing their focus into two forms of information: survival information, such as information related to health, housing and income; and citizen action information needed for effective participation as individuals, or as members of a group in social, political, economic and legal processes. The information types were identified by national and international developmental agents as having high value and hence fit to be disseminated in the process of empowering social groups.

CIS attempted to serve different types of social groups. Starting from geographic community (region, city) to communities of interest, CIS attempted to deliver contextual information for communitarian betterment. Similar to the maintenance of digital repositories in the first phase of organizational knowledge management, efforts to utilize ICT for social cause following the CIS model sought to create and maintain a community information library to serve as an information centre for members. The CIS model mainly adopted a uni-directional information dissemination mode reliant on *combination*. In this phase, explicit knowledge is converted to explicit knowledge, without paying any heed to the tacit knowledge assets that primarily make up a community. The *combination* strategy adhered to at this phase disallows CIS to incorporate communitarian development within its purview. Uni-directional information flow is only successful in passively disseminating information to target group, thereby treating them as inert consumers of information.

In an attempt to commercialize CIS for developmental purposes, Arun Shourie, India's former Union Minister of Information Technologies and Telecommunications, suggested at the World Summit on Information Society, held in Geneva in 2003, the following four projects (Ghosh, 2005):

- Use of ICT to abolish illiteracy.
- Development of a universal networking language, so that a person in India can put his/her data in the internet in any of the recognized languages, which will eventually be translated into a universal networking language to ensure widespread accessibility of the information.
- Development of text-to-voice and voice-to-text software to perfection for the print-disabled.
- That ICT should be made affordable, with extended reach crucial to support a networking infrastructure.

The pledge taken at the world summit reflected international concern over how ICT can be appropriately used to foster developmental issues. The concern gave momentum to several efforts seeking to use ICT to mitigate social maladies.

Joseph Kiplang conducted a study in rural Kenya to examine the opportunities ICT has to offer in improving access, transfer and use of agricultural information by local community (Kiplang, 1999). The findings of the study reiterated the fact that, while ICT can act as a potential medium in disseminating important information to local rural community, it can only achieve positive outcome if it is firmly rooted in and responsive to the needs of the community, instead of being externally imposed (Kempson, 1986). Moreover, the level of expertise and skill needed to digest information is generally low in rural community compared with that of social members residing in urban locales. Therefore, rural community often encounters problems in accessing CIS. Rural environment is crippled with poverty, geographical isolation, low literacy levels and ill-served education, health, transportation, communication and other social services (Kiplang, 1999). The marginalization of the rural sector restricts its material conditions, working possibilities and curtails its store of information in amount and quality. Amidst such a scenario, the CIS model offers scant hope in disseminating information to marginalized groups on a widespread level.

The global scenario became such that multiple models of CIS were initiated by diverse developmental agents, governments and non-profit bodies to implement computerized information systems for communitarian betterment (DeSanctis & Poole, 1994). To enable local experts to reach remote rural Ghanaian villagers, Literacy Bridge adhered to the CIS model to invent a device called Talking Book (Schmidt et al., 2011). The device was designed to make important information accessible to rural communities of Ghana. The Talking Book is a hand-held, battery-operated device designed to enable users to create and listen to audio recordings and to copy recordings between devices. Local experts were appointed, who recorded important survival information such as farming techniques and health guidance into the devices, which were subsequently distributed to local community members. The Talking Book enabled developmental organizations to share information with rural communities, typically information aimed at teaching new practices in order to change local behaviour.

The devices were distributed among the rural community at Ving Ving, located in the upper western region of Ghana. The rural locale is one of the most under-developed parts of Ghana, with no electricity and 77% of the local population having never attended school. In the evaluation phase, 94% of local users reported applying a new health or agricultural practice learned from the Talking Book. Although the study venerates the positive effects triggered by the Talking Book, it needs to be remembered that the uni-directional informational dissemination mode of the device highly restricts its scope. Only certain kinds of information can be delivered through such a device. Transaction of more complex information and knowledge requires a more human interaction intensive framework, which throws open the space for dialogue. Moreover, the success of the device has been justified through user response, where local leaders have randomly selected the respondents. Such sampling runs the risk of favouritism, ushered in by the bias of the selector of the sample. Such a study conducted on a small-scale is in little position to advocate in favour of the effectivity of a CIS-based developmental model because the responses attained, which in turn justify the credibility of CIS, are primarily derived from local users' recollections, which are not incorporated following a critical analysis.

Philip Parker's Toto Agriculture (Toto Agriculture, n.d.) accounts to be another appropriate example of the CIS model. Parker and his team developed Toto Agriculture in partnership with the Bill and Melinda Gates Foundation, Grameen Foundation, Farmer Voice Radio and Farm Radio International to produce online agriculture-related information, such as tips on planting and soil health, weather forecasts, etc. (Laureys, 2016). More than 750 sources are deployed to produce on-demand information in close to 60 formats. The website is divided according to agricultural data themes, and country specific data is also made available on the dashboard; for example, farmers from Uganda are encouraged to use the sub-domain developed specifically to access localized content. There is provision for a crop calendar on the dashboard as well, which indicates the most relevant topic to discuss during a particular time of the year. Toto Agriculture is also in the process of developing a GPS tracker-enabled app which will extract geographical coordinates to find the best weather polling station and share accurate weather forecasts. Through effective deployment of ICT, Toto Agriculture intends to transform the agricultural sector from one reliant on traditional methods to one deploying modern practices by relying on agricultural databases and geo-data systems. However, if we critically investigate Toto Agriculture's operations we will see how the practice is reliant on *combination*: aggregated explicit information is disseminated to the farmers, who are mute consumers in the process. The initiative's inability to target community formation makes it exogenous in nature, which is imposed upon rural producers without adequately considering the specificities of local needs.

Scientific Animations Without Borders (SAWBO, 2018) is a Michigan State University-based programme that transforms extension information on relevant topics such as agriculture, disease and women's empowerment into 2D, 2.5D and 3D animations, which are then voice overlaid into a diversity of languages from around the world (Laureys, 2016). All SAWBO animations are freely available to anyone wishing to use them for educational purposes. Animations can be downloaded from a diversity of SAWBO channels and used on computers, tablets, cell phones, TVs and overhead projection systems. From soil testing for grain moisture levels to bio-control for legume pods, SAWBO produces a variety of informational videos loaded with specific agricultural techniques and makes them accessible on their video library.

The Indian government's e-Arik (e-Arik Center, n.d.) initiative accounts to be another major example of a project categorized under the CIS model. E-Arik is a single-window system for improved agricultural information and technology delivery through computer, internet, phone, radio and television. It provides uni-directional dissemination of specialized information on agriculture production, protection and marketing aspects through ICT in north-eastern India (Saravanan, 2011).

An information needs assessment, undertaken in the villages of East Siang District of Arunachal Pradesh in the 2000s, found that an overwhelming majority of tribal farmers lacked access to agricultural information with which they could address challenges such as pest and disease management. The e-Arik (e-agriculture) project was initiated with the aim to disseminate "climate-smart agriculture practices" and to achieve food security (e-Arik Center, n.d.). Climate-smart farm practices were seen as those that were sustainable, low input and reliant on organic technologies. The initiative was sponsored by India's Department of Scientific and Industrial Research and the Ministry of Science and Technology.

Agricultural information dissemination following the e-Arik model yielded some positive outcomes; north-east Indian farmers were seen to be implementing a number of farm practices, such as vermi-compost, crop rotation, etc (Saravanan, 2008). But when it came to adoption of new methods of cultivation, the response was feeble (only two farmers adopted the system of rice intensification in 2010). The tribal farmers are not easily convinced to deviate from traditional methods followed over generations. Moreover, uni-directional information dissemination did not incorporate provision for dialogue, thereby making the initiative externally imposed, without having any ground-level percolation. In addition to that, English and Hindi languages are used for communication, as the *Adi* dialect spoken by the tribal communities does not have a script. Lack of content in local language further distanced the initiative from the largely illiterate stakeholders. Frequent failure of online connectivity due to fluctuating availability of electricity also posed severe problems.

Poor land and water management and a lack of appropriate governance and regulatory frameworks to deal with increasing pressure on limited resources lead to degradation of the land resources upon which rural communities and society as a whole depend. Established in 1992, the World Overview of Conservation Approaches and Technologies (WOCAT, n.d.) is a global network that launched efforts to compile and disseminate sustainable land management (SLM) information (Laureys, 2016). It was far ahead of others in recognizing the vital importance of SLM and the pressing need to manage information for social purpose. In early 2014, WOCAT's growth and ongoing improvement culminated in it being officially recognized by the UN Convention to Combat Desertification as the primary recommended global SLM database for best practice.

The telephonic advisory service extended to smallholder farmers of Africa accounts to be another potential example of CIS. Smallholder farmers in Africa want to run their farms as a business, but they lack the knowledge required. Early user-experience research found that lack of access to government extension officers prevents most farmers from changing their practices. Changes have to be evidence-based, as low literacy levels in the country are a further barrier to disseminating information. With this in mind, Human Network International (HNI, n.d.) created the 3–2–1 Service, an innovative mobile phone information service to allow resource-poor individuals to take action to improve their health and wellbeing. At a moment of need, men, women, boys and girls can use their simple mobile phones to proactively retrieve information across a range of topics. No internet is required. Callers dial the toll-free number, 3–2–1, anytime, anywhere. They are greeted by a welcome message in their local language. The voice prompts them through the menu of topics until they find the trusted information they need. The messages on the 3–2–1 Service are developed by local, regional and international subject matter experts through content committees convened by a 3–2–1 Service partner in each country where the service is active. It is, thus, not dedicated to agriculture only and differs from country to country, covering topics such as gender, health, etc. The effectivity of such a uni-directional information dissemination mode remains debatable because it is unclear whether the proposed content matches the needs of farmers at all.

The above-mentioned examples highlight that, whatever the context, initial attempts to achieve development through the implementation of the CIS model made no efforts to involve communitarian members in the process of development, thereby seldom empowering the marginalized. This makes it clear that communitarian development was never the motive of the CIS model. The primary aim of the model was to provide explicit specialized information to marginalized target groups to improve their socio-economic conditions through bridging the *information asymmetry*. However, the initiatives could seldom achieve such an improvement because the nature and content of information disseminated was never formulated with communitarian needs in mind. The members of the local community were mainly treated as "disempowered subjects", or consumers of information, who are expected to benefit by applying the information disseminated through CIS. Active participation of local community never featured in the purview of the initial attempts undertaken to implement CIS to achieve communitarian benefit. It was the developmental agents who designed the CIS, without involving the local community in their own developmental process.

Non-involvement of locals has often been cited by many scholars as one of the major reasons for failures of CIS initiatives. Harrison and Zappen (2005) provide the example of "Free Nets" and their gradual extinction to highlight how CIS models face difficulty in attaining sustainability. The National Public Telecomputing Network came up with Free Nets in 1990s. These were fashioned after public broadcasting systems and were intended to provide access across wide areas to computer networks and information about local communities. However, with the decrease in costs of computing equipment and the internet, many Free Nets went out of business. Studies of other community networks funded by national governments also suggest that non-involvement of stakeholders makes it difficult for CIS to sustain themselves beyond their initial funding (Rosenbaum, 1998).

The need for a second generation. The limitations of the uni-directional information dissemination mode of CIS paved the path for a new concern: to design and reform CIS in accordance with community functionalities and conceptual configuration, where the goals, interests and ideologies of locals and others who use CIS in their developmental process will shape the design and impact of technology (Lievrouw & Livingstone, 2002; Sproull & Kiesler, 1991). This new concern paved the path for incorporating users' goals, values and needs within the framework of CIS (Björn-Sören, 2011).

The emergent concern chalked out three parameters crucial to ensuring sustainability of CIS:

- Stakeholder involvement. Schuler (1997) insightfully points out the urgency to establish collaboration between academic researchers and local community in the process of designing community networking projects.
- Commitment from key players. Any person associated with community information systems must be proactively involved and should bear accountability to the informational dissemination taking place via CIS. When Connected Kids was formed in 1999 to employ new technologies to provide services to the local community of Troy, the project attempted to secure commitment from both ends – the local community as well as the governing authorities of Troy (Harrison & Zappen, 2005).
- Critical mass of users. CIS must establish a significant number of regular users, who will enact the technology for at least some of the purposes for which it was originally intended and, in doing so, reproduce communitarian standards that are instantiated in the technology. Through regular interaction, the rules and regulations get disseminated within the community, thereby producing producers and consumers of information, who in alliance will make the CIS interactive, instead of being uni-directional.

With this concern emerged a second generation of practices, undertaken to manage social knowledge for social development. As illustrated in Chapter 7 in the context of organizational knowledge management (KM), first-generation KM schemes began by stressing codification and *combination* issues. Second-generation KM, by contrast, moved the focus to interaction between learning and technology use, because firms gradually realized that access to technology alone could not deliver comprehensive knowledge management. In our current context of managing knowledge for social benefit, the practices belong to second generation and are primarily focused on capturing, accumulating and disseminating knowledge through some form of knowledge management system (KMS) (Boughzala & Dudezert, 2011); an IT-based community-driven information system developed to support and enhance the social processes of knowledge creation, storage/retrieval, transfer and application. This phase, in promoting interaction, attempted to transcend from *combination* strategy, practised in its preceding phase, to *externalization* strategy. The efforts undertaken in this phase, apart from disseminating specialized information, enabled the target group to provide feedback on the disseminated information. In an attempt to address the multi-faceted issues of stakeholders, the efforts in this phase witnessed the conversion of experts' explicit knowledge to tacit knowledge in order to provide contextual solutions.

4 The second generation: Facilitating bi-directional information sharing

The CIS model primarily aimed at providing access to ICT to social actors, who were expected to benefit from the disseminated information imparted using the digital medium. In this phase, the designing of a technological infrastructure by involving academicians and technical experts received precedence, and community involvement took a back seat. While these "ICT for development" attempts, mimicking a top-down exogenous approach, attempted to serve marginalized social communities, non-involvement of local members in the process often restricted efforts to yield grassroot impact. Often it was found that the community themselves lacked awareness regarding the schemes undertaken for their own benefit.

The new wave of deploying ICT for developmental purposes marked a shift from technological development and access to a more human interaction centric focus. The main motive behind implementing the CIS model in the preceding phase was to provide digital access to the marginalized sections of society, thereby attempting to overcome digital divide. However, at this phase, many scholars realized that the divide between the privileged and marginalized social groups is more than digital; it includes knowledge, education and a two-way informational exchange between the haves and the have nots and others (Eglash, 2002; Daniel & West, 2006). Many works have been undertaken by national and international organizations to close the divide between the two groups. Basu et al. (2017) highlight how the rice production sector in India adhered to a bi-directional information and knowledge transaction mode to usher in a peer production model, thereby attempting to make rice farmers equal stakeholders in the production process. The shift towards an interactive focus can be seen as the major aspect, which distinguished the emergent wave of employing ICT for development from its preceding phase. However, it needs to be remembered that for these efforts to have greater impact and sustainability they require a greater communitarian and interactive focus (Gurstien, 2003).

The new wave attempted to employ ICT to mitigate the information asymmetry from which marginalized groups suffer. The approach assumes that, apart from several crucial physical assets, disempowered people significantly lack informational assets, which, in alliance, contribute to sustaining their marginalization. In an attempt to disseminate information in productive ways, efforts in the second phase, instead of focusing on uni-directional information dissemination, attempted to encourage information exchange between policy formulators and target group in a bi-directional mode. This paved the path for externalization strategy, where explicit knowledge of experts was converted to tacit form in order to provide contextual solutions to stakeholders. Although this can be identified as an improvement from its preceding phase, where information dissemination was intrinsically uni-directional, how far the marginalized groups, at this stage, were capable of taking part in such informational exchange is an aspect that needs to be critically investigated.

The difference between information and knowledge, as has been furthered in Chapter 2, becomes pertinent in this context. Marginalized communities are not just information impoverished. Their social and material conditions shape their situations disadvantageously, so externally feeding them with information or throwing them open to an informational network is likely to yield dissatisfying outcomes. Until the marginalized groups acquire skills and experience to process the information (i.e., they become knowledgeable), it is difficult to expect betterment out of efforts seeking to mitigate information asymmetry using digital medium. Following, we will provide practical evidence adopted under the purview of second generation to highlight its strength, weakness and what led to the emergence of a third generation in deploying ICT for development.

The second generation led to the emergence of several information network groups, which attempted to mitigate information asymmetry of local community members using the digital forum. Groups such as the Global Donor Platform for Rural Development, the Swiss Centre for Agricultural Extension and Rural Development, the African Forum on Rural Development and the African Knowledge Network emerged with the aim to deploy ICT to mitigate information asymmetry of the socially marginalized groups (Hess, 2006). These groups came up with digital platforms for farmers, practitioners, researchers and donor agencies to share their experience, information and knowledge. The difference of these initiatives from the former CIS model is that the new initiatives attempted to facilitate interaction between platform participants and developmental agents and experts. However, it needs to be remembered that bi-directional information exchange is incapable of facilitating community formation, which also happens to be the premise of social knowledge. Although the interactive premise of second generation can be seen as an improvement from its preceding phase, its inability to facilitate community formation by enabling multi-directional knowledge exchange restricts the measures to an exogenous nature.

Formulation by Payakpaie et al. (2004) of an information networking portal promoting modern rural energy services (MRES) among ASEAN members accounts to be an appropriate measure undertaken in the second generation. The proposed digital platform employs web service technologies for the enhancement, distribution and utilization of rural energy services among local community. In an attempt to be interactive, the platform, along with enabling stakeholders to access specialized information related to the design and use of MRES, also makes provision to capture users' experience. Although this model fits the theoretical premise of being bi-directionally interactive, there is a need to investigate how far the stakeholders, coming mostly from marginalized backgrounds, are equipped to process the imparted information.

The Fisher Friend Programme, piloted by the MS Swaminathan Research Foundation in partnership with Qualcomm, Tata Teleservices and Astute Technology System, also attempted to disseminate practical solutions to Indian fishermen using digital services. The Fisher Friend Mobile Application (FFMA, 2018), a practical realization of FFP, is a single-window solution for the holistic shore-to-shore needs of the fishing community, providing vulnerable fishermen immediate access to critical, near real-time, knowledge and information services on weather, potential fishing zones, ocean state forecasts and markets (FFMA, 2018). It provides critical information about weather and ocean conditions up to 100 kilometres (about 62 miles) from shore, including disaster alerts, potential fishing zones and current market prices of fish. Exact geographic coordinates of shoals of fish and real-time data on wave length and wind speed are updated regularly (with the help of India's National Centre for Ocean Information Services). The app also marks danger zones such as coral reefs and sunken ships.

An impact study conducted in July 2016 found that the app has benefited several from the fishing communities in Kerala, Andhra Pradesh and Tamil Nadu. The app also has provision for users to list their experiences. However, many fishermen recorded that their lack of digital literacy has posed a major hindrance for them in using and benefiting from the information shared in the app. Moreover, only high-end mobile devices could support the app, which further posed a challenge to the financially impoverished fishing communities. Lack of communitarian knowledge on how to use the app on one hand, coupled with lack of training facilities to educate the users regarding the functionality of the app on the other, limited the scope and extent of the FFMA initiative.

Apart from India, other nations have also attempted to apply technology to improve the community informational pool of its marginalized sections. Countries such as Vietnam have applied advanced technology not only to boost agricultural productivity but also to mitigate the information asymmetry of the farmer community. Agriculture in Vietnam is markedly inefficient and productivity levels are among the lowest in Asia. More than 50% of water is wasted as a result of over-irrigation, up to 60% of the fertilizer is not absorbed by the crops and so runs off and destroys the environment, 20%–30% of the crops are lost due to pests and diseases and more than $700 million is lost in export opportunity because of the overuse of pesticides and chemicals. All of this is caused by the fact that farmers are ignorant of the needs and conditions of the crops.

In order to enable farmers to communicate better over crops, MimosaTEK was founded by Tri Nguyen, an engineer with a passion for agriculture. He applied advanced technology and embarked on a journey to educate farmers on precision agriculture and have them adopt a precision management solution, called "MGreen" (MimosaTEK, n.d.). MGreen implements advanced technology for precision agriculture to help farmers increase productivity while minimizing expenses and mitigating risk. The sensors in hardware devices continuously measure environmental parameters; and the algorithms do the computation to recommend to farmers the optimal irrigation schedule. The devised digital infrastructure reserves sections for the farmers to list their experiences and feedback in the process of applying acquired information.

An impact analysis revealed that MimosaTEK customers believe the product has helped them save as much as 50% of the cost of water and electricity to irrigate their farms, and increased their yields by up to 25%. However, the famers, or the major stakeholders, being mostly illiterate and unfamiliar with hard-core technology, gradually lost interest in the initiative. The incorporation of advanced technology comes with a considerable responsibility and accountability due to security concerns. Farmers are typically hesitant to adapt to new technology and are more likely to rely on methods that might be less efficient but which they believe to be reliable. Although application of advanced technology by MimosaTEK attempted to provide useful information to Vietnamese farmers with an interactive spirit, the specialized digital infrastructure devised by experts to a great extent prevented the community feeling at home with it. Very few attempts were made by the start-up to provide digital training to the local mass on a sustainable basis, which would have helped them become familiarized with the technological infrastructure. Moreover, lack of provision to support peer-to-peer learning and discussion forums made the initiative alien to the target group. As a result, although the business apparently seems to be successful in delivering information to local community, it offered little hope in "educating" the farmers about innovative practices.

As part of the Rural Universe Network Pilot Project (RUNPP, n.d.), several partners – including the Caribbean Agricultural Research and Developmental Institute, the German Centre for Documentation and Information in Agriculture and the Rural Agricultural Developmental Authority – have developed rural information cafes in Jamaica aimed at enhancing the availability of local knowledge by establishing certain systems of rural communication (Laureys, 2016). Their primary communication strategy is to invest in internet tools that will facilitate the exchange of know-how between farmers, researchers and other stakeholders. Each information cafe is equipped with a broadband connection and a library of CDs on relevant subjects. This collection of information happens across multiple forms (print, video or voice recordings) and printers, digital cameras and scanners are made use of. Since most of the efforts by RUNetwork involve interpersonal interaction between farmers and researchers, it enables community participation to a certain extent.

A regional information broker, or RIB, is also appointed to oversee the exchange of information and consolidation of the knowledge base. Since it would be fruitless to provide the rural population with a knowledge base without ensuring their interest in participation, the RIB provides them with training and information on other computer-based services. This entire initiative is based on educating indigenous community with expert knowledge on a bi-directional mode, without facilitating peer-to-peer learning possibilities. While the interaction with the RIB required some communitarian participation, bi-directional information exchange is incapable of evoking deep community development.

IIT Kanpur's Agropedia is another potential example of efforts undertaken with the motto to facilitate bi-directional information exchange in an attempt to empower socially marginalized groups (Agropedia, 2004). Agropedia seeks to address the lacunae in Indian agriculture knowledge and application, specifically the lack of content, organized information and extension services which are serious challenges. It has developed delivery mechanisms such as vKVK-net (Voice Kisan Vigyan Kendra), which are a means to connect extension scientists and farmers based on its web platform, which hosts information on agriculture and rural livelihoods (Hugar et al., 2012). The web platform, Agropedia, is unique in the agricultural domain as it is semantically organized and enabled so as to assist one in getting exactly what information or service he/she is looking for. Along with content in the library section, certified by the Indian Council for Agricultural Research, it also allows space for interaction with the experts in attaining contextual solutions to problems. However, in order to successfully acquire and implement disseminated information, the indigenous communities must possess a literacy level sufficient to grasp the explicit knowledge of experts. Over-emphasis on formal dissemination of information, without creating scopes of peer-to-peer learning, prevents these initiatives from having ground-level percolation. Since these initiatives fall short in triggering communitarian development through collaborative learning, they can do little justice in appropriately managing social knowledge. Social knowledge can only be optimally managed if multi-directional knowledge exchange is facilitated among social agents.

The need for a third generation. An in-depth study of projects undertaken during the first and second phase of deploying ICT to achieve communitarian betterment reveals that not only in the first phase, but also in the second phase, the efforts were practically ineffective in mobilizing local community. While the second phase witnessed efforts that theoretically aimed at disseminating specialized information to marginalized community by adhering to an interactive mode, lack of digital literacy among the locals, absence of adequate training facilities to familiarize the locals with the digital infrastructure, and lack of focus on communitarian development by facilitating peer-to-peer learning worked against its interactive premise. The dissemination of information without imparting skills and experience on how to process the information contributed to making the second generation attempts exogenous, in spite of their theoretical inclination towards an interactive mode.

Efforts to manage social knowledge 183

The third generation attempts to use ICT as a medium to empower the social actors prior to exposing them to information networks and expecting them to benefit from such informational exchange. Facilitating multi-directional knowledge collaboration among social actors, the third generation attempts to deploy ICT to facilitate *socialization* (conversion of tacit knowledge to tacit knowledge) among social agents. Seeds of community development lie hidden in socialization resultant of multi-directional knowledge exchange among communitarian members. It is by making collaboration an effective premise that third generation attempts to deploy the digital infrastructure to manage social knowledge. It is only in this phase, with the help of social technology, that an empowering ecosystem is created that has the potential to effectively tap and manage social knowledge by facilitating effective collaboration between and across communities.

Conventionally, in the preceding phases, ICT has mainly been conceptualized as an information dissemination tool. As we have seen, when the digital medium has been used to disseminate information to marginalized groups it mainly attempted external feeding of information to individual members, without taking into account social factors that shape the life conditions of social members. Individuals are not isolated beings; it is social fabric that determines individual capacities and actions. The objective of third-generation initiatives is to move from bi-directional information dissemination mode and to facilitate multi-directional knowledge exchange, thus enhancing social capital of marginalized groups. The growth of social capital with the aid of social technology in the third generation creates the scope for collaborative learning space by virtue of facilitating peer-to-peer knowledge exchange. It is this peer-to-peer knowledge exchange that truly radiates a communitarian flavour and can be justly concluded as the premise of social knowledge.

While ICT in the preceding phases only enabled users to assume the status of "consumers" of information, the emergent digital infrastructure, in promoting collaborations, gives enormous opportunities to users to participate in the knowledge-creation process. Identifying every social agent to be a potential contributor of knowledge, the third-generation initiatives blur the distinction between producers and consumers of information. These initiatives attempt to design a digital infrastructure that will be sustained through effective collaboration and networking between local community agents and external agents, where each agent will equally be a producer and consumer of information at the same time. The collaboration between these diverse social agents accounts to be the premise of social knowledge.

5 The third generation: Facilitating multi-directional knowledge collaboration

While *combination* accounts to be the strategy followed in the first generation, followed by *externalization* in second generation, *socialization,* or conversion of tacit to tacit knowledge, accounts to be the core of third generation's collaborative premise. In an attempt to facilitate communitarian development by enabling effective networking between and across communities, efforts undertaken in the third generation seek to create a collaborative, social learning space with the aid of social technology. Wenger (1997) furthers four premises of social theory of learning. They are:

- We are social beings and this is the central aspect of learning.
- Knowledge is a matter of competence with respect to valued enterprise.
- Knowing is the matter of participating in the pursuit of such enterprise, namely active engagement in the world.
- Learning cultivates meaning; our ability to experience the world and our engagement with it as meaningful is derivative of our learning capacities.

Wenger's conceptualization highlights the importance of learning in the context of knowledge acquisition and application. In the earlier chapters, where we have discussed the issue of knowledge capability, we have seen how, apart from knowledge possession, it is application of knowledge, or knowledge capability of entities, that has the potential to usher in holistic empowerment by mitigating knowledge asymmetry. The way Wenger differentiates between knowledge and the act of knowing leading to formulation of meaning reiterates a similar concern we have faced in demarcating knowledge from knowledge capability. While knowledge acquisition can be achieved along multiple paths, knowledge capability is a product of learning, or *internalization*, where explicit and tacit knowledge from external sources is converted to tacit knowledge sources by the human agents themselves. It is only amidst a collaborative learning space that we can attempt to enhance the knowledge capability of human participants on a sustainable basis. Apart from enhancing knowledge capability, a collaborative learning space facilitates knowledge exchange within and across communities, which has the capacity to do justice to the management of social knowledge.

Collaborative learning is derivative of effective networking, both within and across communities (Cummings & Zee, 2005). It incorporates within the learning process an act of building relationships with other independent actors to share knowledge, goods and services and experiences, thereby paving the path to learn from each other with a common goal in mind (Plucknett et al., 1990). Effective networking enables an atmosphere of openness by allowing unhindered exchange of skills and expertise and upgrading them in the process. Networking's importance in knowledge-centric developmental models has been insightfully articulated by Cummings and Zee (2005). They argue that networking knowledge, or promoting knowledge exchange among relevant agents, produces the most significant results if the network develops into a space for innovation, experimentation and learning. Capacity-building, institutional building, advocacy and societal change are unthinkable in the absence of a collaborative learning space, which facilitates networking and learning among relevant developmental actors.

The collaborative learning premise of the third generation achieved its practical realization with the emergence and proliferation of social technology. As we have discussed in the preceding chapter, social technology and its inclusive spirit have significantly altered the way socio-economic activities are conducted in the contemporary world. Contemporary social technologies are infused with the potential to virtually integrate different sectors and have a significant role in enabling social functioning by facilitating collaboration among these diverse sectors. It is only with such a supportive digital infrastructure that attempts can be taken to employ the digital medium to attain holistic communitarian betterment. Integration of diverse sectors and relevant knowledge networking between them create a collaborative learning space that is sustained through the spirit of peer-to-peer learning and active communitarian engagement. Such a framework supports multi-directional knowledge exchange.

Engel (1997) highlights how one-sidedness of social and institutional learning processes poses a major hindrance in the development of sustainable solutions. The earlier efforts, based on uni-directional and bi-directional mode, were insufficient in enabling a sustainable learning system. It is with the aid of social technology and the capacity of the medium to establish effective collaboration that attempts can be taken to manage social knowledge by facilitating collaborative learning.

It is the reach and extent of social technology in facilitating and practically realizing effective collaboration that provide the capacity to do justice to third generation's aim to deploy digital services to empower communitarian members. Instead of disseminating information between defined entities, efforts of this genre attempt to empower social actors by facilitating multi-directional knowledge exchange. Social technology-supported multi-directional knowledge exchange is not derivative of inert knowledge sharing but is a dynamic product of knowledge exchange between and across communities. Such a dynamic exchange is only possible when communitarian knowledge sources, apart from possessing relevant knowledge, also develop knowledge-operating capacities or, in other words, become knowledge capable. It is *socialization*, conversion of tacit knowledge to tacit knowledge through collaboration between communitarian members, which has the capacity to mitigate the extant knowledge asymmetry that cripples society and sustains marginalization of the disempowered.

Optimally managing social knowledge relies on collaboration, where social technologies happen to be appropriate tools in facilitating effective networking. A collaborative premise not only enables communitarian members to be producers of knowledge; these efforts successfully blur the distinction and hierarchy between producers and consumers of knowledge. By enabling one and all to contribute, efforts to manage social knowledge assume each entity to be a potential knowledge-contributing source, therefore being both producer and consumer of knowledge simultaneously. Only such an infrastructure has the potential to be self-sufficient and endogenous and optimally extract the potential of crowd knowledge for the cause of social empowerment. Effective collaboration between crowd, or general social members, has the potential to manage social knowledge in a way where the role of external developmental agents will gradually become secondary. Unrestricted knowledge exchange between social members will not only add dynamicity to the pool of social knowledge but will make the entire process of knowledge exchange a voluntary act, therefore self-sustainable and without the intervention of developmental authorities.

In order to have a better understanding as to what managing social knowledge practically entails, we will provide a glimpse of some efforts undertaken in the third phase aimed at managing social knowledge in a community-minded spirit.

WeFarm has built a platform for close to one billion smallholding farmers to help them access basic information and solve problems through real-time multilingual knowledge sharing (WeFarm, n.d.). Headquartered in London, it aims to create an ecosystem for global smallholder agriculture by fostering peer-to-peer learning and networking that addresses issues such as the effects of climate change, sourcing best-quality seeds and availability of loans. Since its founding in 2015, WeFarm has enabled farmers to share information on basic mobile phones via SMS without the need for the internet and was named one of Africa's most innovative companies by FastConnect. WeFarm collaborates with 280,000 smallholder tea, coffee and cocoa farmers on innovative, community-driven projects in Peru, Kenya and Tanzania (Laureys, 2016), for which it received the Google Impact Challenge Award. WeFarm, claiming to be the world's largest farmer-to-farmer digital network, has now transitioned into a for-profit business model to achieve greater financial sustainability and to collaborate with local as well as global organizations in the future. This opens up fertile ground for analysis of farming systems in developing countries though community-driven knowledge management models.

The ambitions of AgriProFocus (AgriProFocus, n.d.) resonate with a similar community-minded spirit. Members of AgriProFocus are dedicated to meeting the challenge of food security through collaboration with farmers, agribusinesses, civil society and governments. Their model of development includes linking, learning and leadership, wherein farmers are linked with change-makers in the agriculture and food industry to solve specific challenges. The digital platform also provides an atmosphere conducive to peer-to-peer learning: share the best practices, experiences, failures and learn from one another. The group also aims to create agripreneurs who can make a large-scale and sustainable impact on the business environment. Converting communitarian members into entrepreneurs through necessary capacity-building training, AgriProFocus radiates a truly community-minded spirit.

As per the AgriProFocus website, the group's knowledge base can be split into several themes, such as Climate Smart, Circular Economy, Nutrition Sensitive and Inclusive Agribusiness. It fosters a community of practice through e-learning opportunities in the form of free online courses, training videos and agricultural libraries that are available on the website. The strength of this model lies in its physical and local networks, and the virtual platform provides an opportunity for knowledge-sharing and teaming of resources.

The *Savannah Young Farmers Network* also successfully qualifies to be an initiative dedicated to optimally managing social knowledge. At SavaNet-Ghana (SYFN, n.d.) they build bridges between research and practical farming while developing products and services in partnership with other users (Laureys, 2016). The initiative supports Ghanaian farmers in deploying the latest knowledge and technology innovatively and efficiently. Savannah remains pivotal in the nurture of Ghana's next generation of transformational leaders in agribusiness for secured food security. Every generation needs its leaders in agribusiness and every leader needs leverage to achieve goals. SavaNet-Ghana has created an innovation ecosystem where various agriculture value-chain actors and agribusiness organizations interact for the development of viable agribusinesses. It serves to be the nation's precision agriculture technology corridor, with the iHub as the flagship agribusiness innovation development initiative. Their agriculture development initiatives are in the area of young farmer development, agribusiness development and leadership, precision agriculture development, natural resource conservation and environmental management, urban agriculture development, etc. The network is made up of various groups of farmers: large-scale commercial farmers, small-scale farmers, semi-commercial farmers, non-poor complex diverse risk-prone farmers and poor complex diverse risk-prone farmers. It is also made up of a wide range of agriculture value-chain actors; for example, produce-buying companies, mechanization service providers, aggregators, financial institutions, angel investors, agri-input companies, agri-processing companies, warehousing companies, etc. The organization remains committed to securing the future of agriculture in Ghana and Africa as a whole for a secured food security.

ICT4dev.ci (ICT4Dev, n.d.) is a start-up founded in 2012 that specializes in the development and integration of ICT solutions to tackle the daily problems of African populations. One of its flagship projects is Lôr Bouôr (Lôr Bouôr, n.d.), which translates as "excellent plantation" and is a technology solution platform targeted at building a modern and efficient agricultural sector. Lôr Bouôr improves connections between different stakeholders in the agri-sector: buyers and sellers, input suppliers and farmer cooperatives, and farmer-to-farmer (ACP-EU (CTA), 2016).

The Lôr Bouôr platform is designed to offer five services to local farmer cooperatives and their partners: a web-portal (www.lorbouor.org), which is an information, training and promotion space dedicated to the agricultural sector; a web-based cooperative management tool; a mobile and SMS application referred to as a "virtual market" that creates an opportunity for agricultural cooperative provision and customers' demands to meet; an SMS market information system application; and a voice mailbox called "Djassi" (news) to directly convey agriculture-related information to producers in local languages. Lôr Bouôr improves connections between different stakeholders in agricultural communities. Its information portal promotes local input suppliers and even cooperatives who would like to increase their visibility; the digital record-keeping platform allows farmers in the same cooperative to track their farm information in the same location, making management infinitely easier; and the online market and market prices connect farmers directly to their buyers, so they can increase their income. Lôr Bouôr manages social knowledge by facilitating dynamic collaboration, both within and across groups. Through digital services, Lôr Bouôr attempts community development by building an empowering infrastructure facilitating unhindered knowledge exchange. Training and guidance for sustenance of the project is provided and delivery of projects follows the private–public–partnership (PPP) model.

All the above-mentioned examples, mainly in the field of agriculture, offer practical evidence of managed social knowledge. Only these sorts of practices, with a holistic vision, can do justice to the collaborative motto of third generation. However, it needs to be remembered that, although the initiatives incorporate peer-to-peer knowledge collaboration, they do so sporadically and without proposing the inter-connected, unified framework vital to sustaining such collaborations. An inter-connected, unified framework, supporting rural producers (supporting both farm and non-farm activities), truly has the capacity to facilitate multi-directional knowledge exchange on an unhindered scale, derivative of voluntary participation of members. In the absence of an inter-connected, unified framework, communitarian development, while attainable, becomes difficult to sustain.

6 Conclusion

The efforts highlighted in this chapter provide a detailed understanding of the way practices to manage social knowledge and information evolved with time and development of technological infrastructure. The existence since time immemorial of practices to achieve social functioning through managing social knowledge and information proves that knowledge management, although formally not commonly applied in social context, has long been in action in the social domain ideologically. Moreover, the aspects of formal knowledge management, yet to be applied in a social context, have been made possible by the collaborative spirit of contemporary social technologies. Thus, to reap the benefits that knowledge management as a strategy has to offer to the fullest, it is necessary to deploy the connecting spirit of social technology to reformulate and redesign attempts to manage social knowledge and information.

Although the collaborative spirit of digital technology has been deployed in the third phase to manage social knowledge through community formation, this has been achieved only sporadically. The reason why community formation has been given precedence in the context of managing social knowledge in its third phase is because community formation has proven itself effective in organizational context, following the concept of *ba*. *Ba* conceptually refers to a shared space or context which leads to creation of new knowledge, innovation and learning opportunities (Suni & Hong, 2011). The concept of *ba* and its relevance in the context of organizational knowledge management has been further developed by Nonaka and Toyama (2003), who conceptualized it as a multiple interacting mechanism explaining tendencies for interactions that occur at a specific time and space. It is socialization, or effective tacit knowledge exchange through community formation, which happens to be the premise articulating the credibility of *ba* in the context of organizational knowledge management. While in social context, the relevance of community formation in the process of managing social knowledge has been recognized in the third phase, such formation has mainly been triggered along sporadic lines. In this context it needs to be remembered that community formation alone cannot yield concrete benefits if purposive community is not formed. In the absence of purposive community, although groups of people can come together and collaborate temporarily, lack of clearly defined purpose and objective will not enable such community formation to be sustainable. It is the lack of purposive community formation that most third-generation attempts to manage social knowledge suffer from.

To evade the inherent shortcomings of extant efforts dedicated to managing social knowledge and information, in the following chapter we will advocate for the credibility and necessity of our *social knowledge management framework* in the context of holistic rural empowerment. Our social knowledge management framework attempts to build an inter-connected ecosystem which has the capacity to facilitate purposive communitarian development on a sustainable scale by encouraging voluntary collaboration between members. Purposive community formation binds the members with a common objective, which happens to be the key for sustainable community development. Through the development of purposive community characterized by strong inter-personal bonds, our proposed framework is designed to justly manage social knowledge. In the following chapter we will provide an account of our social knowledge management framework to highlight its potential in facilitating and sustaining purposive communitarian development through building an inter-connected ecosystem.

References

ACP-EU (CTA) (2016). Innovate for Agriculture: Young ICT entrepreneurs overcoming challenges and transforming agriculture. Retrieved from: https://issuu.com/ashokachangemakers/docs/1924_pdf_ilgfwf6.

AgriProFocus (n.d.). Retrieved from: https://agriprofocus.com/intro.

Agropedia (2004). Retrieved from: http://agropedia.iitk.ac.in/content/about-us.

Basu, S., Jongerden, J. & Ruivenkamp, G. (2017). The Emergence of a Hybrid Mode of Knowledge Production in the Generation Challenge Programme Rice Research Network (GCP-RRN) in India: Exploring the Concept of Commons-Based Peer Production (CBPP). *Geoforum*, 84, 107–116. doi:10.1016/j.geoforum.2017.06.008.

Björn-Sören, G. (2011). Informational Capabilities: The Missing Link for the Impact of ICT on Development. Working Paper Series No.1, The World Bank, March. Retrieved from: http://hdl.handle.net/10986/19011.

Conceptual foundations

Boughzala, I. & Dudezert, A. (2011). *Knowledge Management 2.0: Organizational Models and Enterprise Strategies.* Hershey, PA: IGI Global. doi:10.4018/978-1-61350-195-5.

Bunch, A. (1982). *Community Information Services: The origin, scope and development.* London: Clive Bingley.

Childers, T. (1975). *The Information Poor in America.* Metuchen, NJ: Scarecrow Press.

Cummings, S. & Zee, A. (2005). Communities of Practice and Networks: Reviewing Two Perspectives on Social Learning. *KM4D Journal*, 1(1), 8–22.

Daniel, J. & West, P. (2006). From Digital Divide to Digital Dividend: What will it take? *Innovate*, 2(5). Retrieved from: http://citeseerx.ist.psu.edu/viewdoc/download?doi=10.1.1.193.1957&rep=rep1 &type=pdf.

DeSanctis, G. & Poole, M.S. (1994). Capturing the Complexity in Advanced Technology Use: Adaptive Structuration Theory. *Organization Science*, 5, 121–147.

e-Arik Center (n.d.). Using ICT for educating farmers. Retrieved from: https://leisaindia.org/e-arik-center-using-ict-for-educating-farmers/.

Eglash, R. (2002). A Two-way Bridge Across the Digital Divide. *The Chronicle of Higher Education*, 48(1), 12.

Engel, P.G.H. (1997). *The Social Organisation of Innovation: A Focus on Stakeholder Interaction.* Amsterdam: Royal Tropical Institute.

FFMA (2018). Qualcomm's case study on FFMA. Retrieved from: https://www.qualcomm.com/company/wireless-reach/projects/fisher-friend.

Ghosh, M. (2005). The Public Library System in India: Challenges and Opportunities. *Library Review*, 54(3), 180–191. doi:10.1108/00242530510588935.

Gurstein, M. (2003). Effective Use: A Community Informatics Strategy beyond the Digital Divide. *First Monday*, 8(12). Retrieved from: https://firstmonday.org/article/view/1107/1027.

Harrison, T. & Zappen, J. (2005). *Building Sustainable Community Information Systems: Lessons from a Digital Government Project.* Proceedings of the 2005 National Conference on Digital Government Research, Atlanta, Georgia. doi:10.1145/1065226.1065267.

Hess, C.G. (2006). Knowledge Management and Knowledge Systems for Rural Development. *GTZ Knowledge Systems in Rural Areas*, 1–16.

HNI (n.d.). Retrieved from: http://hni.org/what-we-do/3-2-1-service.

Hugar, L.B., Prabhuraj, A., Nandini & Poornima. (2012). KVK-NET and VKVK: Novel Approaches for Information Communication and Knowledge Sharing in Agriculture. *AIPA*. Retrieved from: http://insait.in/AIPA2012/articles/007.pdf.

ICT4Dev (n.d.). Retrieved from: http://ict4dev.ci/.

International Telecommunication Union (2005). Tunis agenda for the Information Society. Retrieved from: http://www.itu.int/wsis/docs2/tunis/off/6rev1.html.

International Telecommunication Union (2011). The Role of ICT in Advancing Growth in Least Developed Countries: Trends, Challenges and Opportunities. Retrieved from: http://www.itu.int/pub/D-LDC-ICTLDC.2011-2011.

Kempson, E. (1986). Information for Self-reliance and Self-determination: The Role of Community Information Services. *IFLA Journal*, 12(3), 182–191.

Kiplang, J. (1999). An Analysis of the Opportunities for Information Technology in Improving Access, Transfer and the Use of Agricultural Information in the Rural Areas of Kenya. *Library Management*, 20(2), 115–128. doi:10.1108/01435129910251575.

Laureys, F. (2016). Use of ICT for Agriculture in GIZ projects– Status quo, opportunities and challenges. *Deutsche Gesellschaft für Internationale Zusammenarbeit (GIZ)*. Retrieved from: https://snrd-asia.org/download/sector_programme_rural_development/Use-of-ICT-for-Agriculture-in-GIZ-projects_Laureys-F.pdf.

Lekoko, R.N. & Semali, L.M. (2011). *Cases on Developing Countries and ICT Integration: Rural Community Development* (1st ed.). Hershey, PA: IGI Global.

Lievrouw, L. & Livingstone, S. (2002). "Introduction: The Social Shaping and Consequences of ICTs." In *Handbook of New Media: Social Shaping and Consequences of ICTs*. London: Sage Publications. doi:10.4135/9781848608245.n1.

LôrBouôr (n.d.). Retrieved from: http://lorbouor.org/.

MimosaTEK (n.d.). Retrieved from: https://securingwaterforfood.org/innovators/mimosatek.

Nonaka, I. & Takeuchi, H. (1995). *The Knowledge Creating Company: How Japanese Companies Create the Dynamics of Innovation*. New York: Oxford University Press.

Nonaka, I. & Toyama, R. (2003). The Knowledge-Creating Theory Revisited: Knowledge Creation as a Synthesizing Process. *Knowledge Management Research & Practice*, 1(1), 2–9. doi:10.1057/palgrave.kmrp.8500001.

Payakpaie, J., Fung, C.C., Nathakaranakule, S., Cole, P. & Depickere, A. (2004). *A knowledge management platform for the promotion of modern rural energy services in ASEAN countries*. Proceedings of the 2004 IEEE Region 10 Conference TENCON, 535–538. doi:10.1109/TENCON.2004.1414826.

Plucknett, D.L., Smith, N.J.H. & Ozgediz, S. (1990). *Networking in International Agricultural Research*. New York: Cornell University Press.

Rosenbaum, H. (1998). *Web-based Community Networks: A Study of Information Organization and Access*. Proceedings of the American Society for Information Society, 35, 516–527. Retrieved from: http://hdl.handle.net/2022/174.

RUNPP (n.d.). Retrieved from: http://www.runetwork.org/html/d/articles/3456/preview_to_print.html.

Saravanan, R. (2008). *e-Arik: ICTs for Agricultural Extension Services to the Tribal Farmers*. Proceedings of World Conference on Agricultural Information and IT, IAALD AFITA WCCA. Retrieved from: https://www.cabi.org/gara/FullTextPDF/2008/20083298081.pdf.

Saravanan, R. (2011). eArik: Using ICTs to Facilitate "Climate Smart Agriculture" among Tribal Farmers of North East India. Climate Change, Innovation and ICTs. Retrieved from: http://www.niccd.org/wp-content/uploads/2017/11/NICCD_AgricAdapt_Case_Study_eArik.pdf.

SAWBO (2018). What are the genres of vocational schools where the number of students is expected to increase in the future? Retrieved from: http://sawbo-illinois4.org/.

Schmidt, C., Gorman, T., Andrew, B. & Gary, M. (2011). *Impact of Low-Cost, On-demand, Information Access in a Remote Ghanaian Village*. Proceedings of the IEEE Global Humanitarian Technology Conference, Seattle, WA. doi:10.1109/GHTC.2011.88.

Schuler, D. (1997). Community Computer Networks: An Opportunity for Collaboration among Democratic Technology Practitioners and Researchers. Paper presented at Technology and Democracy Workshop, Oslo, Norway.

Sproull, L. & Kiesler, S. (1991). *Connections: New Ways of Working in the Networked Organization*. Cambridge, MA: MIT Press.

Suni, I.M. & Hong, J. (2011). Ba and Communities of Practice in Research and Strategic Communities as a Way Forward. *Handbook of Research on Communities of Practice for Organizational Management and Networking Methodologies for Competitive Advantage*, 46–69. doi:10.4018/978-1-60566-802-4.ch004.

SYFN. (n.d.). *Savannah Young Farmers Network*. Retrieved from: http://savanet-gh.org/.
TotoAgriculture (n.d.). Retrieved from: https://infoagro.net/en/links/toto-agriculture.
Venkatappaiah, V. (1999). Community Information Services. *DESIDOC Bulletin of Info Technology*, 19(1), 1–4.
WeFarm (n.d.). Retrieved from: http://www.wefarm.co/.
Wenger, E. (1997). *Communities of Practice: Learning, Meaning and Identity*. Cambridge: Cambridge University Press.
WOCAT (n.d.). Retrieved from: https://www.wocat.net/en/global-slm-database/.

10 Social knowledge management

A social technology-enabled framework to bridge knowledge asymmetry of rural producers through virtual community formation

1 Introduction

The preceding chapters, after underlying the premise of knowledge in being a valuable resource, have discussed how management of knowledge resources is conducive in boosting socio-economic performance. In discussing knowledge management and the adopted strategies of the practice, the earlier chapters of this part of the book have significantly focused on how the concept gradually gained importance in the business world, and how it evolved in alliance with technological development. Knowledge management, as practised recently in its third generation, has made collaborative creation and modification of content possible, only with the help of contemporary social technologies. The inclusive spirit of social technologies, as fleshed out in Chapter 8, in establishing effective collaboration within and across social groups has significantly contributed to knowledge management transcending to a social practice.

In the preceding chapter we have spoken at length regarding efforts undertaken to manage social knowledge and information using ICT. Although these efforts cannot be formally tagged as "knowledge management practices", their course of action can undoubtedly be traced to managing social knowledge and information for social cause. Tracing the historical evolution of the way efforts to manage social knowledge and information altered, the preceding chapter shows how, only in the presence of social technologies, efforts undertaken for social cause could do justice to the motto of optimally managing social knowledge. However, the sporadic nature of the initiatives and their lack of communitarian focus have often marked the inadequacy of extant initiatives. To mark a disjuncture from extant initiatives and to fully utilize the potential of formal knowledge management as a strategy, we have devoted this chapter to chalk out the credibility and necessity for our social knowledge management framework in the context of holistic rural empowerment.

Many scholars have used the term *social knowledge management* to refer to knowledge management practice of collaborative creation and modification of content using social technologies in organizational context (Helmes et al., 2017). However, while several scholars, even at this stage, articulate the relevance of knowledge management in organizational context (which obviously is a social unit), it is important to investigate the prospects knowledge management as a practice has to offer in the context of overall society. Does knowledge management as a practice remain unaltered when it is applied to a social setting, as compared to that followed in organizational context? Is the nature of utilizing crowd knowledge to boost organizational performance, as a part of knowledge management practice, similar to the knowledge management efforts dedicated to achieving social empowerment through optimal tapping of crowd knowledge? What potential does knowledge management hold for social cause and how can the practice be modified to mitigate social maladies?

This chapter, in an attempt to further our conceptualization of social knowledge management, tries to answer all these questions. It builds on the concept of *social knowledge management* in the context of rural empowerment, which offers a respite from the inadequacies with which current efforts to manage social knowledge suffer from. While earlier versions of technology supported uni-directional and bi-directional information and knowledge transaction among social agents, it is in its most recent phase, with the help of social technology, that efforts to manage social knowledge can facilitate multi-directional knowledge transaction. The empowering and inter-connected virtual infrastructure offered by social technologies has the potential to sustain collaboration among diverse social agents, thereby enabling multi-directional knowledge exchange by empowering all to participate in the process of creating social knowledge.

In this context, it needs it be remembered that, while all knowledge management practices do not qualify to be social knowledge management practices, similarly, all initiatives to manage social knowledge may not be successfully termed as "knowledge management practices". The efforts undertaken to manage social knowledge for social development do not radiate characteristics intrinsic to the formalized discipline of knowledge management. The initial efforts undertaken for social cause, as we have seen in the preceding chapter, primarily attempted to capture and disseminate specialized information for communitarian betterment. The purview of these efforts is not similar to the ones we have articulated as knowledge management practices. Even in the second generation, bi-directional information and knowledge exchange could also offer scant hope to reduce knowledge asymmetry of marginalized participants. Although the efforts undertaken in the third phase, by deploying social technology, could do justice to the practice of managing social knowledge, their lack of purposive communitarian focus disallow these practices from transcending to the status of social knowledge management. Thus, in this chapter, we attempt to articulate what we mean by social knowledge management and the credibility and necessity of our proposed framework in the context of holistic rural empowerment. The chapter bears reference to how social technology can be used in a way to channelize social knowledge management practices in pursuit of mitigating rural–urban knowledge asymmetry.

2 Social knowledge vs. organizational knowledge

In order to clearly articulate the credibility and necessity of our social knowledge management framework we will begin by distinguishing social knowledge from organizational knowledge. Following that, distinguishing between knowledge management as practised in organizational context from efforts undertaken to manage social knowledge will further demarcate the uniqueness of our social knowledge management framework, which employs social technology in a way to rid itself of the hindrances intrinsic to conventional efforts undertaken to manage social knowledge. Although management of organizational knowledge has formal guidelines in the context of an organization, social development through management of social knowledge resources has no formal guiding principles. Also, it needs to be remembered that, in spite of similarities, the operationalization of knowledge management tactics differs from organizational context to social context. Two reasons can be traced as important in demarcating the practice of knowledge management in organizational context to that in social context:

- The premise of society is social knowledge, referred to as a collective body of knowledge produced by our community or social circle. On the other hand, domain specific, fixed, bounded knowledge accounts to be the premise of organizations.
- The composition of a society is heavily heterogeneous in nature. Society is composed of diverse social agents, while organizational workers, being committed to a fixed organizational aim, radiate homogenous characteristics.

These two crucial factors make it mandatory to analyse the practice of organizational knowledge management differently from the efforts taken to manage social knowledge for social development. Following, we will try to distinguish social knowledge from organizational knowledge. However, the difference that arises due the heterogeneity of social setting, as compared to homogeneity of organizations, will be taken up in the latter section of this chapter.

Social knowledge refers to the collective body of knowledge produced by our community or social circle (Study.com, n.d.). Being an asset of the community, social knowledge in reality is created and recreated following the ethics of social convention, where the dominant ideology often determines what can be considered as "authentic" social knowledge. However, in order to accredit social knowledge with a communitarian flavour, from which it primarily owes its origin, it has to be created in a decentralized way, as a product of communitarian collaboration, without the presence of a centralized arbitrator. Social knowledge acquires its true essence when it becomes a product of unhindered knowledge exchange between one and all within and across communities.

Social knowledge, in its truest sense, is a context-specific dynamic body of knowledge which is the product of effective knowledge exchange within a social group. In this context, it must be remembered that social knowledge is not the sum total of a group's knowledge; it acquires its dynamism from collaborations between diverse social agents. Social knowledge paves the path for a knowledge base, which is created through collaborations and participation and is the product of relationships and connections within a particular social group. Drawing its existence from collaborative knowledge exchange between social agents, social knowledge, the way we define it, is unbounded in nature. Unlike organizational context, anybody and everybody can contribute to the social knowledge pool. Social knowledge, therefore, radiates characteristics of openness, unlike organizational knowledge, which is domain-specific, fixed and bounded and committed to a fixed organizational goal.

Processes and strategies of managing knowledge for social cause are, therefore, significantly different from those as practised in organizational context, because the former has to manage social knowledge, which is different in its nature, scope and orientation from organizational knowledge. Hence it is important to chalk out the differences and similarities the practices of managing social knowledge ideologically share with organizational knowledge management. Will knowledge management as practised in organizations yield similar results when applied to social context unaltered? Do the nature, scope and agenda of managing knowledge remain similar in both organizational and social context? The following section attempts to answer these questions by providing a relational study between knowledge management as practised in organizations and the efforts undertaken to manage social knowledge for social benefit.

3 Organizational knowledge management vs. managing social knowledge

We have already demystified the concepts, processes and strategies of knowledge management as practised in organizational context in Chapter 7. Here we will try to differentiate between organizational knowledge management and efforts undertaken to manage social knowledge from different perspectives:

Heterogeneity vs. Homogeneity. Organizational knowledge management mainly attempts to enable effective knowledge exchange among a homogenous mass of organizational members. The organizational value system integrates the knowledge workers of organizations and binds them with a common purpose. Being possessors of similar intellectual, social and economic aptitude, and believing in a unified organizational goal, organizational members resonate characteristics of homogeneity.

Society at large, on the other hand, is intrinsically composed of heterogeneous members, coming from different castes, class, creeds, religion, ethnicity and other ascriptive backgrounds. While knowledge management practices undertaken in a homogeneous organizational setting require the consent and motivation of authorities and stakeholders, practices undertaken to manage social knowledge in a heterogeneous social setting require certain conditions beyond the consent of interested parties. For example, knowledge management practice will gain momentum in a business context if the management authorities, organizational members and organizational culture in alliance support the practice. However, in a social context – say, for example, in a rural sphere – success in managing information and knowledge of social relevance is not solely dependent on the motivation and participation of local governing bodies and local community members. Several factors, such as social conditions, political atmosphere and the cultural practices of locals, have significant impact in shaping which information and knowledge is to be considered ideal and suitable to be exchanged in the particular social setup. The heterogeneity of social setup calls for a management approach with twin focus; the one paying adequate attention to micro dynamics happening at the individual level, coupled with a macro lens to analyse the social whole as an entity beyond the summation of its individual parts.

Top-down vs. Bottom-up Approach. Organizational knowledge management mostly opted for a top-down approach, where knowledge management practices were initially decided upon by management authorities and subsequently imposed on organizational workers. Knowledge management as practised in first and second generations mostly relied on top-down management strategies to boost organizational performance. It is only recently, in its third-generation phase, that a bottom-up approach has been adopted in the context of organizational knowledge management. In trying to be people-centric, knowledge management practices in its third generation rely on self-initiated and voluntary knowledge exchange among organizational members in an attempt to improve organizational performance. At this stage, instead of being enforced or imposed by top authorities, common organizational members and their voluntary knowledge transaction determine the fate of knowledge management practices.

While top-down approaches have dictated organizational knowledge management for a considerable time and yielded positive outcomes, practices undertaken to manage social knowledge can only do justice to its cause in the absence of a top-down approach. A "one size fits all" deterministic top-down approach has been applied in several social contexts, where money and agricultural equipment were delivered to rural locales in developing countries in the hope of reducing poverty (Rawsthorne, 2006). The physical and fiscal help, however, failed to achieve the desired result because the local community lacked the skills and motivation to operate the equipment for communitarian betterment. As a result, the equipment was abandoned and the expected trickle-down effect did not eventuate because little attention was paid to other social, political and cultural factors that impacted adoption of new resources by local community members. The heterogeneity of social setting and its members calls for an approach to managing social knowledge that will address the concerns of the local community following local pace, culture and context. Until the local members are incorporated in the process of managing social knowledge through a bottom-up approach, we cannot expect such efforts to boost social performance.

Competitive Advantage vs. Empowerment. The primary motive behind undertaking knowledge management in organizational context is to boost competitive advantage of firms. The prior motive was to enhance economic efficiency to mark out a firm's identity in a competitive globalized market. In its third generation, when knowledge management practices shifted from a hard-core technological to a human-centred approach, enhancement of competitive advantage retained its supreme position. Knowledge management at this stage is encouraged to be people-centric because firms realized that the business units would suffer if its human resources were not incorporated within the knowledge management practices. However, ultimately, enhancement of competitive advantage of organizations, instead of empowering organizational members, can be identified as the primary motto of organizational knowledge management.

On the other hand, empowerment of social actors accounts to be the ultimate goal, which triggers the practice of managing social knowledge. Sole emphasis on economic efficiency can never be a sufficient motive for practices undertaken for social empowerment. Instead of economic efficiency, communitarian betterment should mostly take precedence in the context of managing social knowledge for social cause. Unlike its organizational counterpart, efforts to manage social knowledge for social benefit can only remain true to its cause by aiming for empowerment of social actors by overcoming the extant knowledge asymmetry that cripples society (Bandyopadhyay et al., 2017).

Restricted Collaboration vs. Open Collaboration. Collaboration accounts to be the premise of both organizational knowledge management and practices adopted to manage social knowledge for social cause. In organizational context, organizational authorities centrally manage knowledge management activities. It is the organizational authorities who decide which knowledge is to be exchanged, who will gain access to the organizational knowledge pool. Even in circumstances where organizations employ crowd knowledge to boost performance, organizational policy determines which knowledge is made accessible to the crowd. Organizational knowledge management reflects practices which resonate the spirit of restricted collaboration.

Efforts undertaken to manage social knowledge mostly promote open collaboration. Instead of having a single authoritative body, social knowledge can only be managed by facilitating knowledge exchange between diverse social agents. Although in its initial phase, efforts of this stature were mainly conceptualized and directed by external developmental authorities. With the passage of time, these practices became increasingly reliant on decentralized and voluntary mobilization of knowledge resources contributed by a diverse range of knowledge sources. This framework identifies every knowledge source to be a potential knowledge contributor. Crowd, which contributes to the pool of social knowledge, has equal and open access to the whole of the social knowledge pool. There is no structured social policy regulating transaction of social knowledge.

The relational study presented above clearly reflects how practices undertaken to manage social knowledge for social benefit require certain conditions, which go beyond activities crucial to retain the success of organizational knowledge management. Conventionally, the term social knowledge management has been used to refer to organizational knowledge management practices conducted with the aid of social technology. However, we need to remember that the term social knowledge has a holistic significance. It refers not just to knowledge but knowledge pertaining to society, created through dynamic collaboration between social members. An organizational knowledge management framework following social technology does not necessarily possess such a holistic purview. Neither does a practice to manage social knowledge in absence of such a holistic purview appropriately qualify to be a social knowledge management practice. It is when the efforts to manage social knowledge for social cause rely on optimal utilization of social technologies to incorporate within its framework the diverse economic, cultural and political contexts in which the social actors are embedded that it transforms into a social knowledge management framework. Such a framework, following social technology with a holistic lens adapted to address diverse aspects, has the credentials to boost social performance by empowering social actors, which we will take up in detail in the following section.

4 Social knowledge management: A functional perspective

Social knowledge management in our context is a framework for knowledge creation, assimilation and dissemination by social agents through digital connections and social collaboration for societal benefits, enhanced by social technologies (Bandyopadhyay, 2013; 2015; 2017). In social knowledge management, people interact and collaborate with each other, establish community norms and values, share knowledge and information resources and build trustful relationships, which are the core values of social capital: a relational resource composed of a variety of elements, most notably social networks, social norms, values, trust and shared physical resources (Bourdieu, 1992; Putnam, 2000). The reason why we think inclusive knowledge management practices can do justice to the term "social knowledge management" is justified below.

As we have explained in the former sections, social knowledge refers to a dynamic knowledge pool, created and sustained due to knowledge exchange between communitarian members. This knowledge can only be managed through democratic collaboration between social agents, instead of feeding communitarian members with information and knowledge externally. While earlier we have seen how management of social knowledge has ensured social functioning since primitive times, in contemporary growing and complex societies many developmental initiatives, in an attempt to manage social knowledge, have tried to deploy ICT to facilitate large-scale knowledge exchange between social members. However, it needs to be remembered that ICT-driven efforts to manage social knowledge must be community-centric, because community forms the premise of social knowledge. Conventional attempts deploying ICT to manage social knowledge have often failed to have trickle-down effects because, instead of facilitating communitarian engagement, the undertaken efforts have largely attempted to disseminate information and knowledge to disempowered groups externally (Basak et al., 2016).

The initiated efforts failed to have a widespread trickle-down effect because it needs to be remembered that ICT for social transformation is more than just making people digitally literate. ICT as a means of sharing knowledge and information is not simply about establishing a connection between people. In order to be effective, ICT as a medium has to serve as a link in the chain of development process. Information and knowledge transaction with disempowered people and groups is a complex process, where ICT can only be an effective link if it is appropriated and used in a way that helps resolve daily concerns (Mansell, 2010). Information and knowledge transaction between disempowered people is generally not amenable in across-the-counter productization and monetization. Only some kind of information – such as agriculture price information or health-related information – could be delivered through kiosk-based models. Other information and knowledge transfer is much more human interaction intensive and is required to be performed in an altruistic and community-minded spirit (IT for Change, 2009).

Recent efforts, which attempt to invest ICT for social cause, have started endorsing a new shift in conceptualization. They advocate that the most important impact related to ICT is not caused by the use of technology but by new forms of informational behaviours that they facilitate, which help in reducing extant knowledge divide. These new behaviours enable connections that offer the potential of new value or transformative change being created in social, political, cultural and economic spaces (Rawsthorne, 2006). A core developmental challenge is to make use of ICT community driven. Only then can we optimally use the potency of digital medium in managing social knowledge.

Efforts dedicated to deploying ICT for social development can be identified as a practice dedicated to managing social knowledge for social cause if, apart from giving local community access to knowledge, they attempt to inculcate information and skills to community members on how to process acquired knowledge. Subsequently, a similar practice of managing social knowledge can justly be termed a social knowledge management framework if it successfully deploys social technology to exploit the potential of community knowledge, making it available to the community and empowering the community to interact, collaborate and participate in the developmental process (Basak et al., 2016). Only such a social knowledge management framework is endowed with the capacity to build next-generation collaborative and responsive community by empowering communitarian members within a social setup with a social technology-enabled "capability framework". This inclusive social knowledge management framework has the capacity to provide specific ways in which social capital of social members can be enhanced. The processes intrinsic to such a framework are:

- Collaboration – social knowledge management framework must facilitate open collaboration among different and diverse social members.
- Content – the framework must harness the potential of crowd to rapidly identify and address challenges.
- Competence – the framework must attempt to further individual ability by facilitating effective networking among relevant parties.
- Enhanced human experience – the social knowledge management framework must provide experience in the form of integration across and between important capabilities, which results in increased social productivity.
- Contribution – the framework must facilitate one and all to contribute in the social knowledge pool. The effective collaboration social knowledge management attempts to foster can only be realized if the framework is successful in blurring the boundary between producers and consumers of knowledge, by viewing every social actor as a potential and unique knowledge source.

These credentials of social knowledge management framework not only distinguish it from organizational knowledge management efforts using social technology but also distance it from efforts undertaken to manage social knowledge for social development using exogenous approaches (Mansell, 2010). The intrinsic characteristics of social knowledge management, as articulated, make it a model that attempts to achieve social empowerment from within. Instead of imposing developmental policies, empowering social actors in tune to their local context and need is the premise of endogenous social knowledge management framework.

It is this inclusive social knowledge management framework that we wish to employ and expand in our research drive to mitigate the marginalization of disempowered social members by facilitating effective knowledge collaboration among them. The unhindered knowledge exchange facilitated by social knowledge management is conducive to effective community formation, which ultimately has the potential to mitigate the knowledge asymmetry faced by marginalized social members. It is the potential of virtual community formation with the help of social technologies that accredits a holistic purview to social knowledge management framework.

The concept of virtual communities was introduced by Rheingold (1993) in his popular book, *Virtual Communities*, where he described them as a "group of people who discuss a topic in a computer-mediated way sufficiently long with sufficient emotional involvement and who form interpersonal relationships". Virtual communities are online social networks in which people with common interests, goals and practices interact to share information and knowledge, and engage in social interactions (Chiu et al., 2011). It is the nature of social interactions and the set of resources embedded within the network that sustain virtual communities. Virtual community thus acts as a medium of interaction and communication that binds community members across geography for the purpose of enhancing both bridging and bonding social capital (Lin, 2001). Social capital is a resource that can combat social exclusion. Trust, social interaction and mutual reciprocity via online communities have the potential to create an interactive environment (Rheingold, 1993). Virtual community formation triggered by social knowledge management – positively enhancing bonding and bridging social capital of marginalized social members – is endowed with the credential to mitigate knowledge asymmetry and ensure holistic social empowerment.

In an attempt to blur the distinction between producers and consumers of knowledge within a virtual community, social knowledge management practices are endowed with the capacity to employ crowd knowledge in facilitating knowledge exchange leading to social empowerment. By considering every social actor to be a potential knowledge contributor, social knowledge management attempts to establish effective collaboration among crowd or otherwise unrelated human entities through social technologies. Effective collaboration enables crowd knowledge to get translated into crowd capital, which is defined as a heterogeneous knowledge resource, described as a "body of very important, but unorganized knowledge ... the knowledge of the particular circumstances of time and place" (Hayek, 1945). In the context of crafting a social knowledge management framework, crowd capital acts as a heterogeneous knowledge resource, derived from dispersed knowledge of the crowd and facilitating productive activity. Social knowledge management captures crowd capital through social technologies and applies acquired crowd resource to facilitate a commons-based peer production in a digitally networked environment (Benkler & Nissenbaum, 2006). A hallmark of this socio-technical framework is to promote socialization among crowd and target holistic development by facilitating voluntary knowledge exchange among these otherwise unrelated social members.

Social knowledge management framework aided by social technology can be considered an empowering strategy because of the positive outcomes it has the ability to usher in (IT for Change, 2013; Basak et al., 2016):

- Social empowerment. Social knowledge management has the potential to usher in social empowerment by improving communitarian access to basic social services. Enhanced access to basic social services includes improved access to formal and non-formal education, knowledge about health practices and about social programmes undertaken by national and international developmental champions.
- Economic development. Social knowledge management has the potential to usher in economic development by promoting a diverse range of economic opportunities to disempowered groups. It positively contributes in improving access to markets and commercialization of products, improving productive activities through inclusive dissemination of enhanced knowledge (for example, knowledge about agricultural practices), coupled with facilitating enhanced capacity to mobilize resources from outside donors.
- Participation in governance. Social knowledge management has the potential to ensure grassroot-level political participation, thereby enhancing transparency in governance. It attempts to secure "voice" and participation of local community

in their own developmental process, improve transparency of political community institutions and enhance local community's decision-making power in political process. The above-mentioned aspects ensure better co-ordination of political activities. It also attempts to encourage direct participation of local community in combating emergency situations such as natural disaster.
- Cultural identity. Social knowledge management has the potential to strengthen the cultural identity of local communities by strengthening the base of indigenous knowledge and language and facilitating improved dissemination of communitarian culture.

Social knowledge management practices thereby prove that they are not just capable in practically realizing the aim of third generation to deploy digital infrastructure in the process of empowering social actors. The inclusive potential of social knowledge management, by facilitating knowledge collaboration through effective community formation, has immense credibility to support the emergence of a new participative socio-economic sphere. With the aid of social technology, such initiatives pave the path for movements to ensure greater and more equitable access to knowledge and promotion of responsive and participatory democracy. This highlights the potential of social knowledge management practices in altering the way socio-economic activities are conducted in the contemporary digitally connected era. While this section highlights at length the necessity of social knowledge management framework in the context of achieving holistic social empowerment, we have reserved the following section to discuss the conceptual and interventional intricacies of our proposed social knowledge management framework.

5 A social knowledge management framework to mitigate rural–urban knowledge asymmetry

In this section we will attempt to give a practical shape to the framework of social knowledge management to mitigate rural–urban knowledge asymmetry through virtual community formation. The objective of our research is to demonstrate how the current internet-based social technology revolution has the potential to build/enhance the existing social capital of rural community by bridging rural–urban knowledge and information asymmetry through this social knowledge management framework. Improving access to knowledge and informational resources through this social knowledge management framework will eventually act as a gateway to make other forms of resources accessible. At the same time, this social knowledge management framework will not only serve as a medium of knowledge and information dissemination but also as a facilitator in bringing together producers and consumers of knowledge and information disregarding geographical boundaries, and thus create a global socio-cultural phenomenon. Such an inter-connected framework not only fosters explicit knowledge exchange among diverse social agents but also attempts to realize practically the spirit of collaboration in its truest essence.

5.1 The conceptual framework

The proposed social knowledge management framework has been conceptualized as an inter-connected digital space, where people can interact and collaborate with each other, establish community norms and values, share resources and build trustful relationships. The stated aspects which such a collaborative learning space promotes have been identified by several scholars as the core values of social capital: a relational resource composed of a variety of elements, most notably social networks, social norms, values and trust and shared resources (Bourdieu, 1992; Putnam, 2000). Our research is ultimately directed at creating rural transformation, where the sharp economic, social and cultural differences between rural and urban gradually disappear. Rural transformation is only possible when there is livelihood enhancement and holistic empowerment of the rural community using modern social information systems.

Creation and building of social capital within rural communities and across rural and urban communities in facilitating effective collaboration between them happens to be the premise of the social knowledge management framework we intend to propose. The right kind of information and knowledge required to increase social capital of rural communities is made up of access to quality educational support, training and advisory services, knowledge about available local opportunities and market links and, finally, access to a forum to discuss local governance. Our social knowledge management framework attempts to boost social capital of rural communities by cultivating effective knowledge transaction between urban and rural communities using social technology.

In order to achieve the above-stated research objective, realization of our social knowledge management framework is primarily reliant on the accomplishment of the following three tasks:

- Developing and implementing an internet-enabled social knowledge management (SKM) platform using social technologies, which will be a collaborative digital platform using local language. This platform will be designed to practically execute the proposed credentials of our social knowledge management framework.
- Equip selected rural communities with smartphones to introduce them to the SKM platform, which will enable need-specific integration of rural–urban communities. Providing rural mass with market connect and knowledge resource, we wish to critically investigate the impact on social capital and community wellbeing through engagement fostered by this SKM platform.
- Integrate an online synchronous and asynchronous e-learning platform with SKM to impart vocational training and to deliver online advisory services for members of rural community.

The above objectives can be achieved by establishing effective knowledge transaction between rural and urban communities in local languages and using local content. Rural communities can make use of the knowledge of various experts who can act as their mentors, guiding them to access quality resources based on their need, enabling them to share their concerns on public forums and providing them with necessary counselling wherever required. Mentors will interact with the rural community to identify their problems, impart their knowledge to solve those problems and, thus, enhance the social capital of the underprivileged community. Experts may also help rural community in assessing their community assets and competence – such as traditional, but extinct, skills, arts, crafts, culture, and natural flora and fauna, wildlife etc. – and help them translate these assets into opportunities. It is through such symbiotic knowledge exchange that social knowledge derives its dynamicity and gets managed through purposeful communitarian engagement.

With such rural–urban knowledge transaction, several virtual communities will be evolved based on the purpose of interaction (Figure 10.1). It is the ability to form virtual communities that marks the credibility of social knowledge management framework in the context of holistic rural empowerment. Unhindered knowledge exchange facilitated through social knowledge management is conducive to cultivating three types of virtual communities. The *communities of*

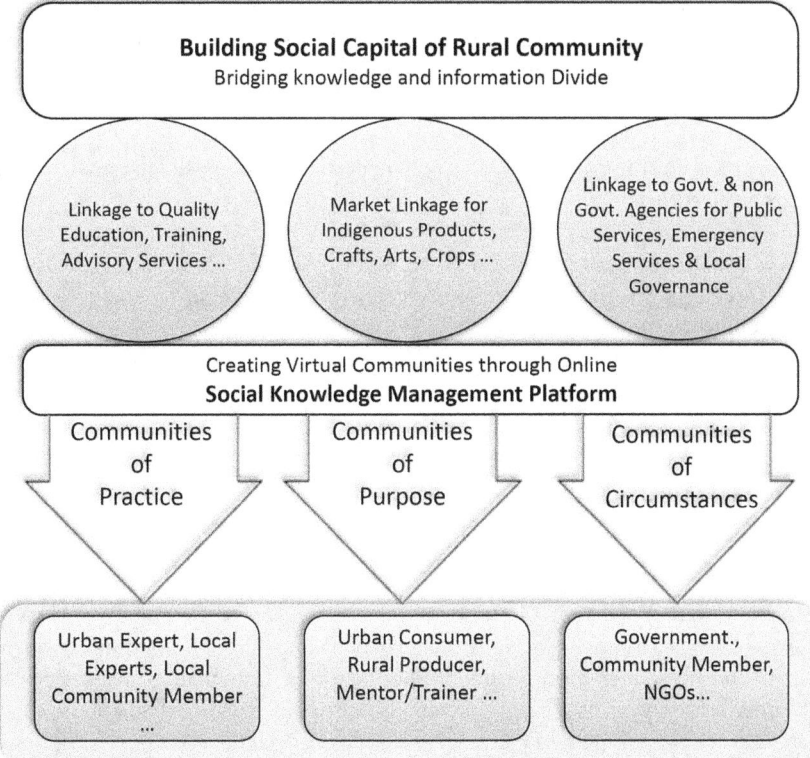

Figure 10.1 Social knowledge management framework facilitating virtual community formation

practice will be formed when the rural people seeking quality educational support and other advice get online training and guidance from the relevant professional experts (academic experts, medical experts, lawyers, etc.). Community of practice (Wenger et al., 2002), facilitating practice-oriented collaborations within and across groups, enables rural members to enhance their individual capability. However, it does not necessarily guarantee translation of enhanced capability into the generation of concrete economic results. Thus community of practice can mitigate knowledge asymmetry of rural producers but cannot improve their linkages to larger opportunity structures leading to economic benefits and livelihood enhancement. In order to achieve both, we subsequently advocate cultivating community of purpose (Stukes, 2016) among rural–urban entities.

Communities of purpose will be evolved through interaction of rural and urban communities to solve their market linkage, livelihood-related problems and to promote local community assets. While communities of practice and purpose contribute in enhancing knowledge capability of individual rural producers and can be rightly identified as drivers of self-development along a socio-economic axis, it is only when the rural community derives collective participatory credentials that they are able to mobilize local resources crucial to achieving resilience through formation of community of circumstance. *Communities of circumstance* will be formed to handle critical emergencies and other circumstantial issues. Such a community can only be formed if the community develops the desired adaptive capacities at a collective level, transcending individual enhancement. This will be illustrated in detail in Part III of our book.

Through the proposed SKM implementation, we wish to answer two research questions:

- How can the agency of rural population be enhanced, along with making greater opportunities available to them, to enable them to achieve degrees of empowerment?
- How can bridging the rural–urban knowledge asymmetry using social technologies empower the rural population to take informed decisions and purposeful choices, thereby making them agential actors?

5.2 The model of intervention

The model of intervention discusses practical means to execute our social knowledge management framework. In order to practically implement the proposed framework, we have designed a digital platform and a mobile app to carry out unhindered knowledge collaboration between rural–urban entities through community formation. In our intervention model, rural producers, who are equipped with smartphones with internet connectivity, are given training to use the SKM mobile app in a local language. The proposed SKM platform will provide social networking opportunities, fostering a high degree of collaboration and connectedness in virtual communities through both synchronous and asynchronous interaction. The overall model of intervention is depicted in Figure 10.2 below, having the following components:

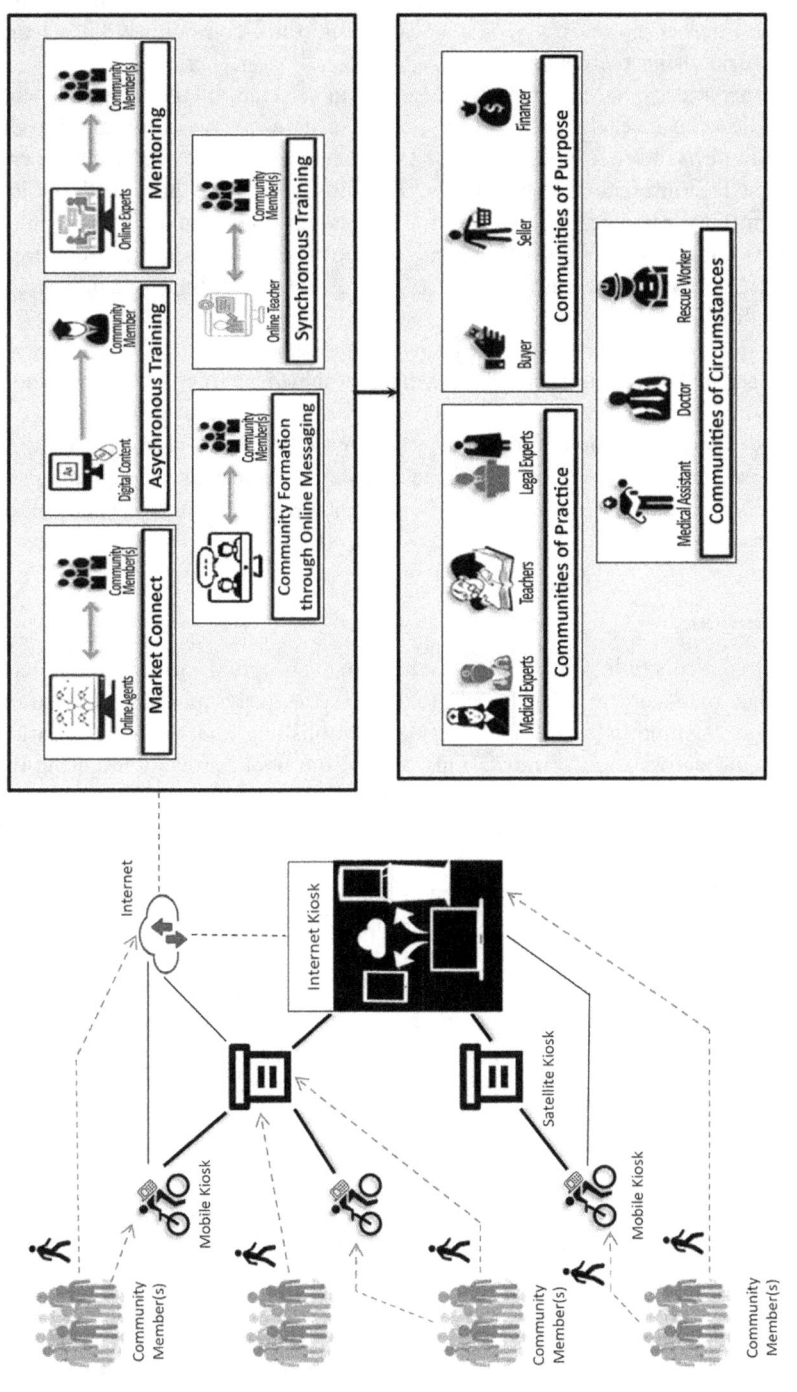

Figure 10.2 SKM framework to mitigate rural–urban knowledge asymmetry

- Members of rural community are equipped with low-cost smartphones with internet connectivity. They can form intra-community knowledge networks using their mobile apps.
- Internet kiosks (wi-fi hotspot) are set up in selected village locations with one desktop in each kiosk acting as a wi-fi gateway with unlimited high-bandwidth internet connectivity. The members of the community can access free internet at these kiosks. The kiosks will also have a discussion room with low-cost LCD projectors to conduct online interactive training/counselling/mentoring sessions and to show (in pre-assigned time slots) online videos such as movies, sports, etc. A local coordinator will manage this kiosk.
- An internet-enabled social knowledge management platform with embedded local/regional content will be designed to implement the model of e-interaction and e-collaboration in order to promote purposive rural–urban knowledge interaction. This platform will provide social networking opportunity, fostering a high degree of collaboration and connectedness in virtual communities through both synchronous and asynchronous interaction.

6 Conclusion

We wish to conclude this chapter with our conceptualization of a social knowledge management framework that can effectively mitigate the extant knowledge asymmetry crippling society by establishing effective collaboration between and across social groups. This part of the book, after highlighting the importance of knowledge management as an effective strategy in boosting both organizational and social performance, articulates our conceptualization of social knowledge management framework and its importance in ushering in holistic rural empowerment by enhancing knowledge capability of rural actors by facilitating effective intra- and inter-group collaboration among them.

The uniqueness of our research contribution lies here. By facilitating unhindered knowledge exchange between and across social groups, our social knowledge management framework does not limit itself to community formation but extends to enhancing knowledge capability of participants by virtue of such formation. An enhanced knowledge capability means that the participants do not exchange knowledge passively but develop the credentials to trigger knowledge collaboration in pursuit of enhancing their opportunity scopes. While efforts to manage social knowledge in the third generation incorporate aspects of community formation, they seldom do so to enhance the knowledge capability of the participants. It is only enhancement of knowledge capability through community formation that sows the seeds for mitigating the extant knowledge asymmetry from which marginalized groups suffer. Mitigation of knowledge asymmetry through enhancement of knowledge capability of marginalized members bears the prospect of attaining holistic rural empowerment through community formation.

So far we have discussed the problems intrinsic to rural context and proposed a social knowledge management framework to usher in holistic rural empowerment by bridging rural–urban knowledge asymmetry. While Part I and Part II of this book are mostly reserved for theoretical articulations, the following part, Part III, has evidence of how the proposed framework can be practically realized to cultivate formation of *communities of practice, purpose* and *circumstance* among marginalized rural populations through the design and development of a *digital social knowledge management platform*. We have designed the social knowledge management platform to enable cultivation of knowledge capability among rural members on a practical level by facilitating practice-oriented, purposive and resilient community formation. It is through active and voluntary formation of such communities that rural members will develop knowledge capability through effective collaboration, which will attempt to realize a holistic vision of rural empowerment through mitigation of extant knowledge asymmetry.

References

Bandyopadhyay, S., Shaw, V., Banerjee, A. & Nag, D. (2013). *Social Knowledge Management: Use of Social Media for Disseminating Informal Wisdom of Elderly to the Youth*. Proceedings of the International Conference on Knowledge, Innovation and Enterprise, London. Retrieved from: https://www.iimcal.ac.in/sites/all/files/sirg/2-1-Social.pdf.

Bandyopadhyay, S., Banerjee, S., Bardhan, A., Dey, P. & Das, S. (2015). *A Social Knowledge Management Framework for Harnessing Collective Knowledge Capital of Senior Citizens*. Proceedings of the 12th International Conference on Intellectual Capital, Knowledge Management & Organisational Learning. Retrieved from: http://toc.proceedings.com/28324webtoc.pdf.

Bandyopadhyay, S., Bardhan, A., Dey, P., Banerjee, S., Das, S. & Mandal, K. (2017). "A Social Knowledge Management Platform for Universal Primary Education Online," in *Harnessing Social Media as a Knowledge Management Tool*. Information Science Reference. Hershey, PA: IGI Global. doi:10.4018/978-1-5225-0495-5.ch005.

Basak, J., Parthiban, R., Roy, S. & Bandyopadhyay, S. (2016). *A Community-driven Information System to Develop Next Generation Collaborative and Responsive Rural Community (NCoRe)*. Proceedings of the ITU Kaleidoscope Academic Conference: ICTs for a Sustainable World (ITU WT), Bangkok, 1–8. doi:10.1109/ITU-WT.2016.7805727.

Benkler, Y. & Nissenbaum, H. (2006). Commons-based Peer Production and Virtue. *Journal of Political Philosophy*, 14(4), 394–419. doi:10.1111/j.1467-9760.2006.00235.x.

Bourdieu, P. (1992). *An Invitation to Reflexive Sociology* (1st ed.). Chicago, IL: University of Chicago Press.

Chiu, C.M., Wang, E.T.G., Shih, F.J. & Fan, Y. (2011). Understanding Knowledge Sharing in Virtual Communities: An Integration of Expectancy Disconfirmation and Justice Theories. *Online Information Review*, 35(1). doi:10.1108/14684521111113623.

Hayek, F.A. (1945). The use of knowledge in society. *The American Economic Review*, 35(4), 519–530.

Helmes, R., Cranefield, J. & Reijsen, J. (2017). *Social Knowledge Management in Action: Applications and Challenges*. Heidelberg: Springer.

IT for Change (2009). ICTs for community development in India: Going beyond the basic CSC model. Retrieved from: http://www.itforchange.net/gov-ict/73-governance/280-csc-model.html.

IT for Change (2013). ICTs for Empowerment and Social Transformation: A Brief Exploration of the Field from the Viewpoint of Organizational Action. Retrieved from: https://itforchange.net/icts-for-empowerment-and-social-transformation-a-note-prepared-by-it-for-change-for-actionaid-0.

Laszlo, K.C. & Laszlo, A. (2002). Evolving Knowledge for Development: The Role of Knowledge Management in a Changing World. *Journal of Knowledge Management*, 6(4), 400–412. doi:10.1108/13673270210440893.

Laszlo, K.C. & Laszlo, A. (2006). *Fostering a sustainable learning society through knowledge-based development*. Proceedings of the 50th Annual Meeting of the ISSS. doi:10.1002/sres.850.

Lin, N. (2001). *Social Capital: A Theory of Social Structure and Action*. Cambridge: Cambridge University Press.

Mansell, R. (2010). Power and interests in developing knowledge societies: exogenous and endogenous discourses in contention. IKM Working Papers (11), IKM Emergent, Bonn, Germany. Available at: http://eprints.lse.ac.uk/29255/.

Putnam, R.D. (2000). *Bowling Alone: The Collapse and Revival of American Community*. New York: Touchstone.

Rawsthorne, P. (2006). Community Knowledge Management for Development: The Creation of Community Learning Environments for Reducing the Knowledge Divide. Available at: www.rawsthorne.org/docs/PeterRawsthorne.CKMS4D.pdf.

Rheingold, H. (1993). *The Virtual Community: Homesteading on the Electronic Frontier*. Cambridge, MA: MIT Press.

Study.com (n.d.). Social Knowledge: Definition & Networks. Retrieved from: https://study.com/academy/lesson/social-knowledge-definition-networks-quiz.html.

Stukes, F. (2016). Communities of Purpose (Doctoral thesis, The University of North Carolina, Charlotte). Retrieved from: https://eric.ed.gov/?id=ED572119.

Wenger, E., McDermott, R. & Snyder, W.M. (2002). *Cultivating Communities of Practice*. Cambridge, MA: Harvard Business Press.

Part III
Social knowledge management in action
Some empirical studies in rural India

11 Cultivating online communities of practice to facilitate practice-oriented rural–urban knowledge exchange through collaborative learning spaces

1 Introduction

The earlier part of this book, after tracing the evolution of knowledge management practices and technical architecture, furthered a conceptualization of our social knowledge management framework. The effectivity of social knowledge management, in relation to former knowledge management versions, rests in its capability to implement social technology to establish widespread collaborations among diverse social agents. It is social technology-supported social knowledge management that has the potential to facilitate unhindered multi-directional knowledge exchange. The concluding chapter of the preceding section bears reference to our conceptualization of social knowledge management and its credibility in facilitating holistic rural empowerment. Part III of the book discusses the utilization of social knowledge management framework in creating different forms of virtual communities, which would eventually enhance knowledge capabilities of rural producers by bridging rural–urban knowledge divide. In this part we have articulated the conceptual and implementational dynamics of our social knowledge management platform, which has been designed to facilitate different types of community formation between rural–urban agents: a practical way to realize the potential of our devised social knowledge management framework.

We will highlight the effectivity of social knowledge management framework by showing how its collaborative premise is conducive to cultivating different communities, both within rural members and across rural–urban members. Part III of this book spells out the effectivity of social knowledge management in terms of *cultivating* three types of community: *community of practice, community of purpose* and *community of circumstance*. While community of purpose and circumstance will be dealt with in detail in subsequent chapters, we have reserved this chapter to discuss how our proposed framework supports the formation of community of practice.

Community of practice refers to a group of people who share a particular practice. Collaborations among the members of community of practice, or practitioners in other words, result in collective learning, which makes community of practice a collaborative learning space. This chapter is dedicated to spelling out the conceptual framework of community of practice and its practical credibility in achieving holistic empowerment of rural marginalized population.

The chapter is divided into five sections:

- It begins by articulating what community of practice is, the reason behind its inception and its credential in facilitating knowledge collaborations among its members.
- The second segment gives a historical account of how collaborative learning spaces have enabled inter- and intra-generational knowledge transmission for some time, long before such spaces were formally identified as community of practice.
- The third segment highlights how the idea of community of practice and the knowledge collaboration among members, which it supports, gradually gained ground. With the passage of time, this section bears reference as to how this concept is influenced by several other concepts like the Japanese concept of *ba,* which has been conceptualized as a shared space of learning, crucial to boosting organizational performance.
- The fourth section expands on the relational study between *ba* and community of practice, as presented in the third section, to highlight the importance community of practice has in organizational context. The section provides examples of companies that have attempted, by cultivating community of practice, to facilitate knowledge exchange among its members, thereby attempting to boost overall organizational performance through such exchange.
- The final section highlights the importance of cultivating community of practice in context of rural empowerment. By providing first-hand field insights, the section concludes with how cultivating community of practice using social technologies creates a collaborative learning environment, which has the potential to justly manage social knowledge.

2 Conceptualizing community of practice

Social actors are continuously – either spontaneously, or in a more organized way or both – trying to build relationships with each other to pave the path for opportunities facilitating collaborative learning. Collaborative learning can act as a potential driver in improving awareness level and current practices of social actors. This collective learning results in practices, which is property of a kind of community, created over time by the sustained pursuit of shared enterprise. Wenger calls this community of practice. He defines communities of practice (CoP) as "groups of people who share a concern or a passion for something they do and who interact regularly to learn how to do it better" (Wenger, 1997). Community of practice can evolve naturally because of members' common interest in a particular domain or can be created and cultivated deliberately with the goal of gaining knowledge related to a specific field (Wenger et al., 2002). According to Wenger et al., communities of practice are like "gardens" that "benefit from cultivation". There is a growing interest within organizations to cultivate communities of practice in order to benefit from shared knowledge that may lead to higher productivity (Wenger et al., 2002; Wenger et al., 2000). Communities of practice are now viewed by many organizations as a means to capturing tacit knowledge, the knowledge that is not so easily articulated. It is through the process of sharing knowledge that members learn from each other and have an opportunity to develop personally and professionally (Lave & Wenger, 1991).

The origin and primary use of community of practice has been in learning theory. It started with Jean Lave and Etienne Wenger, who coined the term community of practice while studying apprenticeship as a learning model. They studied the relationship between student and master and concluded that, instead of being a simple relationship, the master–student relationship involves complex sets of social relationships through which learning takes place (Lave & Wenger, 1991). Their research let them look at how apprenticeships help people learn. Initially, newcomers in an organization learn and watch the activities of older members to get familiar with the operational dynamics of the particular organization. It is through this process of socialization that learning becomes a participatory practice, which Lave and Wenger named "situated learning" (Lave & Wenger, 1991). This proves that, since its very inception, community of practice has been intrinsically linked to the concept of collaborative or networked learning (Cummings & van Zee, 2005).

In order to facilitate geographically distributed work practices, the concept of *virtual communities of practices* (VCoPs) has evolved that supports online interactions among members through the use of internet-enabled social technologies (Dubé et al., 2005). With pervasive penetration of mobile technologies, the concept of "mobile communities of practice" (MCoP) (Kietzmann et al., 2013) is also emerging, where members communicate with one another via smartphones and participate in community work on the go. These virtual communities enhance innovative and productive growth of the community members as well as the communities as collective entities beyond the degree of formal organizational structures (Wartburg et al., 2006).

Two viewpoints characterize community of practice (Hoadley, 2012): the feature-based view and the the process-based view.

The *feature-based view* of community of practice emphasizes the principle of sharing: a community that shares practices (Hoadley, 2012). According to this viewpoint, learning was not a property of individuals and the representations in their heads (the cognitive view), but rather a more *relational property of individuals* in context and in interaction with one another (the situated view).

The *process-based view* of community of practice emphasizes the process of knowledge generation, application and reproduction through community participation. Through participation, learners enter a community and gradually take up its practices. In fact, a primary focus of Wenger's more recent work is on learning as social participation, where an individual constructs his/her identity through active participation in these communities (Wenger et al., 2002).

2.1 Factors leading to the cultivation of community of practice

After the joint work with Lave, Wenger embarked on the journey to give a theoretical and practical base to the devised concept of community of practice. He identified seven factors as leading to the cultivation of community of practice (Wenger, 1997):

- The community should be designed in a way so that it evolves naturally. It should be flexibly designed to incorporate shift in focus with changing surrounding conditions.
- The created community must facilitate open dialogue within and with outside perspectives.
- The community must welcome and allow different levels of participation among members.
- The community should accommodate both private and public spaces within the practice to adequately enable shared context on a wide range.
- The community should put special emphasis on the value of the community.
- The community should provide opportunities to members to shape their learning experience through collective brainstorming sessions.
- The community should facilitate a thriving cycle of activities and events that motivates the members to regularly meet, reflect and evolve.

2.2 Components of community of practice

After articulating the prerequisites in the process of cultivating community of practice, Wenger goes on to articulate the three components of community of practice (Wenger, 1997):

- Domain – Community of practice has an identity defined by a shared domain of interest.
- Community – Within the shared domain of interest, members engage in joint activity and discussions, help each other and share relevant information and knowledge. This collaborative learning environment leads to the formation of community.
- Practice – Community of practice is not just a community of interest. A key paradigm is the fact that members of community of practice are practitioners, who enliven the community through their active participation. The shared practice enables the members to develop a shared repertoire of resources, such as experience, stories and tools.

2.3 Structure of community of practice

Based on the components of community of practice, Wenger proceeded to produce a formal structurization of community of practice. Wenger postulated that the structure of community of practice consists of three inter-related terms (Wenger, 1997, p. 72–73):

- Mutual engagement. In community of practice, through participation, members establish norms and build collaborative relationships, which have been identified as mutual engagement. These collaborative relationships bind the members of community together as a social entity and enhance both bridging and bonding social capital.
- Joint enterprise. Through interactions, the members create shared understandings of what binds them together. This is referred to as joint enterprise. Joint enterprise can be referred to as the "domain" of the community.
- Shared repertoire. As a part of shared practice, community produces a set of communal resources. These communal resources have been identified as shared repertoire and are derivative of the common practice that integrates the members of community of practice.

2.4 Factors determining sustainability of community of practice

It is the simultaneous and sustained cultivation of the above-mentioned aspects that contribute to formation of community of practice. The sustenance of community of practice is thought to be dependent on three factors (Battistella, 2015):

- Social presence: Communicating with others in community of practice includes creation of social presence. Tu (2002) defines social presence in terms of degree of salience of another person in an interaction and consequent salience of an inter-personal relationship. Social presence affects the likelihood of an individual's participation in community of practice.
- Motivation: Motivation of members to share knowledge is critical in sustaining community of practice (Ardichvilli et al., 2003).
- Collaboration: Effective networking between members accounts to be both the necessary and sufficient condition for thriving community of practice.

The above descriptions reaffirm the potential community of practice has in enabling democratic knowledge exchange, where one and all is accredited with the potential to contribute to the collective knowledge pool. By connecting individuals with other relevant social actors, community of practice not only enables formation of a dynamic knowledge repository but also facilitates discussion forums through expert connect, enlivened by voluntary collaboration between communitarian members. While community of practice can be formed

218 *Empirical studies in rural India*

physically, contemporary social technology and its connecting spirit has promising prospects to offer in the domain of cultivating such practice-oriented communities in virtual space. Optimal cultivation of online community of practice can be achieved both through synchronous (live online interactions, such as video conferencing) and asynchronous (offline interactions, such as instant online messaging and discussion forums) mode. Such a setup transcends providing communitarian members access to relevant knowledge resources. Through effective exchange, community of practice thereby successfully cultivates knowledge-operating capacities or knowledge capability of communitarian members.

As Figure 11.1 highlights, online community of practice can act as a facilitator to create knowledge repository, initiate discussion forums, provide access to experts and promote relevant exchange over synchronous and asynchronous mode of operations. Only such an optimal facilitation through creation of practice-oriented community offers the potential to simultaneously cultivate

Figure 11.1 Community of practice: A conceptual framework

social capital and knowledge capability of communitarian members through the creation of collaborative learning spaces. The multi-dimensional credentials of community of practice in enabling democratic knowledge exchange are increasingly marking its importance in academic, developmental and business domains.

However, it needs to be remembered that, although the formal inception of the concept can be traced to recent times, collaborative learning space, which happens to be the premise of community of practice, is not a new activity. Historically people have been learning and sharing knowledge and experience through the act of storytelling. It is through such informal knowledge exchange within community – long before formal association with community of practice – that collaborative learning spaces have evolved and facilitated inter- and intra-generational knowledge transmission. In the following section we will focus on collaborative learning spaces of early society to draw a continuum between these informal collaborations of early society and the one recently formulated as community of practice.

3 Collaborative learning spaces of early society

Community of practice and the collaborative learning it supports have gained much prominence in the field of development and management studies. However, it needs to be remembered that, although the linkage between the two is derivative of recent research attempts, collaborative learning and knowledge exchange within community has been a persistent practice since time immemorial. It is through informal knowledge exchange and creation of a collaborative learning space that, historically, community members have been enabled to achieve intra- and inter-generational knowledge transmission.

Gymnasium of ancient Greece accounts to be a perfect example of a collaborative learning space of early society. The gymnasium functioned as a training facility for competitors in public games and was also a place for members to socialize and engage in intellectual pursuits. Although the gymnasium started with a health concern, as it pronounced itself as a place for exercise, soon it became more than that (Hugh, 1911). This development arose through recognition by the Greeks of the strong relationship between athletics, education and health. Accordingly, the gymnasium became connected with education on the one hand and medicine on the other. Except for time devoted to cultural pursuits such as music, the education of young men was solely conducted in the gymnasium, where provisions were made not only for physical pedagogy but also for instruction in morals and ethics.

The early Greek gymnasia thrived on active participation of the members, who collaboratively participated in the learning process. Although the members frequenting the gymnasia were not recognized to formally form "community of practice", the collaborative learning environment of the institution thrived on peer-to-peer interaction, which also happens to be the premise of community of practice.

Early Indian teaching methods also reflected a practice of collaborative learning. The ancient *ashrams*, or hermitage, happened to be the premise of the *guru-shishya* (teachers and disciples in traditional Indian culture) learning model, where youths were sent to learn not only curriculum-based pedagogy but also ethics and morals and religious preaching. The learners stayed at the ashrams and practised acquired knowledge in collaboration. This proves that, although community of practice and the collaborative learning environment it supports is of recent origin, the practice of peer-based learning is not a new phenomenon and has enabled informal inter- and intra-generational knowledge transmission across the ages.

4 Community of practice in action

The emergence of community of practice following Lave and Wenger's conceptualization and its gradual proliferation proved the concept's effectivity in sharing best-practices and creation of new knowledge to advance a domain of professional practice. Forming a community accounts to be crucial in furthering best practices for professional pursuit, because intra- and inter-group collaboration is increasingly becoming important in today's connected world for both individual and collective performance improvement (Cambridge et al., 2005).

As community of practice can be rightly identified as a triggering factor in facilitating collaborative learning, it bears relevance even outside the domain of learning theory, from where it first originated formally. The role community of practice plays in facilitating informal collaborations through exchange of tacit knowledge marks the relevance of the concept in the domain of knowledge management, undertaken to boost organizational performance (Lesser & Prusak, 1999). The emergence of the Japanese concept of *ba*, in an attempt to enhance business performance, seems to share a lot of commonality with community of practice.

Ba conceptually refers to a shared space or context which leads to creation of new knowledge, innovation and learning opportunities (Suni & Hong, 2011). *Ba* was initially used by Japanese researchers as a knowledge management strategy to boost performance of Japanese firms. Several guidelines emerged in Japan regarding how companies can use *ba* for successful knowledge transfer, in initiating intangible benefits for workspace, by facilitating effective collaboration between organizational workers through a shared space or context. The concept of *ba* was originally proposed by Kitaro Nishida (1921) and further developed by Hiroshi Shimizu. The early scholars defined *ba* as a shared context, in which knowledge is created, shared and utilized.

The shared space, characteristic of *ba*, marks a departure from the command and control model of traditional pyramid management. The shared space can only be set up by voluntary membership within an emerging and stimulating environment through care and mutual respect (Suni & Hong, 2011). The concept of *ba* was later developed by Nonaka and Toyama (2003), who conceptualized it as a multiple interacting mechanism explaining tendencies for interactions that occur at a specific time and space, instead of thinking of *ba* as a strictly physical space such as a meeting room. Following the scholars' conceptualization, *ba* can be articulated as an existential space where participants share their context and create new meanings through interactions. This shared space, enlivened through collaborations, serves as a foundation for knowledge creation and exchange (Von Krogh et al., 2000). The concept of *ba* unifies physical, virtual and mental spaces involved in knowledge creation. It is a space for emerging relationships. The space can be physical (office, business space), virtual (teleconference, e-messaging) and mental (shared experience, idea).

The concept of *ba* is very much congruent with Nonaka and Takeuchi's SECI model of knowledge sharing, which to a great extent has revolutionized the domain of organizational knowledge management. While we have explained the SECI model in detail in Chapter 7, we have reserved this section to discuss the categorization of *ba* in relation to the SECI model of knowledge transfer. Based on the SECI model, there are four types of *ba* that correspond to four stages in the SECI model (Nonaka & Noboru, 1998). They are:

- *Originating ba* – Individual face-to-face interaction offers a context for socialization. From this emerge care, love, trust, commitment. In today's connected world, this face-to-face interaction can also happen in virtual space through video conferencing/video chat.
- *Dialoguing ba* – Refers to collective face-to-face interaction. It is the place where individuals' mental models and skills are shared, converted to common terms, and articulated as concepts, or, in other words, individuals are able to give explicit form to their tacit knowledge resource through externalization. Tacit knowledge is shared and articulated through dialogues among participants.
- *Systematizing ba* – Offers the context for a combination of existing explicit knowledge. IT such as online groupwares and networks offer a virtually collaborative environment for the creation of systematizing *ba*.
- *Exercising ba* – Offers a context for internalization, where individuals embody explicit knowledge communicated via virtual media.

A brief discussion on *ba* reflects how the concept shares a similar premise to that of community of practice. Both *ba* and community of practice are useful in bringing together people from different backgrounds who share a common interest and express willingness to share those, including knowledge and practices through effective networking (Wenger & Snyder, 2000; Nonaka & Toyama, 2003). As a result, both the concepts have been identified as an integrating tool in bringing together people from diverse backgrounds to develop something new together. Moreover, both *ba* and community of practice cannot be stimulated through forced participation. It is only through voluntary participation in a conducive environment that the concepts can usher in democratic knowledge exchange. Given the similarity *ba* and community of practice share conceptually, it can be rightly concluded that community of practice, similar to *ba*, has the potential to impact the field of organizational knowledge management through activation of democratic knowledge exchange. In the following section, before delving into the potential of cultivating community of practice to facilitate social development, we will highlight the relevance of the concept in ushering organizational knowledge management on a holistic level.

5 Building community of practice in organizational context

Lesser and Prusak (1999) have shown how community of practice accounts to be a major building block in creating, sharing and applying organizational knowledge. In an attempt to justify the relevance of the concept in the domain of knowledge creation, storage and use, the authors highlight how cultivating community of practice acts as an accelerating force in enhancing social capital, a social resource, which provides value to themselves and their organization. This social resource is a necessary condition for knowledge creation, sharing and use.

Nahapiet and Ghoshal (1998) attempted to link social capital at organizational level with an organization's ability to manage its knowledge resources. According to them, social capital has three characteristics:

- Structural. Cultivation of informal networks through which individuals gain the provision to identify, connect and collaborate with others possessing potential resources.
- Relational. Addresses inter-personal dynamics between individuals within the network. The relational dynamics lead to the cultivation of cementing elements of trust, shared norms, values, obligations and expectations.
- Cognitive. Addresses the need for common context and language, mandatory to building social capital.

Communities of practice share similar characteristics with those of social capital, as mentioned above (Lesser & Prusak, 1999):

- Structural. Community of practice gives individuals the opportunity to develop a network of individuals having similar interests.
- Relational. Community of practice fosters interpersonal interactions necessary to build a sense of trust and obligation critical to building social capital.
- Cognitive. Since they tend to be organized around a common issue, community of practice is instrumental in maintaining the common context and language behaviours used by members.

The above-mentioned factors not only imply the relevance of community of practice in the domain of establishing effective networking but also hint at the potential the concept has to boost organizational performance through informal creation and exchange of knowledge among organizational members. The concept of social capital, the web of social relationships that influence individual behaviour, has recently gained credence as a means to achieve sustainable economic growth. Effective networking between organizational workers generates a value, which has the potential to yield socio-economic outcomes, without the intervention of external agents (Nahapiet & Ghoshal, 1998).

A *community of practice* refers to an inter-personal bonding space enlivened by a common practice, which can be referred to as a dynamic process, knowledge in action, through which individuals learn how to do their jobs by actually performing tasks and interacting with others performing similar tasks. While teams/groups are formal and specifically task-oriented, *community of practice* on the other hand is informal and premised on a shared context. In most organizations, community of practice exists without formal charters or organizational mandates. It is viewed as a means to capture the tacit knowledge or the organizational know-how that is not so easily articulated.

Lesser and Storck (2001) articulate the dimensions along which cultivation of community of practice benefits organizational performance:

- Decreasing the learning curve of new employees.
- Responding more rapidly to customer needs and inquiries.
- Reducing rework.
- Spawning new ideas of products and services.

In order to exemplify the effectiveness of community of practice in organizational context, we will cite the example of Xerox Corporation to show how the company boosted its performance by cultivating community of practice. Xerox attempted to cultivate a community of practice among customer service representatives who were entrusted with repairing machines in the field (Brown & Duguid, 2000). The representatives exchanged tips and tricks with each other over informal meetings, which were recognized by Xerox as valuable. As a result, the company captured these interactions and launched the Eureka project to allow these interactions to be shared across the network of representatives globally. This attempt by Xerox to build a community of practice among customer service representatives not only enabled a space of collaborative learning but also attempted to enhance the social capital of organizational workers through purposive exchange of contextual knowledge, thereby enhancing the overall organizational performance on a sustainable basis.

While this section articulates the relevance of building community of practice in context of boosting organizational performance, we have reserved the following section to explore how community of practice can be cultivated within rural communities and between rural–urban communities by using social knowledge management framework. This is having significant implications in reducing knowledge asymmetry of rural producers, leading to holistic rural empowerment.

6 Cultivating online communities of practice in rural context

According to Wenger et al. (2002), communities of practice are like "gardens" that "benefit from cultivation". They proposed that "even though communities [of practice] are voluntary and organic, good community design can invite, even evoke, aliveness". We use this section to explore how cultivating communities of practice among rural producers can create and strengthen the knowledge network of the marginalized rural sector. And, in a subsequent section, we will show how our proposed social knowledge management framework can help cultivate the communities of practice.

Unhindered knowledge exchange facilitated through community of practice, leading to a collaborative learning space, offers the prospect of improving the livelihoods of rural participants. Active participation of rural populations in the process of knowledge exchange, not only within their own communities but also with other communities including urban entities, enables them to apply newly acquired knowledge in pursuit of self and communitarian benefit. As we have mentioned in Part I, in spite of significant concern from multiple sectors to uplift and enhance rural livelihood, attained results have been unable to achieve desired outcomes. Two reasons can be cited as key hindering aspects: (i) lack of information and knowledge flow among rural members; and (ii) rural–urban information and knowledge divide. Since, in our research drive, we have primarily traced marginalization of rural sector to the knowledge asymmetry they suffer from, building community of practice and facilitating unhindered knowledge exchange offer rich prospects in our model of rural empowerment.

Wenger defines communities of practice as "groups of people who share a concern or a passion for something they do and who interact regularly to learn how to do it better" (Wenger, 1997). The characteristics of these communities include: "shared ways of engaging in doing things together; mutually defining identities; knowing what others know; what they can do and how they can contribute to an enterprise and a rapid flow of information and propagation of innovation" (Roberts, 2006, p. 625). It is to be noted that the primary focus here is on learning through social participation, where the individual is an active participant in the practices of social communities and he/she constructs identity through these communities (Wenger et al., 2002). In this context, a community of practice is a group of individuals participating in the knowledge-sharing activity, and, at the same time, experiencing/creating their shared identity through practice-oriented collaborations.

Alexandra Talpau remarks on how internet-enabled social media platforms have ushered in a new era of communication (Talpau, 2014). In the same context, digital technologies have shown their immense potential in fostering and nurturing communities of practices where groups of strangers communicate and mutually engage each other with the purpose of reaching a common goal. These virtual spaces have thus been successful in reducing spatial (physical space) and temporal (time) distances, enabling people from anywhere and at any time to join the community and perform their practice. Knowledge creation (generation) and sharing (exchange), considered to be crucial resources for a community of practice, can be successfully cultivated in such a virtual space (Ardichvilli, 2008).

In our research initiative described below we have used social technologies to cultivate virtual community of practice among rural communities and rural–urban communities to mitigate the extant knowledge asymmetry of rural participants.

Following, we will provide examples of research efforts we have undertaken with selected segments of Indian rural population, scattered across the state of West Bengal, to validate practically the effectivity of our proposed implementation framework.

6.1 Examples from some field studies with self-help group women in rural India

6.1.1 The universe of the study

The universe of the study entails women self-help groups from the rural communities of West Bengal, India, having reasonable infrastructure in villages in terms of electricity and internet connectivity.

A large proportion of the population of rural India is comprised of marginal farmers, landless labourers, petty traders and rural artisans who are socially and economically backward (including the tribal population). They suffer from issues related to poverty, illiteracy, lack of knowledge and skills, health care, etc. Mainstream institutional efforts, exogenously thrusting developmental initiatives on rural mass, largely fail to enhance financial prospects and livelihood options of the Indian indigenous community. Moreover, the problems they face are such that these cannot be solved through individual, sporadic attempts. They can only be addressed through group efforts. With this objective in mind, small groups are formed within a village with the purpose of solving common problems. These groups, commonly known as *self-help groups* (SHGs), are micro-communities (with 10 to 15 members) within a village community. These micro-communities have been identified by public and other developmental bodies as potential vehicles of change for the poor and marginalized (VOICE, 2008; Sreedhar, 2012).

The SHG movement in India involves the voluntary association of people (mostly women) in small groups to address their lives and livelihood issues. Savings and credit activities act as unifying factors for them in most cases. However, SHGs are not solely focused on aspects of micro-finance, and have been popularly conceived as potential institutions of change and aid in human development in order to empower local members. They have great potential to address social issues such as gender discrimination, thereby acting as potential drivers of female empowerment. Such a holistic approach can be identified as a major contributor in strengthening local governance through facilitating local community participation. In India there are three major streams through which SHGs have gained prominence in public discourse: NABARD's SHG Bank

Linkage Programme (BLP); *Swarnajayanti Gram Swarozgar Yojana* (SGSY), a self-employment programme launched by the Indian government to promote micro-entrepreneurship and provide sustainable income to poor people; and, finally, non-government organizations (NGOs) and their dedication to the uplifting of marginalized sectors. In BLP alone, about 94 million poor villagers, linked with banks through 7.5 million SHGs, have mobilized an amount of Rs33,000 crores (US$5.5 billion) as savings, and issued loans to the tune of Rs66,000 crores (US$11 billion) (Narender, 2015; NABARD, 2014).

6.1.2 Problems faced by self-help groups

In spite of significant concern from multiple sectors to enhance life and livelihood-related aspects of rural settings, attained success is still limited (Savitha & Rajashekar, 2014; Misra, 2015). Lack of inter-group, group-to-agency (NGO, bank or government) and group-to-external world communication and coordination can be cited as potential reasons sustaining the marginalization of rural sector. A secondary study (Thileepan & Soundararajan, 2013; Misra, 2015) reveals a set of problems faced by SHGs in India, as given in Table 11.1.

To summarize, there is a huge information and knowledge divide not only within the local SHG communities but also between SHG communities and external agencies (Basak et al., 2016; Basak et al., 2017). There is a lack of

Table 11.1 Analysis of gaps from an information-sharing perspective

Themes	Analysis of gaps in SHG developments from information-sharing perspective
Networking and external links	Limited inter-group interactions; no knowledge about SHGs outside the group's locality; referential (word of mouth) growth of SHGs; enrolment of new members only through member references.
Market awareness	Personal selling of group's products; no knowledge of market outside the locality.
Supporting agencies	Low interaction with the NGOs; no knowledge about other supportive agencies; harassment by the banking system.
Government schemes	Limited knowledge about the benefits of government schemes.
Health	Lack of knowledge about procurement of health insurance; limited awareness about seasonal epidemic disease.
Miscellaneous examples	Lack of task independence within the group; regular and manual maintenance of multiple record books, which is cumbersome.

connectivity among people with common interests that results in weak relationships and weak network ties within the community (low bonding social capital) and outside the community (low bridging social capital). At the same time, knowledge exchanges are poor, leading to less access to ideas and low awareness of new developments that could have helped the groups to take an informed decision.

Digital exclusion of SHG members is one of the main reasons for the above-mentioned problems (Basak et al., 2016). However, providing mere access to digital technology alone is not the solution. Muir (2004) argued that, apart from access to and basic training in internet technology usage, community *connection* is the most important aspect that would enhance proper digital inclusion. This motivates us to cultivate online communities of practice among SHG members.

6.1.3 How community of practice among SHGs would help?

In this context, building a virtual community of practice is important (Cambridge et al., 2005), because it:

- **Connects people:** The distributed and disaggregated nature of rural life entails weak communication ties within the rural community. Members of SHG communities therefore have limited possibilities to interact with each other, as well as with the outside world. ICT can act as a potential medium enabling both intra- and inter-group communication for rural community. Through enhanced communication, a virtual knowledge repository can be created which rural members can resort to in times of need. This increases the chances of solving local issues and helps them to find business opportunities.
- **Provides a shared context:** Easy and smooth communication paves the path for inter- and intra-group sharing of information and personal experiences, which has the provision to enhance life and livelihood prospects of SHG communities. Most of rural India has restricted access to the internet and inadequate provision of ICT services. A knowledge repository, supported by suitable technologies, serves as a mandatory prerequisite in sustainable development of rural business and livelihood. The knowledge repository, by giving rural members affordable access to specialized knowledge content, can be identified as a major mitigator of contextual problems.
- **Enables dialogue:** CoP enables its members to explore new possibilities, solve challenging problems, and create new, mutually beneficial opportunities. It can be identified as a potential driver in securing communitarian participation in local governance by triggering active involvement of rural members as active citizens.
- **Stimulates learning:** CoP serves as a vehicle for authentic communication, mentoring, coaching and self-reflection. By facilitating effective collaboration between different members, it contributes to cultivating a collaborative learning environment. Such a stimulating learning environment educates the members and urges them to innovate by getting informed about others' successes and failures.

- **Captures and spreads existing knowledge:** CoP helps members to improve their practice by providing a virtual platform to identify solutions to common problems. The primary objective of such practice-oriented community formation is to facilitate effective creation, assimilation and exchange of various knowledge resources through ICT. Such practice-oriented exchange enables members to connect with the facilitators and senior teachers/trainers who are located across the globe.
- **Introduces collaborative processes:** CoP facilitates easy and unhindered exchange of ideas and information among community members, thereby enabling collaboration based on shared practice.

6.1.4 The study design

Forty-eight SHG women enlisted under the Kandi Block Mahila Cooperative Credit Society Limited (Kandi Federation) accounts to be the sampling frame of our study. Kandi is a small town in Murshidabad district of West Bengal, India. Kandi Federation is a civil society organization working to empower local women registered under Kandi Block. There are 307 SHGs under the federation. Women here have been trained in tailoring, handicrafts, kitchen gardening, pickle making, etc.

In order to address the issues faced by rural Indian SHG women, we attempted to cultivate online community of practice by incorporating both rural members and urban experts to facilitate exchange of specialized knowledge (Basak et al., 2017). Such practice-oriented community formation among rural–urban communities is not solely to enhance the skill set of rural SHG women; practice-oriented exchange is also expected to enhance their market prospects by keeping them informed regarding crucial market information.

The forty-eight SHG women from Kandi Federation possessing basic tailoring, stitching and painting skills were randomly selected for the purpose of our study. Being members of the SHG federation, these women attended group meetings once or twice a month. Apart from their limited activities as SHG members, the women were involved in household activities. The financially impoverished status of most of these women has compelled them to undertake market activities on a local scale, which is why they attempted to cultivate their artistic skills and thereby produce marketable products (such as fabric-painted blouse pieces, garments, etc.). It is the local market that serves as the primary, and in most cases only, selling site for the hand-made produce of local women. Using the limited resources available in the local market, coupled with their insufficient knowledge regarding contemporary urban market trends, the women's products lacked the credentials to get acknowledged on a global scale.

We distributed smartphones with internet facility to the 48 women in the self-help group in collaboration with Panasonic India and Airtel. After the distribution of the mobile phones, our field workers gave the selected women training in use of the smartphones and basic social media platforms such as WhatsApp in their native language (Bengali) (Figure 11.2).

Cultivating online communities of practice 229

Figure 11.2 Training SHG women to use smartphones

A WhatsApp group was created to enable the SHG women to regularly connect with urban-based domain experts. These women utilized the WhatsApp platform to asynchronously share ideas and ask questions of senior trainers in relation to the making of different hand-made products such as soft toys, clothes, paper-made flowers or paintings. Most of these women expressed explicit eagerness in enhancing their opportunities for financial independence. The bi-directional communication flow taking place in WhatsApp between the SHG women and the senior trainers through the sharing of product images is shown in Figure 11.3.

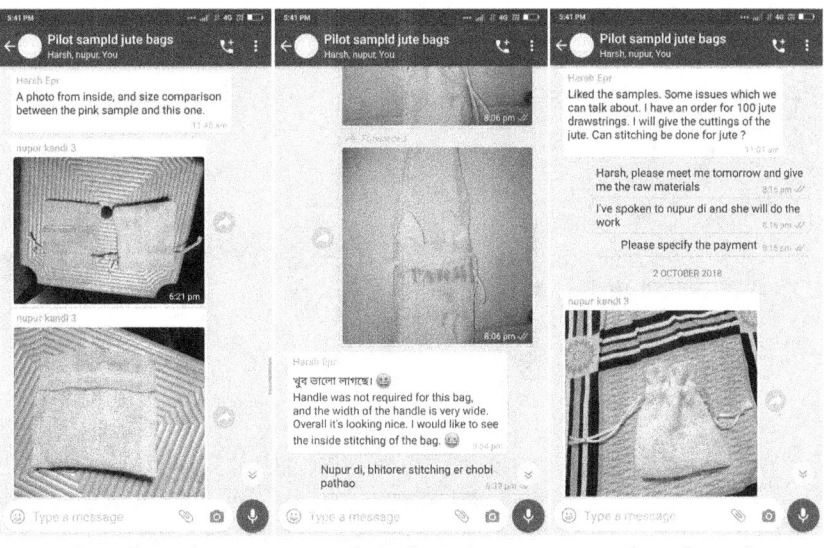

Figure 11.3 Sample WhatsApp communications: Sharing information

230 *Empirical studies in rural India*

Apart from getting connected via WhatsApp, our field workers (who are also a part of this community so formed) had also given some online training, demonstrating stitching and different types of textiles and fabric painting using pre-recorded videos of senior teachers/trainers. The hands-on activities in blended mode within the group enabled the SHG women to develop and upgrade various skills having significant market value. Practice-oriented exchange portrayed immense potential in fostering peer-to-peer learning among these women (Figure 11.4). This was followed by synchronous Skype interactions with remote teachers.

Figure 11.5 illustrates online training sessions conducted on synchronous mode with the women of Kandi. The training session was on fabric-painting, which was imparted by an urban-based artist. The training sessions and live interactions with urban experts, both individually and collectively, created a collaborative learning space where the members not only gained the provision to acquire specialized knowledge but also got the chance to learn from peers. Live interactions with experts also ensured immediate doubt clearing of the target

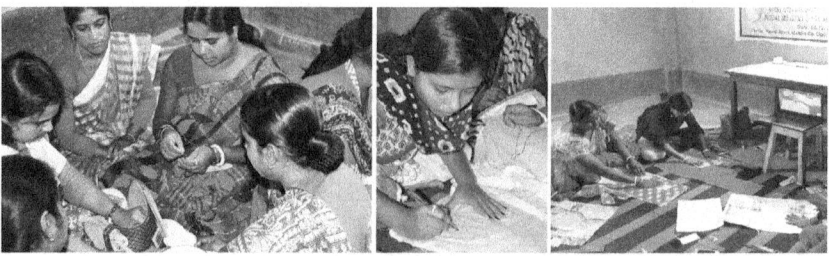

Figure 11.4 Video-based asynchronous training, followed by online interactions

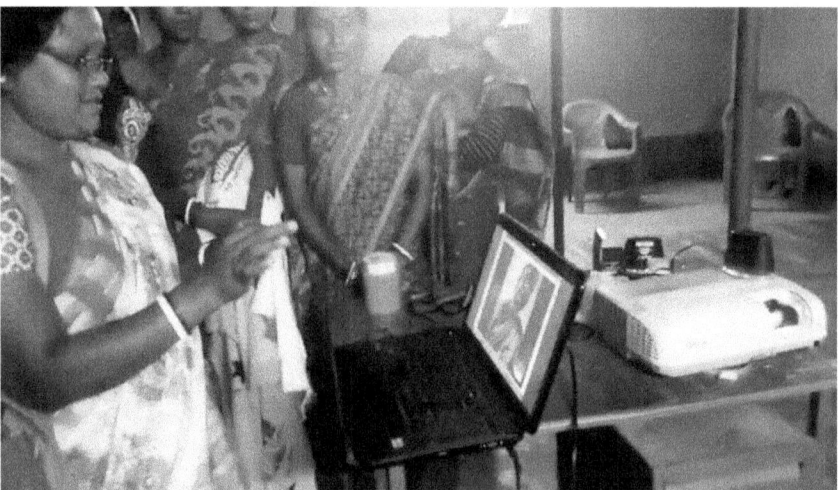

Figure 11.5 Online feedback sessions provided by urban experts to women of Kandi

group, where the feedback provided by experts served as contextual solutions to problems and facilitated better internalization of disseminated knowledge. Feedback provided by experts paved the path for building a skill set of rural producers, which is more suited to enhancing socio-economic performances.

6.1.5 Results and discussion

After six months of regular WhatsApp group activity among the community members and the trainers it was observed that many women, who were previously unconnected with each other, now conducted practice-oriented exchange on a regular basis. WhatsApp acted as a potential platform to these women, enabling them to easily share their needs and their created products, which was not possible earlier. Most of the women were previously unaware of what the other SHG group members produced and sold. This intervention, enabling inter- and intra-group collaborations, created willingness among SHG participants to learn and replicate others' products and business pathways. The women also started sharing their own product images and thoughts, which indicates a strengthening of bonding social capital.

Regular interactions with urban-based domain experts enabled the selected group of women to have better awareness regarding contemporary market trends and demands. This is reflective of an increasing "bridging social capital" that connects rural women of Kandi with facilitators outside the immediate rural locality. Here, social capital grows by gaining access to global knowledge and resources, such as information regarding the availability of raw materials, market, design ideas, etc.

Daily recorded usage of WhatsApp is shown in Figure 11.6. The nature of the graph shows that, at the beginning, WhatsApp usage among SHG women was high as they were enthusiastic about using this new form of communication. However, over time the frequency of usage dropped due to lesser exchange of concrete information. In order to increase WhatsApp usage of rural women we included some urban-based trainers to conduct concrete practice-oriented exchange within the cultivated virtual community. Over time it was observed

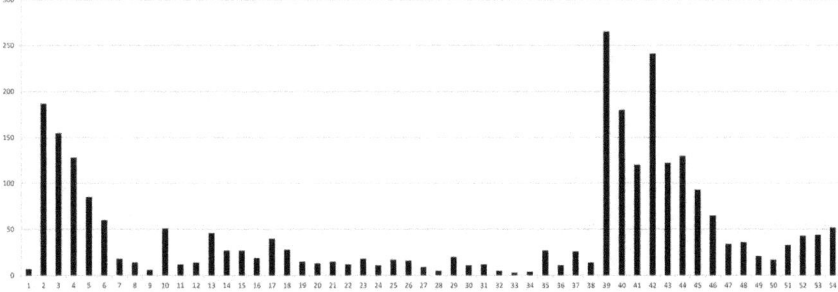

Figure 11.6 Daily usage of WhatsApp by SHG members

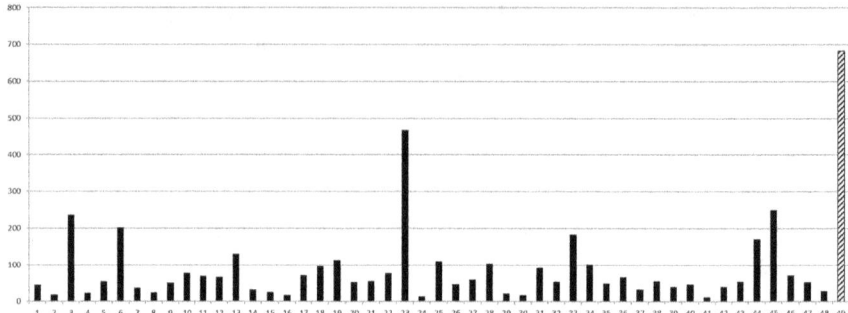

Figure 11.7 Contribution of individual members in terms of total number of messages

that video-based training workshops and live interactions (synchronous) with urban-based trainers and facilitators, followed by asynchronous sharing of video clips on product designs, significantly contributed in enhancing the frequency of WhatsApp usage among the selected group of women. This indicates that a proper form of reciprocation, the inclusion of mediating agency and the sharing of relevant resources can make an enormous impact on the usage characteristics. All spikes indicate a contribution from external trainers/facilitators with newer inputs/suggestions/feedback, which boosted WhatsApp interaction periodically. Hence it can be rightly concluded that the presence of external agents is mandatory to make CoP active.

As is evident from Figure 11.7, the contribution of individual members, in terms of total number of messages during this six-month period, varied widely. Out of 48 members, 11 members can be identified as aggressive participants (with a total number of messages >= 100), whose contributions made the CoP alive. In this regard, it is also to be noted that the aggregated number of messages contributed by external facilitators (user-id: 49) is also quite high, indicating that involvement of external agents is a significant factor in sustaining community engagement.

In this context, it needs to be reiterated that although 48 accounts to be the number of women we intervened, only 11 of them can be identified as active participants. Although the training given to all was similar, Figure 11.7 indicates non-uniform usage of social media platform by the intervened women. This proves that even though measures to empower the marginalized have been adopted, local orientation and hindrances often get in the way of generating holistic benefits for all. Educating rural mass in digital usage and enabling them to utilize the same to conduct purposive collaborations is a processual activity, which cannot be achieved overnight. Specifically in developing countries, such an activity faces multiple social obstacles in its way to successful translation. Some of our field insights capture the issues at stake.

The majority of the SHG women with whom we interacted have very low literacy levels, making it difficult for them to use smartphones and other digital devices freely. Hence contextual digital literacy training is mandatory, which will not only introduce the rural mass to the digital medium but will generate avenues to sustain their interest. Second, a strong gender bias omnipresent in rural India often disallows women to participate freely in the public medium. Although digital services offer such marginalized women the space to express themselves freely, introducing local women to the digital medium requires a lot of awareness at the local level. It is only when the immediate surrounding is socially supportive that we can expect the rural marginalized to show an inclination towards unhindered digital usage.

While introducing a digital solution, we need to remember that digital usage and virtual collaborations, although offering immense prospects in mitigating knowledge asymmetry of rural community, are quite new to extant rural context. When we started the process of familiarizing rural women of Kandi with virtual collaborations we faced several obstructions from the local authority, restricting local women from taking part in our research activities freely. Over time we convinced the said authorities, who only gave permission for us to carry out our research activities with the women whom the local authority identified as fit to be in our target group. This proves that having a holistic empowering plan for the marginalized is not enough to generate desirable results. We need to give time to the rural mass to familiarize themselves with the digital medium first, coupled with negotiating with the immediate surroundings, and only then can we expect the rural community to see the difference that using the digital path makes.

To analyse the impact of the cultivated CoP on the community members, a post-study was conducted after five months of this intervention. A total of 46 questions in 10 different categories were asked, with the five different answering options being Strongly Agree, Agree, Neutral, Disagree and Strongly Disagree. A sample set of questions – under the statement "After becoming members of the WhatsApp community" – is shown in Table 11.2.

To calculate the aggregated response of community members to these questions, we combine the total number of responses, as shown in Figure 11.8. From the graph it can be concluded that the benefits of this CoP, as perceived by its members, are significantly high and it has created a positive impact on their lives and livelihoods. Our personal interviews with SHG members reveal that all of them are quite enthusiastic, even though some of them were passive listeners.

It can be inferred that the rural producers not only learnt from live training sessions; they also resorted to the images and videos provided to them via the asynchronous mode, using them to make similar products and thereby enhancing both their skill set and market prospects. Formation of community and subsequent development of effective inter-personal relation between the members contributed in enhancing the motivation level among rural participants, derivative of having access to professional advisory services. The experiential accounts of the rural respondents (some sample testimonials are given in Table 11.3) thereby hint at how successful cultivation of communities of practice can be done through social technology-supported blended learning environments,

Table 11.2 Sample questions (translated into the native language) used to assess the impact of CoP on individual members "After becoming members of the WhatsApp community"

	Question	Category
1	I have used ideas from other community members and trainers to expand my business	Livelihood enhancement
2	I have earned money using ideas or knowledge acquired from community members	
3	We can discuss our health-related problems and seek help from our mentors	Health-related issues
4	We can learn more about health-related risks and how to mitigate them	
5	I have become more professional in my work attitude	Productive activity
6	I have become more productive and enthusiastic about my work these days	
7	I am learning new things I did not know before	Education
8	I am now more eager to learn new things related to SHG	
9	I am more aware of avenues through which I can help my children to study	Family
10	I am feeling more confident as I can now provide significant contribution in my family	
11	I am now more equipped to combat sudden disaster	Security
12	I can find solutions to mitigate disaster through this participatory community	
13	I feel positive about myself these days	Subjective wellbeing
14	I am more confident in my approach nowadays	

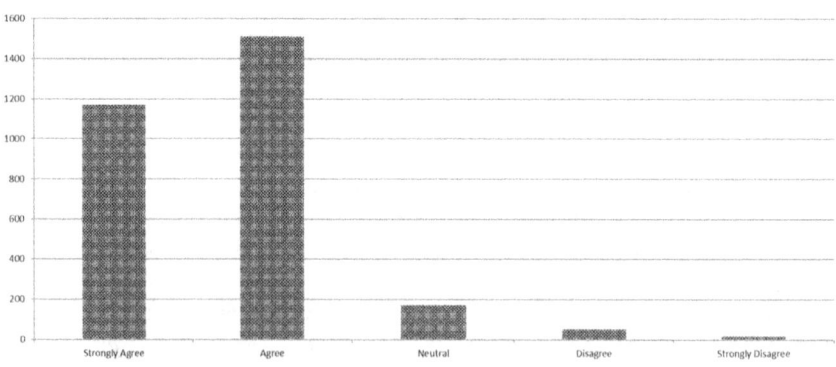

Figure 11.8 Total response of all queries from community members

Table 11.3 Effect of community of practice on rural SHG women (translated from Bengali)

Supporting testimonials (First-order concepts)	Second-order themes
"I get ideas for new designs by communicating with my trainers through messaging app"	Self-induced learning, derivative of purposive rural–urban exchange
"In the messaging group, people share the images of what they produce. We can learn from each other that way"	Fostering peer-to-peer learning
"The training sessions help us in learning better. Regular interactions with the teacher enrich our knowledge regarding fabric painting"	Prospects of contextual professional guidance and advisory services
"We can get our doubts cleared anytime from the teachers through online live training sessions, as well as through personal messaging. This helps us to learn anytime, anywhere, faster and better"	Promoting a conducive and collaborative learning environment

which offers the prospect of facilitating social knowledge exchange on a democratic level.

The second-order themes, or conceptual derivations, are summarized below:

- *Self-induced learning derived from purposive rural–urban exchange*: Cultivation of community of practice within rural and urban communities following social technology-aided blended learning mode enables rural participants to learn while actively contributing. Heightened motivation level is derivative of active participation, which makes learning a voluntary activity.
- *Fostering peer-to-peer learning*: Collective learning, taking place in blended mode, not only ensured dissemination of specialized and contextual expert knowledge but also facilitated a collaborative learning environment. Relevant knowledge exchange between communitarian members paved the path for peer-to-peer learning, giving the members the provision to learn from others' successes and mistakes.
- *Prospects of contextual professional guidance and advisory services*: Easy availability of contextual professional guidance and advisory services through regular interactions with urban experts on a blended mode made provisions for sustainable enhancement of rural skill set and an increased awareness regarding contemporary market trends, operations and demands.
- *Promoting a conducive and collaborative learning environment*: Peer to-peer learning, easy access to professional guidance and advisory services and immediate resolution of queries through virtual connection with experts create a learning environment that offers prospects of social knowledge collaborations. Such a conducive and collaborative learning environment is derivative of building a successful community of practice between rural and urban communities, which can only be realized through social knowledge management framework premised on a blended mode.

6.2 A field study with rural youth in India

Diamond Harbour is a semi-urban space located in South 24 Parganas of West Bengal. While in Kandi our attempt to cultivate communities of practice manifested along vocational lines, in Diamond Harbour it was cultivated along academic lines. A group of rural youth was selected, mostly female, to whom online spoken English training was imparted in synchronous mode to improve their personal and job prospects. A WhatsApp messaging group was formed – comprising the English teacher, members of the rural group and members of our research unit – to asynchronously supplement the lessons learnt through synchronous classes.

Universe of study: A significant section of rural population accounts to be rural youth. Although possessing some levels of education, the physical and knowledge distance they share from urban job markets contributes significantly to aggravating the issue of educated unemployment. Mostly taught in local languages, the youth lack proficiency in English, which today's society considers to be a mandatory skill required to enter the professional job sphere. In this context, it needs to be remembered that providing passive teaching sessions on English will fail to motivate the community of rural youth to use the foreign language proficiently. In order to have optimal impact, training in spoken English should be disseminated in an interactive way, where pupils and teachers, through dialogue, will attempt to grasp the nitty-gritty of the foreign language.

Profile of the rural youth selected for our study: We randomly selected five rural youths, mostly female, from Diamond Harbour. Our research group collaborated with BRWAS group, a local NGO working to improve the lives and livelihood prospects of local residents through education. With the help of the NGO we selected our target group, who, although educated, are driven to poverty by the unavailability of suitable jobs. The selected target group has received some education in the local Bengali language, but a pre-study conducted by our research group recorded how their lack of fluency in English contributed to diminished job prospects. In an attempt to educate the target group in English language and to subsequently enhance their job prospects, our research group provided synchronous online sessions with urban English teachers, supplemented by knowledge exchange via an asynchronous messaging tool, to create a collaborative learning space imbued with the potential to enhance socio-economic prospects of target group.

Blended learning environment: In an attempt to improve the English proficiency of target group, we organized synchronous online classes through video conferencing with urban-based English teachers. The curriculum covered reading, writing and speaking in English, with special emphasis on enhancing the English-speaking fluency of target group. Such an emphasis made the classes significantly interactive, where the rural learners were encouraged to learn in dialogue with each other and with the teacher.

A supplementary asynchronous messaging tool was used in the process of creating a collaborative learning space derivative of community of practice. The

Cultivating online communities of practice 237

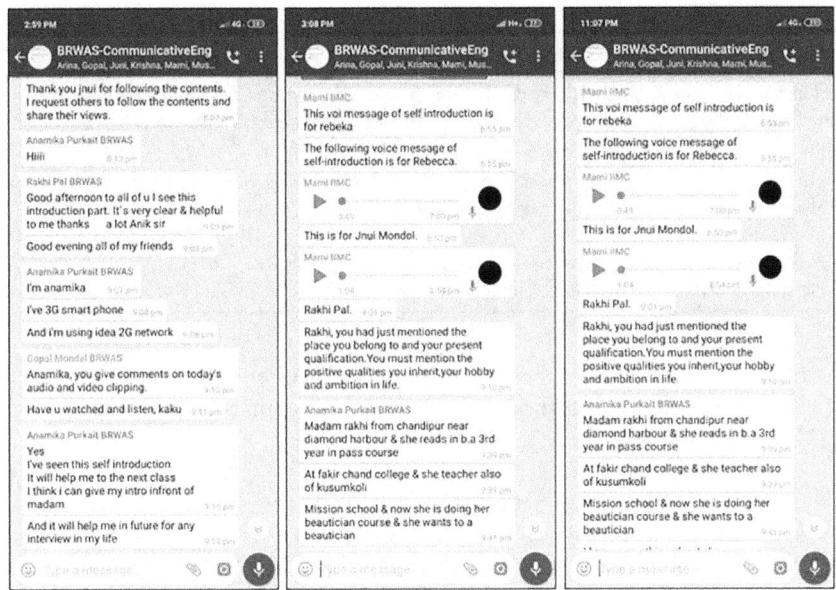

Figure. 11.9 Screenshots of communications taking place over messaging tools

learning tool enabled sharing of reading materials related to the topics taught in online classes, which were going on simultaneously. It also facilitated sharing of topic-related images, videos and texts, which improved prospects for the learners to learn faster. Learning fostered via this blended mode ensured immediate resolution of doubts and queries, not only by professional experts but also by fellow classmates. This triggered effective and faster learning. The following screenshots (Figure 11.9) depict the communication pattern which took place between rural learners and urban-based academic professionals. They demonstrate how such communication eased the process of learning.

Findings: Jensen (2003) highlighted how cultivation of community of practice can improve the process of learning English as a second language. Several researchers have also illustrated the use of WhatsApp as a teaching/learning tool in improving the learning experience (Jafari & Chalak, 2016; Bouhnik & Deshen, 2014; Gon & Rawekar, 2017; Cetinkaya, 2017). In our context, we conducted a post-study to record the effect of blended mode (synchronous + asynchronous) in fostering collaborative learning. The personal narrations of rural respondents (Table 11.4) explicitly brought out the effectivity of learning experience within the virtual community so formed. The learners stated that, although at times they felt shy to ask the teacher some questions in front of the whole class, doubt-clearing provision through personal messaging made the learning process easier. The community of practice that was built around spoken English training sessions fostered peer-to-peer learning, where students were given the provision to learn from each other's mistakes and queries. Even the teacher recorded the process of

Table 11.4 Effect of community of practice on rural youth (translated from Bengali)

Supporting testimonials (First-order concepts)	Second-order themes
"I have learned new English words through the online classes. The flexibility of communicating with teacher through messaging, other than the fixed time in class, has helped me in learning".	Promoting a flexible and conducive learning environment
• "In class, as well as in the messaging group, we the students also discuss our doubts and queries, which eases the process of learning" • "Videos sent through the messaging tool on relevant topics have helped me in revising the lessons taught in class"	Fostering peer-to-peer learning

learning as getting easier and more interactive through the use of a blended mode of learning and subsequent formation of virtual community of practice.

The second-order themes are explained below:

- *Promoting a flexible and conducive learning environment*: Creation of a collaborative learning space through formation of a community of practice between urban teachers and rural youths facilitated learning, different from conventional classroom teaching. The flexibility of learning hours, easy interaction with the teachers anytime, anywhere and the immediate resolution of doubt via the virtual asynchronous messaging application (WhatsApp in this case) promoted a flexible and conducive learning environment, suited to disseminating specialized knowledge following local pace, context and need.
- *Fostering peer-to-peer learning*: The collaborative learning environment created through community of practice encouraged peer-based learning, where the rural learners had the provision to consult and learn from others voluntarily in the process of learning. This triggers efficient and faster learning by ensuring a better rate of internalization of newly acquired knowledge.

7 Cultivating online communities of practice using a social knowledge management platform

Based on the above experiments, we propose to design and develop an integrated social knowledge management platform supporting cultivation of communities of practice. The way we have attempted to cultivate community of practice among rural participants follows a two-fold process. First, we have designed a social knowledge management platform, which will holistically support knowledge exchange both within rural community and between rural–urban communities. We have incorporated domain experts within the platform, with whom rural participants are given the provision to interact, collaborate and exchange knowledge with in a synchronous mode. Second, we have tried to supplement the collaborations taking place in the synchronous domain with an asynchronous messaging tool, which enables the community members to interact with each other personally whenever they feel the need to. It is in this fashion that we have attempted to cultivate community of practice using a generic social knowledge management platform to usher in holistic rural empowerment, as shown in Figure 11.10.

The platform traces the journey of the user via both synchronous and asynchronous mode in order to highlight his/her successful participation in the formed community of practice.

- The journey begins with *user interface*, which is a place between the user and the social knowledge management platform that enables users to access and control the knowledge resources effectively. In our system, the user interface is visualised in two ways: (1) web browser and (2) mobile applications.
- The second step is the *authentication module*, which verifies the users and prevents unauthorized users from gaining access to the system. It also ensures that authorized users can access the resources they need. Authentication plays an important role in maintaining the overall security of software applications and systems.

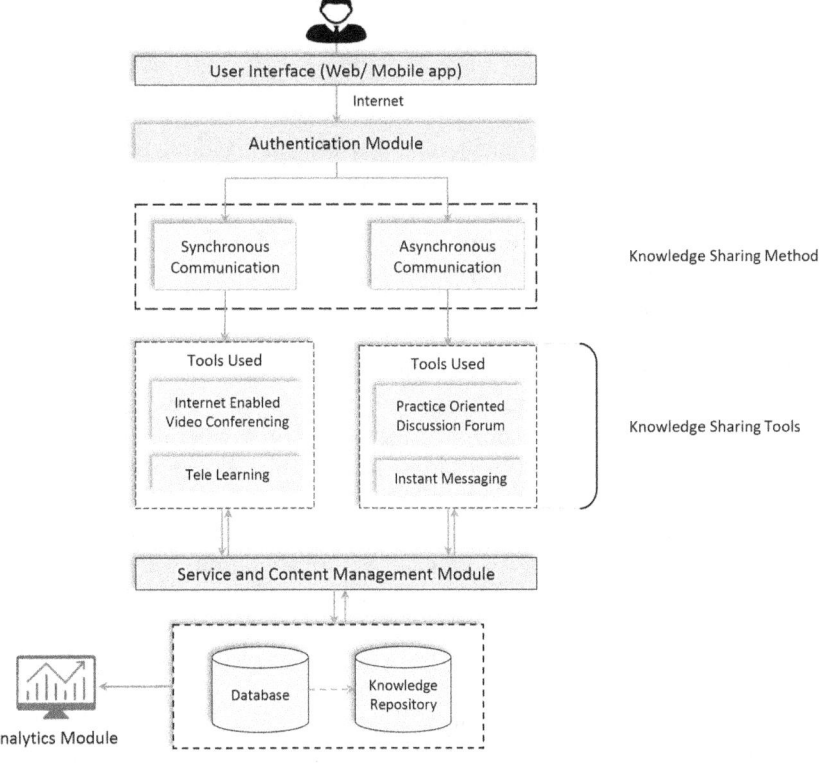

Figure 11.10 A social knowledge management platform to cultivate community of practice

- After authentication, the user can access the knowledge-sharing method, through both s*ynchronous* and *asynchronous communication*. While the knowledge-sharing tools of synchronous mode comprise *internet-enabled video conferencing* and *tele-learning* through live interactions, *practice-oriented discussion forum* and *instant messaging* accounts to asynchronous knowledge sharing tools.
- The *service and content management module* manages shared knowledge resources. The *service management module* helps in assigning services and resource capacities to specific users. This module enables formation of different user groups based on users' preferences and manages all services related to real-time knowledge sharing with other users. The *content management module,* on the other hand, is a logical block that facilitates creating, storing, organizing, accessing and publishing content.
- Optimal management in service and content module phase enables the creation of a *database and knowledge repository*, on which we apply an *analytics module* to judge the effectivity of fostered collaboration through our platform. The *knowledge repository* module captures the tacit knowledge of users (in the form of chat-logs in messaging apps) and manages the explicit knowledge pool, which can be accessed and augmented based on specific transactional requirements.

8 Conclusion

The above-mentioned experiments highlight how cultivation of community of practice through facilitation of collaborative learning spaces has a positive impact in enhancing the social value of marginalized rural producers. Through formation of community, rural producers get the provision to access and apply specialized knowledge through expert guidance, thereby enhancing the quality of their skill set and awareness level. In Part I of this book we have clearly stated how lack of information and knowledge regarding market operations and allied factors significantly contributes to sustaining the marginalization of the overall rural sector. Formation of community of practice not only offers the prospect of empowering the rural community with access to relevant knowledge but also endows in them the applicability of its usage derived through expert supervision. Collaborative learning scopes, coupled with knowledge regarding product design, market operations and other related livelihood issues derivative of effective collaboration within the formed community of practice, thereby transcend simply being an aspect of social value. Such effective collaboration and its impact on rural producers' skill set and awareness levels offer promising prospects in enhancing market performance of rural producers.

In the following chapter we will therefore attempt to show how community of purpose can be cultivated among rural–urban communities to mitigate the poor performance of rural economy. While community of practice has the potential to usher in a space for collaborative learning to cultivate a specific practice, community of purpose refers to the formation of purposive communities, where the purpose is mostly identified along economic lines. We attempt in cultivating community of *practice, purpose* and, subsequently, *circumstance* between rural–urban entities to realize the promise of social knowledge management in the domain of rural empowerment. While community of practice and purpose, in amalgamation, attempt to usher in socio-economic development, community of circumstance attempts to build resilience on a communitarian level. It is the cultivation of all three in amalgamation that has the potential to establish the proposed social knowledge management framework as an effective strategy in mitigating knowledge divide and subsequently ushering in holistic rural empowerment.

References

Ardichvilli, A. (2008). Learning and knowledge sharing in virtual communities of practice: Motivators, barriers and enablers. *Advances in Developing Human Resources*, 10(4), 541–554. doi:10.1177/1523422308319536.

Ardichvilli, A., Page, V. & Wentling, T. (2003). Motivation and Barriers to Participation in Virtual Knowledge Sharing in Communities of Practice. *Journal of Knowledge Management*, 7(1), 64–77. doi:10.1108/13673270310463626.

Basak. J., Bandyopadhyay. S., Bhaumik. P. & Roy. S. (2017). *Cultivating Online Communities of Practice as Rural Knowledge Management Strategy in India.* Proceedings of the 18th European Conference on Knowledge Management, Barcelona.

Basak, J., Parthiban, R., Roy, S. & Bandyopadhyay, S. (2016). *A Community-driven Information System to Develop Next Generation Collaborative and Responsive Rural Community (NCoRe).* Proceedings of the ITU Kaleidoscope Academic Conference: ICTs for a Sustainable World (ITU WT), Bangkok, 1–8. doi:10.1109/ITU-WT.2016.7805727.

Battistella, C., Annarelli, A. & Nonino, F. (2015). *Exploring the Impact of Organizational and Working Models, Incentives and Collaboration Strategies on Innovation Development in Online Communities of Practices.* Proceedings of the 16th European Conference on Knowledge Management, Udine, Italy.

Bouhnik, D. & Deshen, M. (2014). WhatsApp goes to school: Mobile instant messaging between teachers and students. *Journal of Information Technology Education: Research*, 13, 217–231. Retrieved from: http://www.jite.org/documents/Vol13/JITEv13ResearchP217-231Bouhnik0601.pdf.

Brown, J.S. & Duguid, P. (2000). Balancing Act: How to Capture Knowledge without Killing It. *Harvard Business Review*.

Cambridge, D., Kaplan, S. & Suter, V. (2005). *Community of Practice Design Guide – A Step-by-Step Guide for Designing & Cultivating Communities of Practice in Higher Education.* Retrieved from: https://library.educause.edu/resources/2005/1/community-of-practice-design-guide-a-stepbystep-guide-for-designing-cultivating-communities-of-practice-in-higher-education.

Cetinkaya, L. (2017). The Impact of WhatsApp Use on Success in Education Process. *The International Review of Research in Open and Distributed Learning*, 18(7). doi:10.19173/irrodl.v18i7.3279.

Cummings, S. & van Zee, A. (2005). Communities of Practice and Networks: Reviewing Two Perspectives on Social Learning. *KM4D Journal*, 1(1), 8–22.

Dubé, L., Bourhis, A. & Jacob, R. (2005). The Impact of Structuring Characteristics on the Launching of Virtual Communities of Practice. *Journal of Organizational Change Management*, 18(2), 145–166.

Gon, S. & Rawekar, A. (2017). Effectivity of e-learning through WhatsApp as a Teaching Learning Tool. *MVP Journal of Medical Sciences*, 4(1), 40–46. doi:10.18311/mvpjms.v4i1.8454.

Hoadley, C. (2012). "What is a Community of Practice and how can we support it?," in D.H. Jonassen and S.M. Land (Eds.), *Theoretical Foundations of Learning Environments* (pp. 287–300). New York: Routledge.

Hugh, C. (1911). *Gymnastics and Gymnasium, Encyclopedia Britannica* (11th ed.). Cambridge: Cambridge University Press.

Jafari, S. & Chalak, A. (2016). The role of WhatsApp in teaching vocabulary to Iranian EFL learners at junior high school. *English Language Teaching*, 9(8), 85–92. doi:10.5539/elt.v9n8p85.

Jensen, P.M. (2003). Learning ESL (English as Second Language) in a Community of Practice. (Master's thesis in Information Technology, IT Learning). Retrieved from: https://projekter.aau.dk/projekter/files/6143918/report.pdf.

Kietzmann, J., Plangger, K., Eaton, B., Heilgenberg, K., Pitt, L. & Berthon, P. (2013). Mobility at work: A typology of mobile communities of practice and contextual ambidexterity. *Journal of Strategic Information Systems*, 3(4), 282–297.

Lave, J. & Wenger, E. (1991). *Situated Learning: Legitimate Peripheral Participation*. Cambridge: Cambridge University Press.

Lesser, E. & Prusak, L. (1999). Communities of Practice, Social Capital and Organizational Knowledge. IBM Institute for Knowledge Management. Retrieved from: http://www.providersedge.com/docs/km_articles/cop_-_social_capital_-_org_k.pdf.

Lesser, L.E. & Storck, J. (2001). Communities of Practice and Organizational Performance. *IBM Systems Journal*, 40(4), 831–841. doi:10.1147/sj.404.0831.

Misra, N. (2015). Problems Faced by SHGs and Suggestion to Minimize It (Social Capital as a Public Policy Tool Project Report). Policy Research Initiative: Ottawa. Retrieved from: http://www.yourarticlelibrary.com/india-2/self-help-group/problems-faced-by-shgs-and-suggestion-to-minimize-it/66720.

Muir, K. (2004). Connecting Communities with CTLCs: From the digital divide to social inclusion. The Smith Family. Sydney. Retrieved from: http://library.bsl.org.au/jspui/bitstream/1/609/1/Connecting%20communities%20with%20CTLCs.pdf.

NABARD. (2014). Status of microfinance in India. Retrieved from: https://www.nabard.org/Publication/SMFI-2015r-new.pdf.

Nahapiet, J. & Ghoshal, S. (1998). Social Capital, Intellectual Capital and The Organizational Advantage. *Academy of Management Review*, 23(2), 242–266. doi:10.2307/259373.

Narender, K. (2015). The self-help groups movement in India: Impatient Optimists. Bill & Melinda Gates Foundation. Retrieved from: http://www.impatientoptimists.org/Posts/2015/01/The-Self-Help-Groups-movement-in-India#.V3-I8dJ9600.

Nishida, K. (1921). *An Inquiry into the Good*. London: Yale University.

Nonaka, I. & Noboru, K. (1998). The Concept of *Ba*: Building a Foundation for Knowledge Creation. *California Management Review*, 40(3), 1–15. Retrieved from: http://home.business.utah.edu/actme/7410/Nonaka%201998.pdf.

Nonaka, I. & Toyama, R. (2003). The Knowledge-Creating Theory Revisited: Knowledge Creation as a Synthesizing Process. *Knowledge Management Research & Practice*, 1(1), 2–9. doi:10.1057/palgrave.kmrp.8500001.

Roberts, J. (2006). Limits to Communities of Practice. *Journal of Management Studies*, 43(3), 623–639. doi:10.1111/j.1467-6486.2006.00618.x.

Savitha, V. & Rajashekar, H. (2014). Evaluation of Major Problems Faced by the Members of Self-Help Groups: A Study of Mysore District. *International Journal of Research in Applied, Natural and Social Sciences*, 2(6), 59–64.

Sreedhar, N. (2012). Self-Help Groups' Performance in India. *Arth Prabandh: A Journal of Economics and Management*, 1(8).

Suni, I.M. & Hong, J. (2011). *Ba* and Communities of Practice in Research and Strategic Communities as a Way Forward. *Handbook of Research on Communities of Practice for Organizational Management and Networking Methodologies for Competitive Advantage*, 46–69. doi:10.4018/978-1-60566-802-4.ch004.

Talpau, A. (2014). Social Media – A New Way of Communication. *Bulletin of the Transilvania University of Braşov, Series V, Economic Sciences*, 7(56). Retrieved from: http://rs.unitbv.ro/BU2014/Series%20V/BULETIN%20V/I-06_TALPAU-1.pdf.

Thileepan, T. & Soundararajan, K. (2013). Problems and Opportunities of Women SHG Entrepreneurship in India. *International Research Journal of Business and Management*, VI. Retrieved from: http://irjbm.org/irjbm2013/December/Paper9.pdf.

Tu, C. (2002). The Measurement of Social Presence in an Online Learning Environment. *International Journal on E-learning*, 34–45. Retrieved from: https://pdfs.semantic scholar.org/4802/ 54715d32d2c5d3b0a14bf5e205912e6a0fe7.pdf.

VOICE (2008). A Report on the Success and Failure of SHGs in India: Impediments and Paradigm of Success. Submitted to Planning Commission, Government of India. Retrieved from: http://planningcommission.nic.in/reports/sereport/ser/ser_shg3006.pdf.

Von Krogh, G., Ichijo, K. & Nonaka, I. (2000). *Enabling Knowledge Creation: How to Unlock the Mystery of Tacit Knowledge and Release the Power of Innovation*. Oxford: Oxford University Press. doi:10.1093/acprof:oso/9780195126167.001.0001.

Wartburg, I.V., Rost, K. & Teichert, T. (2006). The creation of social and intellectual capital in virtual communities of practice: shaping social structure in virtual communities of practice. *International Journal of Learning and Change Volume*, 1(3), 299–316. doi:10.1504/IJLC.2006.010972.

Wenger, E. (1997). *Communities of Practice: Learning, Meaning and Identity*. Cambridge: Cambridge University Press.

Wenger, E. & Snyder, W. (2000). Communities of Practice: The Organizational Frontier. *Harvard Business Publishing*, 139–145.

Wenger, E., McDermott, R. & Snyder, W.M. (2002). *Cultivating Communities of Practice*. Boston, MA: Harvard Business School Publishing.

12 Cultivating communities of purpose to enhance market opportunities of rural producers through collaborative knowledge transaction

1 Introduction

Community of practice helps in nurturing and exchanging specific practice-related knowledge among communitarian members. While such community formation positively enhances the knowledge capability of members or virtual practitioners, it may or may not have purposive outcomes. In this context, it needs to be remembered that our research initiatives advocate community formation using a social knowledge management platform to mitigate extant rural–urban knowledge divide. The socio-economic marginalization of the rural population, in comparison to their urban counterparts, urges us not to limit communitarian formation solely along practice-oriented lines.

Community of practice (Wenger et al., 2002), facilitating practice-oriented collaborations within and across groups, enables rural members to enhance their individual capability. However, it does not necessarily guarantee translation of enhanced capability into generating concrete economic results. Thus community of practice can mitigate knowledge asymmetry of rural producers but not their market separation. In order to address our dual goal, in this chapter we have advocated cultivating *community of purpose* (Stukes, 2016) among rural–urban entities. The community of purpose, although under-defined in existing literature, can be defined as a community of people, unified with a common goal, purpose or objective. The reason why we think community of purpose can be a prospective means to mitigate both knowledge asymmetry and market separation of rural target group is because of the promise of purposive collaboration and networking that it assures.

Community of purpose is defined as a community of people who are going through the same process or are trying to achieve a similar objective with a defined purpose. While shared practice accounts to be the premise of community of practice, it is purpose or a clearly defined objective that unites the members of community of purpose. In rural context, while practice-oriented community formation has huge prospects in enhancing the social benefits of the members, it is also important to augment the social benefits with economic pursuit. This highlights that both community of practice and purpose, in amalgamation, have the credentials to counter marginalization of rural sector along a socio-economic axis. When economic pursuit, being a specific and defined purpose, triggers community formation in rural context, the outcome assures socio-economic benefits on a holistic scale.

Community of purpose, in spite of possessing enormous potential to uplift rural communities, is under-defined in research literature. Barring a few sources – such as Wikipedia and a white paper published by e-Moderation, a social media management group – community of purpose has not received much attention, both in academic and developmental spheres. The few sources that mention the concept primarily define it along the premise of a shared objective, a common and clearly defined goal with a fixed purpose (Happe, 2010). Since the concept has immense prospects in facilitating relevant knowledge exchange among communitarian members, it is crucial to demystify how to construct, nurture and sustain an ecosystem which will support formation of community of purpose.

In our research framework we have attempted to build community of purpose among rural–urban agencies, where market incentives are the unifying purpose. If economy is to be taken as the unifying purpose, then we can see there have been many attempts to unify rural producers with urban buyers, along both physical and virtual lines (described in detail in Part I). However, it needs to be remembered that forming community of purpose is different from conventional direct-selling physical marketplaces and e-commerce sites. Cultivating a community of purpose to boost the market prospects of rural producers, apart from taking into account aspects related to market transactions, also serves to be a product of social knowledge management. In rural context, participants not just lack access to market but also suffer from other ancillary factors, which in amalgamation contribute to sustained marginalization. Since they account to be disempowered groups, economic initiatives with a solely economic focus are insufficient to generate desired outcomes. It is through community formation, through relevant dialogue and collaboration, that attempts can be undertaken to empower the rural marginalized on a holistic scale. Cultivating community of purpose through social knowledge management offers hope here because, apart from providing relevant market-related connections, it attempts to develop knowledge capability of rural members through purposive collaborations.

The chapter is divided into five segments:

- The first part provides a conceptual description of community of purpose.
- The second part attempts to flesh out the relevance of community of purpose in bridging market separation of rural producers. The section ends by hinting at the connecting spirit of contemporary digital technologies and the relevance it plays in building community of purpose in rural context.
- The third part is dedicated to spelling out a digital framework, which has the potential to support the formation and sustenance of online community of purpose for rural community, comprising relevant rural–urban agents.

246 *Empirical studies in rural India*

- The fourth part demonstrates an integrated social knowledge management platform, NCoRe, which has the capacity to cultivate community of purpose among rural–urban communities to ensure active participation of rural producers in the process of market transactions.
- The chapter concludes with in-depth reference to our field insights, which validate our conceptualization and implementation initiative of building community of purpose through social knowledge management platform.

2 Community of purpose: A conceptual framework

Community of purpose can be defined as a community of people, unified with a common goal, purpose or objective. Over time and with technological development, the traditional significance of community as a territorial phenomenon has declined. Instead, the conceptualization that community is a relational phenomenon has gained ground over the years. Relational communities are not limited by geography and are primarily characterized as relational bonds and the psychological sense of belonging to a community or an integrated whole (Royal & Rossi, 1996). Such a community is concerned with the quality of character of human relationships and to the effectivity of collaborations that it facilitates, without referring to location or other individual traits (Gusfield, 1975). Community of purpose, in this context, is not a strictly geographical phenomenon. It is a clearly defined purpose, rather than territorial or ascriptive traits, which unites the members of community of purpose. And both physical and virtual lines can act as a potential medium of unification.

In our research initiatives we have identified cultivation of community of purpose among rural–urban communities as a potential vehicle to mitigate economic hindrances faced by rural producers. The reason why we think community of purpose can be a prospective means in our research initiatives is because of the promise of purposive collaboration and networking that it assures. (Stukes, 2016) articulates the parameters responsible for a successful community of purpose-supported network as:

- *Bridging structural holes* – Structural holes are characterized by interaction gaps, which prevent connections and therefore create holes within network structures. Purposive collaboration supported by community of purpose positively contributes in bridging structural holes.
- *Mobilizing social capital* – Community of purpose by triggering effective purpose-oriented networking helps in mobilizing social capital of communitarian members.
- *Mediating societal barriers* – Open and purposive interactions help members to counter negative perceptions about themselves, which are gifted to them by the stringencies of social conventions. Moreover, commitment to the common purpose, instead of ascriptive traits or geography, accounts to be the premise of community of purpose, which makes it defiant of social conventions, which largely guide community formations.

- *Awareness of the isolated* – Community of purpose, by triggering purposive collaborations, attempts to enhance the knowledge capability of members, thereby enhancing their awareness and operative capacities in the process.
- *Decentralized leadership* – Transactions taking place through community of purpose are the result of purposive collaborations among members, without the presence of a centralized authority determining transactional dynamics.
- *Capturing dynamic processes* – Community of purpose is constantly changing, adapting and innovating and expanding beyond its immediate local context. The flexible nature makes community of purpose suited to accommodating changes in alliance with alterations in surrounding settings.

These credentials highlight how community of purpose, in triggering the above-stated factors, has the capacity to transcend its immediate purpose and can be rightly identified as the product of social knowledge management. Since marginalized rural context happens to be our research premise, community of purpose and its relation to social knowledge management makes this an effective strategy to usher in empowerment in an already under-privileged social setting. In order to further establish the effectivity of cultivating community of purpose to enhance socio-economic prospects of rural producers, in the following section we will discuss the relevance of cultivating community of purpose to bridge the market separation of rural producers. The section, by highlighting the credentials of community of purpose in enhancing economic prospects of rural producers, articulates why such a purposive community formation is appropriate in rural context, where the members are already striving to make a living amidst a marginalized setting.

3 The role of communities of purpose in bridging market separation of rural producers

Rural producers lack access to market sites and are also ignorant of relevant knowledge regarding market dynamics, operations, trends and nature. This reiterates that problems cannot be solved by making additional provision for market connect. While additional channels of market connect are necessary in the context of rural producers, they have to be coupled with supplementary factors to enhance the overall market-related knowledge capability of rural actors. This points to the importance of forming a community of purpose, which, through supporting purposive collaborations, offers immense potential to boost the overall performance of rural economy.

Rural economy accounts to be the livelihood of most of the world's citizens, with the proportion highest in developing nations (Singh et al., 2015). In spite of being the source of livelihood for a significant number of people, rural economy is mostly informal and disenfranchised. Sales are limited to the inconsistent and unpredictable local markets and, as a result, the rural producers are trapped in the vicious cycle of low investment capacity, low productivity, weak market linkage and inconsistent revenue.

By using naturally available raw materials and indigenous methods, production processes in the rural economy have a low carbon footprint; the indigenous base of the rural production process minimizes environmental damage. But despite the promise it holds, rural producers face a number of problems that threaten the industry's very existence. At the root of the issue is the fact that the sector it is largely informal and unorganised, with a majority of the producers working as independent entities on a freelance basis (Ghouse, 2012).

The fallout of this is the inability of the rural producers to leverage the benefits that organized entities enjoy, creating a number of hurdles in the process (Parthiban et al., 2018). For example, the rural producers have limited access to quality raw materials, limited awareness about consumer demand in non-local markets, limited ability to produce high-quality products that can satisfy global markets, limited access to non-local markets, etc. (Aref & Aref, 2011; Olayiwola & Adeleye, 2005; Rogerson & Sithole, 2001; Shah et al., 2017). These barriers impede the aspirations of rural producers to sustainably follow their trade, and force them to look for alternate options for their living, thus endangering their current livelihood options and the future of indigenous talent and culture.

These reasons have compelled most rural producers to rely on exploitative intermediaries in order to sell their produce in the market. The first part of this book details how an entire class of middlemen capitalize on rural producers' ignorance of market operations. This factor not only paves the path for low economic performance but also contributes significantly in sustaining the producers' isolation. The market separation faced by rural producers can be understood by using the theoretical lens offered by Bartels (1968).

According to Bartels, there are four types of market separations. These are:

- *Spatial separation.* The location of rural producers in remote villages acts as an obstacle for them to connect with different consumers in non-local markets (Ghouse, 2012). Even if they target non-local markets using some channels, the dearth as well as expense of logistics providers force the rural producers themselves to individually travel to customer locations, thereby causing them to waste both time and money. In the case of rural artisans, they participate in handicraft and handloom fairs. But they need to spend 15–20 days in the same location and run the risk of not covering expenses through sales (Singh et al., 2015). As a result, the rural producers are forced to sell to middlemen who pick up their products near their home, allowing the middlemen to get the products at prices well below market rates.
- *Financial separation.* Limited access to financial capital is responsible for financial separation experienced by rural producers. It hinders rural producers' ability to buy raw materials or tools needed for improved production (Shah et al. 2017). Also, the local money-lenders take the opportunity to gain from the low financial capacity of rural producers, often putting the rural producers in a debt trap (Sonne, 2012).

- *Informational separation.* This has been discussed in detail in Chapter 4 under "Information asymmetry and rural producers". Limited use of communication infrastructure (for example, the internet) and devices (especially smartphones), coupled with the spatial separation of rural producers from customers, inhibit them in gauging market demands, both in terms of quantity and type of produce. Accordingly, this makes it difficult for the rural producers to plan their production schedules (Singh et al., 2015).
- *Temporal separation.* This refers to the time-lag between production and consumption. The primary reasons are remote location of rural producers and poor transportation infrastructure, including poor road conditions, dearth of logistics providers, etc. This temporal separation necessitates the creation of warehousing facilities, which is a difficult option for rural producers (Tarafdar et al., 2012).

Apart from the four market separations articulated by Bartels, our close investigation of the dynamics of the rural sector prompts us to add two more categories of market separation (Parthiban et al., 2018). They are:

- *Capacity separation.* This refers to the difference between the order assigned by the customer and a producer's limited capacity to satiate the same because of operative hindrances. The issues intrinsic to rural production often impede easy production, thereby creating significant obstacles in the path of rural producers to cater to lucrative market demands. The distributed and disaggregated nature of rural life, characterized by weak communication ties within the community, further disallows the rural producers to take the help of communitarian members for fulfilling bulk order requirements. Due to capacity separation, rural producers often lose out on lucrative market orders, even though they possess the skills necessary to complete the order.
- *Capability separation.* The indigenous skills possessed and practised by rural producers, both in the agro- and non-agro domain (for example, handicrafts and handlooms), are often gifted to them by hereditary sources. Generations of rural producers practise a particular skill set that has been handed down and will subsequently be transferred to future generations. This highlights the fact that, although most rural producers possess sound core skills, they derive these skills mostly from the specialized knowledge of their immediate family and surrounding, which may or may not perform well in the context of contemporary markets. In today's world, market demand is heavily driven by upcoming trends and styles, which infest the market for a time and then make way for newer trends and designs. Capability separation of rural producers from fast-changing urban market trends contributes to reducing the market value of their produce. Lack of exposure, ignorance about innovative market designs and inadequate knowledge on how to employ technology to enhance production capabilities contribute to sustaining the poor market performance of rural producers (Tarafdar et al., 2012).

The problems of rural economy make it crucial to undertake efforts to reorganize the current supply-chain practices of rural production following a fairness principle. The need to reorganize explicitly spells out the importance of active participation and interaction of all the actors involved in the production process. The problems intrinsic to rural economy can be vastly mitigated by facilitating effective collaboration between rural–urban actors. With the promise of collaboration in mind, we wish to restructure extant supply-chain practices into a more decentralized model, which would provide additional opportunities to each actor to reap economic benefits from resultant networking.

Cultivating *community of purpose* bears promising prospects to boost the performance of rural economy by ushering in a decentralized production mode, enlivened and sustained by collaborations between communitarian members. Effective collaborations between rural–urban entities through *community of purpose* significantly contribute in improving mutual awareness of market dynamics, thereby having positive influence in mitigating market separation of rural producers. Communities of purpose, as mentioned earlier, are groups of people who have an ability to influence, can share knowledge and learn from others, and be committed to achieving a common purpose. In this context, communities of purpose, comprising relevant rural–urban entities (Figure 12.1), will not only ease the process of economic return for rural producers but will also holistically affect them by facilitating knowledge transaction along the following axes:

- Connect rural producers with urban designers/experts, under whose guidance the rural producers will have better knowledge of existing market trends, thereby enabling them to build their business ventures in accordance with market demands.
- Link rural producers with government professionals, where they will have scope to interact and know about public policies devised to ease the procedure of rural production.
- Connect rural producers with trainers to receive training sessions and workshops in blended mode (both synchronous and asynchronous), which will enable the rural community to upgrade their skill sets and initiate innovative production.
- Connect rural producers with micro-financers to ensure finance and financial advice, which has the potential to enable the rural producers to frame a cost-effective and profitable business strategy.
- Connect rural producers with a range of raw-material providers, allowing the rural producers to have a wide array of options, from where they can choose the most cost-effective procurement sources.
- Link rural producers with logistics suppliers to reduce time, effort and money in the context of delivery of finished products and procurement of raw materials from non-local markets.

Cultivating communities of purpose 251

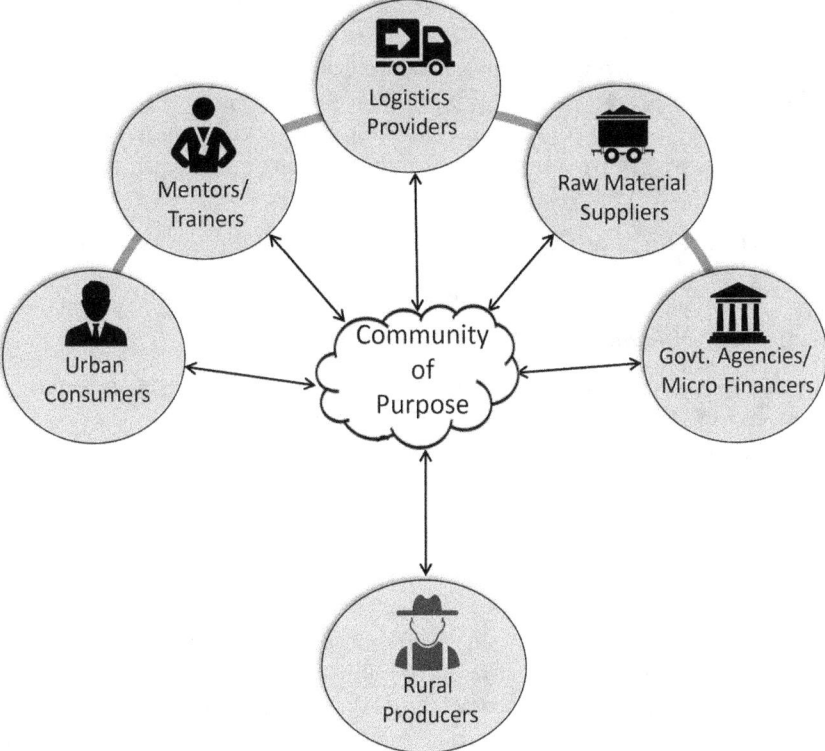

Figure 12.1 Community of purpose

These inter-personal communitarian bonds will not only secure rich economic benefits for rural participants but will facilitate peer-to-peer learning. This will enable them to learn and act accordingly, following others' mistakes and success stories. The poor economic performance of rural producers, due to their physical and virtual isolation from market dynamics, makes purposive community development a crucial prerequisite in the process of empowering them. The cultivation of community of purpose in rural context and the multi-agent knowledge transaction it supports have the capacity to enable rural producers to actively participate in collaborative decision-making, thereby enabling the members to engage in problem-resolution processes to bring collective agreement. The voluntary participation of rural producers, which community of purpose ensures, makes it a strategy more suited to address the problems intrinsic to rural production and its practitioners. The physical and virtual isolation of rural producers from urban markets, unlike their urban counterparts, have significantly contributed to reducing rural producers to passive labourers, whose skills are exhaustively used by urban markets without giving proper recognition and a deserving wage.

Although the need for cultivating community of purpose is well-understood, the question remains: how do we create it, especially in the context of disempowered rural community? Communities of purpose cannot be created or built out of a vacuum; there has to be a framework that facilitate formation of community of purpose. In the following section we propose a digital framework, suited to build and operationalize communities of purpose in rural context. The advocated framework attempts to convey how the connecting spirit of contemporary ICT can be used to cultivate effective community of purpose among rural–urban communities.

4 A digital framework towards building online community of purpose for rural producers

4.1 Conceptual foundations

The conceptual foundations of the framework that we propose here to cultivate online communities of purpose for rural producers are primarily derived from two industry trends of the 21st century, driven by social technologies: the sharing economy as a form of platform economy and virtual enterprises.

4.1.1 Industry trend 1: The sharing economy as a form of platform economy

The flow of *value* in the traditional *pipeline* business model is linear from a producer to a consumer, and this is the model of the industrial era where supply-chain practices in industries have followed the pipeline structure. "Pipeline businesses create value by controlling a linear series of activities—the classic value-chain model. Inputs at one end of the chain (say, materials from suppliers) undergo a series of steps that transform them into an output that's worth more" (Alstyne et al., 2016, p. 4).

With the advent of the internet and mobile technologies, a new economic model has emerged that is having a profound impact on the existing business models: it is called the **platform economy** (Figure 12.2). A *platform* presents the digital infrastructure and rules for a marketplace that connect producers and consumers. Examples are Uber, Airbnb, Amazon and similar companies that disrupted the markets. The main asset of a platform is its network of producers and consumers. In contrast to pipeline strategies, "*resource orchestration* is more important than *resource control*, and facilitating interactions and managing relationships have a higher priority than internal optimization" (Alstyne & Parker, 2017; Cui et al., 2017; Parker et al., 2016; Parker et al., 2017).

Platform businesses create an ecosystem comprised of four components:

- *Owners* of the platform (controller and arbiter; for example, Uber owns the Uber platform but not the cars).
- *Providers* who serve as the platform's interface (e.g., the mobile device running Uber apps).
- *Producers* who create their offerings (e.g., a car with drivers in Uber).
- *Consumers* who use those offerings (e.g., the passengers who hire the car as and when needed).

Cultivating communities of purpose 253

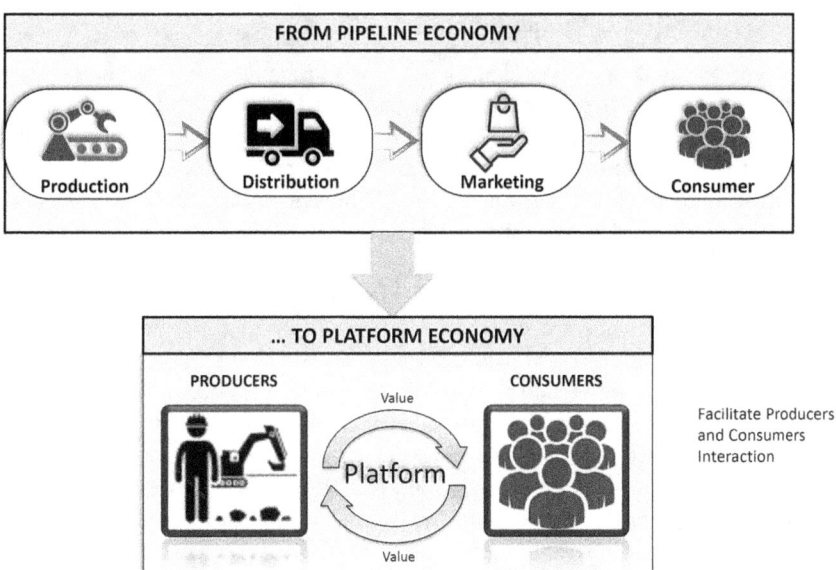

Figure 12.2 From pipeline to platform economy

This notion of platform economy also brings about the concept of a sharing/collaborative economy, which includes shared creation, production, distribution, trade and consumption of goods, services and ideas by different people and organizations. The motivation and philosophy behind the collaborative building of value that results from sharing goods and services is termed "sharism". Billions of connected individuals can now actively participate in social development and they collectively have the capacity to solve social problems. Sharing economy may be defined as "any marketplace that brings together distributed networks of individuals to share or exchange otherwise underutilised assets" (Koopman et al., 2015, p. 4). Extant research on the sharing economy (SE) has posited that SE-based ventures have four commonalities between them: focus on resource sharing, both tangible (for example, physical resource) and non-tangible (e.g., knowledge resource); belief in the commons; trust between strangers; and critical mass (Botsman & Rogers, 2010). Researchers believe the use of social technologies, especially mobile apps and web 2.0, has ushered in a new era of *crowd-based capitalism* that could enable marginal producers to enter the mainstream economy through collaborative efforts (Sundararajan, 2016).

The framework of our communities of purpose is derived from platform economy in general and sharing economy in particular. Whereas the decentralized resource mobilization of our framework is based on the principles of *platform economy*, the peer-to-peer knowledge exchange and work norm in the community is derived from *sharing economy* principles.

4.1.2 Industry trend 2: Virtual enterprises

Collaboration can be understood as the act of working together to produce outputs that may be beneficial for all the participating actors/entities. Information and communication technology (ICT) in general, and social technologies in particular, facilitate the flow of information to support collaborative work organizing. In this context, extant research has defined e-collaboration as: "business-to-business interactions facilitated by the Internet" (Johnson & Whang, 2002, p. 8). It may be noted that these interactions are beyond simple market transactions and can be better described as relationships. They could include activities such as information and knowledge sharing, process sharing, decision sharing and resource sharing (DeMattos & Laurindo, 2015). Researchers have indicated that, in a supply-chain context, "e-collaboration facilitates coordination of various decisions and activities beyond transactions among supply-chain partners" (Lee & Han, 2009, p. 1).

One of the outcomes of e-collaboration in the manufacturing space is the emergence of the notion of a virtual enterprise (VE). A VE may be defined as "a series of co-operating 'nodes' of core competence which form into a supply-chain in order to address a specific opportunity in the market place" (Camarinha-Matos et al., 1998, p. 1). Essentially it is a *temporary association* of independent agents that may act as suppliers, logistics firms, producers and others to share risks, costs and benefits to satisfy a business opportunity (Pires et al., 2001). Each of the agents within a VE is an autonomous entity that joins the same to cater to a specific business opportunity (or a set of similar ones) and is free to exit the VE on completion of the same (Camarinha-Matos & Pantoja-Lima, 2001). However, from a customer perspective, a VE appears as a single organizational entity wherein the different entities are physically distributed but the management of which is logically coordinated (Camarinha-Matos et al., 1998).

Extant research on VEs has identified seven distinguishing characteristics of the same: its customer-centric focus, wherein the consortium appears as a single entity; the VE itself owns very little, with resources mostly owned by individual entities; use of ICT to manage geographically dispersed entities; each participating entity contributing its core competency; temporary lifetime, with it being dissolved after the completion of the business opportunity; partner equality, wherein each entity has equal responsibility to ensure success of the VE; and dynamic and changing partners according to the type of opportunity (Hao et al., 2016).

Based on the conceptual foundations of the proposed digital framework discussed above, we will now focus on the operational dynamics of the same, which will highlight how the framework supports mobilization of communitarian members in the process of forming purposive community among rural urban entities.

4.2 Operationalizing the framework: Mobilizing rural–urban community towards purposive collaboration

The facilitating of purposive exchange by multiple rural and urban actors, connected through the digital platform (as shown in Figure 12.3), results in the

Cultivating communities of purpose 255

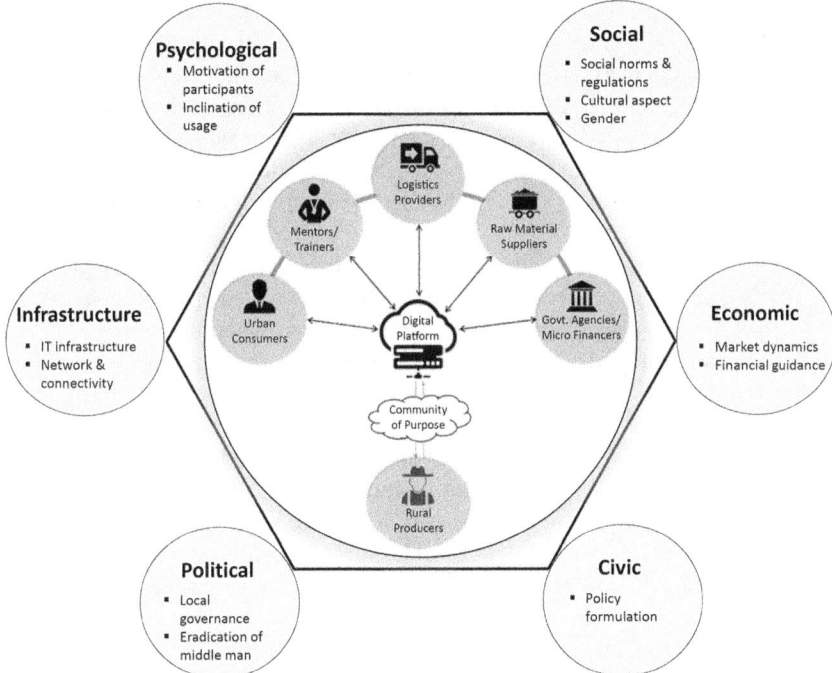

Figure 12.3 A digital framework to cultivate online community of purpose

formation of online community of purpose. Collaborative connections of rural producers with other agencies (urban consumers, mentors/trainers, logistics providers, raw material suppliers and government agencies, including microfinancers) through social technologies undoubtedly contribute in enhancing the efficiency of rural production.

Six enablers are needed for successful operationalization of the proposed framework of online communities of purpose. They are:

- *Social* – Social factors, such as social conventions, norms and regulations immensely hinder rural producers in carrying out profitable and efficient production. For example, social conventions, significantly discriminating along gender lines, make it additionally difficult for female rural producers to freely participate in market affairs. Virtual community of purpose can offer innovative prospects for these marginalized producers. This highlights that we need a supportive social environment to optimally operationalize community of purpose between rural and urban entities.
- *Economic* – Flexible economic parameters are required to operationalize community of purpose. Community of purpose, promoting purposive collaboration between rural–urban agents, has to be supported by a market condition, which has the potential to monetize the skill set of rural producers and generate lucrative demand of the same.

- *Political* – Rural setting is stricken with the presence of exploitative middlemen, who hinder rural producers' profitable ventures. By now, the class of middlemen has become so prominent that they are indispensable in most of the market ties that rural producers share with urban transaction sites. In order to cultivate community of purpose, there is a need for a local governance structure, which would contribute in securing active participation of rural members by bypassing exploitative intermediaries.
- *Civic* – Cultivation of community of purpose, derivative of optimal mobilization of rural–urban entities, can only be achieved in the presence of a supportive civic structure. Contextual policies to support rural–urban collaboration, coupled with developmental initiatives undertaken to achieve communitarian participation in the rural sphere, serve to be crucial enablers in the said context.
- *Infrastructure* – We have proposed an inter-connected digital infrastructure to support cultivation of online community of purpose. Contemporary digital technologies have immense reach to incorporate remote places within the parameters of virtual networking. Such an enabling e-infrastructure is required to cultivate and sustain online community of purpose among rural urban entities.
- *Psychological* – The psychological dimension, referring to the attitudes and motivation levels of individual members in the community, is a decisive factor in not only cultivating, but also sustaining, community of purpose. It is the voluntary participation of the members from which community of purpose derives its life. This highlights the need to cultivate conducive psychological dimensions of social actors in order to secure their participation in the cultivated community of purpose.

Cultivating online community of purpose attempts to bridge the different dimensions of market separation faced by rural producers as follows:

- *Spatial separation* – The separation rural producers face from market agents significantly contributes to deteriorating market performance. Cultivation of community of purpose among rural–urban communities has the potential to trigger effective multi-agent collaborations, therefore nullifying the hindrances faced due to spatial separation. Contemporary digital technologies act as a potential medium in this context, virtually connecting geographically isolated rural producers with relevant market agents and facilitating effective collaboration among them.
- *Financial separation* – The financial separation of rural producers significantly restricts their production capacities. Direct linkage to diverse agents, such as government agencies and micro-financers, financially empowers rural producers through formation of community of purpose. This linkage gives them easy access to financial resources and financial advisory services, crucial to boosting their market performance.

Cultivating communities of purpose 257

- *Informational separation* – Lack of access to adequate information has been cited by many as an important factor in sustaining marginalization of rural producers. Purposive exchange of information and knowledge triggered through cultivated community of purpose immensely contributes in enhancing the awareness level of rural producers by equipping them with relevant information and knowledge, which subsequently enhance the market performance of these marginalized producers.
- *Temporal separation* – The time difference between production and consumption, referred to as temporal separation, hinders rural producers in participating in speedy market affairs. Purposive collaborations triggered through online community of purpose can act as an effective compensating force for poor rural infrastructure. Active participation of rural producers and urban customers in the process of collaborative creation, derivative of cultivating community of purpose, significantly equips rural producers to offer on-demand delivery of products, thus reducing the negative effects caused by temporal separation.
- *Capacity separation* – Purposive intra- and inter-group collaboration facilitated through cultivating community of purpose between rural–urban entities contributes in enhancing the capacity of rural producers, thereby making them better suited to cater to bulk market orders, without compromising on quality.
- *Capability separation* – Purposive collaboration not only enables rural producers to have enhanced market performance but also has the capacity to enhance overall capability of rural producers through facilitating necessary knowledge exchange between urban experts and rural producers. Enhancement of capability, leading to innovative production, therefore has a direct impact in boosting rural producers' production capacities.

It is only the dynamic collaboration supported by online community of purpose that has the potential to bridge the above-mentioned market separations faced by rural producers. Articulating the multi-faceted issues faced by rural producers solely along economic terms will be a typically reductionist understanding. This proves the inadequacy of conventional economic incentive schemes adopted for rural producers to improve market performance. Although existing promotional schemes, including e-commerce sites, attempt to provide rural producers with enhanced market prospects, they remain ineffective in rural context because of their lack of emphasis in purposive community formation. It is only the dynamic interpersonal exchange, facilitated by community of purpose, that has the potential to economically empower rural producers on a holistic scale.

While this section explicitly narrates the conceptual foundations and operational dynamics of a digital platform needed to cultivate online community of purpose for rural producers, the following section bears explicit reference as to *how this digital platform is realized or implemented in real-life*. In Chapter 8 we showed how community of purpose is a product of social knowledge management. In the next section we will demonstrate the architecture of an integrated social knowledge management platform, NCoRe, which has the capacity to cultivate online community of purpose among rural–urban communities to ensure active participation of rural producers in the process of market transactions. In other words, we will now expand the notion of digital platform, as depicted in Figure 12.3, into a social knowledge management platform, driven by social technology.

5 Architecting a social knowledge management platform to cultivate online communities of purpose for rural producers

In this section we will extensively talk about a social technology-enabled social knowledge management platform – called NCoRe (**N**ext generation **Co**llaborative and **Re**sponsive rural community) – cultivating community of purpose for rural producers on an integrated scale. NCoRe is an e-connecting and e-supporting platform hosting on one platform a diverse range of entities, including urban consumers, mentors or trainers, logistics providers, raw material suppliers, financial investors and rural producers. The platform, by housing diverse agents, attempts to build a community of purpose among them by facilitating purposive collaborations. This section is dedicated to spelling out the system architecture and validation of NCoRe, to give the readers a holistic vision as to how NCoRe attempts to cultivate community of purpose for rural producers.

5.1 NCoRe: System design

The NCoRe platform facilitates communication, collaboration and trade between rural producers, urban consumers and other actors in the system. Specifically, it promotes transactions between rural producers, urban consumers and other stakeholders (raw-material providers, logistics suppliers, etc.) by providing a standardized, flexible and open platform that not only improves productivity but also ensures fairness and financial benefits to all. The collaboration facilitated by this platform ensures transparency and helps in optimizing the positions of all stakeholders in the business. This platform provides a virtual space through which multiple actors in this system can exchange knowledge between themselves. We termed this virtual space as "community". Thus this platform (Figure 12.4) can be defined as a temporary association space of autonomous crowd workers who establish dynamic peer-to-peer connections to collaborate with each other through coordinated sharing of skills, resources, information, risks, costs and benefits in order to satiate a given business opportunity.

The different modules of NCoRe, as depicted in Figure 12.4, are discussed below:

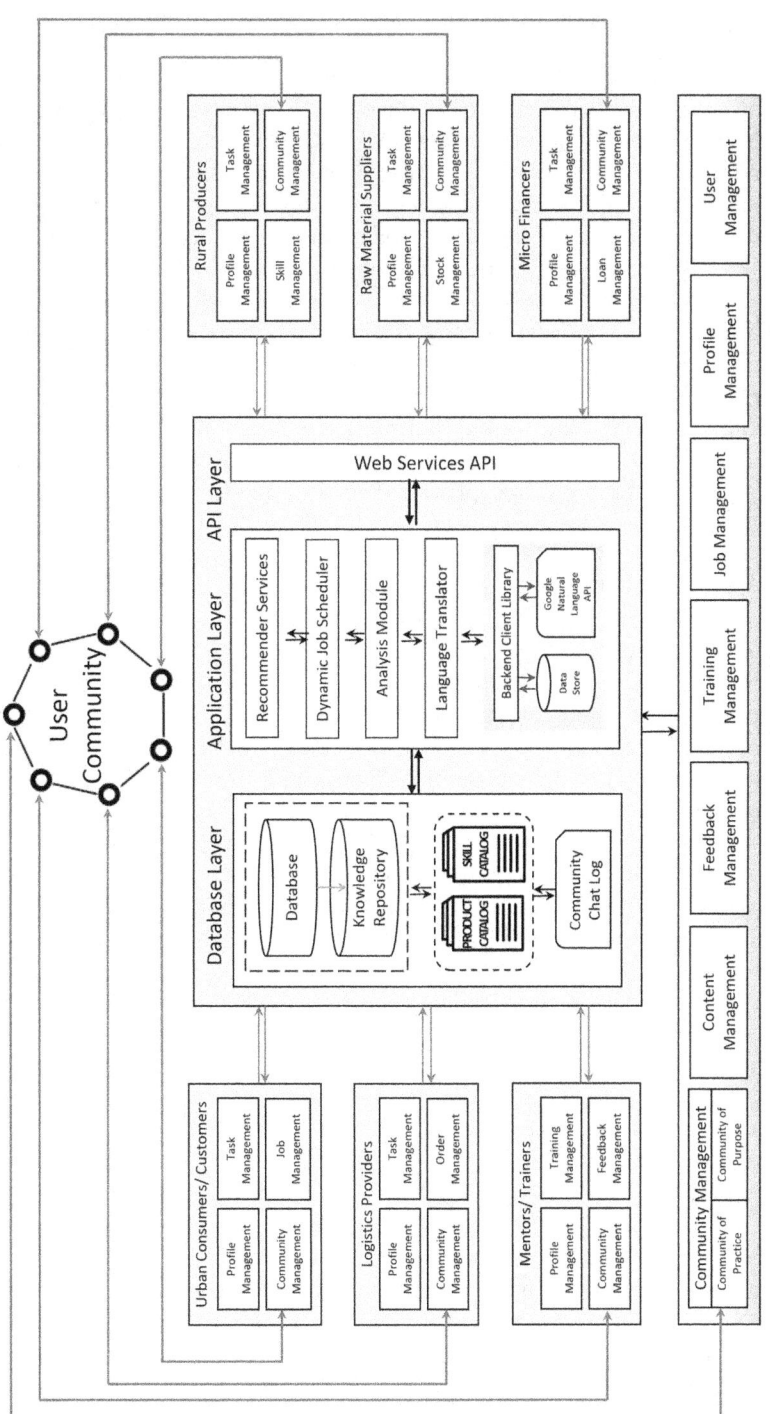

Figure 12.4 NCoRe: System design

5.1.1 Users

There are six types of users in the system: (i) urban consumers; (ii) rural producers; (iii) logistics providers; (iv) mentors/trainers; (v) raw-material suppliers; and (vi) government agencies/micro financers. They are connected to this platform via an online digital interface on their mobile phones (mobile apps).

Urban consumers: The urban consumers are micro-entrepreneurs or independent urban consumers. They can view profiles of rural producers in digital catalogues and "post a job" for prospective rural producers, where the job's details, budget and timeline are mentioned. An urban consumer may need to customize a selected product/design to cater to a sizable market need. In that case, he/she may need to train the rural producers to make that customization and then place an order for the customized product through the same module; and can also access the training module to train the selected rural producers online. Following the release of the suggested rural producer list for a specific job, urban consumer shortlists finalize rural producers, provide them with the necessary training and make regular checks on the progress of the job through the app.

Rural producers: The rural producers can advertise their product details, contact details, skill sets, production capacity and product feedback, which will be maintained in a digital catalogue. The rural producer is also encouraged to view other rural producers' samples to broaden their outlook and learn from peers, while at the same time making better and more informed decisions about enhancing skills and price-quoting. The bidding activity is an important event as it allows rural producers to quote their own prices and bargain effectively for maximum profit and healthy competition. Every rural producer participates in community activities under "user community", which will be detailed later.

Logistics providers: Logistics providers in this platform will do location-specific enrolment and handle and manage the movement of goods from the one place to another place, based on the requirements of different actors in our platform.

Mentors/trainers: Responsibility of a mentor/trainer in the NCoRe platform is to provide training on skill upgrading of any rural producer or to give expert advice to rural producers on any issue of concern. They will conduct various training sessions remotely (through platform) to any individual user or to a group of users on a particular topic. A trainer can also post asynchronous video clippings on any specific topic to train the users in the platform.

Raw-material suppliers: It enables the suppliers of raw materials to enrol and participate in transactions as and when needed. They advertise their stock of raw materials, contact details, price, delivery time, etc., which will be maintained as a digital catalogue in the platform. If an order is placed and the platform selects rural producers to execute the order, order details will be sent to the mailbox of possible raw-material suppliers dealing with the ordered product so that he/she can act accordingly.

Government agencies/micro financers: They can provide financial assistance, advisory service, information related to different government schemes and subsidies, etc. to rural producers or other targeted individuals as and when needed.

5.1.2 Application layer

Analysis module. The order distribution, product demands, customer comments, feedback, product ratings, etc. for individual rural producers will be fed into this module, which will be analysed to suggest the scope of future improvement in the business of a rural producer.

Dynamic job scheduler (DJS) module. This module is responsible for carrying out the scheduling activity between urban consumers and rural producers. The DJS module examines the availability of resources and coordinates and selects relevant actors to form a supply-chain to process any particular activity. This module engages multiple actors – rural producer(s), raw-material provider(s), logistics provider(s), trainer(s) and micro-financer(s) – to carry out collaborative activity. The DJS may aim at one or more of the following goals. For example:

- *Efficient load balancing*: Keeping all available resources uniformly busy.
- *Ensuring quality of service*: Selecting resources to ensure QoS.
- *Minimizing response time*: Time from work becoming enabled until it is finished.
- *Maximizing fairness*: Granting equal opportunity to all users according to the priority and workload.

Language translator module. This module uses a backend client library and integrates Google API to translate the content of this platform from one language to another language. Since we have designed this platform keeping in mind rural context, the platform provides provisions for rural users to navigate using native language.

5.1.3 User community management

Basic messages and discussion themes are the core content of NCoRe community. A message is information passed from one person or a group of people to another with the intention of producing an effect. Discussion themes are information or ideas designed specifically to focus the attention of a group on a problem and generate dialogue about possible actions to be taken. Actors in our system can participate in the *user community* module by sending a request to the system administrator. Based upon the approval status of the system administrator, an actor can post messages in the form of text or image. This module also allows different actors to post short videos related to any specific topic. Other actors can also reply to the same by typing some text or attaching an image file. Every communication between community members will be subsequently analysed by the system and a short record will be kept in the database in the form of a "chat-log" for future use.

Several studies indicate that most talented rural producers are fragmented and geographically not well connected. In this context, the "community" (a virtual knowledge-sharing space) serves multiple purposes. First, it will bridge the communication gap between the community members by creating a digital knowledge repository/space that allows for the provision of knowledge accumulation and sharing, which equally increases the chances of solving local issues and helps rural communities achieve business prospects through inter- and intra-group virtual networking. Second, it allows the creation of a digital repository among all stakeholders in the rural–urban production system to necessitate cultivation of their skill set.

5.1.4 System administrator

The system administrator is responsible for the upkeep, configuration and reliable operation of the platform. The functional description of each activity of the system administrator is given below:

- *User management*: User management describes the ability of administrators to manage user access to various components of the systems. A directory service is maintained that has the capacity to authenticate, authorize and audit user access in the platform.
- *Profile management*: Profile management auto-consolidates and optimizes user profiles in order to minimize management and storage demands. It needs minimal administration, support and facilities while offering enhanced options for users.
- *Job management*: There are few activities which are performed by this module. They are: (i) organize and search by open jobs; (ii) manage the list of rural producers, who are available to handle any job; (iii) flag unassigned work orders; and (iv) manage jobs through an easy-to-use job console.
- *Community management*: Community management is one of the most important activities in our platform. Here we deal with two types of virtual communities: (i) community of practice, which is a group of actors who share a concern or a passion for something they do, and learn how to do it better as they interact regularly; and (ii) community of purpose, which is a group of actors in our platform who are going through the same process of job execution.
- *Order management*: This is a module in the NCoRe platform that facilitates and manages the execution and tracking of orders.
- *Training management*: The training management module keeps track of all training-related activities, which are conducted through our platform.
- *Feedback management*: This module captures and processes the feedback of different actors and performs analytical operations to produce meaningful results.
- *Content management*: This module is a set of processes that supports the collection, managing and publishing of digital content in our platform in any form or medium. Modification or adding new content to the platform can be done through this module.

5.2 Validation of the NCoRe system

To validate the NCoRe platform we have worked extensively in more than seven districts in West Bengal, India, and have a detailed profile data set of more than 200 rural artisans. This dataset is used by the analytics module of the platform to understand the level of artisan skills, market and resource-related problems. Apart from the artisan profiling, we have also empanelled the other related entities of the craft eco-system in the platform, such as urban entrepreneur, raw-material supplier, logistics provider, trainer and micro-financer. We have also designed a mobile app to interact with the platform.

Several experiments were conducted in order to understand the entire artisan–entrepreneur ecosystem and to identify ways to bridge the gaps between them. For this purpose, a team of researchers was engaged as *enablers* to connect the rural artisans and their products directly with urban boutique entrepreneurs and sellers. During this process of market connect we have validated our NCoRe platform's provision to connect rural artisans with urban buyers directly through the NCoRe app. At the same time, urban boutique entrepreneurs can directly contact rural artisans to execute their orders and see the status of their order. In our mobile app we use Google's *"Language Translator API"* module to translate the content of the NCoRe platform from English to Bengali and vice versa. This language translator module helps rural artisans understand and communicate with urban entrepreneurs in their native language.

5.3 Discussion

The architectural framework of NCoRe presented above is an integrated and decentralized social knowledge management platform that can facilitate formation and cultivation of both communities of practice and communities of purpose among relevant rural–urban actors. The proposed platform, besides its present purpose, has scope to handle added modules and the introduction of desired scalability. In coming days the platform may serve to provide insights and solutions to a range of issues governing rural producers and their livelihoods, some of which are hinted at below:

- Notifications, for instance, presently serve the purpose of advising rural producers and other entities in the system about upcoming markets and other government and non-government initiatives to exhibit or sell products. In a broader view, these push notifications may take up the role of emergency news dissemination and impending disaster-related information. For example, many of the villages based in the fringe areas of the Bengal delta regularly face floods and storms. Emergency notifications and high-alert danger signals may be passed on to the region's clusters of rural producers.
- Intelligent analysis of the collected data may reveal more than a few statistics in terms of livelihoods of rural producers and the standard of living, along with economic and social impacts in the rural producers' communities. This will, later on, serve as an information-base to formulate focused policy decisions.

In the next section we will narrate our pre-pilot field observations conducted in Kandi, a remote village in rural India. In these pre-pilot studies we attempted to cultivate community of purpose among rural–urban communities using social technology and conducted a qualitative pre- and post-study to analyse the impact.

6 Some field observations on cultivating communities of purpose

In an attempt to observe the formation and cultivation of communities of purpose to enhance market opportunities of rural producers, we undertook a pre-pilot study with the rural producers of Kandi, a remote village in India. For the pre-pilot study we used social technology-enabled platforms to establish purposive collaborations between rural producers of Kandi, urban consumers and other relevant actors in the supply-chain. This experimentation was the continuation of our research attempt, undertaken in Kandi, to build community of practice among rural–urban entities. To transcend practice-oriented exchange, we attempted to cultivate community of purpose for these rural producers to enable them to take part in collaborative creation, and subsequently enhance their market prospects.

6.1 Objective of the study

The objective of this study is to investigate the potential of communities of purpose to enhance market opportunities of rural producers. Cultivation of community of purpose has been identified as an effective strategy to solve the problem of market linkage to boost the rural economy. The economic impoverishment of rural producers and the reasons for the sustenance of such impoverishment is well known. The marginalized status of rural producers further prevents them participating in the production process, where urban markets primarily treat them as mute entities or a passive labour force. Facilitating effective collaboration through formation of community of purpose not only has the capacity to enhance market performance of rural producers but, by ensuring their active involvement, also accredits a sense of creative worth among rural producers.

6.2 Background of the study

The women of Kandi, who were involved with us in our prior research drive of cultivating community of practice (described in the previous chapter), explicitly recorded that, in spite of possessing basic productive skills, they lack market opportunities to sell their produce. Being members of a SHG (self-help group) federation, these women were involved in producing garments, soft toys, fabric painting on clothes, etc., and they were in search of non-local market opportunities to earn more by cultivating their creative skills. Lack of adequate knowledge regarding contemporary market trends, coupled with lack of direct access to urban market sites, heavily hinders the market prospects of these rural producers. We attempted to cultivate community of practice by distributing 50 smartphones to 50 women of Kandi, who underwent phases of skill-upgradation training in blended mode from urban-based experts (discussed in detail in Chapter 11). From this group, 12 women, who were more skilful and had good creative senses, were selected through purposive sampling. The selected group of women comprised mainly non-farm producers who possessed basic cutting, stitching, tailoring and painting skills. The selection was based on three criteria: the motivation level of the members to engage in productive activities; their performance in the prior skill upgradation training; and their familiarity with the digital device. Before a community of purpose was formed with these rural craft producers and other relevant market agents a qualitative pre-study was conducted among the women, which tried to capture the market hindrances faced by them. The resultant community of purpose was cultivated in accordance to the hindrances cited, so that the purposive exchange was suited to address the needs of the rural producers.

6.3 Insights from field work

In an attempt to explore the potential that community of purpose has to offer in boosting market possibilities of rural producers, we attempted to link virtually the selected group of rural producers from Kandi with urban consumers and other relevant agents of the supply-chain (raw-material suppliers, logistics providers, etc.). Social technology-enabled platforms (promoting both synchronous and asynchronous interactions) were used to trigger collaborative creation via blended mode among the above-mentioned agents. The rural producers received the market orders from urban consumers digitally. Provisions were made for easy communication among rural producers, urban consumers and other actors of the supply-chain using both synchronous and asynchronous mode. Such communications were aimed at enabling each entity to perform their role-specific task in accordance with the needs of the others, thereby achieving perfect execution of the customized order through the spirit of collaboration. Following, we will discuss instances of two real market orders, which were fulfilled by facilitating community of purpose among rural urban entities.

Puja (name changed) is a semi-skilled producer residing in Kandi who is proficient in basic tailoring, cutting and stitching skills. She participated in our prior research and was an active member of our cultivated community of practice. She was a very enthusiastic member and expressed a high motivation level in employing newly acquired skills to make innovative products. In order to enable Puja's enthusiasm to yield concrete outcomes, our team procured a series of time-bound real customer orders (using online channels) that were offered to and accepted by Puja. The raw materials required for the order were either given by the customer or were supplied by designated raw-material providers. The timeliness and quality of the produce were monitored periodically. The primary objective of this study was to understand and demonstrate how online community of purpose could be created to cultivate purposive collaborations among rural–urban members. We used the digital platform to remotely drive every aspect of order fulfilment, including order procurement, raw-materials sourcing, design input, production scheduling, monitoring, logistics and order fulfilment.

The assigned order required Puja to make earrings as part of a wedding gift. The urban-based customer gave specificities of the designs to her during synchronous online sessions. The synchronous sessions between the urban-based consumer and Puja were conducted using online video-conferencing tools. An asynchronous messaging tool played a big role in conducting conversations between the buyer and the producer during the course of production. WhatsApp, as a messaging tool, was used in this context. A group was formed – comprising Puja, members of our research group, the customer who placed the order and some local community members of Kandi who could act as potential logistics providers – to keep the provision of easy communication during the course of production.

Doubts arising during the course of production were resolved with the aid of blended mode. Most of the queries arising in the process were solved through discussion in asynchronous mode. We dealt with the more complex issues in synchronous online sessions. The customer also requested that Puja make videos explaining the problem she was having and to send the same through WhatsApp. The customer drew the specificities of the designs and sent the image via WhatsApp, which Puja could refer to at her convenience. Instances of such asynchronous conversations are depicted in Figure 12.5.

In order to ensure perfect customization, Puja sent through WhatsApp pictures of her daily work, which was then ratified by the customer who had placed the order. Here we can see how Puja actively participated in the production process, instead of being a passive source of labour, which indicates the collaborative nature of production in this case. Production taking place through dialogue between buyer and producer makes it a collaborative creation. When the deadline approached, Puja had to hire a women artisan from her

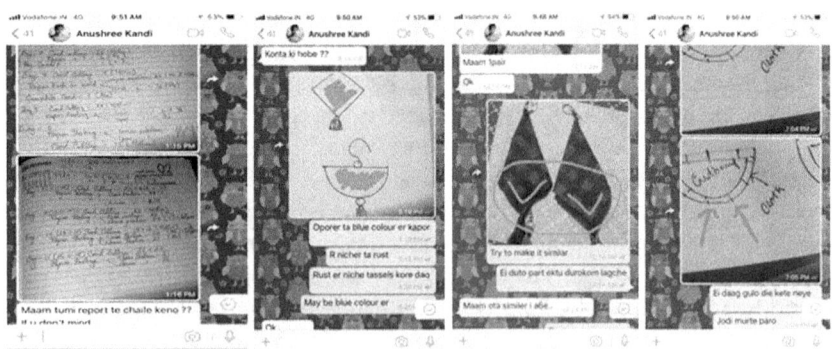

Figure 12.5 Asynchronous discussions over WhatsApp during production process

neighbourhood, who was also a member in the messaging group, to complete the job within deadline. Discussions in the messaging group regarding shortage of time prompted the artisan to offer her help, and she got paid by Puja on an on-demand basis. Finally, Puja's brother, who was also enlisted in the messaging group, acted as logistics provider and travelled to the city to deliver the products. The customer feedback was very positive and the customer's payment ensured reasonable profitability. After completion of other similar orders, we helped Puja set up an online shop on Instagram where she displayed her new products. We continued sending her new designs and product ideas and trained her wherever needed. We also observed that she slowly started improvising and creating her own designs, quite in tune to urban demands and trends.

The second experiment narrates Riya's experience from the real order she secured via our cultivated community of purpose. A middle-aged woman, Riya, possessing cutting, stitching and designing skills, has been a consistent participant in all the programmes we have conducted at Kandi. After attending the online vocational training organized by our research group, her upgraded skill set made her a potential producer capable of carrying out real orders. Consequently we connected Riya virtually with an urban-based entrepreneur involved in the production of eco-friendly items out of jute. After providing an online synchronous training, where the urban micro-entrepreneur explained to the rural producer the details of the customization, a WhatsApp group was created with the entrepreneur, Riya and other members, including members from our unit. The WhatsApp group was created to ensure smooth communication between involved parties during the course of production. The rural producer periodically posted images of work completed, on which the urban entrepreneur added his corrective insights in an attempt to achieve perfect customization.

On completion of the assigned order within the stipulated time, the rural producer used a logistics provider to deliver the finished goods. A subsequent WhatsApp group was formed with the urban entrepreneur, rural producer and the logistics provider in order to track every step of delivery through necessary communication within relevant agents. The delivery was successful, marking the completion of the collaborative production process.

A qualitative post-production study was conducted to assess the sentiments of both the producer and buyer towards the production. While both the entities explicitly recorded satisfaction pertaining to the production, they additionally stated how the innovative usage of both synchronous and asynchronous modes of communication (online sessions coupled with communication over WhatsApp) had eased the production process and helped both the parties achieve perfect customization by working together. In a qualitative interview, Riya stated, "I have never used digital medium before to cater to orders. Now, after using it, I have realized its worth. I could produce from home and get deserving wages, more than the wage I can get by selling locally … Sharing images through WhatsApp helped me to get instructions and produce accordingly, which helped me in learning better and faster, anytime, anywhere." The urban-based micro-entrepreneur expressed a similar satisfaction. He said, "With

WhatsApp, it has been easier to instruct my rural producer on specificities of my demand. Moreover, the provision of communicating with my producer anytime, anywhere helped both of us in producing together; where Riya helped me in executing my ideas and gave a concrete shape to my dream production."

6.4 Findings from field work

The experiments with Puja and Riya explicitly show their positive market experiences from the cultivated community of purpose. The response of the other executed orders, using similar pathways with the selected group of women in Kandi, also recorded a satisfying post-production experience from both ends; the urban consumers and the rural producers. In order to chart the experience after the completion of every transaction, we conducted a qualitative post-production study to record production-related sentiments of both the urban consumer and rural producer.

In the following table (Table 12.1) we will present a comparative analysis of the responses of rural producers obtained from the pre- and post-study. The comparative analysis of responses articulated prior to cultivation of community of purpose, as compared to the ones posted since cultivation, will highlight the impact that purposive collaborations had on the lives of rural producers.

The responses of Kandi's rural producers attained in the post-study, when compared with their pre-study responses, explicitly highlight the positive influence cultivated community of purpose ushered in to boost their business prospects. As Table 12.1 narrates, purposive collaborations facilitated through cultivated community of purpose enhanced the market-related prospects of these producers. Effective networking also explicitly improved civic and social aspects of the selected group of rural producers, thereby having a holistic impact in the process of empowering them. The positive response attained through this pre-pilot field observation inspired us to cultivate community of purpose for rural producers on a larger scale. While the observation included a small group of 12 women, who are craft producers, the hindrances faced by them can be considered as generic and suffered by most rural producers (both farm and non-farm). Hence the experience of rural non-farm producers of Kandi can be considered a proper premise on which we can attempt to utilize an integrated and scalable digital platform to cultivate community of purpose.

6.5 Discussions

In order to expand the reach of purposive community formation across different rural–urban regions we have designed and developed a social knowledge management platform called NCoRe (Next generation Collaborative and Responsive rural community), which has been described in detail in the previous section. The designed platform has the capacity to cultivate community of purpose for rural producers on an integrated scale, by hosting a range of prospects to stimulate blended (synchronous and asynchronous) collaborations

Table 12.1 Comparative analysis of pre- and post-study conducted with rural producers in Kandi

Functional area	Broad functional area	Findings of pre-study	Findings of post-study
Market sphere	Knowledge asymmetry between rural producers and urban marketplace	Over 80% of the interviewed women in Kandi recorded extreme dependency on the local market in context of both procuring raw materials and selling finished products. However, lack of information pertaining to the appropriate selling price of their products compel the majority of them to sell their goods at undeserving rates.	All the respondents recorded an enhanced awareness regarding the dynamics of the market because of increased communitarian communication occurring through created community of purpose. Over 95% of them expressed how they have utilized the fruits of collaboration derived through purposive exchange for practical benefits. They now have better knowledge pertaining to selling channels, contemporary market demands and innovative designs, which enhanced the rural producers' capacity to produce in accordance to market demands.
Civic sphere	External assistance for sustaining business ventures	Over 90% of the women interviewed recorded not receiving any governmental assistance to aid their entrepreneurial ventures. At the same time, the same majority expressed willingness to receive external assistance to transform their business initiatives into profitable ventures.	Barring three out of the total number of women interviewed, every one of them expressed strong agreement in favour of receiving innovative business and investment-related ideas from cultivated community of purpose. A big majority of them also recorded practically utilizing those ideas for profitable outcomes. The ability to implement the knowledge acquired for practical benefits paves the path for an elevated confidence level among rural producers.
Social sphere	Inter-communitarian solidarity	The majority of the female rural producers interviewed recorded no prior adherence to digital networks to communicate with members of their own community. Inter-communitarian communication was mostly performed by virtue of physical and telephonic connection. As a result, they were mostly unaware of what others in their community were producing.	Findings of post-study recorded widespread usage of social technology platforms among the intervened women of Kandi to communicate with members of their own community, outside their community, in order to establish purposive collaborations. Easy and smooth communication fostered through the cultivation of community of purpose enabled the women to have better knowledge regarding what others in their community are producing and gave them an opportunity to frame their business strategy by learning from others' success stories and failures.

among relevant rural–urban entities. However, this requires the rural participants to be equipped with sufficient knowledge and confidence to use digital technology. Although the rural participants have some knowledge about smartphone usage, it will take some more time and hand-holding to enable them to use those devices in a *smarter* way, so that they can take part independently to form and cultivate community of purpose using a full-scale social knowledge management platform like NCoRe. Hence NCoRe, in spite of having immense prospects, must address the following social factors in order to be successful in implementing and operationalizing the platform in a rural context:

- Purposive collaborations account to be the premise on which NCoRe attempts to empower rural producers. Securing voluntary participation of rural producers in the production process makes NCoRe adhere to an endogenous model of development. However, building community empowerment and transferring power from the external development agencies to community members requires time, financial resources and appropriate skills. Steiner and Farmer (2017) argue that, to reach endogenous empowerment, exogenous empowerment practices are useful and effective for some communities. Capacity building might be emergent (in endogenous community development) but in some cases it may need to be nurtured via external sources (by exogenous development). Thus successful implementation of a digital platform like NCoRe requires creation of appropriate support structures that enable decentralization of transactional processes.
- Even though purposive collaboration accounts to be the premise of NCoRe, it will fail to do justice to its goal if the surrounding environment is not conducive to facilitate such purposive collaboration between rural urban agents. This highlights that, apart from endorsing endogenous developmental initiatives, we are also in dire need of supportive external agencies interested in sustaining ventures undertaken to empower rural community from within. NCoRe can only be successful in mobilizing community of purpose for rural producers in the presence of an inter-connected developmental ecosystem, comprising symbiotic exogenous and endogenous developmental efforts. This has been discussed in Section 4.2, where we have explained six enablers that are needed for successful operationalization of online communities of purpose.

7 Conclusion

The chapter highlights the importance of cultivating community of purpose to enhance market opportunities of rural producers. Purposive collaborations between relevant rural–urban entities not only contribute in mitigating the market separation of rural producers but also secure allied social benefits for the same. Such community of purpose, going beyond the purview of its immediate objective (economic enhancement in this case), has the potential to holistically empower rural producers by enhancing their knowledge capability by triggering collaborative knowledge transaction. We have also crafted a social knowledge management platform that would assist in formation and cultivation of online communities of purpose.

Communities of both practice and purpose contribute in enhancing knowledge capability of individual rural producers and can be rightly identified as drivers of self-development along a socio-economic axis. However, it is only when the rural community derives collective participatory credentials that they are able to mobilize local resources crucial to achieving resilience through formation of community of circumstance. Communities of practice and purpose, undoubtedly, can be identified as major driving forces to enhance individual credentials and knowledge capability. Community of circumstance, on the other hand, can only be formed if the community develops the desired adaptive capacities on a collective level, transcending individual enhancement.

The following chapter discusses our research efforts undertaken to cultivate community of circumstance among rural urban communities to enhance community resilience. It is by ensuring active participation on a collective level in the process of enhancing communitarian adaptive capacities that cultivating community of circumstance can truly be identified as an important milestone in the process of achieving holistic empowerment.

References

Alstyne, M.W.V. & Parker, G.G. (2017). Platform Business: From Resources to Relationships. *GfK Marketing Intelligence Review*, 9(1), 25–29. doi:10.1515/gfkmir-2017-0004.

Alstyne, M.W.V., Parker, G.G. & Choudary, S.P. (2016). Pipelines, Platforms, and the New Rules of Strategy. *Harvard Business Review*. Retrieved from: https://hbr.org/2016/04/pipelines-platforms-and-the-new-rules-of-strategy.

Aref, A. & Aref, K. (2011). Rural Empowerment for Sustainable Agricultural Development in Iran. *Journal of American Science*, 7(11), 350–353. Retrieved from: http://www.jofamericanscience.org/journals/am-sci/am0711/042_7032am0711_350_353.pdf.

Bartels, R. (1968). The General Theory of Marketing. *Journal of Marketing*, 32(1), 29–33.

Botsman, R. & Rogers, R. (2010). *What's Mine Is Yours: The Rise of Collaborative Consumption*. New York: Harper Collins Publishers.

Camarinha-Matos, L.M. & Pantoja-Lima, C. (2001). Cooperation Coordination in Virtual Enterprises. *Journal of Intelligent Manufacturing*, 12(2), 21.

Camarinha-Matos, L.M., Afsarmanesh, H., Garita, C. & Lima, C. (1998). Towards an Architecture for Virtual Enterprises. *Journal of Intelligent Manufacturing*, 9(2), 189–199.

Cui, M., Pan, S.L., Newell, S. & Cui, L. (2017). Strategy, Resource Orchestration and E-Commerce Enabled Social Innovation in Rural China. *Journal of Strategic Information Systems*, 26(1), 3–21.

DeMattos, C.A. & Laurindo, F.J.B. (2015). Collaborative Platforms for Supply Chain Integration: Trajectory, Assimilation of Platforms and Results. *Journal of Technology Management and Innovation*, 10(2), 79–92.

Ghouse, S. (2012). Indian Handicraft Industry: Problems and Strategies. *International Journal of Management Research and Review*, 2(2), 345–353.

Gusfield, J.R. (1975). *Community: A Critical Response*. New York: Harper & Row.

Hao, Y., Helo, P. & Shamsuzzoha, A. (2016). Virtual Factory System Design and Implementation: Integrated Sustainable Manufacturing. *International Journal of Systems Science: Operations & Logistics*, 2674, 1–17.

Happe, R. (2010). Communities of Purpose (eModeration Whitepaper). Retrieved from: https://communityroundtable.com/definitions-best-practices/emoderation-whitepaper-communities-of-purpose/.

Johnson, E. M. & Whang, S. (2002). E-Business and Supply Chain Management: An Overview and Framework. *Production and Operations Management*, 11(4), 413–423.

Koopman, C., Mitchell, M. & Thierer, A. (2015). The Sharing Economy and Consumer Protection Regulation: The Case for Policy Change. *The Journal of Business, Entrepreneurship & the Law*, 8(2), 530.

Lee, M. & Han, M. (2009). E-Business Model Design and Implementation in Supply-Chain Integration. Proceedings of the 2009 International Symposium on Web Information Systems and Applications. Retrieved from: https://pdfs.semanticscholar.org/6385/8f26b13656ef131be90d6297f8d6448f1621.pdf.

Olayiwola, L.M. & Adeleye, A.O. (2005). Rural Development and Agro-Industrial Production in Nigeria: Concepts, Strategies and Challenges. *Journal of Social Sciences*, 11(1), 57–61.

Parker, G., Alstyne, M.W.V. & Choudary, S. (2016). *Platform Revolution: How Networked Markets are Transforming the Economy, and How to Make Them Work for You*. New York: W.W. Norton.

Parker, G., Alstyne, M.W.V. & Jiang, X. (2017). Platform Ecosystems: How Developers Invert the Firm. *MIS Quarterly*, 41(1), 255–266. Retrieved from: https://misq.org/platform-ecosystems-how-developers-invert-the-firm.html.

Parthiban, R., Bandyopadhyay, S. & Basak, J. (2018). *Towards a Nex-Gen Cottage Industry in the Digital Age: Insights from an Action Research with Rural Artisans in India*. Proceedings of 22nd Pacific Asia Conference on Information Systems, Yokohama. Retrieved from: https://aisel.aisnet.org/ pacis2018/196.

Pires, S.R.I., Nucleus, C.F.B., Eulalia, S. & Goulart, C.P. (2001). Supply Chain and Virtual Enterprises: Comparisons, Migration and a Case Study. *International Journal of Logistics Research and Applications*, 4(3), 1–19.

Rogerson, C.M. & Sithole, P.M. (2001). Rural Handicraft Production in Mpumalanga, South Africa: Organization, Problems and Support Needs. *South African Geographical Journal*, 83(2), 149–158.

Royal, M. & Rossi, R. (1996). Individual-level correlates of sense of community: Findings from workplace and school. *Journal of Community Physiology*, 24: 395–416.

Shah, A., Vidyapith, G., Patel, R. & Vidyapith, G. (2017). Problems and Challenges Faced by Handicraft Artisans. *Voice of Research*, 6(1), 57–61.

Singh, R., Agarwal, S. & Modi, P. (2015). Market Separations for BOP Producers: The Case of Market Development for the Chanderi Cluster Weavers in India. *International Journal of Rural Management*, 11(2), 175–193.

Sonne, L. (2012). Innovative Initiatives Supporting Inclusive Innovation in India: Social Business Incubation and Micro Venture Capital. *Technological Forecasting and Social Change*, 79(4), 638–647.

Steiner, A. & Farmer, J. (2017). Engage, Participate, Empower: Modelling Power Transfer in Disadvantaged Rural Communities. *Environment and Planning C: Politics and Space*, 36(1), 118–138. doi:10.1177/2399654417701730.

Stukes, F. (2016). Communities of Purpose. (Doctoral dissertation, University of North Carolina). Retrieved from: https://eric.ed.gov/?id=ED572119.

Sundararajan, A. (2016). *The Sharing Economy: The End of Employment and the Rise of Crowd-Based Capitalism.* Cambridge, MA: MIT Press.

Tarafdar, M., Singh, R. & Anekal, P. (2012). Market Development at the Bottom of the Pyramid: Examining the Role of Information and Communication Technologies. *Information Technology for Development*, 18(4), 311–331.

Wenger, E., McDermott, R. & Snyder, W.M. (2002). *Cultivating Communities of Practice* (Hardcover: ISBN: 9781578513307). Boston, MA: Harvard Business School Publishing.

13 Cultivating communities of circumstance to enhance community resilience through knowledge sharing using collaboration and connections

1 Introduction

Detailed descriptions of *communities of practice* and *purpose*, as provided in Chapter 11 and Chapter 12, explicitly highlight how the formation of such communities are crucial to enhance the knowledge capability of communitarian members. The said communities act as engagement premise, because of which *communities of practice* and *purpose* can be rightly identified as drivers of self-development along a socio-economic axis. While cultivating communities of practice and purpose using social knowledge management framework yields positive outcomes in rural context, it does not ensure creation of a *resilient community*, a community "that can withstand hazards, continue to operate under stress, adapt to adversity, and recover functionality after a crisis". However, communities of practice and purpose account to be mandatory prerequisites in building *community of circumstance* among rural urban communities. Communities of practice and purpose serve as engagement premise, which, by contextually involving rural participants, subsequently act as facilitating platforms in cultivating participatory abilities of rural members. It is only when the rural community derives collective participatory credentials that they are able to mobilize local resources crucial to achieving resilience through formation of community of circumstance.

According to the International Federation of the Red Cross, a disaster is defined as "a sudden, calamitous event that seriously disrupts the functioning of a community or society and causes human, material, and economic or environmental losses that exceed the community's or society's ability to cope using its own resources. Though often caused by nature, disasters can have human origins." The ability to withstand disaster can only be derived from collective participation on a communitarian level. *Communities of circumstance* refer to mechanism towards building a *resilient community*, possessing a high rate of adaptive capacity to withstand disaster on a collective level. Communities of practice and purpose, undoubtedly, can be identified as major driving forces to enhance individual credentials and knowledge capability. Communities of circumstance, on the other hand, can help a community to develop the desired adaptive capacities on a collective level, transcending individual enhancement and thus making it a resilient community.

Development of collective capacities on a communitarian level is impossible to achieve in a short time. It is a gradual process, where only a prior democratic engagement premise (communities of practice and purpose in this context) can pave the path for a participatory premise, mandatory to mobilize local resources. This collective participatory premise is the base of community of circumstance, which offers communitarian resilience.

Communitarian resilience refers to the collective power to act locally using local resource and agency. External developmental agencies are undoubtedly important in devising beneficial policies and undertaking measures that promote resilience on a communitarian level. However, it needs to be remembered that the presence of a conducive external environment, while accounting to be a necessary condition, is not a sufficient one. A community can only develop and advance its adaptive capacities through active participation of communitarian members, not individually but as a connected collective.

This reiterates the indispensability of an inter-connected developmental ecosystem where, although external developmental agents have a significant role, the network is primarily enlivened by communitarian participation on a collective scale. While communities of practice and purpose can be rightly identified as crucial drivers towards enhancement of individual knowledge capability, community of circumstance can be identified as a precursor towards achieving communitarian empowerment on a collective scale. Such empowerment is the product of a community actively participating in the developmental process as an integrated collective (Steiner & Farmer, 2017). Communities of circumstance facilitate communitarian resilience by building on the social capital of the entire community as a single entity, an integrated collective, which enables them to get connected to different agencies and thereby improve their adaptive capacities as a collective. It is by ensuring active participation on a collective level in the process of enhancing communitarian adaptive capacities that cultivating communities of circumstance can truly be identified as an important milestone in the process of achieving holistic empowerment. This makes development along communitarian axis an intrinsic aspect of communities of circumstance, different from the comparatively individualized focus of communities of practice and purpose.

This chapter is organized as follows. It starts by introducing the concept of *community resilience* from the perspective of rural empowerment and highlights major components or characteristics of a resilient community. The characterization of community resilience indicates that making a resilient community primarily depends on: (i) formation of a network that connects intra- and inter-community stakeholders; and (ii) collaborative knowledge transactions among various agents (the nodes) of this network. Moreover, building a resilient community doesn't come from a top-down, government-only, command-and-control approach; it comes from a combination of top-down and bottom-up approaches through establishing collaborative connection among community members and external agencies. Thus, building an active community is a precursor to the formation of a resilient community. We call them communities of circumstance.

However, communities of circumstance cannot be created or built out of vacuum; there has to be a framework that facilitates formation of community of circumstance. In Section 3 we illustrate how a distributed framework towards building online communities of circumstance can be created and operationalized that would mobilize a community towards resilience. The conceptual foundations of the framework that we have proposed to build an active online community of circumstance are primarily derived from two industry trends of the 21st century, driven by social technologies: *sharing economy*, as a form of *platform economy*, and *virtual enterprises*.

Finally, in Section 4, we have highlighted some empirical investigations from the area of disaster management to show a three-stage process, exploring how community participation can be enhanced through collaborative knowledge transaction, which eventually will lead to development of resilient community. Taking a cue from the Engagement-Participation-Empowerment model (Steiner & Farmer, 2017) indicating stages in transferring power from external actors to local communities, we have shown that the process of community resilience starts with engagement, is followed by participation and subsequently facilitates community empowerment, a precondition for realizing a resilient community.

2 Understanding community resilience

The discussions on rural empowerment would be incomplete unless we talk about how community empowerment can lead towards developing *resilient community*. In simple terms, resilient communities "can withstand hazards, continue to operate under stress, adapt to adversity, and recover functionality after a crisis" (National Research Council, 2011). One of the greatest challenges encountered by governments, organizations and communities today is how to cope with large-scale crisis situations faced by the communities in the event of natural or man-made disasters, be they political, social, environmental or economic. Interventions from external agencies, both public and private, are undoubtedly needed to manage large-scale crises. However, several policy documents from across the world suggest that community participation in crisis management helps to deliver more effective services (Steiner & Atterton, 2014). And, to engage the community members in a participatory service, community empowerment is important in facilitating local democratic participation and developing confidence and skills among local people (Scottish Government, 2014). For example, the Scottish Community Empowerment Bill highlights that "communities are a rich source of talent and creative potential and the process of community empowerment helps to unlock that potential. It stimulates and harnesses the energy of local people to come up with creative and successful solutions to local challenges" (Scottish Government, 2012). Several studies report the positive influences of participatory processes on community empowerment (Fraser et al., 2005).

Although the concept of empowerment goes beyond participation and researchers have perceived empowerment as an "enabling and motivational construct that leads to the transformation of power structures through collective action and individual capacity-building" (Mohan & Stokke, 2000), empowerment is a process of self-mobilization in which individuals participate in the process of community-building and become agents of their own development (Elliott, 1999). Philips and Pittman (2009) suggested that "community development consists of capacity building (developing the ability to act), social capital (the ability to act), and community development outcomes (community improvement)". Zimmerman (1995, p. 583) indicated that "community development programs must develop empowering processes where people create or are given opportunities to control their own destiny and influence the decisions that affect their lives". Hence community development is a process that enhances the capability of citizens to act collectively towards betterment of the community (be it social, economic and/or cultural) (Steiner & Farmer, 2017).

The notions of empowerment and resilient community development are intimately related, where people acquire the ability to act collectively in order to improve the adaptive capacity of their community (Perkins & Zimmerman, 1995; Steiner & Farmer, 2017). McAslan (2010) defines resilience as "the ability of something or someone to cope in the face of adversity – to recover and return to normality after confronting an abnormal, alarming and often unexpected threat. It embraces the concepts of awareness, detection, communication, reaction (and, if possible, avoidance) and recovery."

Resilience is a term that has been used in physics, psychology and environmental sciences for many years, but use of this concept is relatively new in the context of community development. For example, in physics, resilience refers to the ability of material to bend and bounce back, rather than break (Skerratt, 2013). Folke (2006, p. 259) defined the term from an ecological perspective as "the capacity of a system to absorb disturbance and re-organise while undergoing change so as to still retain essentially the same function, structure, identity, and feedbacks". In a community setting, resilience is conceptualized as "the existence, development, and engagement of community resources by community members to thrive in an environment characterised by change, uncertainty, unpredictability, and surprise", and that "resilience, simply, is about the capacity to adapt to change" (Magis, 2010). This adaptive capacity enables a community to flourish in spite of disruptive changes in a dynamic socio-economic as well as natural environment (Milman & Short, 2008; Steiner & Atterton, 2014). Aked et al. (2008) argued that community resilience fosters wellbeing among community members by creating common objectives and motivations to work together for the benefit of the community at large.

On July 29, 2009, Janet Napolitano, US Secretary of Homeland Security, articulated the spirit of resilient community in a presentation to the American Red Cross when she said: "Building a resilient nation doesn't come from a top-down, government-only, command-and-control approach; it comes from a bottom-up approach; it comes from Americans connecting, collaborating; it comes from asking questions and finding new solutions. And it comes from all of us as a shared responsibility."

3 Components of community resilience

Patel et al. (2017) undertook a systematic literature review and identified the following main components as important within the concept of community resilience. They are:

Local knowledge: This comprises a community's understanding regarding its existing vulnerabilities and local knowledge about the mitigation strategies against the onset of sudden crisis. For example, Rahman et al. (2017) highlight how the Smong tradition of indigenous knowledge of tsunami risk embedded in communities successfully alerted people to the 2004 tsunami on the island of Simeulue, Indonesia. Thus local knowledge helps to build resilience within a community. Apart from specific indigenous knowledge, the *factual knowledge base* of the community members also plays an important role, including specific learned information and knowledge related to disaster preparedness, mitigation, response and recovery (for example, knowledge about first aid; knowledge about basic health and hygiene, knowledge about other agencies to be contacted for rescue and relief operations, etc.). *Training and education* play an important role in this context. For example, community education, including public disaster education (Moore et al., 2012), community training and exercises, etc. are important to build local knowledge and capacity. A community must have adequate knowledge and understanding about its own resources and processes to endure and respond to a disaster (Chandra et al., 2011). This is achievable only through collaboration and connection between community members.

Community networks and relationships: One of the primary characteristics of a resilient community is collaborative connectedness, which allows the community to function as a cohesive whole. The connectedness of a community allows its community members to interact and form social relationship locally as well as with other members outside their community, thus forming bridging and bonding social capital (Aldrich & Meyer, 2015; Lin, 1999; Lin, 2001). The community cohesion depends on the strength of these links, including trust and shared values among community members.

Communication: An effective communication practice among both intra- and inter-community members is an important determinant of community resilience. Norris et al. (2008) have defined communication as "the creation of common meanings and understandings and the provision of opportunities for members to articulate needs, views, and attitudes". This implies that effective communication should premise not only on a framework facilitating common understanding but should also provide opportunities for open dialogue. Another related aspect is the accessibility of communication infrastructure, enabling multiple modes of communication – for example, voice, text, graphics, video, etc. – which is now possible with the pervasive use of social technology. Chandra et al. (2011, p. 20) noted that "strong communication networks are critical for resilience" with "diversity of mode and content". Dawes et al., (2004) identified the need for open communication during a crisis to share up-to-date situational information with members of the affected community and other stakeholders as a part of crisis communication. Houston et al. (2015) highlighted the need for strategic communication processes to enhance community resilience through information and knowledge sharing using community narratives and community systems and resources. This would enable effective request–response coordination between agencies, organizations and community members.

Health: Since both public health and public health services are severely affected by any disaster, knowledge about community health vulnerabilities and health service provisioning is an important factor in building community resilience. Community participation in healthcare services can be enhanced through appropriate training and capacity-building at the community level to handle mass casualties (Camacho et al., 2016; Haldane et al., 2019).

Governance/leadership: Steiner and Farmer (2017) suggest that "empowering communities should harness community development techniques that use both external actors and sources of support (i.e., exogenous practices), and those that utilise assets from within the community (i.e., endogenous practices)". This implies that governance and leadership should come both from outside and inside the community in order to build community resilience. There are two components to look at: *infrastructure and services* and *involvement and support of external agencies* (both public and private). Community resilience is attainable only when the community has access to adequate infrastructure and has the required operating capability to use and control the infrastructure (be it physical or virtual; e.g., informational). Involvement and support of external agencies would enhance the bridging social capital of the community, which in turn would help to improve community resilience.

Resources: Numerous types of resources, such as natural (e.g., water), physical (e.g., food, shelter), human (e.g., doctors, technicians) and financial (financial aid), are widely available and distributed in the community during and post-disaster. A resilient community must be able to harness these resources and allocate them appropriately within the community using fair distribution mechanisms.

Preparedness: Involvement of community stakeholders in pre-disaster planning process and running training sessions/practice drills with a focus on disaster risk reduction contributes to improved community resilience (Moore et al., 2012). Altogether, the involvement of community members in the planning process to improve mitigation measures and overall preparedness can enable a community to become resilient to disaster.

Mental outlook: The mental outlook of a community determines the ability and willingness of community members to participate in the process of disaster management activities in the face of uncertainty (Twigg, 2009). *Adaptability* can be defined as the ability and willingness to change after a disaster while accepting that things will be different. Bahadur et al. (2010) identified *"acceptance of uncertainty and change"* as the main characteristic of a resilient system.

The above characterization of community resilience is only indicative and may not be comprehensive. Even then, this list gives us a guideline on what constitutes community resilience. However, a more important question in this context is: how do we build a resilient community? What specific socio-economic, socio-technical and socio-political processes are important in making a community resilient? The above characterization indicates that making a community resilient primarily depends on: (i) formation of a network that connects intra- and inter-community stakeholders; and (ii) collaborative knowledge transactions among various agents (the nodes) of this network. In the next section we will illustrate how creation of *online communities of circumstance*, enabled by social technologies, has the potential to enhance community resilience using collaboration and connections.

4 A framework towards building online communities of circumstance: Mobilizing community towards resilience

4.1 Communities of circumstance

The National Research Council (2011) indicates the importance of community participation in decision-making in the event of an emergency. For example, Herbst and Jacqueline (2013) illustrate how community participation is an important parameter in every stage of disaster management: disaster mitigation, preparedness, response and recovery. Effective collaboration among members of the affected communities, together with private and public agencies, can lead to the formation of a *community of circumstance*, which would help community to take part in decision-making. The UK Cabinet Office (2011) describes communities of circumstance as follows: "These communities are created when groups of people are affected by the same incident, such as a train crash. These groups of individuals are unlikely to have the same interests or come from the same geographical area but may form a community in the aftermath of an event. Although this sense of community may be temporary, some communities of circumstance grow and are sustained in the long-term following an emergency." Communities of circumstance harness the potential of community knowledge, making them available to the community and empowering the communities to interact, collaborate and participate in the development of society, transforming the way they live, learn and work.

In designing the guideline for a community resilience strategy, the Red Cross proposed to engage community members in a network enabling formation of communities of circumstance to empower them to build disaster resilience (Herbst & Jacqueline, 2013). However, to accomplish this the Red Cross proposed working collaboratively "with networks under non-emergency circumstances, so that when a disaster occurs, the community not only is better prepared, but also has the critical partnerships and systems in place to effectively respond and recover well". This indicates that communities of circumstance cannot be created in isolation. Both *communities of practice* and *purpose* account to be mandatory prerequisites in building community of circumstance among rural urban communities. Communities of practice and purpose serve as engagement premise, which, by contextually involving rural participants,

Cultivating communities of circumstance 281

subsequently act as facilitating platforms in cultivating participatory abilities of rural members. It is only when the rural community derives collective participatory credentials that they are able to mobilize the local resources crucial to achieving resilience through formation of community of circumstance.

Although the need for a community of circumstance is well-understood, the question remains: how do we create it, especially in the context of a disempowered rural community? Communities of circumstance cannot be created or built out of vacuum; there has to be a framework that facilitates formation of community of circumstance. In the following section we propose a framework to build and operationalize communities of circumstance in rural context.

4.2 An operational framework for cultivating online communities of circumstance

Using the concept of platform economy and virtual enterprise as explained in Chapter 12, Section 4.1), we propose to operationalize online communities of circumstance, connecting intra-community and inter-community stakeholders, as shown in Figure 13.1. The aims are to achieve three main objectives, as illustrated in Herbst and Jacqueline (2013): "(i) foster 'connected' communities, in which linkages and relationships form between and across sectors; (ii) promote

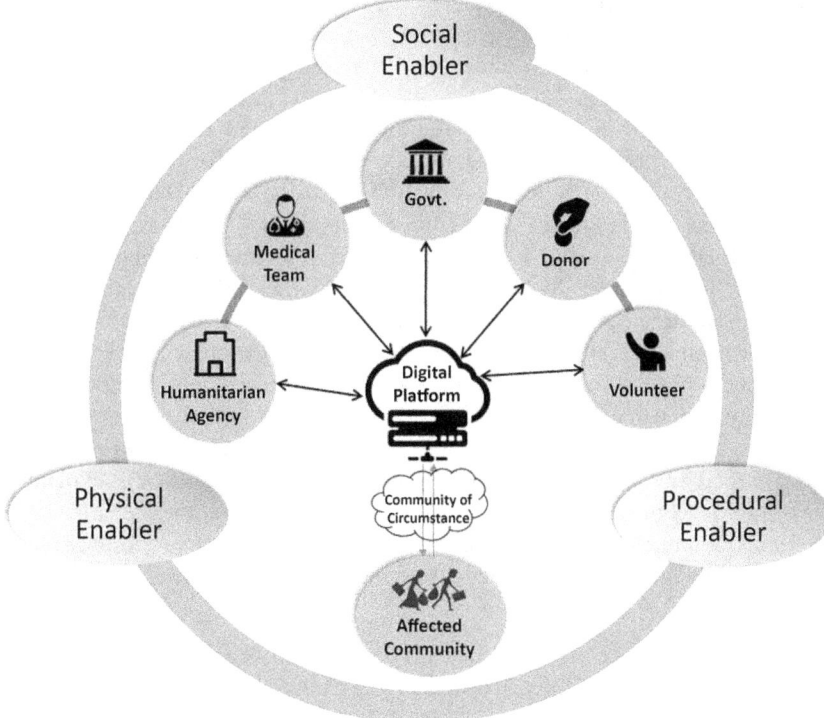

Figure 13.1 Creating community of circumstance in emergency management

'problem-solving' communities, in which community stakeholders trust one another and are able to work together to form solutions and take action; (iii) build 'prepared' communities, which have the capacity to prepare, respond and recover for any type of disaster that might occur" (Herbst & Jacqueline, 2013).

Three enablers – physical, procedural and social – are needed for successful operationalization of communities of circumstance (McAslan, 2010):

Physical enablers refer to accelerating factors that enable communities to mobilize physical resources and infrastructure to help in cultivating resilience on a communitarian level. The mobilizing capacity of physical and infrastructural resources, granted by physical enablers, includes utilities (water, electricity and gas), food, health services, transportation, communications and banking in the event of a crisis. Physical enablers allow the communities to operate at a level which, by triggering effective collaboration on a collective level, helps in enhancing adaptive capacities of individuals and groups.

Procedural enablers aim at ensuring knowledge creation, sharing and transaction capability of members of the communities, so that they can enhance their adaptive capacities in the process, thereby possessing better preparedness to recover from a major disruptive event. Such information and ideas are derived from past experiences, operational practices (gained through lessons learnt and experimentation) and a thorough analysis of immediate risks and future threats. Procedural enablers encourage target-oriented actions on a collective level, thereby endowing policy-makers, emergency planners, community leaders and individuals with the ability to understand the context in which effective action needs to be undertaken.

Social enablers aim at ensuring community cohesion and motivation. Amidst a restrictive social scenario, individuals need to develop credentials mandatory to sustain collective existence and survival. The social component of resilience is about getting people prepared and willing to confront and overcome dangerous and difficult circumstances. *Community cohesion* occurs when willing individuals voluntarily want to form a collective to achieve a common outcome; it draws on shared experiences, a common sense of worth and an expressed collective identity, which is sustained by shared values and beliefs. *Motivation* is the product of a common will to survive and the confidence to recover from crisis using protective measures, effective local leadership, mutual respect and a clear understanding of the threats and risks. Adger (2003) and Morrow (2008) have insightfully articulated the relational dynamics between social capital and resilience in explaining community-level participation in combating different natural disasters. The resilience of communities is dependent on social bonds and collective action based on networks of relationships, reciprocity, trust and community norms.

5 Developing resilient community through collaborative knowledge transaction: Some examples from disaster management

This section explores how community participation, in the context of disaster management, can be enhanced through collaborative knowledge transaction, which eventually will lead to development of resilient community. Taking a cue from the Engagement-Participation-Empowerment model (Steiner & Farmer, 2017) indicating three stages in transferring power from external actors to local communities, we show that the process of community resilience starts with engagement (Section 5.2) and follows with participation (Section 5.3) – both representing a precondition of community empowerment, leading to a resilient community (Section 5.4). To begin with we explore the role of knowledge management in combating disaster situations.

5.1 The role of knowledge management in disaster situations: An introduction

Responses to any disaster situation involve extensive cross-organizational coordination among several agencies. Multiple government and non-government agencies, including local volunteers/field workers, have to respond in a coordinated manner to handle a disaster situation. Therefore there is a serious need for both intra- and inter-organization information and knowledge transactions at various stages. In order to carry out *situation analysis* of a disaster-stricken region, to determine the *need* for various types of resources and to ensure fair and efficient *allocation and distribution of those resources*, all the agencies have to depend on coordinated and collaborative information and knowledge transactions. Since the scope of managing disasters is unstructured in nature, this is difficult to control centrally. Hence there is a need for a decentralized and hierarchy-independent approach, where even the end users (i.e., the disaster victims) are empowered to take quick and effective action.

Disaster management is inherently a knowledge-intensive (Ciccio et al., 2014) and collaboration-heavy process, involving all public safety-related organizations and affected community members (Abobakr & Majed, 2017). Therefore, managing knowledge becomes crucial in ensuring accessibility and usability of accurate and reliable disaster-related information whenever required and taking actionable decisions based on that (Seneviratne et al., 2010). Since knowledge in any disaster, both during and after the incident, is inherently fragmented, there is a huge problem in integrating this fragmented knowledge, which would, in turn, lead to inefficient coordination and sharing of resource (Mohanty et al., 2006; Seneviratne et al., 2010). According to UNESCO (2005), we do have plentiful knowledge on risk and vulnerability to hazards, but its access and utilization at the community level has yet to reach its full potential. During the Asian tsunami, for example, "the lack of knowledge management resulted in re-inventing the wheel in terms of setting up and managing construction programs and projects within the tsunami recovery operation" (Koria, 2009).

Knowledge management systems (KMS) have been used extensively by several government agencies to collect and distribute disaster-related information (Hassan, 2011). For example, in India the National Disaster Risk Management Programme of the Ministry of Home Affairs developed a KMS portal to connect several government departments and selected non-government agencies to share disaster-related knowledge and information. Highlighting the example of

Hurricane Katrina, Murphy and Jennex (2006) concluded that KMS should be integrated with all disaster management activities. Another example is the use of the information management system for hurricane disasters (IMASH) (Iakovou & Douligeris, 2001). However, in most of the cases, the centralized, non-interactive and static nature of these KMS make them ineffective.

Use of knowledge management practice to enhance community resilience has not been widely explored by academics and practitioners (Rahman et al., 2017). The members of a resilient community need to have the capacity to not only use and share existing knowledge but also to generate dynamically new knowledge for communitarian benefits. This would strengthen the capacity of all the members of the community individually as well as the community as a whole (Twigg, 2009). This also enables use of local perspectives and initiatives that increase the capacity of the community as a whole to recover from an adverse situation (Aldrich & Meyer, 2015). Although the concept of community resilience to disaster is complex and based on multiple factors, one of the specific characteristics that builds up community resilience is a focus on knowledge and education (Twigg, 2009).

Community resilience, thus, more particularly refers to how local communities develop their capacity to cope with disaster by (i) reusing local resources and (ii) mobilizing external resources by getting connected to external agencies for collaborative knowledge transaction. As illustrated in Rahman et al. (2017), resilience is "communities' capacity to adapt to, reduce, manage, and recover from the worst impacts of hazards by utilizing available resources through appropriate, actionable decisions in pre-disaster, disaster, and post-event phases.... Communities' knowledge, both existing within the communities and acquired from outside agencies, is central to ensuring community resilience."

Emergency response processes are unpredictable, unrepeatable, complex, time-critical, knowledge-intensive, unstructured and very dynamic (Kushnareva et al., 2015). Therefore emergency response processes must be scalable, flexible and adaptable enough to enable a collaborative response. Community-sourcing of real-time data (as opposed to crowd-sourcing) from the entities who are physically present in an affected area is inevitably much more accurate than any other passive source and is better for appropriate resource allocation and effective planning of response operation. We will discuss the issues of community participation in disaster knowledge management in subsequent sections.

5.2 Use of social media to engage community members during disaster for situational information and knowledge transaction

Several researchers in the emergency management field believe that using social media will help build community disaster resilience. For example, White (2012, p. 187) states that "community resilience should include a grassroots effort where social media is utilized in a number of ways to support the safety of the community." Dufty (2012) promotes the use of social media by emergency agencies to assist in "learning for disaster resilient communities". The objective of this section is to discuss prospects and limitations of social media in this context.

Social media promote public participation in emergency management through knowledge and information transactions over various social media channels, such as Twitter, Facebook, different blogs and discussion forums, etc. This exhibits a new form of information-sharing behaviour where social media users share information not only to request assistance but to offer assistance to others (Palen & Liu, 2007). Through social media, community members provide multi-modal information that would contribute to information required for analysing crisis situations (Hughes & Palen, 2012).

Social media facilitate formation of online communities where members share information during emergency situations (Wang, 2010). Hurricane Katrina in 2005, for example, has shown the potential of blogs and online forums where displaced US citizens could connect with members of their communities (Macias et al., 2009; Palen & Liu, 2007). Torrey et al. (2007) found that several citizens used online means to coordinate distribution of relief materials to help others. There are also evidences where social media is used to find missing persons as well as housing for victims (Macias et al., 2009; Palen & Liu, 2007).

During a major crisis, users' participation in social media with crisis-related data contributes significantly in conducting situation analysis (Cameron et al., 2012; Vieweg et al., 2010). For example, analysis of tweets sent during the Oklahoma City fires and Red River floods, both in 2009, helped to improve situational awareness (for example, fire locations and flood levels) (Vieweg et al., 2010). Researchers also have attempted to develop natural language processing (NLP) tools to analyse social media text to help identify social media posts that would assist in a disaster situation (Corvey et al., 2012). However, the technology is not yet mature enough to derive meaningful insights from these free-formatted, multi-modal social media posts. In fact, the use of social media has become so widespread that during a major crisis the huge amounts of social media posts generated are difficult to monitor and analyse (Castillo, 2016). For example, the University of Colorado Boulder collected over 26 million tweets during Hurricane Sandy (Anderson & Schram, 2011). With the available technology it is very difficult to consolidate and derive actionable insights from this large amount of socially-generated data available during an emergency (Palen & Anderson, 2016). Real-time collection, analysis and interpretation of multi-modal, multi-lingual social media posts during a crisis situation still poses a challenge to the research community.

Of course, various social media channels can be potential tools to engage community members in crisis preparedness, response and recovery, which may enhance community resilience (Belblidia, 2010; Dufty, 2012). But, because of the limitations stated above and the informal and unregulated nature of social media data with low information credibility, social media adoption in formal emergency response has lagged behind that of public uptake (Hughes & Palen, 2012). Furthermore, traditional social media platforms may not generate any useful benefits to members of disempowered/rural communities who are not used to them because of access and/or language barriers (Cinnamon & Schuurman, 2012). However, it is true that social media can provide an engagement platform for the member of the communities to interact with each other and other agencies during emergency situations.

5.3 Interactive community-sourcing: A participatory knowledge management practice during disaster

As indicated earlier, efficient management of disaster requires accurate and timely information from the disaster location so that the situation can be analysed, community needs can be assessed and, accordingly, resources can be mobilized to mitigate the effect of disaster. Traditional methods of information collection by the agencies involved in disaster management are time consuming and inaccurate, as they rely on survey results conducted by deployed volunteers/ agencies. Because of various constraints – such as anonymity of contributors, journalistic narratives, subjectivity of information, etc. – other media-generated data, including from social media, cannot be relied on to supply accurate and authentic situational information that can enable proper need assessment.

In a study we conducted on the use of Twitter during the Uttarakhand flood disaster in northern parts of India in 2013 (North India floods, n.d.), a total of 2,921 tweets spanning 19 days (from 14th June, 2013, to 3rd July, 2013) were collected. After data filtering, a total of 2,390 unique users were identified, of which 2,086 tweeted only once. With this evidence that most Twitter users tweeted only once in the crisis situation, the implication is that users tweeted out of sentiment or impulse, and not specifically to help or pass on some useful information. Some 54% of tweets were found to be 'retweets' and these were posting news-URLs collected from other media such as television, newspapers and other websites. This reveals another pattern of Twitter use – to communicate or circulate the latest news headlines among the Twitter communities. Very few tweets were found that could be examples of Twitter providing useful and authentic information. Typically, 47% tweets in this dataset contained anguished comments on government or political parties, which corrupts the usefulness of the tweets as sources of information and makes it difficult to identify important pieces of information in the dataset through analytics.

This is where community-generated credible and useful information plays a significant role. With the help of social technologies it is possible not only to engage affected community members but also to encourage their participation in providing authentic situational information from identifiable users to help manage disaster. This can be termed *community-sourcing*, as opposed to *crowd-sourcing*.

The term "crowd-sourcing", coined by Jeff Howe (Howe, 2006), describes how businesses can involve "an undefined (and generally large) network of people" to carry out some tasks through an open call. Crowd-sourcing can also be used to describe a practice of obtaining task-based information or input from large numbers of people, either paid or unpaid, and typically via the internet. For example, Chen et al. (2014) used an automated question–answer system for spontaneous reporting of adverse drug reactions (ADR) in a crowd-sourced manner. They showed that information crowd-sourcing is an efficient way to track and discover cases of ADR. In the context of disaster management, social media, as discussed in the previous sub-section, use a crowd-sourced model to collect citizen-generated information in the context of disaster. In this context, Ushahidi is an effective example of collating and analysing citizen-generated data from affected locations to generate a *crisis map*.

On the other hand, community-sourcing can be defined as a way of getting a task done through a defined group of people who share a common interest and belong to a community. In crowd-sourcing, users are anonymous and there is no need for any affiliation to be engaged. The objective is to involve "everyone" with a hope that "someone" will contribute. Contrary to this, in community-sourcing, members are part of a defined community and, hence, identifiable; and they have a common interest in contributing, which satisfies not only the individual's need but also the need of the community. The community-sourcing model, therefore, is more targeted, sustainable and effective for all concerned.

Since participants in community-sourcing are identifiable, they can be encouraged to interact and to participate in the process in a more intimate manner. This interaction model can be termed as interactive community-sourcing. This is derived from the notion of interactive crowd-sourcing, where the users in a crowd-sourcing process are made to interact to fulfil the purpose of crowd-sourcing. For example, in the context of designing innovative products through crowd-sourcing using a co-creation model, the participants from the crowd are made to interact and work closely together from the selection of the idea through to the production and marketing of the innovation (Djelassi & Decoopman, 2016). Basu et al. (2016) in their visionary paper introduced an interactive crowd-sourcing system that includes the human factor in interactive crowd-sourcing.

Using a similar notion, Das et al. (2016) and Basu et al. (2016) have illustrated how interactive community-sourcing can help to collate useful data and enable community participation in providing vital information related to damage assessment. Basu et al. (2016) conducted a field trial where a set of post-disaster situational awareness questions were put to people in a disaster-affected region. Their answers were collected with the help of 20 volunteers from a NGO in three remote villages in the Namkhana region of West Bengal, India, namely North Chandanpiri, South Chandanpiri and Haripur. Around 20 need-assessment questions, picked up from the need-assessment questionnaire normally used by disaster management authorities for situational data collection, were arranged in nine different categories (viz., affected area profile, health and medical infrastructure, food aid and nutrition, water and sanitation, education, and others). An automated system was developed for interactive community-sourcing to connect with the affected community members (disaster victims/volunteers/first responders in our case) and to collect interactive

SMS-based responses from them to help the system build a structured repository of situational information.

The field trial took place six months after the said region was affected by a flood in mid-2015 and was aimed at assessing the post-disaster "social continuity". Social continuity can be defined as the process of returning to the originally prevailing socio-economic conditions of the local inhabitants after being disturbed by a disaster. The volunteers interacted with more than 150 inhabitants/responders of the villages and mobilized each of them to respond to around 20 interactive questions framed in the context of social continuity. Around 3,000 responses were collected (around 150 responses per question) through SMS-based interactive crowd-sourcing in order to gain actionable insight directly from the affected communities. Once the answers were collected, state-of-the-art text summarization algorithms were used to assess the answers and acquire situational awareness. Such summarized information will potentially assist the disaster management authorities in taking decisions regarding time-critical assessment of damage and needs. Interactive community-sourcing can supplement social media posts to generate effective insights.

Using a case study of the great deluge in Kerala, India, Ajay (2019) shows how mobile phone and social media in combination can be used as effective tools in rescue and relief operations. As part of a large digital volunteering team, the author collated social media posts from various platforms, and phone calls were made to the individuals who posted these online messages between 16th August and 18th August, 2018, with the objective to verify the authenticity of the messages and to collect more relevant details that might help the emergency service providers on the ground to provide specific support. Use of messaging apps (for example, WhatsApp) was found to be effective in this context, which provided a platform towards not only information sharing but also supporting interactions with affected members.

5.4 Cultivating online communities of circumstance using a collaborative knowledge management platform: Towards a disaster-resilient community

Following the Engagement-Participation-Empowerment model (Steiner & Farmer, 2017) that illustrates three stages in transferring power from external actors to local communities, we have shown that the process of community resilience starts with engagement (Section 5.2) and follows with participation (Section 5.3). However, in order to achieve community empowerment, leading to a resilient community, we need to have a *platform* (as described in Section 4.2) that promotes more deep-rooted participation of the community members, enabling them to participate not only in information and knowledge exchange but also in decision-making. In this context, it is essential to create a collaborative knowledge management platform for disaster management that will help all stakeholders to interact via knowledge and information sharing and derive actionable insights. The platform eventually helps its users to visualize the location-based snapshots of situations, resource demands and available resources in near real-time, extract meaningful knowledge out of these "local snapshots" and integrate them to build a coherent picture of the overall disaster scenario. The functional description of such a platform, CORDS (COmmunity dRiven Decision System), is described below.

CORDS is a simple multiplatform (web and app-based) system that transforms *crowd* to a contributing *community* for community empowerment, disaster management and social continuity management. It provides an environment to integrate disaster management authorities with community members to promote active involvement of the affected community members. The use of social technologies enables the platform to manage community formation and support interactions (*socialization*). The system architecture is shown in Figure 13.2. It has the following modules:

Data collection module: Situational data from the disaster-affected sites is not only collected from designated volunteers/agencies but also from members of affected communities through various communication channels (phone, mobile app, interactive SMS).

Analytics and report generation module: This module does the data authentication, filtering and aggregation to assess the damage and need for resources.

Resource management module: The task of this module is to match resource need with available resources. The platform helps to view a list of resource requests made by any stakeholders, including affected community members, authenticate the request and allocate available resources to match the request. Both demand and supply of resources are dynamic in nature and need collaborative coordination among various stakeholders to ensure fair distribution of resources.

Community management module: Apart from sharing knowledge and providing query-response processing and decision support for disaster management, such a platform can also be used for enabling regular interaction among community members for sharing and resolving their daily concerns (life and livelihood related), getting advisory and other support from external service providers and for bridging the information and knowledge gap faced by the information- and knowledge-deprived communities. Regular interaction among the community members over such a platform may eventually foster a sense of community. Members of community start sharing an emotional connection and, as the members satisfy their own needs, they also meet the community's needs. Gradually, community resilience is developed which ensures that community may respond to, withstand and recover from any kind of adverse situations (for example, economic collapse to global catastrophic risks) utilizing their available resources.

The users of the platform are: (i) the administrator (controller and arbiter of the platform: see Chapter 12, Section 5.1.4); (ii) affiliated disaster management agencies (both government and non-government); (iii) rescue and relief workers (volunteers); (iv) victims (affected population)/other affected community members; (v) resource donors; and (vi) medical teams.

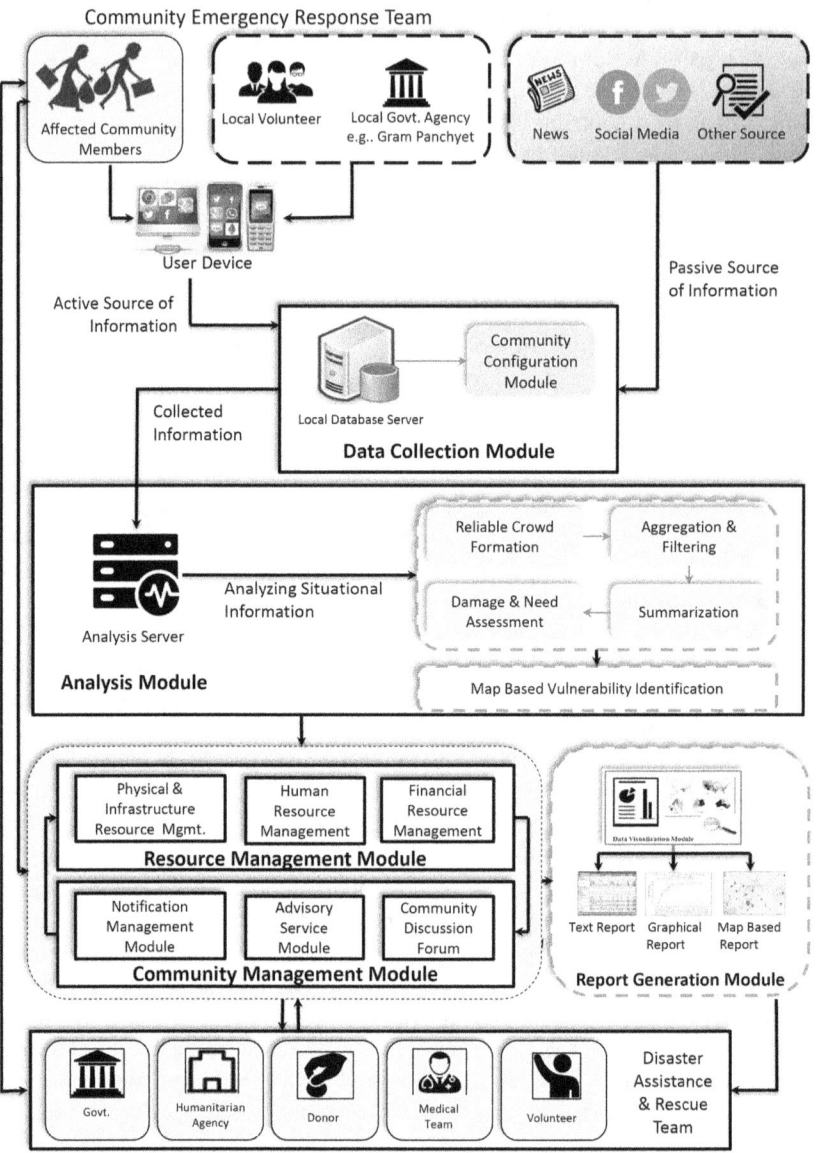

Figure 13.2 System architecture for CORDS: Knowledge sharing using collaboration and connection

Cultivating communities of circumstance 291

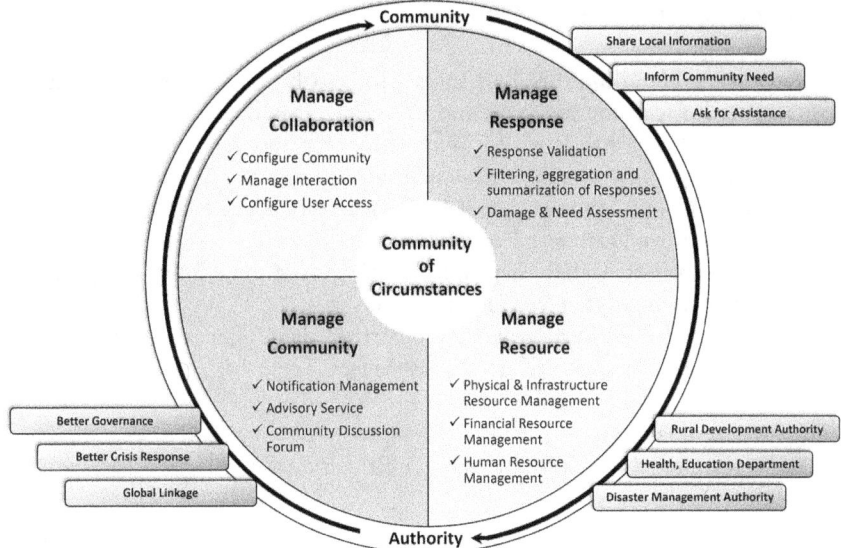

Figure 13.3 Software framework of CORDS

The CORDS software framework (Figure 13.3) incorporates four essential functional modules: (i) manage collaboration, (ii) manage response, (iii) manage resource and (iv) manage community. The components, purpose and functionalities of each module are briefly explained below.

Manage collaboration is the most important module in the CORDS system. It introduces the community to the platform with an aim to engage the community, help them to connect and collaborate online around the platform:

- *Configure community:* The basic profile and contact details of community members are fed into the CORDS platform for enabling online interaction between community and the system. Apart from the community members, other location-based service providers as well as government/ non-government supporting agencies can also register on this platform for providing various supports to community. Intra- and inter-community conversation can be initiated as and when necessary using the community contacts stored in the system.
- *Manage interaction:* This enables interactive community-sourcing for gathering knowledge on various community-related matters during normal situations (such as need for support, need to connect with external agencies, etc.) and/or emergency situations (such as emergency resource needs, available resources, etc.).
- *Configure user access:* Community members are allowed to interact with the system and with other community members using various role-based accesses. A community member may sometimes be a resource requester and/or resource provider and/or may even be an emergency volunteer and so on.

Manage response module performs the following tasks:

- *Response validation:* The responses gathered by the system as a result of information community-sourcing are authenticated (sourced from reliable crowd) and then processed for duplication and inconsistency removal.
- *Filtering, aggregation and summarization of responses:* Validated responses are filtered and categorized according to the responders' locations and topics. Topic-based or location-based aggregations of responses are performed for building an integrated snapshot of the situation. Finally, aggregated responses are analysed and summarized.
- *Damage and need assessment:* Summarized data offer actionable insights (for example, damage and need assessment).

Manage resource module allows the system to record the location-based available resources and allocate them efficiently to fulfil the corresponding resource demands:

- *Physical and infrastructure resource management:* A location-based pool of available physical and infrastructure resources is validated by the administrator and is maintained by the system. If any sort of demand is raised in the system for such resources, the administrator may allocate them from the available resource pool.
- *Financial resource management:* Donors from the community or from outside the community may donate resources/money, which is recorded in the system. On the other hand, location-based financial needs may be captured from the community conversations. Financial resource management may be done efficiently based on these two inputs.
- *Human resource management:* It is possible to capture the human resource requirements at various sites and use idle human resources available at different locations so that demand for human resources may be satisfied through proper match-making by the system.

Manage community module offers three functions:

- *Notification management:* This enables the administrator to configure any emergency alerts or administrative notifications through the system. The system also offers the flexibility to withdraw any earlier notifications once its relevance or validity is over.
- *Advisory service:* If affected community members express their need for any advisory services, such requirements may be satisfied from the pool of registered advisory service providers from external agencies.
- *Community discussion forum:* The CORDS platform offers a discussion forum that enables its users to share their views on any topics of their concern.

Although interactions over such a collaborative platform are autonomous in nature, as the platform does not impose any kind of control over the participation of entities, such platforms are inherently quasi-controlled as the community interactions are not only governed by the norms and policies supported by software but also invisibly monitored and moderated by the regulatory authority (admin), if required, to confirm trustworthiness of members, authenticity and appropriateness of content and fairness in information and knowledge transactions.

6 Conclusion

The process of developing community resilience is not uniform. As pointed out by Rose (1996), it is possible that some communities do not have the necessary capabilities for rational self-management. Specifically in the context of rural empowerment, Herbert-Cheshire (2000, p. 213) notes that "community-based strategies for self-help will increase the division and inequality in rural towns by empowering a small, fairly powerful minority who are better positioned to mobilize themselves". This highlights that community empowerment may be unevenly distributed, with those of higher social status tending to participate most in civic activity (Brackertz & Meredyth, 2009).

It should be recognized that levels of capability and willingness to participate in governance and to become a resilient community differ between communities. To facilitate community participation in governance, social and political readiness of community members is important (Somerville, 2005). So a pertinent question in this context is: how is a community mobilized towards resilience when capability and willingness to participate in community development initiatives are far less than expected?

Steiner and Farmer (2017) suggest an EPE model (Engage-Participate-Empower) that highlights a process of community resilience starting with engagement, followed by participation and subsequently facilitating community empowerment, a precondition for realizing a resilient community. Communities that have not previously engaged can benefit from external support. Hence exogenous initiatives can provide necessary guidance and supports, which could be a pre-condition as well as a facilitator towards endogenous development of a weaker community. Steiner and Farmer (2017) argue that "to reach endogenous empowerment, exogenous empowerment practices are useful and effective for some communities. Capacity building might be emergent (in endogenous community development) but in some cases it may need to be nurtured via external sources (by exogenous development)". Thus successful implementation of empowerment policies requires creation of appropriate support structures that enable the transfer of power from state to community. Exogenous agencies could add value by providing an enabling environment where endogenous development occurs. This calls for developing an *empowering ecosystem* to foster *connection* and collaboration between external agencies and rural communities, leading towards holistic development of the communities. This will be discussed in the next chapter.

References

Abobakr, Y. & Majed, A. (2017). Adaptive Case Management Framework to Develop Case-Based Emergency Response System. *International Journal of Advanced Computer Science and Applications.* 8(4). doi:10.14569/ijacsa.2017.080408.

Adger, W.N. (2003). Social Capital, Collective Action, and Adaptation to Climate Change. *Economic Geography*, 79(4), 387–404. doi:10.1111/j.1944-8287.2003.tb00220.x.

Aked, J. & Thompson, S. (2008). Five Ways to Wellbeing. Retrieved from: https://b.3cdn.net/nefoundation/d80eba95560c09605d_uzm6b1n6a.pdf.

Aldrich, D.P. & Meyer, M.A. (2015). Social Capital and Community Resilience. *American Behavioral Scientist*, 59(2), 254–269. doi:10.1177/0002764214550299.

Ajay, A. (2019). Role of technology in responding to disasters: insights from the great deluge in Kerala. *Current Science*, 116(6). Retrieved from: https://www.currentscience.ac.in/Volumes/116/06/0913.pdf.

Alstyne, M.V. & Parker, G.G. (2017). Platform Business: From Resources to Relationships. *GfK Marketing Intelligence Review*, 9(1), 25–29.

Alstyne, M.W.V., Parker, G.G. & Choudary, S.P. (2016). Pipelines, Platforms, and the New Rules of Strategy. *Harvard Business Review*. Retrieved from: https://hbr.org/2016/04/pipelines-platforms-and-the-new-rules-of-strategy.

Anderson, K.M. & Schram, A. (2011). *Design and implementation of a data analytics infrastructure in support of crisis informatics research.* Proceedings of the 2011 International Conference on Software Engineering, 844–847. doi:10.1145/1985793.1985920.

Bahadur, A.V., Ibrahim, M. & Tanner, T. (2010). The resilience renaissance? Unpacking of resilience for tackling climate change and disasters. Institute of Development Studies. SCR Discussion Paper 1. Retrieved from: https://www.gov.uk/dfid-research-outputs/the-resilience-renaissance-unpacking-of-resilience-for-tackling-climate-change-and-disasters-scr-discussion-paper-1.

Basu, M., Bandyopadhyay, S. & Ghosh, S. (2016). Post Disaster Situation Awareness and Decision Support through Interactive Crowdsourcing. *Procedia Engineering*, 159, 167–173. doi:10.1016/j.proeng.2016.08.151.

Basu, S.R., Lykourentzou, I., Thirumuruganathan, S., Amer-Yahia, S. & Das, G. (2013). *Crowds, not drones: Modeling human factors in interactive crowdsourcing.* VLDB Workshop on Databases and Crowdsourcing, Trento, Italy. Retrieved from: https://hal.inria.fr/hal-00923542/document.

Belblidia, M.S. (2010). Building community resilience through social networking sites: Using online social networks for emergency management. *International Journal of Information Systems for Crisis Response and Management*, 2(1), 24–36. doi:10.4018/jiscrm.2010120403.

Botsman, R. & Rogers, R. (2010). *What's Mine Is Yours: The Rise of Collaborative Consumption.* New York: Harper Collins Publishers.

Brackertz, N. & Meredyth, D. (2009). Community consultation in Victorian local government: A case of mixing metaphors? *Australian Journal of Public Administration*, 68(2), 152–166. doi:10.1111/j.1467-8500.2009.00627.x.

Cabinet Office (2011). *Strategic National Framework on Community Resilience.* London: Cabinet Office. Retrieved from: https://m.oxfordshire.gov.uk/cms/sites/default/files/folders/documents/fireandpublicsafety/emergency/StrategicNationalFramework.pdf.

Camacho, N.A., Hughes, A., Burkle, F.M., Ingrassia, P.L., Ragazzoni, L., Redmond, A. & Schreeb, V.J. (2016). Education and training of emergency medical teams:

Recommendations for a global operational learning framework, *PLoS currents*, 8. Retrieved from: https://www.ncbi.nlm.nih.gov/pubmed/27917306.

Camarinha-Matos, L.M. & Pantoja-Lima, C. (2001). Cooperation Coordination in Virtual Enterprises, *Journal of Intelligent Manufacturing*, 12(2), 21. Retrieved from: www.academia.edu/248722/Cooperation_Coordination_In_Virtual_Enterprises.

Camarinha-Matos, L.M., Afsarmanesh, H., Garita, C. & Pantoja-Lima, C. (1998). Towards an Architecture for Virtual Enterprises. *Journal of Intelligent Manufacturing*, 9(2), 189–199.

Cameron, M.A., Power, R., Robinson, B. & Yin, J. (2012). *Emergency situation awareness from Twitter for crisis management*. Proceedings of the 21st International Conference Companion on World Wide Web, 695–698. doi:10.1145/2187980.2188183.

Castillo, C. (2016). *Big crisis data: Social media in disasters and time-critical situations*. Cambridge: Cambridge University Press. doi:10.1017/CBO9781316476840.

Chandra, A., Acosta, J., Stern, S., Uscher-Pines, L., Williams, M. & Yeung, D. (2011). Building community resilience to disasters: A way forward to enhance national health security (technical report). Retrieved from: https://www.ncbi.nlm.nih.gov/pubmed/28083162.

Chandra, A., Williams, M., Plough, A., Stayton, A., Wells, K.B. & Horta, M. (1999). Getting actionable about community resilience: the Los Angeles County Community Disaster Resilience project. *American Journal of Public Health*, 103(7), 1181–1189. doi:10.2105/AJPH.2013.301270.

Chen, C., Huang, Y., Liu, Y., Liu, C., Meng, L., Sun, Y., Bian, K., Huang, A., Duan, X. & Jiao, B. (2014). *Interactive Crowdsourcing to Spontaneous Reporting of Adverse Drug Reactions*. Proceedings of the IEEE International Conference on Communications, Sydney. doi:10.1109/ICC.2014.6883992.

Ciccio C.D., Marrella, A. & Russo, A. (2014). Knowledge-intensive processes: Characteristics, requirements and analysis of contemporary approaches. *Journal on Data Semantics*, 4, 29–57.

Cinnamon, J. & Schuurman, N. (2012). Confronting the data-divide in a time of spatial turns and volunteered geographic information. *GeoJournal*, 1–18. doi:10.1007/s10708-012-9458-6.

Corvey, W.J., Verma, S., Vieweg, S., Palmer, M. & Martin, J.H. (2012). *Foundations of a multilayer annotation framework for Twitter communications during crisis events*. Proceedings of the Eighth International Conference on Language Resources and Evaluation, Istanbul. Retrieved from: https://www.aclweb.org/anthology/volumes/L12-1/.

Cui, M., Pan, S.L., Newell, S. & Cui, L. (2017). Strategy, Resource Orchestration and e-Commerce Enabled Social Innovation in Rural China. *Journal of Strategic Information Systems*, 26(1), 3–21.

Das, A., Mallik, N., Bandyopadhyay, S., DasBit. S. & Basak, J. (2016). *Interactive information crowdsourcing for disaster management using SMS and Twitter: A research prototype*. Proceedings of the IEEE International Conference on Pervasive Computing and Communication Workshops, 1–6. doi:10.1109/PERCOMW.2016.7457101.

Dawes, S.S., Cresswell, A.M. & Cahan, B.B. (2004). Learning From Crisis: Lessons in Human and Information Infrastructure From the World Trade Center Response. *Social Science Computer Review*, 22(1), 52–66. doi:10.1177/0894439303259887.

De Mattos, C.A. & Laurindo, F.J.B. (2015). Collaborative Platforms for Supply Chain Integration: Trajectory, Assimilation of Platforms and Results. *Journal of Technology Management and Innovation*,10(2), 79–92. doi:10.4067/S0718-27242015000200006.

Djelassi, S. & Decoopman, I. (2016). Innovation through interactive crowdsourcing: The role of boundary objects. *Recherche et Applications en Marketing* (English Edition), 31(3), 131–152. doi:10.1177/2051570716650160.

Dufty, N. (2012). Using Social Media to Build Community Disaster Resilience. *Australian Journal of Emergency Management*, 27(1), 40–45. Retrieved from: https://www.researchgate.net/publication/279861590_Using_Social_Media_to_Build_Community_Disaster_Resilience.

Elliott, J.A. (1999). *An Introduction to Sustainable Development*. London: Routledge.

Eric, T.W. (2014). The Application of Social Media in Disasters. How Can Social Media Support an Effective Disaster Response? Retrieved from: https://aboutiigr.org/wp-content/uploads/2014/08/The-Application-of-Social-Media-in-Disasters-Final-Product.pdf.

Folke, C. (2006). Resilience: The emergence of a perspective for social-ecological system analyses. *Global Environmental Change*, 16, 253–267. doi:10.1016/j.gloenvcha.2006.04.002.

Fraser, E.D., Dougill, A.J., Mabee, W.E., Reed, M. & McAlpine, P. (2005). Bottom up and top down: analysis of participatory processes for sustainability indicator identification as a pathway to community empowerment and sustainable environmental management. *Journal of Environmental Management*, 78(2), 114–127. doi:10.1016/j.jenvman.2005.04.009.

Haldane, V., Chuah, F.L.H., Srivastava, A., Singh, S.R., Koh, G.C.H. & Seng, C.K., (2019). Community participation in health services development, implementation, and evaluation: A systematic review of empowerment, health, community, and process outcomes. *PLoS ONE*, 14(5). doi:10.1371/journal.pone.0216112.

Hassan, N.A. (2011). The Implementation of Knowledge Management System for the Support of Humanitarian Assistance/Disaster Relief in Malaysia. *International Journal of Humanities and Social Science*, 1(4). Retrieved from: https://pdfs.semanticscholar.org/e4b2/d4a672450020dcbd316ec0bf547325855dda.pdf.

Hao, Y., Helo, P. & Shamsuzzoha, A. (2016). Virtual Factory System Design and Implementation: Integrated Sustainable Manufacturing. *International Journal of Systems Science: Operations & Logistics*, 5(2), 116–132. doi:10.1080/23302674.2016.1242819.

Herbert-Cheshire, L. (2000). Contemporary strategies for rural community development in Australia: a governmentality perspective. *Journal of Rural Studies*, 16, 203–215. doi:10.1016/S0743-0167(99)00054-6.

Herbst, K. & Jacqueline, Y. (2013). *Guidebook on Creating Resilience Networks*. Washington, DC: The American Red Cross. Retrieved from: https://www.preparecenter.org/sites/default/files/guidebook_on_creating_resilience_-_domestic.pdf.

Houston, J.B., Spialek, M.L., Cox, J., Greenwood, M.M. & First, J. (2015). The Centrality of Communication and Media in Fostering Community Resilience: A Framework for Assessment and Intervention. *American Behavioral Scientist*, 59(2), 270–283. doi:10.1177/0002764214548563.

Howe, J. (2006). Crowdsourcing: A Definition. Retrieved from: https://crowdsourcing.typepad.com/cs/2006/06/crowdsourcing_a.html.

Hughes, A.L. & Palen, L. (2012). The evolving role of the public information officer: An examination of social media in emergency management. *Journal of Homeland Security and Emergency Management*, 9(1). doi:10.1515/1547-7355.1976.

Iakovou, E. & Douligeris, C. (2001). An information management system for the emergency management of hurricane disasters. *International Journal of Risk Assessment and Management*, 2(3/4), 243–262. Retrieved from: https://doi.org/10.1504/IJRAM.2001.001508.

Johnson, E.M. & Whang, S. (2002). E-Business and Supply Chain Management: An Overview and Framework. *Production and Operations Management*, 11(4), 413–423. doi:10.1111/j.1937-5956.2002.tb00469.x.

Koopman, C., Mitchell, M. & Thierer, A. (2015). The Sharing Economy and Consumer Protection Regulation: The Case for Policy Change. *The Journal of Business, Entrepreneurship & the Law*, 8(2), 530. Retrieved from: https://digitalcommons.pepperdine.edu/cgi/viewcontent.cgi?article=1130&context=jbel.

Koria, M. (2009). Managing for Innovation in Large and Complex Recovery Programmes: Tsunami Lessons from Sri Lanka. *International Journal of Project Management*, 27, 123–130. Retrieved from: https://www.infona.pl/resource/bwmeta1.element.elsevier-c7f343cd-0905-336e-a441-99c433587654.

Kushnareva, E., Rychkova, I. & Grand, B.L. (2015). *Modeling business processes for automated crisis management support: Lessons learned*. Proceedings of the 9th International Conference on Research Challenges in Information Science, 388–399. doi:10.1109/RCIS.2015.7128900.

Lee, M. & Han, M. (2009). *E-Business Model Design and Implementation in Supply-Chain Integration*. Proceedings of the International Symposium on Web Information Systems and Applications. Retrieved from: https://pdfs.semanticscholar.org/6385/8f26b13656ef131be90d6297f8d6448f1621.pdf.

Lin, N. (1999). Building a Network Theory of Social Capital. *Connections*, 22(1), 28–51. Retrieved from: https://pdfs.semanticscholar.org/16a9/441c05a3bb9e359c868dde882889c6ef8df9.pdf.

Lin, N. (2001). *Social Capital: A Theory of Social Structure and Action*. Cambridge: Cambridge University Press. Retrieved from: https://assets.cambridge.org/97805214/74313/frontmatter/9780521474313_frontmatter.pdf.

Macias, W., Hilyard, K. & Freimuth, V. (2009). Blog functions as risk and crisis communication during Hurricane Katrina. *Journal of Computer-Mediated Communication*, 15(1), 1–31. doi:10.1111/j.1083-6101.2009.01490.x.

Magis, K. (2010). Community resilience: An indicator of social sustainability. *Society and Natural Resources*, 33, 401–416. doi:10.1080/08941920903305674.

McAslan, A. (2010). The Concept of Resilience: understanding its origins, meaning and utility. *Information and Security*. Retrieved from: http://infosec-journal.com/article/concept-resilience-understanding-its-origins-meaning-and-utility.

Milman, A. & Short, A. (2008). Incorporating resilience into sustainability indicators: An example for the urban water sector. *Global Environmental Change*, 18, 758–767. doi:10.1016/j.gloenvcha.2008.08.002.

Mistilis, N. & Sheldon, P. (2005). Knowledge Management for Tourism Crises and Disasters. *Tourism Review International*, 10(1/2), 39–46.

Mohan, G. & Stokke, K. (2000). Participatory development and empowerment: The dangers of localism. *Third World Quarterly*, 21, 247–268. doi:10.1080/01436590050004346.

Mohanty, S., et al. (2005). Knowledge Management in Disaster Risk Reduction. The Indian approach. Retrieved from: https://www.ndmindia.nic.in/images/public-awareness/knowledge-manageme.pdf.

Moore, M., Chandra, A. & Feeney, K.C. (2012). Building community resilience: What can the United States learn from experiences in other countries? Disaster medicine and public health preparedness. *Disaster Medicine and Public Health Preparedness*, 7(3), 292–301. doi:10.1001/dmp.2012.15.

Morrow, B.H. (2008). Community Resilience: A Social Justice Perspective. CARRI Research Report 4. Retrieved from: https://www.academia.edu/4313849/Community_Resilience_A_Social_Justice_Perspective.

Murphy, T. & Jennex, M.E. (2006). Knowledge Management, Emergency Response, and Hurricane Katrina. *International Journal of Intelligent Control Systems*, 11(4), 199–208. Retrieved from: http://citeseerx.ist.psu.edu/viewdoc/download?doi=10.1.1.455.2376&rep=rep1&type=pdf.

National Research Council (2011). *Building Community Disaster Resilience Through Private-Public Collaboration*. Washington, DC: The National Academies Press. doi:10.17226/13028.

Norris, F.H., Stevens, S.P., Pfefferbaum, B., Wyche, K.F. & Pfefferbaum, R.L. (2008). Community Resilience as a Metaphor, Theory, Set of Capacities, and Strategy for Disaster Readiness. *American Journal of Community Psychology*, 41(1/2), 127–150. doi:10.1007/s10464-007-9156-6.

North India floods. (n.d.). In Wikipedia. Retrieved from: https://en.wikipedia.org/wiki/2013_North_India_floods.

Palen, L. & Anderson, K.M. (2016). Crisis informatics – New data for extraordinary times. *Science*, 353(6296), 224–225. doi:10.1126/science.aag2579.

Palen, L. & Liu, S.B. (2007). Citizen communications in crisis: anticipating a future of ICT-supported public participation. *CHI*, 727–736. Retrieved from: http://www.hcitang.org/uploads/Teaching/palenliu-chi07.pdf.

Parker, G., Alstyne, M.V. & Choudary, S. (2016). *Platform Revolution: How Networked Markets are Transforming the Economy, and How to Make Them Work for You*. New York: W.W. Norton.

Parker, G., Alstyne, M.W.V. & Jiang, X. (2017). Platform Ecosystems: How Developers Invert the Firm. *MIS Quarterly*, 41(1), 255–266. Retrieved from: https://misq.org/platform-ecosystems-how-developers-invert-the-firm.html.

Patel, S.S., Rogers, M.B., Amlôt, R. & Rubin, G.J. (2017). What Do We Mean by "Community Resilience"? A Systematic Literature Review of How It Is Defined in the Literature. *PLOS Currents*. doi:10.1371/currents.dis.db775aff25efc5ac4f0660ad9c9f7db2.

Perkins, D. & Zimmerman, M.A. (1995). Empowerment theory, research, and application. *American Journal of Community Psychology*, 23, 569–579. doi:10.1007/BF02506982.

Philips, R. & Pittman, R.H. (2009). *An Introduction to Community Development*. New York: Taylor and Francis.

Pires, S.R.I., Nucleus, C.F.B., de Eulalia, S. & Goulart, C.P. (2001). Supply Chain and Virtual Enterprises: Comparisons, Migration and a Case Study. *International Journal of Logistics Research and Applications* 4(3), 1–19. doi:10.1080/13675560110084111.

Rahman, A., Sakurai, A. & Munadi, A. (2017). Indigenous knowledge management to enhance community resilience to tsunami risk: lessons learned from Smong traditions in Simeulue Island, Indonesia. *Earth and Environmental Science*, 56. doi:10.1088/1755-1315/56/1/012018.

Rose, N. (1996). *Inventing Our Selves: Psychology, power, and personhood*. Cambridge, UK: Cambridge University Press.

Scottish Government (2012). A consultation on the proposed Community Empowerment and Renewal Bill. Retrieved from: http://www.gov.scot/Publications/2012/06/7786.

Scottish Government (2014). Community Engagement and Empowerment. Retrieved from: http://www.scotland.gov.uk/Topics/People/engage.

Seneviratne, T.K.K., Dilanthi, A., Haigh, R. & Chaminda, P. (2010). Knowledge management for disaster resilience: Identification of key success factors. CIB 2010, University of Salford. Retrieved from: http://usir.salford.ac.uk/id/eprint/9759/.

Shahrah, A.Y. & Majed, A. (2017). Adaptive Case Management Framework to Develop Case-Based Emergency Response System. *International Journal of Advanced Computer Science and Applications*, 8(4). doi:10.14569/IJACSA.2017.080408.

Skerratt, S. (2013). Enhancing the analysis of rural community resilience: Evidence from community land ownership. *Journal of Rural Studies*, 31, 36–46. doi:10.1016/j.jrurstud.2013.02.003.

Somerville, P. (2005). Community governance and democracy. *Policy & Politics*, 33(1), 117–144. doi:10.1332/0305573052708438.

Steiner, A. & Atterton, J. (2014). The contribution of rural businesses to community resilience. *Local Economy*, 29(3), 228–244. doi:10.1177/0269094214528853.

Steiner, A. & Farmer, J. (2017). Engage, Participate, Empower: Modelling Power Transfer in Disadvantaged Rural Communities. *Environment and Planning C: Politics and Space*, 36(1), 118–138. doi:10.1177/2399654417701730.

Steiner, A. & Markantoni, M. (2014). Exploring community resilience in Scotland through capacity for change. *Community Development Journal*, 49, 407–425. doi:10.1093/cdj/bst042.

Sundararajan, A. (2016). *The Sharing Economy: The End of Employment and the Rise of Crowd-Based Capitalism*. Cambridge, MA: MIT Press.

Torrey, C., Burke, M., Lee, M., Dey, A., Fussell, S. & Kiesler, S. (2007). *Connected Giving: Ordinary People Coordinating Disaster Relief on the Internet*. Proceedings of the 40th Annual Hawaii International Conference on System Sciences. doi:10.1109/HICSS.2007.144.

Twigg, J. (2009). Characteristics of a disaster-resilient community: a guidance note (version 2). Retrieved from: https://www.researchgate.net/publication/305615592_Characteristics_of_a_disaster-resilient_community_a_guidance_note_version_2.

UNESCO (2005). Towards knowledge societies. UNESCO World Report. Retrieved from: https://unesdoc.unesco.org/ark:/48223/pf0000141843.

Vieweg, S., Hughes, A.L., Starbird, K. & Palen, L. (2010). *Microblogging during two natural hazards events: What Twitter may contribute to situational awareness*. Proceedings of the SIGCHI Conference on Human Factors in Computing Systems, Atlanta. doi:10.1145/1753326.1753486.

Wang, J. (2010). Beyond information: The sociocultural role of the internet in the 2008 Sichuan earthquake. *The Journal of Comparative Asian Development*, 9(2), 243–292. doi:10.1080/15339114.2010.528299.

White, C.M. (2012). *Social Media, Crisis Communication, and Emergency Management: Leveraging Web2.0 Technology*. Boca Raton, FL: CRC Press.

Zimmerman, M.A. (1995). Psychological empowerment: Issues and illustrations. *American Journal of Community Psychology*, 23, 581–599. doi:10.1007/BF02506983.

Part IV
What tomorrow may bring

14 Summary and discussions

1 Introduction

The collaborative premise of our social technology-enabled social knowledge management framework offers a promising alternative to empower rural masses by triggering effective and purposive virtual community formation. The resultant community formation, by facilitating easy and smooth knowledge exchange between rural–urban entities, has the potential to usher in holistic rural empowerment by mitigating the knowledge asymmetry of rural participants, to which they primarily owe their marginalization. While our empowering paradigm offers a respite from the stringencies of conventional developmental models, our decentralized framework is not easy to implement, specifically in the rural context of developing nations. Marginalized spaces of developing nations have their own orientation and operational dynamics with which it is mandatory to negotiate while implementing an empowering effort in the said context. An undertaken effort can only yield desired outcomes over time and once it has negotiated with the needs, orientation and specificities of the local context.

In this chapter we articulate our research journey by looking at operative hindrances, the prospective means to overcome them, and the ethical concerns, following which we have tried to practically implement our research proposition in the rural sectors of India. This chapter is divided into three sections:

- The first section narrates a brief and conclusive summary of our entire work.
- The second section highlights the hindrances we have faced while implementing our social knowledge management framework in the context of rural India and discusses the plausible ways to overcome the operative hindrances, which will ultimately help in practically realizing the potential of our proposed framework in generating desired results.
- The final section mentions the ethical concerns which we have addressed while implementing our research proposition.

2 Summary of work

In this book we have chalked out a holistic framework to usher in rural empowerment from within by facilitating effective community formation between rural–urban entities through our proposed social knowledge management framework. We conceptualize rural empowerment from a knowledge-theoretic perspective and demonstrate how the proposed social knowledge management platform can enhance the knowledge capabilities of rural actors by facilitating connection and collaboration among various rural–urban entities through the formation of purposive virtual communities using social technologies. The uniqueness of our research contribution rests in cultivating knowledge capability among rural members through effective community formation. Formation of effective community enables the members to freely participate in knowledge collaboration and exchange as active agents, thereby enhancing their knowledge-operating abilities in the process. An enhanced knowledge capability of rural members not only gets reflected in their enhanced agency. Endowed with such transactional capacities, knowledge capability positively influences rural members' bridging and bonding social capital. It is knowledge collaboration, both within and across communities, that bears the prospects in enhancing rural members' life and livelihood conditions. An enhanced bridging and bonding capital allows the rural mass to translate the activity of their knowledge exchange in pursuit of generating better opportunity scopes. It is the positive influence of enhanced knowledge capability on the agency, social capital and opportunity structure of rural target group that bears the prospect of mitigating overall knowledge asymmetry of rural participants. Amidst the backdrop of an enhanced agency, social capital and opportunity structure, the rural members are endowed with the capacity to exploit their knowledge-operating abilities in pursuit of generating concrete life and livelihood benefits. This helps to mitigate the knowledge asymmetry rural members face along multiple axes, thereby targeting attainment of rural empowerment on a holistic scale.

In this context, it needs to be iterated that our conceptualization of rural empowerment entails empowering rural mass from within. Such an endogenous empowering framework contradicts centralized developmental paradigms, which externally thrust welfare policies on target group. On the contrary, community formation happens to be the core of our endogenous paradigm, which we have attempted to cultivate through a decentralized, social technology-enabled social knowledge management framework. It is only the collaborative premise of contemporary social technologies that has the power to effectively deploy social knowledge management framework in pursuit of attaining holistic rural empowerment. While our empowering paradigm, by virtue of being endogenous, offers respite from the stringencies of conventional developmental paradigms, it does not imply that deploying the same will ensure immediate results. In the next section we will articulate the hindrances we have faced while trying to achieve rural empowerment through our social knowledge management framework.

3 Hindrances faced during the research journey and prospective solutions

Chalking out strategies to empower rural mass using the collaborative potential of social technologies is indeed promising. However, envisioning rural empowerment using ICT essentially entails several obstacles, which have to be addressed in order to expect the adhered strategy to yield desirable results. Our research experience shows that, while similar training and capacity building were provided to all members of our target group, only a few of them actually utilized these in enhancing their life and livelihood prospects. This proves that even though measures to empower the marginalized are adopted, local orientation and hindrances often get in the way of generating holistic benefits for all. Educating rural mass in digital usage and enabling them to utilize the same to conduct purposive collaborations is a processual activity, which cannot be achieved overnight. Specifically, in developing context, such an activity has to confront multiple social hindrances in order to generate desirable results. Some of our field insights can properly capture the issues at stake.

Literacy level. Most of the self-help group women with whom we interacted have very low literacy levels, making it difficult for them to use smartphones and other digital devices freely. Hence contextual digital literacy training is mandatory, which will not only introduce the rural mass to the digital medium but will generate avenues which will sustain their interest over the medium.

Gender bias. Second, a strong gender bias omnipresent in rural India often disallows women the privilege to participate freely in the digitized public medium (for example, social media). Although digital services offer such marginalized women the space to express themselves freely, introducing local women to the digital medium requires a lot of awareness at the local level. When we started the process of familiarizing rural women of Kandi to initiate virtual collaborations we faced several obstructions from the local authority, restricting the local women from taking part in our research activities freely. With time we won over the said authorities, who only gave permission for us to carry out our research activities with the women whom the local officials identified as fit to be in our target group. Hence it is only when the immediate surrounding is socially supportive that we can expect the rural marginalized to show an inclination towards unhindered digital usage.

Local dynamics. Third, extant collaborations with middlemen operative in rural India follow traditional transactional patterns, and virtual collaborations can often pose a threat to these patterns. If a direct virtual connectivity is established between rural women and urban entities it will not support the interests of the powerful middlemen, who generate profit by being an intermediary. A disjuncture can only be brought with time, where the power of virtual collaborations will urge the rural mass to abandon extant exploitative relations and embrace a much fairer knowledge acquisition and collaboration process supported by digital collaborations.

Cost of internet access. Almost three in five of the world's people are still not connected to the internet. This digital divide hampers economic and social progress. Broadband markets that price internet access out of reach for the majority of people are neither socially nor economically efficient. Liberalizing the telecommunications industry is not enough; the state also has to facilitate strategic investments, subsidizing access for underserved communities and implementing effective and transparent regulations, including open access to subsidized infrastructure.

While introducing a digital solution, we need to remember that the concept of digital usage and virtual collaboration is quite new to extant rural context. This proves that having a holistic empowering plan for the marginalized is not enough to generate desirable results. We need to give time to the rural mass to familiarize themselves with the digital medium, coupled with negotiating with the immediate surroundings, and only then we can expect the digital path to make a difference for rural community.

In an attempt to overcome the hindrances and make our research strategy effective, it needs to be remembered that the marginalized rural spaces of developing nations happen to be our core research context. The rural sectors of developing nations are ridden with poverty, inequality, illiteracy and other socio-economic adversities, which have to be addressed prior to an attempt to overcome the marginalization of those spaces. While, in our research, we have analysed the socio-economic conditions of rural spaces of developing nations in a single lens, the practical execution of empowering parameters requires a serious consideration of local contexts, needs and specificities, which are intrinsic to any particular rural locale.

Our strategy to bring holistic rural empowerment is based on utilization of social technologies to trigger community formation among rural–urban entities. Although adhering to the digital path to provide empowering solutions that offer redemption from conventional developmental parameters, it is important to spell out that the digital medium, even today, is alien to most rural populations of developing nations. Thus contextual digital literacy training has to be provided to rural members before expecting them to make positive change using the medium. Contextual digital literacy training can only be provided once a detailed need analysis of the implementing zone, prior to research intervention, has been conducted. This requires an in-depth analysis of the local orientation so that the process of technological adaptation can be context specific. Once the need analysis has been conducted, it is mandatory to train the rural community in digital usage in accordance with their specific needs. Such an activity is required to sustain the interest of the rural mass towards the digital medium. While rural population can be sporadically introduced to the digital medium, such an intervention often fails to sustain their interest. If local mass is not adequately interested and drawn towards the medium, usage can never be sustained and the community is prevented from utilizing the medium to address daily needs and prospects.

Digital usage is an activity alien to the local orientation of the rural locales of developing countries. Hence, prior to the introduction of the rural community to the digital forum, it is necessary to familiarize them with the intricacies and working dynamics of the medium. This entails familiarizing the local community with how the digital medium works, the benefits it brings, how virtual collaborations are conducted and sustained and how to generate benefits from such collaborations. This guideline will eradicate the fear any alien medium attracts in native context. It will also help the community identify the benefits the digital medium offers by assuring them that the medium will not harm their local culture and operations. Such training must be context specific, thereby increasing the potential of reaping desirable results. However, even context specific digital training is unable to attain rural empowerment immediately. Familiarizing the rural mass to the digital forum and expecting them to benefit from the same is a processual activity, which can only be achieved with time and need-specific adaptation of technology. For example, if we are introducing rural craft practitioners to the digital medium it is better we show them YouTube videos on craft designing and production so that they can derive avenues to use the medium to further their artistic interests. Only then can we expect the rural community to have a sustained interest in utilizing the digital medium and voluntarily use it to address their daily concerns.

While in the earlier sections we addressed the hindrances faced and the prospective means to overcome the obstacles in the context of attaining holistic rural empowerment, an empowering strategy remains incomplete without addressing the ethical concerns intrinsic to any research. Welfare measures undertaken for the marginalized cannot be empowering if ethical parameters are not maintained. In the final section of this chapter we will talk about the ethical concerns we have addressed during the course of our research.

4 Ethical concerns addressed in the research

Any activity undertaken to empower marginalized groups inherently encounters ethical concerns. Overlooking these can restrict the scope and intention of empowering measures; ignoring them can also leave the loopholes that developmental initiatives suffer from. In our research we attempt to empower the marginalized rural groups, giving them the ability to participate in inter- and intra-group knowledge collaboration. Provision to exchange knowledge freely contributes to enhancing the agency, social capital and opportunity scopes of rural members, thereby making the role of external developmental agents redundant in the process of empowering community. However, empowerment will remain a far-fetched dream if ethical issues are not addressed during the course of empowering the marginalized.

Selection of the target group was done in consultation with the local authoritative body and operative NGO, to give our research the element of insider perspective. In cases where personal experiences from our target group have been given as research examples, we have done so without disclosing the identity of our respondents. By maintaining anonymity of the information shared by our respondents we have attempted to preserve the ethical grounds of our research. We also obtained consent from the local authoritative body and our respondents before involving them in our research study. Prior to conducting the study we told them in detail the objectives of our research, their role in it, how they could expect to benefit from the study and how we would utilize the information provided by them in our research. Finally, since in this study we could only include a few from the rural community of our selected locale, we proposed to undertake efforts to extend our research interventions to the entirety of the community. As our research bears positive outcomes, as highlighted in this work, it would be unethical to bar the rest of the intervened community from such empowering interventions. It is only by maintaining ethical parameters that our research can attempt to target holistic rural empowerment in the truest sense.

5 Conclusion

We conclude our book by affirming the effectivity of cultivating community formation among rural–urban entities using our social knowledge management framework in the context of attaining holistic rural empowerment. Different types of virtual communities and the effective inter- and intra-group collaboration they support is conducive to the process of achieving holistic rural empowerment by effectively mitigating rural–urban knowledge, information and opportunity divide. The credibility of the supported collaboration rests in positively influencing enhancement of agency, social capital and opportunity prospects of rural target group, thereby making our proposition crucial in the backdrop of achieving holistic rural empowerment. Capacity building for marginalized communities might be emergent (in endogenous community development) but it needs to be nurtured via external sources (by exogenous development) (Steiner & Farmer, 2017). This calls for developing an *empowering ecosystem* to foster *connection* and *collaboration* between external agencies and rural communities, leading towards holistic development of the communities.

The following chapter focuses on the future prospects for our research. It endorses a vision towards building a developmental ecosystem that combines exogenous and endogenous development process by connecting billions of individuals all over the globe as external agents (the *crowd capital*) and including traditional development agencies for collaborative knowledge exchange. Democratization of science and technology, an increase in global connectivity using social technologies, and greater availability of data will facilitate a movement that will shift control away from centralized development through a handful of traditional development agencies to decentralized development involving *crowd capital* – billions of development agents (Dehgan, 2012). Effective community formation and facilitation of inter- and intra-group collaboration are crucial prerequisites in the process of building an inter-connected developmental ecosystem. Such an ecosystem can only be formed once every member is equipped with sufficient knowledge and its operating abilities, thereby creating value out of knowledge exchange. Amidst this backdrop lies the possibility of a mitigated rural–urban knowledge, information and opportunity divide.

References

Dehgan, A. (2012). Creating the New Development Ecosystem. *Science*, 336(6087), 1397–1398. doi:10.1126/science.1224530.

Steiner, A. & Farmer, J. (2017). Engage, Participate, Empower: Modelling Power Transfer in Disadvantaged Rural Communities. *Environment and Planning C: Politics and Space*, 36(1), 118–138. doi:10.1177/2399654417701730.

15 Building a developmental ecosystem for rural empowerment

1 Developmental ecosystem: Theory and practice

The term "ecosystem" was first used in 1935 by a British ecologist, Arthur Tansley, who devised the concept to draw attention to the complex exchange of materials taking place between organisms and their environment (Tansley, 1935). Following Tansley's theorization, an ecosystem therefore refers to a community of living beings (animals, plants and microbes), coupled with the non-living components of environment (air, water, soil, etc.), interacting as a system. It is this complex network or inter-connected system, enabling living beings to interact with each other and with their environment, which primarily paves the path for social functioning. The decentralized nature of an ecosystem considers each of its components to be indispensable to the whole, where the credentials of the whole exceed the summative valuation of individual components.

Instead of having a standardized and centralized institutionalized conceptualization of development, our mission to attain rural empowerment primarily gets inspiration from the inter-connected spirit that an ecosystem ensures, where each actor is considered indispensable to the process of social development. Moreover, a developmental model deriving ideological nourishment from the inter-connected system of an ecosystem will subsequently attempt to address social maladies by creating an inter-connected ecosystem, which, instead of externally imposing sporadic measures, attempts capacity building of local community by exploiting the potential of *crowd*. An inter-connected developmental ecosystem will enable social actors to empower themselves by establishing connections with other social actors involved in the developmental process (Dehgan, 2012). This purposive exchange will enable rural mass to be true stakeholders in their developmental process, instead of being passive recipients of institutional change.

The idea of devising a developmental ecosystem in the context of rural empowerment rests in creating a new form of socio-economic setup, where development progresses based on collaborative production and consumption initiated by strangers. Such a developmental ecosystem has the potential to connect billions of people and transform them into true stakeholders in their developmental process by cultivating strategies of self-sustenance and self-development among target groups (Capgemini Consulting, 2018). Inter-connectedness among strangers facilitated by the ecosystem is infused with the prospect of reshaping socio-economic activities in innovative ways. Neglecting traditional hierarchy, a developmental ecosystem has the credential to establish purposive collaborations among different entities, belonging to diverse backgrounds, who are involved in the developmental process. Collaborative wealth creation and social development, accounting to be major premise of a developmental ecosystem, have positive effect in collective advancement of arts, culture, science, education, governing infrastructure, economy, etc. (Tapscott & Williams, 2006; Horton & Chilton, 2010).

The inclusive potential of a developmental ecosystem has the capacity to transform crowd to be true stakeholders in the developmental process. By involving the mass in the decision-making process and making them active determinants of their own course of development, developmental ecosystems and their method of achieving social transformation contradict the centralized institution-driven conventional developmental models.

Collaborations facilitated by developmental ecosystem create an atmosphere of healthy dependence, which has redefined the way contemporary socio-economic activities are conducted in today's connected age. The emergence and rapid proliferation of "sharing economy" is the living proof of how purposive collaborations have transformed industries globally and bears severe implications for social development (Sundararajan, 2016). Sharing economy is premised on peer-to-peer relationships, instead of relying on existing and defined market actors to mediate exchange. Such an economic structure is in stark contrast to mainstream economic frameworks reliant on structured economic institutions, with their standardized market principles. We can identify the collaborative premise of sharing economy as an attempt to create an ecosystem, infused with liberatory potential, which can only get realized if the different actors involved in the transactions are accredited with adequate capabilities required to conduct profitable partnerships. Digital technologies, offering promising prospects of virtual linkage, have contributed in easing the process of collaborating by enhancing intra- and inter-communitarian linkage. This interconnected spirit of contemporary ICT has not only given impetus to sharing economy but has offered enticing prospects of creating developmental ecosystem by virtually linking different agents involved in the developmental process.

The notion that social developments cannot be influenced from outside and do not unfold in linear fashion is gaining importance in contemporary academia. The emerging concern increases the urgency to create a field of development cooperation by shifting implementing power from structured institutions to common mass. It is with this intention to create a developmental ecosystem that the United States Agency for International Development (USAID) and its partners crowd-sourced the world to apply science, technology and innovation against seemingly intractable barriers to solve the Grand Challenges for Development (GCDs) and to catalyse global action to achieve scale, sustainability and impact (Dehgan, 2012). Democratization of tools for self-expression using social technologies (for example, social media, where anyone can create and exchange content), availability of anytime-anywhere mobile connectivity using social technologies, and greater opportunity towards resource mobilization using the principles of sharing economy (e.g., mobilizing crowd resources using digital platforms) will facilitate a movement that will shift control from centralized development through a handful of traditional development agencies to decentralized development involving *crowd capital* – billions of development agents.

Purposive knowledge exchange fostered via virtually connected developmental ecosystem subsequently paves the path for creating an ecosystem characterized by collaborative creation, assimilation and dissemination of knowledge (Frohardt & Jones, 2018). This developmental ecosystem considers every social actor to be a potential producer and consumer of information and knowledge. The symbiosis, facilitated via such an approach, is in stark contradiction to the linear informational dissemination mode followed worldwide by the "Rurban" missions. While the Rurban missions attempt to disseminate information following a one-way track from urban to rural communities, the premise of such measures are based on a compassion-driven ideology which conceptualizes rural community as "inferior" consumers, unsuitable for producing information. Consequently, the measures remain exogenous in nature, where external imposition of the schemes fails to create deeper impact.

It is undoubtedly true that the rural community, by virtue of their physical and informational isolation from mainstream transactional sites, shares knowledge asymmetry with urban agents. Lack of adequate knowledge on market operationalizations affecting the economic performance of rural community needs to be immediately addressed by facilitating effective collaboration among rural–urban entities. In this context, it needs to be remembered that the rural community's lack of knowledge on market dynamics is not sufficient to justify any informational/knowledge dissemination model premised on a uni-directional mode. The indigenous knowledge resources possessed by rural members make them potential contributors to the knowledge pool, thereby ensuring a two-way symbiotic knowledge creation/dissemination mandatory to the process of rural empowerment. It is by proposing an idea of a developmental ecosystem facilitating two-way knowledge exchange between urban and rural communities that we have attempted to chalk out an endogenous developmental paradigm premised on effective collaboration.

2 The need for a developmental ecosystem for holistic rural empowerment

As we have already discussed in the book, rural sectors suffer from multi-faceted hindrances, which significantly hinder active participation of rural actors in mainstream discourse. If we are to initiate developmental attempts to empower rural community, then we need to realize that rural empowerment cannot happen overnight. Multi-faceted issues that have deprived the rural sector for generations must be tackled along diverse axes in order to have a holistic idea regarding the cause of rural marginalization. This will subsequently help in formulating contextual solutions to address the operative issues. And, throughout this process, mobilization of local community and securing their active involvement in the developmental journey serves to be a mandatory prerequisite in not just ushering in rural empowerment but also sustaining it.

Grove (2014) articulates empowerment as the act of freeing marginalized people through participatory programmes targeted at building resilience on a communitarian level. Optimally mobilizing local community and ensuring active communitarian engagement in rural context is a gradual process, which needs to be nurtured and cultivated over time to attain effective results. If developmental initiatives are thrust on rural community externally, without developing in them the potential required to avail the given opportunities, then the measures remain redundant and cannot create any sustainable impact. That is why, in our research initiatives, the proposed social knowledge management framework for rural empowerment is premised on securing active participation of rural members by connecting them with diverse social actors. In our framework we are not trying to directly ensure concrete socio-economic benefits for the rural community. Rather, by initiating a collaborative pathway for them, we are trying to enable them to enhance their own socio-economic prospects through voluntary participation. Our research initiatives, therefore, strive to achieve this active participation of rural members in an attempt to empower them.

Steiner and Farmer (2017) rightly identify empowerment as something more than participation, something which enhances the ability to participate in decision-making and accredits social actors with the power to undertake transformative actions. While securing the active participation of rural members accounts to be one aspect in the process of empowering them, the other one is cultivating a conducive environment, which will positively influence the ability of rural participants to sustain their participation. Achievement of this dual goal is only possible in the presence of synergistic union between exogenous and endogenous developmental attempts, which ensures creation of an effective developmental ecosystem.

Steiner and Farmer (2017) suggest an EPE model (Engage-Participate-Empower) that highlights a process of community empowerment starting with engagement, followed by participation and subsequently facilitating community empowerment. Communities that have not previously engaged can benefit from external support. Hence exogenous initiatives can provide necessary guidance and support, which could be a pre-condition as well as facilitator of endogenous development of a weaker community. Steiner and Farmer (2017) argue that "to reach endogenous empowerment, exogenous empowerment practices are useful and effective for some communities. Capacity building might be emergent (in endogenous community development) but in some cases it may need to be nurtured via external sources (by exogenous development)." Thus successful implementation of a developmental ecosystem requires creation of appropriate support structures that enable the transfer of power from state to community. Exogenous agencies could add value by providing an enabling environment where endogenous development occurs.

3 Building a developmental ecosystem for rural empowerment

While we have already highlighted in Parts I and II of this book the importance of knowledge and knowledge-operating capability in organizational and social context, now we will proceed to show the importance of knowledge and knowledge-operating capabilities of the social actors in the manifestation of a developmental ecosystem. A developmental ecosystem can function effectively only when each individual and collective unit is involved in purposive exchange and achieves overall social welfare in terms of their social interconnections. The effectivity of developmental ecosystem rests in its decentralized spirit, which gives equal importance to each unit in the process of achieving development. While this dimension of developmental ecosystem enables successful translation of "crowd" to "member of the community", we must remember that the transition will remain superfluous if each unit is not adequately empowered with knowledge resources.

A developmental ecosystem can only function effectively if each of its units derives the capability to take informed decisions, by exhibiting adequate knowledge possession and knowledge-operating capabilities. This marks the indispensability of knowledge and knowledge capability in facilitating and manifesting a developmental ecosystem, which targets transformation from within by involving local community in the decision-making process, by simultaneously mobilizing exogenous agencies to support communitarian participation.

Apart from cultivating knowledge capability of rural members, we have also demonstrated the importance of creating a supportive environment through collaborative connections with other actors that will secure and sustain communitarian participation of rural members. We have attempted to practically realize our social knowledge management framework through the formation of *communities of practice, purpose* and *circumstance* (as described in Part III). In the context of community formation, we have explicitly stated the importance of external agencies in sustaining the community through triggering purposive exchange. These communities, by attracting urban-based domain practitioners from various fields, not only empower rural actors but also inform urban agents on the intricacies of rural life by facilitating symbiotic exchange. Attempting to achieve rural empowerment through proposed social knowledge management framework therefore incorporates a dual-natured initiative – an endogenous one, by securing active participation of communitarian members, coupled with contextually developing exogenous agencies to support communitarian involvement so that effective collaboration can be derived as a product.

Building a developmental ecosystem 315

The resultant developmental ecosystem, enlivened and sustained through curious co-existence of endogenous and exogenous initiatives, therefore can be identified as an integrating force, connecting stakeholders with policy formulators. Co-existence of endogenous and exogenous measures creates an ecosystem that ensures development for rural actors along diverse domains (Grameen Foundation, n.d.). These are:

- *Information and knowledge.* Open and unrestricted collaboration between rural–urban agents, derivative of an inter-connected developmental ecosystem, has the potential to enhance information and knowledge assets of rural community.
- *Peer support.* The inter-connected spirit of developmental ecosystem, by facilitating effective networking, has the capacity to enhance social capital through utilizing peer support structure.
- *Access to products and services.* A developmental ecosystem, by linking members of rural community with relevant agents, provides them access to products and services and contextual guidance on how to operate the same, thereby enhancing life and livelihood prospects of rural community in the process.
- *Gender equity.* Unrestricted collaboration supported by developmental ecosystem helps rural members to counter atrocities imposed by social conventions, such as restrictive norms for female members, gender discrepancies, etc. Effective collaboration derivative of such ecosystem ensures gender equity and other allied fairness-based prospects for rural community.
- *Market engagement.* Effective networking supported by developmental ecosystem positively contributes in mitigating the market separation faced by rural producers by linking them with relevant agents. This ensures positive outcomes in the domain of market engagement of rural producers.

The developmental ecosystem proposed here is heavily depended on usage of contemporary social technologies, including internet-enabled communications, platforms and tools (for example, web 2.0, mobile 2.0, social media, social software, etc.). One of the major challenges in designing digital platforms for rural community is that the digital maturity levels of our rural users are poor in the following three dimensions (Vardisio and Chiappini, 2015; Dey and Bandyopadhyay, 2018):

- *E-awareness.* The aptitude to understand the opportunities of digital technology.
- *Digital literacy.* Competencies to use digital technologies to fulfil personal and professional objectives.
- *Informational literacy.* The ability to retrieve, understand and interpret information coming from digital sources.

Thus efforts towards building an ecosystem need to be tuned according to the learning context and capacities of rural users, and exogenous agencies are needed to handhold the members of rural community. Most of the contemporary policies devised to employ ICT in rural context follow a development model imposed from outside. While existing public schemes have made ICT infrastructure a public good, the proposed developmental ecosystem encourages communitarian usage of existing infrastructure, apart from providing equal and open access to these infrastructures. It is only through contextual use of ICT infrastructures that we can enhance the possibility of adding or creating value. For example, easy availability of smartphones at affordable rates can enable even the economically challenged to possess the device, enabling smooth transaction of informational and knowledge resources among people from diverse backgrounds.

As the United Kingdom's Cabinet Office recognized in 2004: "Digital inclusion is not about computers, the internet or even technology, it is about using technology as a channel to improve skills, to enhance quality of life, to drive education, and to promote economic well-being across all elements of society. Digital inclusion is really about *social* inclusion, and because of this, the potential for technology to radically improve society and the way we live our lives should not be underestimated" (Cabinet Office, 2004). Muir (2004) argued that *access, basic training* and *community connections* (the ABC of digital inclusion) help to shift the focus away from technology towards people and the community. At the same time, the "C" also stands for *content*, which is equally important in rural context. Appropriate local content is crucial in attracting new users to ICT. The dominance of the English language in internet content may be a problem for rural community in many countries, including India.

We need to remember that digital technologies are neutral by themselves. Their potential can only be realized through coordinated efforts from human organizations to foster social and economic equality. As an example, if practical implications of the social knowledge management platform reflect the platform's potential to empower rural community by mitigating rural urban knowledge divide, then the Common Service Centres (CSCs) in India, following a similar pathway, can be transformed into an e-knowledge hub with such digital engagement platforms. Market connect and advisory services available through this e-knowledge hub would help develop rural entrepreneurs, thereby enhancing prospects of community ownership of CSCs. Once the rural population is sufficiently armed with knowledge, they can devise sustainable ways to utilize the CSCs for communitarian benefit (Bhattacharyya et al., 2019).

The developmental ecosystem has the potential not only to facilitate contextual policy formulation but also to enable modification of existing schemes by giving prior importance to community formation. Only such an ecosystem has the potential to employ the spirit of social technology in cultivating exogenous and endogenous developmental initiatives along symbiotic lines to usher in holistic rural empowerment.

References

Bhattacharyya, S., Dey, P., Basak, J., Roy, S. & Bandyopadhyay, S. (2019). *Building Resilient Community Using Social Technologies: A Precursory Measure for Effective Disaster Management*. Proceedings of the International Conference on Distributed Computing and Networking. 405–408. doi:10.1145/3288599.3295591.

Cabinet Office (2004). Enabling a Digitally United Kingdom: A Framework for Action. Retrieved from: http://www.cabinetoffice.gov.uk/publications/reports/digital/digitalframe.pdf.

Capgemini Consulting (2018). Empowering Ecosystems: Realizing Joint Ambitions in Networks (Alliances and Chains Report). Retrieved from: https://www.capgemini.com/consulting-nl/wp-content/uploads/sites/33/2017/03/Empowering-Ecosystems_English.pdf.

Common Services Centres (2006). Retrieved from: http://meity.gov.in/content/common-services-centers.

Dehgan, A. (2012). Creating the New Development Ecosystem. *Science*, 336(6087), 1397–1398. doi:10.1126/science.1224530.

Dellemijn, R. (2012). Knowledge Asymmetry in Inter-Firm Relationships: A Suggestion for a Knowledge Sourcing Strategy for the Ministry of Oil of Iraq. (Student thesis, University of Twente, Netherland). Retrieved from: http://essay.utwente.nl/61982/.

Dey, P. & Bandyopadhyay, S. (2018). Blended learning to improve quality of primary education among underprivileged school children in India. *Education and Information Technologies*, 24(3), 1995–2016. doi:10.1007/s10639-018-9832-1.

Durkheim, E. (1933). *The Division of Labour*. (Trans. by G. Simpson) (10th ed). New York: Free Press.

Frohardt, M. & Jones, S.B. (2018). Why Information Matters. The Rockefeller Foundation. Retrieved from: https://www.rockefellerfoundation.org/report/why-information-matters/.

Grameen Foundation (n.d.). Retrieved from: https://grameenfoundation.org/what-we-do.

Grove, K. (2014). Agency, Affect, and The Immunological Politics of Disaster Resilience. *Environment and Planning D: Society and Space*, 32, 240–256.

Horton, J.J. & Chilton, L.B. (2010). *The Labor Economics of Paid Crowdsourcing*. Proceedings of the 11th ACM Conference on Electronic Commerce. 209–218. doi:10.1145/1807342.1807376.

Muir, K. (2004). *Connecting Communities with CTLCs: From the digital divide to social inclusion*. Sydney: The Smith Family. Retrieved from: http://library.bsl.org.au/jspui/bitstream/1/609/1/Connecting%20communities%20with%20CTLCs.pdf.

Steiner, A.A. & Farmer, J. (2017). Engage, Participate, Empower: Modelling Power Transfer in Disadvantaged Rural Communities. *Environment and Planning C: Politics and Space*, 36(1), 118–138.

Sundararajan, A. (2016). *The Sharing Economy – The End of Employment and the Rise of Crowd-Based Capitalism*. Cambridge, MA: MIT press.

Tansley, A. (1935). The Use and Abuse of Vegetational Concepts and Terms. *Ecology*, 16(3), 284–307.

Tapscott, D. & Williams, A.D. (2006). *Wikinomics: How Mass Collaboration Changes Everything*. London: Portfolio.

Vardisio, R. & Chiappini, P. (2015). *Digital maturity: What it is and how to build it*. Proceedings of the International Conference the Future of Education, Florence. Retrieved from: https://www.researchgate.net/publication/303683893_Digital_maturity_what_is_and_how_to_build_it.

Index

Abbot, T. 104
Adger, W.N. 282
Adolf, M. 18–9, 117
agency: agency and opportunity 40, 42; agency opportunity structure 33
agriculture 60, 87, 174–75, 182, 186–87
Ahmed, S. 126
Ajay, A. 288
Aked, J. 277
Akerlof, G.A. 72, 98
Alavi, M. 120–21, 136
Alberghini, E. 148–49
Aldrich, D.P. 278, 284
Ali, L. 38, 42
Allee, V. 25
Alsop, R. 33, 39, 45
Alstyne, M.V. 252
Andersen, K.N. 148
Anderson, P. 151, 285
Andreeva, T. 126
Appleyard, M. 125
Ardichvilli, A. 217, 225
Aref, A. 61–2, 66, 248
Arrow, K. 72
asymmetry: information 72–76; knowledge 97, 106
asynchronous learning 204, 206, 218, 230–33, 237
Auronen, L. 72

Ba: Ba and community 26, 155; concept of Ba 137, 188, 220–22
Bahadur, A.V. 279
Baiman, S. 98
Ballon, P. 100, 102, 107
Bandyopadhyay, S. 3, 29, 43, 198–99, 315
Bartels, R. 74, 248
Basak, J. 54, 62, 68, 200, 202, 226–28
Basu, M. 287

Basu, S.R. 17, 178
Bebensee, T. 154
Belblidia, M.S. 285
Bell, R.H. 24
Benkler, Y. 148, 150, 158, 202
Bernard, J.G. 121
Bhat, J. 73
Bhattacharyya, S. 316
Bjorn-Soren, G. 66, 177
Blackie, M. 57–8
Blank, G. 149–50
blended learning 233, 235
Bohn, R. 129
Bonson, E. 153
Botsman, R. 253
Boughzala, I. 136, 178
Bouhnik, D. 237
Bourdieu, P. 30, 130–31, 199, 204
Boyera, S. 151
Brackertz, N. 293
bonding social capital 42, 201, 278, 304
bridging social capital 42, 131
Brooking, A. 16
Brousseau, E. 146
Brown, J.S. 223
Bunch, A. 172
Burke, P. 16, 23
Byukusenge, E. 127

Camacho, N.A. 279
Camarinha-Matos, L.M. 254
Cambridge, D. 220, 227
Cameron, M.A. 285
capability approach: cultural 25–6; of individual 23–4; of organizations 103, 107; theories 104–05
capacity building 276–77, 279
Carr, C.T. 151–52
Castells, M. 146

Castillo, C. 285
Cetinkaya, L. 237
Chaghouee, Y. 46
Chandra, A. 278
Chatti, M.A. 154–56
Chen, C. 101, 287
Childers, T. 172
Chiu, C. 101, 201
Christy, R. 57
Chui, M. 7, 148–49
Ciccio, C.D. 283
Cinnamon, J. 286
Clarke, J. 55
Cloward, R.A. 34
Cohen, W.M. 23
Cole, J. 57
collaborative: connectivity 145–46; economy 147, 252–53; learning 184–85
collaborative knowledge: exchange 116, 196, 308; management 288; transaction 244
community, online: of circumstance 274, 280–81; of practice 213–17; of purpose 244–47; based organizations 65; driven development 59–60; empowerment 276, 288; information systems 168, 172, 177
community resilience 276–79
Cook, K.S. 131
Corvey, W.J. 285
Cress, U. 156
crowd: capital 158, 202; knowledge 158–59, 202; crowd-based capitalism 147, 253; crowdsourcing 147, 286–87
CRT 86–7
CSC, common service centre 64–5
Cui, M. 252
Cummings, S. 184, 215

Dahiya, D. 127
Dalkir, K. 29
Daneshfard, A. 43
Daniel, J. 178
Das, A. 287
Dass, R. 64
Dave, M. 16–7
Davenport, T. H. 16, 43
David, N.S. 71, 76, 87–8
Dawes, S.S. 278
Dawson, R. 25
DeMattos, C.A. 254
Dehgan, A. 29, 55, 59, 68, 308, 310
Dellemijn, R. 16–17, 90–1, 93, 97–100
Derksen, M. 148
DeSanctis, G. 173

developmental: ecosystem 275, 310–12, 316; framework 38–9; endogenous development 308, 313;
exogenous development 308, 313
Dey, P. 315
digital literacy, digital literacy training 306
disaster, disaster management 280, 286
disempowered 176, 185
Djelassi, S. 287
Doctor, R.D. 94
Duan, W. 157
Duarte, A.T. 148
Dubé, L. 215
Dufty, N. 284–85
Dutta, S. 137
Dutton, J. 129

Earl, M.J. 134
ecosystem *see* developmental ecosystem
Eglash, R. 178
Eicher, C. 57
Eisenhardt, K. 98
Elliott, J.A. 277
empowerment: of rural community *see* rural empowerment; and agency 42; and social capital 33, 37, 40; and opportunity structure 42
Engel, P.G. 185
EPE model (Engage-Participate-Empower) 313
Epetimehin, F.M. 122
externalization 125–26, 133–34, 156

Fan, W. 157
Faraj, S. 154
Fehling, M. 55
Fernandez, B. 45
Fichter D. 156
Fitzgerald, M. 146
Flap, H.D. 131
Folke, C. 277
Fong, P.S. 124
Foucault, M. 23
Fraser, E.D. 276
Freeze, R. 101
Frohardt, M. 61, 66, 312

Gao, T. 29, 43, 116, 122, 126–27
Gebert, H. 157
Ghosh, M. 172
Ghouse, S. 74, 248
Gibbs, D. 55
globalization 119
Gold, A. 124, 130

Gon, S. 237
Gordeyeva, I. 155–56
Gorman, M. 95, 123
Grant, R. 97
Greenstein, S. 146
Greiner, M. 127–28
Grootaert, C. 33–34
Grove, K. 313
Gur, A. 132
Gusfield, J.R. 246

Haldane, V. 279
Hansen, M.T. 128, 134
Hao, Y. 254
Happe, R. 245
Harms, E. 52
Harrison, T. 176–77
Hassan, N.A. 283
Hayek, F.A. 202
He, W. 157–58
Helmes, R. 161, 193
Hemsley, J. 44
Herbert-Cheshire, L. 293
Herbst, K. 280–82
Hess, C.G. 43, 90, 179
Hildrum, J.M. 156
Hoadley, C. 215
Hopkins, L. 132
Horton, J.J. 147, 311
Horwitch, M. 122
Houston, J.B. 279
Howe, J. 286
Hugar, L.B. 182
Hugh, C. 219
Hughes, A.L. 285
Hughes, T.P. 28
Hung, S.Y. 127

Iakovou, E. 284
IBM 160
Ibrahim, S. 37–8
indigenous knowledge 21, 312; practices 85
information and opportunity 308; asymmetry 72–5
Inkpen, A.C. 129
ITU 168

Jadav, D. 88
Jafari, S. 237
Jalonen, H. 153
Jarche, H. 156
Jejeebhoy, S.J. 38
Jena, P.K. 82
Jensen, P.M. 237

Jin, Y. 158
Johnson, E.M. 254
Johnstone, J. 24, 28
Jupp, D. 37

Kamaraj, K. 64
Kayworth, T. 124
Kempson, E. 173
Khan, W. 72
Kiernan, P. 119
Kietzmann, J. 151, 215
Kim, D.J. 150
Kiplang, J. 173
Kirby, W. 123
knowledge: acquisition 47, 124, 184, 305; and agency 44–5; and opportunity 47; asymmetry 93, 96–7, 102, 193; capability 15, 23–5, 93, 100–03; centric approaches 17–8, 20; collaboration 107, 182; creation 19, 100, 155, 199; distribution 20, 22; divide *see* rural-urban divide; hub, e-knowledge hub 316
knowledge management, organizational: first generation 134; second generation 135; third generation 136
knowledge management, social: first generation 172; second generation 178; third generation 182; framework 189, 195, 203, 205; platform 238, 258, 288
knowledge operating capabilities 25, 93, 101, 109
knowledge sharing, knowledge sharing tools 47, 127, 129, 134, 240
knowledge society 17, 46
knowledge theoretic approach 34
Kockelman, P. 44
Koo, C. 149
Koopman, C. 253
Koria, M. 283
Kress, G. 156
Krishna, A. 131
Kumar, D. 47, 82
Kummitha, R. 58
Kunst, K. 147, 157
Kushnareva, E. 284

Laroche, M. 157
Laszlo, K.C. 17, 22, 29, 115, 123
Laureys, F. 174–75, 181, 186–87
Laurillard, D. 137
Lave, J. 215–16, 220
learning capability 26–7
Lee, M. 138–39, 254
Lekoko, R. 2, 62, 168

Leonard, D. 128
Lesser, E. 220, 222–23
Lewis, B.K. 152
Li, C. 148
Liao, S. 126
Liebskind, J. 125
Lievrouw, L. 94–5, 177
Limaye, R. 115, 137
Lin, N. 130–32, 201, 278
Lindqvist, J. 153

Macias, W. 285
Magis, K. 277
Malhotra, Y. 128
Mannheim, K. 19
Mansell, R. 51, 67–8, 200–01
marginalized rural community 42, 46, 56
market: inefficiency 71–3, 82; opportunities 244; performance 78, 249; separation 247
marketplace, online 252
Marx, K. 104, 106
McAslan, A. 277, 282
McElroy, M.W. 132, 135–36
McLellan, D. 106
MDG, millennium development goals 54–5
Meja, V. 18
Milman, A. 277
Minkes, A. 39
Misra, N. 226
Mitra, S. 75
Mohan, G. 277
Mohanty, S. 283
Moore, M. 278–79
Morrow, B.H. 282
Mtega, W.P. 27
Muhammed, M. 58
Muir, K. 227, 316
Mujadi, H. 154
multi-agent collaboration 169, 258
Murphy, T. 284

NABARD 226
Nahapiet, J. 130, 222–23
Narender, K. 226
National Research Council 276, 280
Nelson, R.R. 148
Newell, S. 158
Ning, Y. 25–7, 101–02, 107, 129
Nishida, K. 220
Nonaka, I. 26, 120, 122, 125, 128, 133–37, 155, 170, 189, 220–21
Norris, F.H. 278
North, D. 57, 148
Nussbaum, M. C. 24, 27

O'Reilly, T. 137–38, 149, 151
O'Sullivan, P.B. 152
Olayiwola, L. 58, 248
opportunity: divide 308; prospects 107–09; structure 33–4, 37–9

Palen, L. 285
Pangannavar, A. 63
Parashar, M. 25
Parker, G. 147, 174, 252
Paroutis, S. 154
Parsons, T. 52
Parthiban, R. 248–49
Patel, S.S. 278
Pauleen, D.J. 123
Payakpaie, J. 179
peer learning, peer to peer learning 154–55, 235
peer production 148, 158, 178, 202
Pelikan, P. 148
Pelsue, B. 58
Perkins, D. 277
Philips, R. 277
Pires, S.R. 254
Pizziconi, V. 115, 118–19, 124
platform economy 252–53
Plucknett, D.L. 184
Polanyi, M. 97, 100
Portes, A. 131
private-public-partnership (PPP) model 188
Prpic, J. 158
Putnam, R. 29–30, 40–1, 131–32, 199, 204

Quintas, P. 44

Rahman, A. 278, 284
Raisanen, T. 156
Rasula, J. 126
Rawsthorne, P. 197, 200
Razmerita, L. 156
Reddy, K.P. 82
Reijsen, J. 46
resilience *see* community resilience
resilient community, disaster resilience community 282–84, 288
resource management 292
Rheingold, H. 132, 201–02
Rieu, A. M. 22
Roberts, J. 224
Rogerson, C.M. 248
Rosenbaum, H. 177
Rosenberg, B. 150
Ross, D. 103–04

Rouse, M. 123
rural: artisans 77, 225, 248; communities 27, 38, 71, 204, 312; development 37, 46, 68; empowerment 42–6, 51–5, 310; rural empowerment framework 102, 106; rural empowerment models 52, 56; rural India 63–4, 225; marginalization 51, 86, 93, 172; producer 74–5, 267; rural-urban divide 53, 75
rurban, rurbanization 52–3
Russo, A. 152

Saito, A. 128–29
Samman, E. 34, 37–38
Saravanan, R. 175
Savitha, V. 226
Scheler, M. 19
Schmidt, C. 173
Schoen, H. 157
Schotter, A. 148
Schuler, D. 177
Scrase, T. 85
SDG, sustainable development goals 35, 55
SECI model 120, 125–26, 135–36, 155
self-help group 64, 79, 87, 225–36
Semple, E. 29, 129
Sen, A. 17, 24, 38, 45, 94, 103–07
Serenko, A. 115
Shah, A. 248
sharing economy 147–48, 252–53, 311
Sharma, A. 90, 93, 97, 99
Sherif, K. 121
SHG (Self-Help Group) *see* self-help group
Singh, K. 25, 39
Singh, R. 74, 247–49
Skerratt, S. 277
Skyrme, D.J. 122
Smith, A. 104
Snowden, D. 135–36
social: capital 33, 37, 40; knowledge 113, 167–70, 193, 196; networking sites 149–57, 159; software 145, 148–49, 159–60; technology 145–48, 154–55
social knowledge management: first generation 134; second generation 135; third generation 136; framework 203, 205; platform 238, 258
social media: analytics 157–58; applications 153, 157; platforms 147, 157, 228
socialization 125–26, 128–29, 134, 155, 170–71

socially enabled applications 149, 151
sociology of knowledge 19
Soltani, Z. 43
Sonne, L. 248
Sorokin, P. 52
Sproull, L. 177
Sreedhar, N. 225
Stehr, N. 18–9, 117
Steiner, A. 270, 275–77, 279, 283, 288, 293, 308, 313
Stenberg, E. 120–21
Stillman, L. 44
Stinchcombe, A. 97
Stukes, F. 206, 244–46
Styhre, A. 46
Sugden, R. 119, 148
Sundararajan, A. 147–48, 253, 311
Suni, I.M. 188, 220
supply chain practices 250
sustainable development goals *see* SDG
sustainable rural development 35, 37
Sveiby, K.E. 137
Swacha, J. 127

tacit knowledge: exchange 171, 189; resources 123, 138–39; sharing 155–57
Talpau, A. 224
Tansley, A. 310
Tapscott, D. 29, 147–48, 311
Tarafdar, M. 249
Thileepan, T. 226
Tohidinia, Z. 127
Torrey, C. 285
Tu, C. 127
Turner, J.R. 124
Twigg, J. 279, 284
Tzortzaki, A. 115, 126, 136–37

Umemoto, K. 129
UNESCO 21, 35, 46, 86–7, 283
United Nations 54–5
user generated content 151–52, 156

Vardisio, R. 315
Veen, E. 56
Venkatappaiah, V. 172
video sharing sites 147, 150
Vieweg, S. 285
virtual: collaborations 137, 305–06; community formation 244; community of practice 213–17
Vong, W. 42
VonKrogh, G. 137, 221
Vuori, V. 153

Walther, J.B. 152–53
Wang, J. 285
Wang, K.Y. 123
Wartburg, I.V. 215
Weingart, P. 19–21
Wenger, E. 27, 184, 206, 214–17, 221, 224
Wiig, K. 115–19. 124
Williams, B. 29, 147, 311
Wong, Y.K. 120
WSHG, women self-help group *see* SHG

xerox 223
Xue, C. 116, 127

Young, I.M. 94,100
Young, J. 132, 137–38

Zack, M.H. 127
Zaim, H. 124
Zembik, M. 157–58
Zheng, Y. 155
Zimmerman, M.A. 277
Zyl, A.S. 149

For Product Safety Concerns and Information please contact our EU representative GPSR@taylorandfrancis.com
Taylor & Francis Verlag GmbH, Kaufingerstraße 24, 80331 München, Germany